BEHOLD THE MONSTER

CONFRONTING AMERICA'S MOST PROLIFIC SERIAL KILLER

JILLIAN LAUREN

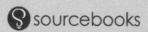

This publication is designed to provide accurate and authoritative information in regard
to the subject matter covered. It is sold with the understanding that the publisher is not
engaged in rendering legal, accounting, or other professional service. If legal advice
or other expert assistance is required, the services of a competent professional person
should be sought. —*From a Declaration of Principles Jointly Adopted by a Committee
of the American Bar Association and a Committee of Publishers and Associations*

Published by Sourcebooks
P.O. Box 4410, Naperville, Illinois 60567–4410
(630) 961-3900
sourcebooks.com

Cataloging-in-Publication Data is on file with the Library of Congress

Printed and bound in Canada.
MBP 10 9 8 7 6 5 4 3 2 1

FOR:

Mary Brosley · 1971

Karen O'Donoghue · 1971

Unknown ("Emily") · 1970s

Unknown · 1970–71

Unknown ("Linda") · 1971

Unknown · 1971

Unknown ("Sarah" or
   "Donna") · 1971

Unknown ("Marianne") · 1971–72

Unknown · 1971–72

Unknown · 1972

Sarah Brown · 1973

Agatha White Buffalo · 1973

Linda Belcher · 1974

Unknown · 1974

Unknown · 1974

Unknown · 1975

Martha Cunningham · 1975

Miriam "Angela"
   Chapman · 1976

Pamela Kay Smith · 1976

Unknown ("Jo") · 1976–79

Unknown · 1976–79

Unknown · 1976–79 or 1993

Mary Ann Jenkins · 1977

Dorothy Gibson · 1977

Lee Ann Helms · 1977

Clara Birdlong · 1977

Unknown · 1977

Unknown · 1977

Unknown · 1977–78

Unknown · 1977–82

Julia Critchfield · 1978

Evelyn Weston · 1978

Karleen Jones · 1978

Brenda Alexander · 1979

Valeria Boyd · 1980

Mary Ann Porter · 1980

Hilda Nelson · 1980

Unknown · 1980–84

Linda Sue Boards · 1981

Patricia Parker · 1981

Annie Lee "Anna" Stewart · 1981

Leila McClain · 1981

Unknown · 1981

Fredonia Smith · 1982

Rosie Hill · 1982

Dorothy Richards · 1982

Patricia Ann Mount · 1982

Melinda LaPree · 1982

Unknown · 1982

Unknown · 1982

Unknown · 1982

Willie Mae Bivins · 1984

Mary Jo Peyton · 1984

Hannah Mae Bonner · 1984

Ida Mae Campbell · 1984

Frances Campbell · 1984

Laurie Kerridge (Barros) · 1984

Tonya Jackson · 1984

Unknown · 1984

Unknown · 1984

Unknown · 1984

Unknown · 1984

Unknown · 1984

Unknown · 1984

Sonja Collette Austin · 1987

Carol Alford · 1987

Unknown · 1987

Unknown · 1987

Unknown · 1987

Unknown · 1987

Unknown · 1987

Unknown · 1987

Unknown · 1987

Unknown · 1987–early 1990s

Unknown · 1988 or 1996

Audrey Nelson · 1989

Guadalupe Apodaca · 1989

Zena Marie Jones · 1990

Alice Denise Duvall · 1991

Rose Evans · 1991

Roberta Tandarich · 1991

Unknown · 1991–92

Alice Denise "Tina"
   Taylor · 1992

Tracy Lynn Johnson · 1992

Unknown · 1992

Unknown · 1992–93

Unknown · 1992–93

Unknown · 1992–93

Ruby Lane · 1993

Bobbie Ann Fields-
   Wilson · 1993

Unknown · 1993

Denise Christie Brothers · 1994

Jolanda Jones · 1994

Melissa Thomas · 1996

Daisy McGuire · 1996

Unknown ("Sheila") · 1996

Unknown ("T-Money") · 1996

Unknown · 1996

Nancy Carol Stevens · 2005

Who holds the Devil, let him hold him well,
He hardly will be caught a second time.

—*Johann Wolfgang Von Goethe*

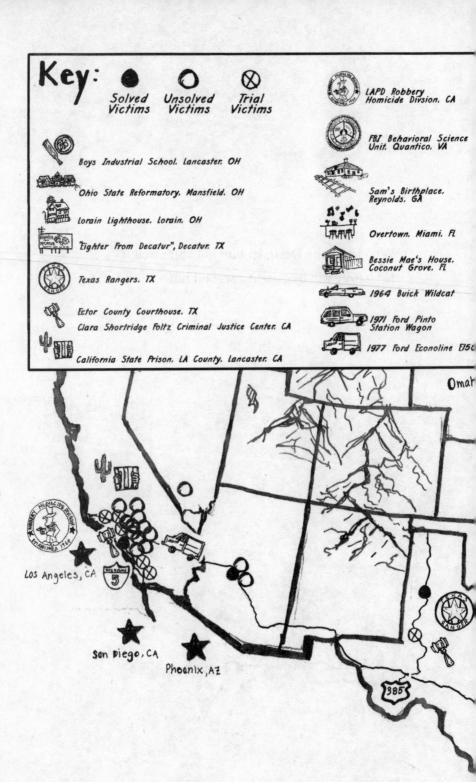

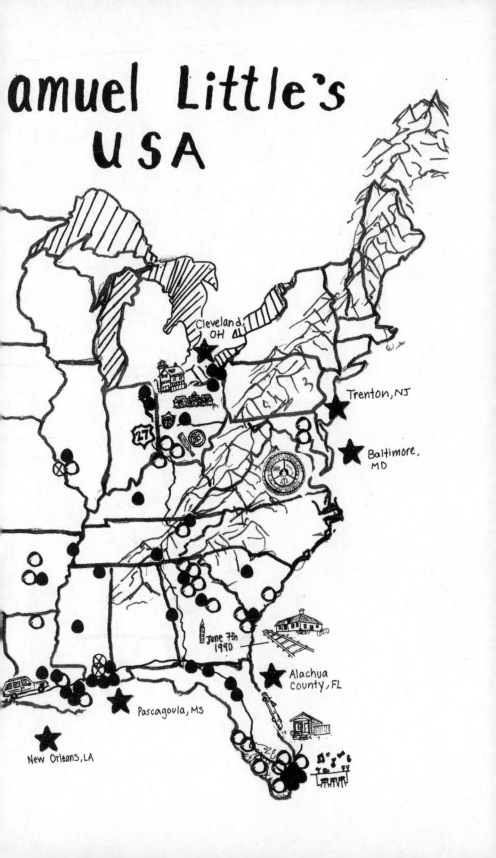

Author's Note

Behold the Monster covers almost four years of research that took me across the country and back, in pursuit of what I clocked as a career-maker of a story. I'd nabbed an interview with an underreported serial killer named Samuel Little, who was already behind bars.

What was meant to be my first eight-thousand-word stab at classic true crime reportage morphed into the unwieldy book-length hybrid of memoir, journalism, true crime, and audacious invention you now hold.

In hindsight, I watch myself first enter California State Prison Los Angeles with half-covered eyes, as if watching that first dummy in a slasher film edge her toe toward the basement stairs.

Is every horror movie a magical universe in which no one has ever seen a horror movie?

Don't go down to the basement, dumbass!

Many of the events on these pages were recounted to me by a liar, a thief, and a murderer. He always tried not to leave witnesses and was therefore often my only source. My only source was not just unreliable. He was terrifying.

Proceed with caution. *Don't go down to the basement, dumbass.* Or follow me, and we'll feel our way through the darkness together.

I corroborated Little's stories with any public documents I could get my hands on, sending blank checks to coroner's departments in places with names like Pascagoula, Escatawpa, Plaquemine. I talked to everyone and anyone I could find who knew him, hunted him, survived him, or grieved the ruin in his wake. I overpaid the vendors selling wilted carnations at the gates of cemeteries.

There were moments of thrilling discovery along the way. Still, for every unlikely solved murder, another dark star hung silent in the sky, a life folded into history on a vicious whim.

When people learn I interviewed a serial killer at length, they ask, inevitably:

How many?

They want a number of victims at which to gasp. I have that number. I have several. I don't believe we'll ever know the answer with exactitude. The number changes as cases close and new information arises. There is no official comprehensive record of Samuel Little's victims.

The oft-quoted number of confessions is 93. As of today, the official FBI number of confirmed cases is 60, surpassing Gary Gilmore's previous 49, to make Sam the most prolific serial killer in American history, of record.

There is no easy list. The sources are vast and conflicting,

Like bodies insufficiently weighted down, checkable facts bob to the surface of the murky waters of Sam's confessions, enabling cold case detectives from across the country to slowly close the gap between the two numbers.

You can find a partial list of cleared cases, as well as confessions still unmatched, at the end of this book. Some of their names, their lives and deaths, will likely remain forever hidden.

You may also ask, how could I have possibly know what was in the minds of Little's victims in their final moments. I didn't. Those are not checkable facts. I knew what I could piece together from the stories of others, fragments, love letters, old Polaroids floating around in dresser drawers, a box of hand-sewn costumes in the attic.

Did I dare try to speak from their perspective? One particularly difficult writing night I stood barefoot on my front lawn and looked to the clear midnight sky, its vast spread of stars the only thing that seemed to echo the sheer scope of the carnage I faced. I asked Sam Little's victims for permission to walk in their shoes, to enter their worlds, to do my best to give them back their voices and their names.

This book is a work of both fact and imagination. This is my best effort at the truth.

Foreword

I write novels about people who are fearless and fierce when it comes to sticking their noses into the things that are wrong. It is a basic formula: F + F = F. That third F is for fulfillment, meaning fulfillment for me the writer hidden behind the words and fulfillment for the reader consuming those words. It is not an original formula. Variations on it can be found in many a crime novel and non-so-called genre books alike. The formula is part of a larger scheme to use fiction to ensure and reassert social order. That's why the formula is so important in crime fiction. From a moment of disorder—a murder or any crime—comes a character who steps in to restore order.

This is the detective or sometimes the lawyer or even sometimes the reporter. The variations on that character and the form of disorder they encounter are endless, and perhaps that is why bookstores and bestseller lists are stocked with novels that feature protagonists who are fearless and fierce. These are the people we want to ride with in our imaginations. These people step forward when others step back. We all want to be one of those who steps forward, and these books show us the way.

This construct is not unique to fiction but rare to find in the real world—the nonfiction world. It is easier to construct a story about a hero than to find a real one. But what you have here is a real one. Jillian Lauren is fearless and fierce. She has seen what is wrong and stuck her nose into it. What has emerged is a story that transcends a crime story to be a story that threatens social order. Sam Little is the monster in this story and Jillian Lauren is the slayer. She is the one who stuck her nose into it, saw something was not right, was dreadfully wrong, in fact, and did something about it.

In Lauren's story are the stories of the many women whose names seemed lost in time until she found them, gave them their names back, and told their stories, made them bigger and stronger than Sam Little. Each one is given loving care in these pages. Under Lauren's skillful and empathic eye, they become real to us, and in becoming so, we see the depth of despair and pain in their loss. This is art and this is not easy to do. It's why I take the easy road and make it up while Lauren chooses to tell the true story with such grace and dignity, a story that cuts into the cancer of what is wrong in our world.

Michael Connelly, Los Angeles

Prologue

The day I was almost strangled to death was an oddly warm and fog-less one, in the late summer of '97, in the gentrifying Mission District of San Francisco. The single kitchen window framed a clean, blue sky.

I'd meant to put a curtain on that window for the entire year and change I'd lived there but never got around to it. That day, its naked-ness seemed a glaring indictment.

I loved the place when I moved in. It was a postage stamp–sized, shotgun flat in a buttercup-yellow Victorian. I hand-stitched the leopard-print pillows on the bed myself. The only other furniture was a set of overflowing IKEA bookshelves, a trash-picked dresser, and a vintage kitchen table with rusted chrome legs. I had moved in with happy dreams of graduating college, finally. Writing, ultimately. It seemed a possibility.

Not three feet away, my soon-to-be-ex-boyfriend Billy sat at the table, arms outspread, palms down, forehead on the marbled red Formica. A tangled mop of sandy-brown hipster hair fell over his face, and his shoulders shook with sobs I found both heartrending and embarrassing.

Though it was still morning, the world shimmered with a lazy, hazy gloss, imparted by the pea-sized dollop of black tar heroin I had just smoked off my last sheet of aluminum foil. You couldn't see the shine anymore, it was so streaked with smears of brown-black sludge smuggled across the border in the ass of some poor fuck way less fortunate than I.

When I was being realistic—as drug addicts are apt to do only first thing in the morning, when the jones sets your nerve endings alight—I knew it was demented that I was regularly ingesting a drug that had recently killed two acquaintances of mine. They had unwittingly fired up not just the precious opiate but also a flesh-eating bacteria. Over the next three days, both they and their friends helplessly watched as their bodies dissolved, cell by decimated cell, into the bloody hospital sheets beneath them. There was nothing the doctors could do to arrest the progress of the bacteria. There was nothing we bystanders could do but watch in shock and awe as our friends fell to pieces in front of our eyes.

At the time, it seemed to me the worst way to die—medieval torture where you die being eaten by rats, starting with your toes. Start with my brain, my heart. Overdose. Myocarditis. Anything other than flesh-eating bacteria.

I continued to suck a cloud of heroin smoke through a rolled-up dollar bill so caked with tar it held together by itself.

To the outside world, I was a functional human being. I held down a job at a high-end women's clothing boutique. I was the fun sales girl, dressed in a vintage cocktail number and Keds, always looking like I was going swing dancing straight from work. I flirted with the well-heeled women and their bored chaperones alike, working it for a pathetic commission. I had terrific sales numbers. My father always said I could sell sand in the Sahara. I had honed the skill during years as a stripper "putting myself through college," though I never seemed to actually finish.

I was through with all that now, trying to get my life together. Even though I had just dropped out of school mere moments before graduating (again), I was not entirely bereft of ambition.

I could still walk away from these poisonous drugs, this equally poisonous guy. I was chipping: using on weekends. Though little by little, the weekends had been growing longer. Friday was now solidly a weekend day. Thursday too, occasionally. As long as you were clean come Monday morning, you wouldn't get strung out and wind up under a bridge.

This was Monday, and I was high. But it *was* an especially horrible Monday.

"I love you," I'd told Billy the night before, after he had placed the heel of his hand against my sternum and pushed me up against the wall one too many times. "And I'm leaving you anyway."

That morning, I wrapped each mismatched piece of glassware in packing paper, placed it in a box, and struggled to manipulate the tape gun under his gaze. Heeding the advice of concerned friends, I had secretly rented a storage facility the week before. For weeks, I had been making plans to move out of town. A clean break. Los Angeles. New Orleans. Austin. Paris. Madrid. Marrakesh.

Los Angeles was good enough for now.

I'd visited the City of Angels a couple of times over the years and noted how literally they take the name. Never was there a city with so many representations of wings. You could find a majestic expanse of white painted on any available flat surface. It was so on the nose, and still, no one could resist.

Wings were a possibility. With wings, you could soar, if you could just figure out how to turn into the wind. A mother's wings could fold around you, a downy soft tent.

Wings could also break, the hollow armature fragile as a wafer. Wings could appear strong, even work fine at first, but prove to be held together with wax from a birthday candle. Wings could get too close to the sun and melt, dropping feathers one by one until you fell like a stone into the ocean.

I had a friend in Los Angeles who was a high-end hairdresser. She told me if I got my cosmetology license, I could come work for her. It sounded like a palm-tree-lined day job.

Something to support me while I plugged away at my novel.

I placed one glass after another into the box to the rhythm of Billy's sobs. He had a right to express his pain. I deserved it. Who hadn't I hurt in the swath of destruction I cut?

Nevertheless, it was time to go. And when it's time to go... I whirled around.

"Why are you doing this to yourself? Why don't you leave?"

"Because if I leave," he said without taking his head off the table, "I'll come back and you'll just be gone."

I almost doubled over. Instead, I imagined my spine to be fashioned of steel. *You can do this. You can leave.* I turned on one bare heel toward the cabinets.

I didn't spin more than a few degrees before the world was upended like glitter in a shaken snow globe. I have no memory of the time in between plucking a mason jar from a shelf of peeling paint and waking up, confused, aware at first only of the throbbing back of my head against the linoleum. Slowly, my shoulder blades, my upper arms, my wrists, my hips, the backs of my calves, my heels existed again, even if they belonged to a different body.

I was underwater. It was so quiet. I wondered if I was dead and my soul would begin to rise. Would I look down at my candy-apple-red hair, nerdy glasses, cutoff jeans, chipped blue nail polish and see, in death, what I suspected the rest of the world saw every day of my life? Another entitled, reckless, college girl gone a little bit too wild. A whorish junkie. A junkie whore. A girl who had been too hungry. A girl who had asked for it.

My neck burned, and then it itched. I swallowed a tennis ball on fire, and it lodged in my esophagus. I clawed at it. I still have the white threads of scars you'll only notice if I inadvertently get a tan.

I was alive.

Billy straddled my chest, hands in a position of surrender, face a mask of disbelief. I studied him for what felt like a long time.

The night I met him was wildly tilted, humming with possibility, fizzy with laughter. We were at a house party in the Castro. There had been a drag queen selling Tupperware, a bowl of punch floating with shrooms, a lesbian band with a topless singer, a famous porn star turned tantric healer, flashes of color, sparkling twinkle lights, a roomful of people delighted with their youth and beauty, enthralled by their cleverness. Billy held court in the corner—the most beautiful and cleverest of them all. We talked about college things, like Milton and Jung and Elliott Smith. It was morning when he went home to the girl he lived with.

The next day, he called to tell me he was walking his dog outside my door. I hadn't recalled even giving him my number, much less telling him where I lived, but there was plenty I had forgotten about the previous night. I blew him off at first. He lived around the corner with some girl who had a trust fund and two shar-peis. Who needed that shit?

He wore me down. He pursued me relentlessly, prolific with the poetry—a dilettante James Dean, the same tortured azure eyes. I felt adored.

I looked up into those eyes—bloodshot, deranged, exhilarated. I wasn't sure if the exhilaration came from the fact that he had stopped himself or the fact that he had finally strangled me.

This sadistic loose cannon on top of me had been there the whole time, if I had looked. If I hadn't been so busy inventing him.

I didn't know anything about anyone.

As if we'd reached a tacit understanding, Billy stood, wiped his palms on his jeans, and held out a hand. I took it and allowed him to pull me upright. To this day, it is the moment I most regret about the incident. I still fantasize about running into him and saying, "I could have made it back onto my feet on my own."

Maybe he fantasizes about saying, "I could have killed you, you broken bitch. So easily. And you never would have had the chance."

1

THE BLACK DAHLIA

LOS ANGELES, CALIFORNIA
OCTOBER 2017

One of LA's most infamous murders is that of the Black Dahlia: twenty-two-year-old Elizabeth (Beth) Short, whose bisected, exsanguinated body was discovered on January 15, 1947, at the edge of a field in Leimert Park. The media went nuts for this baroque and brutal murder of a young white woman. Widely mythologized and never solved, the murder of the Black Dahlia fascinates to this day: the ultimate cold case.

In the fall of 2017, I was writing a mystery novel called *How to Saw a Girl in Half*, with references to Beth Short's famous murder. Every cold case in Los Angeles has a custodial detective. The Dahlia will never be solved, in spite of several competing ghost stories and an endless parade of TV miniseries. There is no physical evidence and no reason to prioritize the case beyond the insistence of its cultish following. Being the custodial detective of the Black Dahlia case means you'll be inundated with tips, conspiracy theories, creeps, and kooks. Every detective knows that one is a dog.

Legendary Robbery Homicide Division Cold Case Special Section Detective Mitzi Roberts took the case. She couldn't resist. Only she and her captain held the keys to the battered, gray filing cabinets stuffed with the original Dahlia archives. All sorts of rumors floated about what they held.

While researching the novel, I scored a much-coveted, rarely granted interview with Roberts. I hoped to gossip about Black Dahlia, but I was also hungry for any current leads I could charm out of Roberts: something no one else had done.

I'd been planning to write fiction, but truthfully, into the late hours of the night, after every baseball practice, after I got my two kids to bed and made the lunches, I dug deeper into the world of true crime. Was I obsessed? Not quite yet. I saw a glimmer of opportunity to make a meaningful change, bringing to light stories from which most people turned their heads. I had a strong stomach, insatiable curiosity, and the dead calm afforded me by PTSD. I was hooked.

When I first faced Detective Mitzi Roberts across a booth at Little Dom's in Silver Lake on a warm October day in 2017, I felt only the faintest tug of the undertow that was about to drag me into far deeper waters than I'd planned.

The real person behind Michael Connelly's wildly popular fictional Detective Renée Ballard was laid-back and hawkeyed, wearing a pin-striped suit and shiny badge.

"I envy that you get to go through people's drawers," I said to Roberts.

The waiter refilled our iced tea.

"So you're weird and want to read people's diaries and shit," she said. "Okay, so how that works—when we're at a search warrant, we have a protocol. You get there, you can't touch anything until the photographer comes, so we can prove we didn't jack up the house. I scope out the best-looking room with the good shit. I don't want the kid's room. Anyway, it's mostly gross. Roaches and dirty chones and some cop always waving a dildo around. I more want to look through a murder book. I want to be the one to find that thing somebody didn't. Find that nexus. Solve it. Go to these families. It's true to some it didn't mean anything. To a lot, it meant everything."

I asked Roberts what case she was most proud of.

"I'm proud of them all." She stirred the last watery remains of her drink while watching the parade of almost supermodels pushing strollers and Reiki healers headed to the cold-pressed juice bar.

"I did catch a serial killer named Sam Little once. That was pretty cool."

"How did we skip that?"

"I'm not the one doing the questions."

Roberts told me she suspected this killer of many more murders across the country. Little got away with it for decades by cherry-picking his victims—drug addicts and prostitutes on the fringes, largely women of color. "Less dead" homicide victims, a term credited to criminologist Steven Egger, have historically been not as thoroughly investigated as their wealthier, whiter, and perhaps more sober counterparts. Pretty white college students are the most dead. Black transgender hookers with addiction issues are the least dead.

A stone of recognition dropped into my gut. I knew the concept well. I had talked to cops who worked in the 1980s, when hooker after hooker turned up in dumpsters every morning in South LA.

The calls came in: "There's 187 [a homicide] corner of Fifth and Main. NHI."

NHI: No humans involved. Or simply a no one. "Body found in a dumpster on the corner of Fifty-Fifth and Central. It's a no one."

Roberts had tried to mobilize other police departments across the country to investigate their cold case files for possible connections to Little's patterns, possible evidence that might still hold his DNA. To her frustration, not much happened. She'd recently heard seventy-eight-year-old Little, sitting in prison just miles away in Los Angeles, was in poor health.

"Who knows how many victims are out there? How many families will never know?"

My midnight dives into evolving forensic technology led me to believe in the possibility of leveling the playing field, restoring the names of unidentified victims from marginalized and often dismissed populations. Attitudes in law enforcement were changing, as were its demographics. And an intriguing detective had just dropped an underreported serial killer into my lap, with potentially many more victims to be identified.

What my research turned up that night set me down the path toward a years-long dialogue with a serial killer. In a wild stroke of luck, I landed in the middle of a current investigation. Little was about to spill his gruesome well of secrets to the FBI and the Department of Justice (DOJ), with a cocksure Texas Ranger in a tall hat at the helm, who would bring in hundreds of detectives from local jurisdictions. It was the story of a lifetime. Dozens of victims long lost in boxes of buried evidence might find justice, and their families would finally know the truth.

Samuel Little would eventually be identified as the most prolific serial killer ever to stalk America's streets. I had no earthly idea about the scope of his crimes when I first wrote to Little, but I sensed an energy gathering behind the man, the monster.

By the pricking of my thumbs, something wicked this way comes.

In 2014, Samuel Little was convicted for three murders committed in the late eighties in Los Angeles. I scrolled through mug shot after mug shot of this evasive drifter and smooth criminal, with a one-hundred-page rap sheet that spanned twenty-four states and included arrests for theft, battery, assault, rape, and even murder. For this sixty-year swath of crime he cut across the country, forty of those years involving murder, he'd served a combined total of approximately ten years before the triple life sentence he was serving when Roberts mentioned him to me.

I'd had my own run-ins with drugs and violent men and usually talked my way out. People want to talk to me. If I don't feel like hearing anyone's life story, I wear headphones in public. I've always imagined myself an undercover private detective, a member for life of the Nancy Drew Fan Club. I like asking the questions. What if I could get this guy talking? Think of the questions I could ask.

While the media might lead us to believe society is littered with serial killers, in reality, they are quite rare. It would be a once-in-a-lifetime kind of thing. I might be able to bring a little heat to the story, get law enforcement interested in these long-cold cases. I could make a difference.

Corny? Overreaching? Maybe. In any case, it was a hell of a story.

I pitched the story to my editor, Laurie Abraham, at *New York* magazine. She agreed the idea was intriguing.

"Keep at it. There's something, but we're not going to do another gruesome serial killer story. You need an angle."

We agreed. I needed an angle. I wrote Samuel Little a letter.

The letter I received in return and those that followed didn't disappoint—if I was looking for a spooky movie prop. He wrote voluminously on torn scraps of yellow legal pads, in handwriting that veered from careful cursive to serial killer ALL CAPS. He included doodles of what I think was either a monkey or just a man with enormous ears. When the monkey had a sad face and tears, you were in for a creepy letter. When the monkey had a happy face, it was worse.

He maintained his innocence and railed against the lies and injustices of his "upside-down case," with the constant refrain that DNA just proved he was there, not that he did it.

I also did my homework on psychopaths. If all went well, I was about to talk to one. You don't want to be underprepared. As many mistakes as I made, at least I knew not to underestimate a sexual serial killer.

Through a diagnostic lens, opinions differ as to whether psychopathy and sociopathy are the same. The American Psychiatric Association acknowledges neither as a clinical disorder. The clinical designation is antisocial personality disorder, or ASPD.

The Mayo Clinic website describes it as such, based on the psychopathic traits as laid out by Dr. Bob Hare, one of the early innovators in the field of antisocial behavior, in his classic psychopathy checklist.

Antisocial personality disorder, sometimes called sociopathy, is a mental disorder in which a person consistently shows no regard for right and wrong and ignores the rights and feelings of others. People with antisocial personality disorder tend to antagonize, manipulate or treat others harshly or with callous indifference. They show no guilt or remorse for their behavior.

Antisocial personality disorder signs and symptoms may include:

- Disregard for right and wrong
- Persistent lying or deceit to exploit others
- Being callous, cynical and disrespectful of others
- Using charm or wit to manipulate others for personal gain or personal pleasure
- Arrogance, a sense of superiority and being extremely opinionated
- Recurring problems with the law, including criminal behavior
- Repeatedly violating the rights of others through intimidation and dishonesty
- Impulsiveness or failure to plan ahead
- Hostility, significant irritability, agitation, aggression or violence
- Lack of empathy for others and lack of remorse about harming others
- Unnecessary risk-taking or dangerous behavior with no regard for the safety of self or others
- Poor or abusive relationships
- Failure to consider the negative consequences of behavior or learn from them
- Being consistently irresponsible and repeatedly failing to fulfill work or financial obligations

If you're wringing your hands and wondering...breathe. The answer is almost certainly no.

I spent hours on the phone with my aunt, a psychiatrist at Massachusetts General Hospital and Harvard University for forty years. She's known for being an incisive diagnostician. I asked about her experience with ASPD. My father's twin sister is a brilliant, odd beauty, with wild red hair. I loved her Cambridge condo as a kid. A sixties black-and-white photograph of her naked in a field of tall grass hung in the entryway. Her closet smelled of cloves, not Bounty.

My grandfather, their father, was a proctologist and also the family physician at Bamberger's department store in Newark, New Jersey—when there was such a thing as Bamberger's and family physicians. He was dismissive of the soft science of psychiatry, but the two still came up with names for the shingle they'd hang outside their shared practice:

Odds and Ends
Rears and Queers
Nuts and Bolts

Our clan came from Polish Ashkenazi stock who turned turnip carts into one of the biggest discount supermarket chains in the tri-state area:

Why pay more? Shop at a ShopRite Store!

If you didn't work for the company store, the only options were MD or the president of a local Hadassah chapter.

I grew up surrounded by brilliant and eccentric proctologists, cardiologists, psychiatrists, teamsters, social climbers, Wall Street tightrope walkers, and Ponzi schemers who took holidays in the Caymans. Not much freaks me out.

The night before I faced Samuel Little, I freaked out.

I rubbed my neck and paced my upstairs hallway, demanding my psychiatrist aunt give me the magic key to unlock the mystery of this monster I was about to face.

"Psychos? Meh," said my aunt. "Everyone wants to talk about psychopaths because they're an aberration. If you're almost anyone, psychos make you look good, feel good…in comparison. You didn't bludgeon coeds to death in their beds? Hey! You're okay! Any diagnosis is a moving target. I usually start with trauma and move from there.

"Psychopathy is like *Jeopardy*," she continued. "All answers are questions, and don't expect to win. Psychopaths have a way of being extraordinary liars while telling you exactly what they're doing. I can tell you what it *feels* like to be around a psychopath. It works better than the questionnaire: He will steal the shirt off your back. He'll tell you he's stealing the shirt off your back. Still, you will be inexplicably compelled to give him the shirt off your back."

"It'll be an adventure," I said.

"It will be what it will be. Don't expect to tease the truth from the lies. He may not even know. This takes time. Don't wear an underwire," she concluded, sounding strangely sad. "You'll set off the metal detectors."

2

THE SERIAL KILLER

CALIFORNIA STATE PRISON, LOS ANGELES COUNTY, CALIFORNIA
AUGUST 2018

California State Prison, Los Angeles County, is located in the city of Lancaster, roughly eighty miles northeast of the palm tree–lined boulevards of Beverly Hills, but it might as well be eighty million. The prison is an ecosystem unto itself, where over three thousand men live sandwiched between a sunbaked terrain inhospitable to much more than scrub brush and a wide, unforgiving sky. In the early morning hours, when dawn lights up the desert in dusty shades of rose, there's something almost peaceful about the way the outside world recedes quickly, beyond the fifteen-feet-high, maximum-security-specification mesh fencing. In the flat heat of midday, when temperatures regularly reach one hundred and ten degrees in the shade and the desert winds blow so hot and wild they could sear the eyelashes off your face, the landscape holds a biblical feeling of punishment.

The prison campus is strewn with identical two-story tan-colored buildings that blend into the expanse of sand and rocks beneath them. The only flashes of color are the garish turquoise doors with industrial grade locks and matching windows the width of butter knives. On the morning of August 8, 2018, after waiting for seven hours for my number to come up, I finally faced its iron security gates, but I kept setting off the metal detector. I couldn't believe I'd forgotten my aunt's advice. I wound up having to pry the underwire out of my bra with my teeth, because there were no sharp objects available. The prison wives carefully coiffing their children's hair in the bathroom beside me cheered me on.

"You go, girl. Gnaw that shit out. You got this."

It would be my first time inside a men's maximum-security prison. It would most certainly be my first time talking to a serial killer that I was aware of. I was as prepared as I could be, but you always forget something.

Once I made it through the metal detectors, I waited with a group of ten women and children, as a tall iron gate opened. We stepped into the cage that formed the liminal space between freedom and its opposite. I was an impostor. These people were there to visit loved ones, because they had no other choice. I was there to visit a monster, because I wanted a story no one else had.

The gate behind us whirred and clanked closed. We stepped out onto the prison campus. I walked on shaky legs toward B Block, my knees actually knocking together. Such a cliché. But the body is the body, and fear is unoriginal.

I carried a clear plastic baggie full of quarters and a key fob. My friend Sasha had once done time in the same prison, and I'd called him for tips.

"It's impossible to get an appointment," he told me. "You have to show up at six in the morning and wait in a line of cars outside the gate. They don't start letting you in until nine thirty, but if you line up later than six, you'll never see him. Bring quarters. You're not cool if your visitor doesn't bring quarters for the vending machines."

Criminal psychology had fascinated me since my first fix, Manson—the gateway drug for many a true crime buff. The outrageous crimes documented in Vincent Bugliosi and Curt Gentry's seminal true crime classic *Helter Skelter* signaled the end of the sixties. Manson and his family upended the burgeoning ethos of tuning in and dropping out. How can you twist peace and love into the evisceration of innocent human beings?

In the same way, Truman Capote's *In Cold Blood* documented not just the brutal murder of the Clutter family in Holcomb, Kansas, but also the end of the fifties white-bread meritocracy of the American dream. Surely if you were a hardworking, virtuous, cherry pie–making, white, midwestern nuclear family, you would thrive and succeed. You can be anything you want to be if you just try hard enough! Life is a system of just deserts. Isn't it?

No, it isn't. For the Clutters, it wasn't. For the LaBiancas, it wasn't. What do you do with that lesson?

Manson himself was overrated, a mediocre mind at best. At any senior prom, stoned quarterbacks spout deeper platitudes. Manson got press, superfans, fawning groupies for his theatrics, his emptiness, and his "girls."

The gravitational pull of these famous multiple murders could make you give up on not just ideals but humanity in general. How can you still view with anything but cynicism the human animal, capable of such casual cruelty? Or it could be a puzzle. It could be a career maker. I had a voracious and reportedly infuriating level of curiosity, plus a strong stomach for both gore and narcissism. I had a chance.

I approached what I hoped was B Block, as the hot wind lashed my hair to my face and sheriff's deputies passed by me in SWAT vests. Some smiled and said hi or remarked on the weather.

I handed the guard my ID.

"You here to see Little?" he asked. "How you know Little?"

"He's a friend," I said. I wasn't sure how this thing worked, but I knew enough to not say I was a journalist.

"A friend? My ass," the guard said cheerfully as he put an enormous brass key into an enormous brass lock and admitted me to a cinderblock room full of families huddled together at plastic tables. Along one wall was a play area with Astroturf and a few tubs of oversized LEGOs. Next to the play area was a gray seamless background where you could get your picture taken with your loved one for a two-dollar token.

I used the quarters to buy Funyuns, a Coca-Cola, and some Little Debbie Honey Buns. I put them on the table and tried to figure out where to train my eyes. At the door? At the red line behind which the inmates stood until given permission to sit?

Instead, Little wheeled up on me from behind and startled me.

"Hello, Sam."

Sam was wheelchair-bound, suffering from diabetes and a heart condition. He wore standard prison-issue shapeless denim pants, a blue cotton T-shirt with CDC printed on the back in block lettering, and a pair of orthopedic white sneakers due to a toe amputation. The tail end of a baby-pink heart surgery scar the size of an earthworm peeked out from the top of his T-shirt. He sported a thinning pelt of kinky white hair and a beard to match. Age spots discolored his skin, giving him the appearance of a molting lizard. At first glance, he appeared a frail and pitiable grandpa, but you could see the evidence of the man he once was: a six-foot-one powerhouse with catcher's mitts for hands.

Gravity had done its inevitable work, dragging his jowls into lazy folds around his jaw, but you could still make out the strong cheek-bones, the handsome face, the glittering pale-blue eyes that once put his victims at ease. The sound of children, chatter, and vending machines bounced off the cinder blocks.

Sam wagged a finger at me. "You!" he said. "You my angel come to visit me from heaven. God knew I was lonely and he sent me you. You want a story for your book? Oooooeeeee, do I have a story."

I came prepared to do battle with a dragon, and instead I faced a lonely old man over a bag of Funyuns. Sam spoke in a soft patois, cobbled together from what I would soon learn were his Georgia origins and his years growing up in the Ohio steel town of Lorain. I leaned in, then leaned in some more, until I was approximately a foot from the face of the man I knew had strangled and brutalized at least three women and who knew how many more. My eye twitched.

Sam and I talked that first day about our childhoods, about our first loves, about his family tree, which includes (it really does) both Malcolm X and Little Richard. We talked about my kids. We talked about baseball, boxing, and his long-term girlfriend, Jean, who had been a master shoplifter. We talked about travel. We talked about art. He was good at only two things in his life he told me: art and boxing. Later he'd admit to a third at which he was far better.

Sam had learned to draw in the Ohio State Reformatory as a young man, and it was still his preferred pastime.

"What do you like to draw?"

"Oh, girls. I mean women. I mean ladies," he said, searching for the term I'd find least offensive.

Was the answer "victims"?

"I can draw anything. Paint, pencils, whatever I can get. I can do all the light and dark. Just like I see you right now."

What was he seeing? What had he seen in them? How do you find someone simultaneously worthy of the kind of deep attention it takes to render them and also disposable?

"I live in my mind now. With my babies. In my drawings. Not with these robots in here. The only things I was ever good at was fighting and drawing."

We talked about his hero, Sugar Ray Robinson, and the prizefighting career Sam had almost had. He was once a middleweight champion in the prison boxing ring who'd been called "mad" for his speed and fury. The Mad Daddy. The Mad Machine. The Machine Gun.

I sat with him for hours that first day and returned the next, committed to it being my last go at him. If I couldn't make a dent in his bullshit, it wasn't worth the gas mileage.

After about six hours total, he lingered on a story about a woman in Florida. "I want a TV," he said.

"I want things too."

His eyes went dead flat. I had almost forgotten to be afraid of him. "You going to buy me a TV?"

"I don't know, Sam. Am I?"

He laughed and drummed his half-inch-long, dirty yellow fingernails on the table. "Okay, okay, you got me! What do you want to hear about for your story, little miss? You want to hear about the first one?"

I dug my toes into my shoes. Was this really going to happen? I don't know why it shocked me. We're all dying to spill our secrets. It just takes figuring out what will nudge us over the edge into free fall.

"She was a big ol' blond. Round about turn of the new year, 1969 to 1970. Miami. Coconut Grove. You know Coconut Grove? Nah, you wouldn't know Coconut Grove. She was a ho"—he corrected himself—"a prostitute. She was sitting at a restaurant booth, red leather, real nice. She crossed them big legs in her fishnet stockings and touched her neck. That was my sign from God."

With that, he began an incantation of murders. He remembered eighty-six, give or take a couple. With astonishing detail and near photographic recall, he took me back through his past, when the road was his home and the back alleys and underbelly bars of city after city across the country offered a feast of low-hanging fruit, women whose eyes were half-dead already, women who Sam believed in his heart had only been waiting for him to show up and finish the job. Back to better times, when Sam believed God himself gently placed neck after willing neck, still pulsing with life, into his hungry hands. He imagined himself as some kind of angel of mercy, divinely commissioned to euthanize.

I put every word in my mind's lockbox and stayed on track. If I lost the thread, I'd lose control of the interview. Sentiment, horror, shock: these were things that could wait. What could not wait was the confession: a confession I could do nothing but mentally record while I robotically responded, because this confession was fucking nuts. Eighty-four? Eighty-six? Could he have possibly killed that many women?

My subconscious did the calculus while I looked the man in the face. I kept my legs crossed at the ankles, knees pressed so tight they could hold an aspirin, hands clasped in my lap—when I didn't have a friendly, encouraging palm on his arm. I thank my mother for my Emily Post posture. I used to judge it until I realized all that clenching effort can help you keep a calm face.

"I only ever told this to one other person in my life. Texas Ranger Jimmy Holland. Him and you. You're my only friends," said Sam.

Who? Was Sam delusional? Was that a ridiculous question?

Had I wasted my time on a killer with imaginary friends? A Texas Ranger? Who was next, Buzz Lightyear?

It turned out Texas Ranger James (Jim to his colleagues, Jimmy to his mom) B. Holland, Company B, was real indeed. Passionate about cold cases and famous for eliciting confessions from psychopaths, this cowboy had found what he called a Samuel Little Texas nexus—Denise Christie Brothers—a 1991 Texas murder case likely committed by Samuel Little. It was enough to dig into the case. Like Detective Roberts, he also suspected the man of many more murders across the country and was confident that with the support of the FBI and the DOJ, he'd crack him. He was right.

Sam told me about a day, just months before, on May 17, 2018, in a windowless interview room off a hallway buried deep in B Block, when he sat across from a real live cowboy. A black hat faced a white hat, deciding whether to hold or fold.

It settled in slowly that I'd unwittingly inserted myself into an open federal investigation.

In the months to come, I continued my face-to-face interviews with Sam. I took any relevant details of unsolved crimes to the cops.

During this same time, Holland elicited his mind-boggling series of official confessions and arranged interviews with law enforcement from jurisdictions across the country. He would later describe me as a headache.

I insisted on the essential part played by a free press in any democracy.

Just let the law do their job, young lady.

In Texas?

He sent a rare eye-roll emoji.

I responded, *You and me and the devil make three.*

3

MARY

Mary wished she had brought her cardigan. She hadn't wanted to forget it again at the bar, and the night looked warmer than it felt. She wore a short, flowered cotton dress with bell sleeves, fishnets, and patent leather heels. There was more of a bite to the evening air than usual, and her bum hip was giving her pain. The chill went straight to the metal plate they had put in after she toppled off the porch back home. After the fall, her husband started giving her a hard time about her drinking, and her parents chimed in. She'd come to Miami to escape the cold, the pain, and the shame. Not necessarily in that order.

That kind of drinking is unattractive on a *young* girl, only thirty-three. Pretty funny, coming from cousins like the man who slipped Mary her first slug of whiskey at twelve. Then a hold-your-nose-just-one-more, until one side of her head was heavier than the other. What came next swam in her lopsided brain still. She'd told her mother straightaway.

Mary's mother's face flushed, forehead veins pulsing with the kind of fury you only carry for someone who has put a pin in the balloon of your entire life with one sentence. It would always be the fault of the pin. Just look at her. Mary was that kind of girl. She broke the rules. If anyone asked for it, it was Mary. Ding-a-ling, staring at the sky.

The fall was the final proof of her utter brokenness. Broken enough to turn and not look back. She had neither beauty, nor youth, nor health, nor reputation. Check ya later! She'd go far away, to a land where the rustle of palm fronds in the sea air sometimes sounded like a whisper of hope, a possibility of new beginnings.

In the meantime, there was a night to get through, a morning to face, with the sweats, the teeth-grinding shakes, and the ache that cut straight through her as if the plate they put in her hip had razor blades for edges.

A bar stool would have been a more obvious place to hang her shingle, but instead she ordered herself another gin and tonic and sidled into a red leather booth with a view of the door. One more now, until she found someone to buy the next round. She'd make it up. It was still early.

Mary usually hung out in Overtown, a part of town mostly pop-ulated by Black folks. She felt more at home there, even though she drew stares with her pale skin, thick legs, and platinum hair. In the white bars, she was a piece of furniture, a talking couch. In Overtown, she was something special.

On that night in mid-January 1971, in one of her regular hangs on North Miami Avenue, her only competition was an orange-haired middle-aged woman at the end of the bar, her shoulders already slouched forward so they seemed to hug the glass on the bar in front of her. There was a table full of hippie kids and a Black guy with an

Afro like a bonsai tree sitting in a corner booth with a white woman—likely out somewhere none of their friends would see them. Other than that, a few barflies who wouldn't be good for anything more than goosing her when she walked to the bathroom.

Every time the door opened, her luck could change. The very next person who walked in could be the savior she'd been waiting for. She liked to imagine he'd be someone like Ernest Hemingway. He'd been rumored to visit Overtown once, before he kicked the bucket. He was someone who understood how hard life could be. She'd especially loved that one story about the tiger or whatever it was that froze to death on a mountain somewhere in India. Her mother had called her morbid, said no man wants his lady too thinky-thinky. "They only say they like smart girls. Men like to be right, and they like to be taken care of. The end."

The door swung open, and a rotten waft of the bay's low tide sailed in, followed by a striking man in a wide-collared shirt and a pair of sharkskin bell-bottoms. A light-skinned Black guy, well groomed, with a beard, heavy mustache, wild hair. He carried himself with confidence, chest out like a peacock. He scanned the smoky, windowless room with ice-blue eyes. Hunting for something? Maybe for her?

He caught her eye briefly, then walked toward the bar and ordered a beer. Mary's face flushed. Ignoring her in this crowd? How low could you go?

The man drew several slow swallows before he locked his gaze on her. There was barely a drop left in her glass, mostly melted ice. She looked down at it with a cartoonish pout, pushing her frizzy blond bangs out of her eyes. The man's smile went electric.

A sparkle ran up her spine. She loved that moment. Only problem was it almost always went downhill from there.

"Whatchu doing all alone like this, little kitten?" said the man.

"I'm not alone anymore."

"You need another one of those?"

"Gin and tonic," she said. "Double!"

He brought back a drink, and they shot the shit while she sucked it down through a miniscule straw. He told her his name was Sam.

So many names. How to remember? She gave them nicknames. Sammy Davis Jr.? No. Sam…son. Samson from the Bible. She couldn't remember much from Bible study, but she knew he was strong, and this man was strong. Something about his hair being all that. A little queer, how they go all on and on about his hair. He was kind of vain if you think about it. This man also seemed vain. That was how she'd remember his name.

"Where you from?" he asked. "Because it ain't Overtown."

"No, no, it's not," she said. "From near Boston."

"So far from your family, sweet little thing like you?"

"They just…" She heard herself slur the last word, enough to alert her she was getting a thick tongue. "You know. They want to *control* you. First your own parents. Then you meet some guy and maybe you think he's going to give you some grown-up life where you finally do what you want to do. My sister did everything they wanted her to do. The goddamn Labrador did too. *They* listened and obeyed when everyone said think this and eat this and don't drink that and don't do this and if you do, confess. Well, I'm not a dog, and I'm not my sister."

There it was again, the soft sibilance. The words she couldn't quite call to mind. She hated that. She was talking too much, she knew it. His eyes were already starting to wander. They asked you a question, but they never wanted the answer.

"They didn't understand you."

"They didn't," she slurped the last of her watery drink. Mary toyed with the gold cross she wore on a chain. Her father had bought it at a kiosk at Faneuil Hall when she was a little girl.

"I do."

He had nursed the one beer and she had downed two more G and Ts already. Would have thought there was a crack in the glass for how fast they went. Didn't pack the same punch anymore.

"Come with me for a little cruise, sugar," he said to her necklace.

"Only if it's a Caribbean cruise."

"Sure!" he said. "Caribbean, anywhere you want to go, beautiful little thing you. You're like a queen. Maybe you the queen of whatchu call it...Polynesia!"

He was funny. Maybe it wouldn't be all bad. "You got a car?"

"Your cruise ship awaits," said...Sam. That was it. Sam. "And it's the only cruise that actually pays *you*."

"Fifty."

He got up and half bowed, holding out an arm toward the door.

There was always that moment, when she had to stand. People could be strange about a little thing like a limp, as if it made her a leper. She tried to make it look like a swagger. He didn't mention it. So far, there were a few things she liked about this mysterious stranger.

"Nice ride."

"1964 gold Wildcat. Just got it."

"Made of real gold?"

He opened the door for her but didn't stay to close it. He shuffled around back and hopped in the driver's seat. She'd barely yanked the heavy door shut when he cut the wheel hard. He sure got quiet quick.

He pulled a U-turn and hopped on the 27. "Where we going?"

"Whatchu mean? We're going to the Polynesian Islands."

"I think that's the other way."

"How about we find you another drink?"

"How about we get there?" she said, bitchy, the alcohol leaving her system. He put his arm around her neck, and she leaned into him. The strip malls and low-slung concrete motels grew sparse, swallowed by lush foliage.

She dozed for a moment, and when she woke with a jerk, his arm was still around her shoulders, his palm resting gently on her throat.

"We there yet?"

"We there. Here we go."

He turned off the 27 onto 170th Avenue, which was less of an avenue and more like a dirt path. The car kicked debris off the limestone onto its undercarriage, making a sound like a hailstorm. The radio played "Signed, Sealed, Delivered I'm Yours." To the left, the reflection of the moon shimmered on an otherwise black expanse of water. Beyond that unfolded the vast green expanse of the Everglades. To the right was a cluster of dense brush, probably only ever visited by hunters or teenagers looking for a remote place to neck.

He slowed to a halt, and with the hand that wasn't around her throat, he began to knead her thigh. She crossed her leg to offer him more of it. She may have had a bum hip, but she had plenty of thigh. She sighed and laid her head back against the brown leather upholstery, more from exhaustion than from pleasure.

"Let's get in the back."

Mary lifted the latch and kicked open the door. She took in the smell of the trees, the buzz of the cicadas, the stars caught in a loose net of filmy black clouds. It was a pretty kind of spot for an ugly deed. Maybe she'd get away with just a handy.

He sniffed at her like a dog, kissed her thighs through her fish-nets, dragged them down to her ankles, then licked the embossed diamond pattern they'd left on her skin. He stopped dead and looked her straight in the necklace.

These freaks—there's always a body part they caught sight of when their sister was in the shower, or a mother who made them rub her feet too much, or a nun who spanked them in front of the class.

Mary's throat was dry. She swallowed and swallowed again.

"That's right," he said, lightly kneading her throat. "Swallow for me. I love it when you swallow."

His hand tightened. This one was a little freakier than usual.

He released. Something in her rose to the surface, stone-cold sober. He wasn't a little freakier. He was a lot freakier.

She looked around. Could she even get out if she had to? Where was there to go? She scanned the ground for a rock, a stick, anything.

Nah, nah. She was drunk and paranoid. She reached for his cock but her hand found only air as he closed the vise grip around her neck. Her body instinctively jerked, hands rising in front of her, no more effective than swatting a swarm of flies. Probably he'd just let go after he came. He wouldn't be the first man with one hand around her neck and the other on his cock.

Her vision went starry, then black, and when she returned, her head was in his lap. She looked up at him. Who was he? Where was she again?

"You're beautiful. I own you. You're mine."

He pressed his lips to hers and squeezed again.

"You're trying to kill me?" she spat. "Go ahead then! Go ahead kill me, you son of a bitch."

The man paused, looked up as if thinking or praying. "Okay."

She thrashed and gagged. "Damn you to hell," said Mary. Her chest screamed for breath, collapsing in on itself.

"I love you," he said.

She had been right. She wasn't crazy. They had all also been right. She was doomed.

4

LOVE AT FIRST SIGHT

MIAMI, FLORIDA
JANUARY 1971

Mary...

Sam thought that had been her name. Was he hallucinating? He doubled back, back, back to the bar, the flaxen hair, the gold chain, the pale thick thighs covered with blue veins that looked like highways. Highways leading where?

Her lips had turned a similar shade of blue to the veins in her leg. Foamy, pink liquid spilled from the side of her slack bottom lip. Her eyes were open, staring at him, now ringed with crayon-red spots. He slid his arm from around her neck, and she slumped toward the door. Her arm was limp as an old rag. *Drunk bitch*, he thought, but then he realized he had seen many drunk bitches in his day. This one was different.

He shook her, slapped her cheek. He put his ear to her lips and heard nothing. The world was quiet and dark as a church at midnight. For the first time in Sam's life, so was the restless world inside him.

When the sound crept back in, it was the white noise of crickets, frogs, and wind-rippled water.

She looked cold. She had mentioned she left her coat at home. He wrapped his arms around her to warm her, nuzzled her chin, nibbled her crushed neck, sniffed her silken skin, salty like the ocean, sweet like some flowery perfume that belonged on a fifteen-year-old, and bitter with the unmistakable tang of fear. Fresh kill to a lion.

She was perfect. It was the first time he ever felt that about a woman. She was perfectly his. He had never loved before that moment. He told her so over and over. He finally said the words he had never spoken to a woman other than his mama. He finally understood what the whole world had been going on and on about like a broken record. All the love songs on the radio he blasted with the windows open. All the black-and-white movies with tough guys in fedoras, undone by bitches in dresses tight as lizard skin. He'd watched them and felt nothing other than that the guy was a sap. Now he was the sap. He finally understood what could bring you to your knees.

It was love. It was everything they said it would be. It was wonderful. "I love you, I love you, I love you, I love you."

He put his mouth to hers and drew a breath in case there was a final ounce of oxygen in her lungs that he could take for himself. It was like breathing in a ball of electricity.

The scent of urine reached his nostrils. Only then did he fully comprehend she was a corpse. His beautiful moment with the lifeless body beside him turned to panic and then disgust. He had finally done it.

"What have I done, Lord?" he said aloud.

He was a pervert, sure. He jerked off over strangled and mangled bodies in the *True Detective* magazines he hid under his mattress. He wasn't a killer. That was a terrible thing. Terrible, terrible thing, to take a life like that. He'd never do it again. He vowed to God right there and then.

If he just got away with it, he'd never do it again.

His next thought was—why did it take him so long?

He was used to trouble, but this kind of thing could get you into a different kind of trouble. He instinctively checked his six. He thought about the countless times he had seen those red and blue lights in his rearview, but tonight there was only blackness.

The love of his life instantly turned from an angel to a piece of refuse, and a heavy one at that. He grabbed it by one juicy hank.

You were supposed to bury a body. He could do that. He'd dug a hundred graves when he worked at a cemetery. He even worked for the sanitation department. He was used to disposing of trash.

He yanked it out of the car, and it bounced in a way he found comical, its head catching on the edge of the seat and then the floorboard. He dragged it through the dirt and awkwardly wedged it into some underbrush. He shoved it with his foot, but it kept rolling back.

He tested the unforgiving soil to see if he could scoop out enough of it with his hands to make a shallow grave, but it was hard as granite. There was no way. His only other solution was to run. He left the meat puppet tangled in underbrush and whore rags and drove the speed limit down the 27, thirty minutes or so, back to Coconut Grove.

It was nothing new for Sam to come home late and shuck his duds for someone else to launder. Not even much blood. He washed up and crawled into bed next to a sleeping Yvonne.

Sam replayed the night, vacillating between pleasure and fear. What had been her name?

Marcia? Madeleine? He remembered perfectly her doughy face, her frizzy blond curls that smelled like fresh shampoo, her neck that smelled like gin…

He got up just before dawn and kissed Yvonne goodbye, whispering he'd be going in to work early. He dressed in his green jumpsuit. On his way out, he got down on his knees and grabbed the shovel he'd seen under Mama's porch. He drove back to the body, shovel in the trunk. The adrenaline of the kill was gone, and paranoia gathered in the vacuum. You didn't get away with something like this.

A thought comforted him: that flat-footed ho wouldn't likely be missed. She had told him as much. The night came to him like images in one of those old flip books, each picture leading to the next, creating the sensation of movement. Knew it was coming, didn't she, somewhere deep down?

The radio went in and out as he approached the Everglades.

He slowed onto the turnoff at the dirt road, half expecting to see the familiar blue and red light show that had punctuated every few years of his life since he was thirteen. There was nothing but a thick woman's calf, emerging from the underbrush.

He pulled over next to it, placed a boot solidly on its hip, and shoved until he cleared a space long and wide enough for at least a shallow grave.

How hard does a man have to work?

He rolled up his sleeves and plunged the shovel into the hard limestone soil.

The digging was a drag. Sam was strong on dramatic beginnings but lousy with follow-through. He left the discarded thing with its foot sticking out of the cold ground.

———

A few hours later, a garbage truck lurched down a wide boulevard lined with stately white houses. Sam was strapped into one of the side chairs on the exterior of the truck. The truck hit a pothole, and Sam nearly knocked heads with the two men strapped into the seats next to him.

"You heard they found a foot?" said the Cuban guy on his left.

"A what now?" chimed in the other trash monkey, as Sam thought of them. Fine enough guys, he supposed.

He had helium in his head that morning. Could have sailed over the rainbow, like that fat glassy-eyed bitch in the apron with the pillows for lips used to sing in the black-and-white movies. He imagined the strap that held him to the plastic seat on the side of the garbage truck was the only thing holding him down. He had to bide his time, play the game. He scratched the back of his neck, where he felt a tingle, like a premonition.

"A foot, my man. Glad it's out of our zone."

"What fool thing you talking about? Found a foot?" asked Sam.

"Out in the country."

"They know who did it?"

"The fuck should I know."

"Sure, sure."

"I just know I don't want to see no dead foot. I don't like that creepy movie shit."

"What movie?" asked Sam, sitting on his slightly trembling hands. That fucking foot. "The one about the kid who screws his mom?"

"Kills his mom."

"Screws her and kills her."

"Kills her and screws her."

"Not throwing stones from here, man. Almost killed a blond once."

"Only once?"

It was gossip, nothing more. He laughed along with the puerile jokes of the trash monkeys and did his day's work. A day's work was all they'd ever do. He now had a life purpose. He could feel it rising in his chest, heat high in his cheeks.

As Sam lay next to a snoring Yvonne that night, he thought over and over again about what's-her-name Margaret. Thought about stroking his dick while he closed his iron fist around her throat and squeezed. Thought about the look in her eyes when she realized he wasn't stopping.

He rolled on top of his girl and managed to finally fuck her. She snuggled up next to him after and dropped back off to sleep, her head on his chest. He'd done a good deed.

He knew what he'd done was wrong, but it wasn't his fault. He wondered how sex and death and love and hate could get all twisted up inside a person. Hadn't his ideas of right and wrong eroded long ago, starting at Boys' Industrial School, where thirteen-year-olds who stole bicycles wound up fucked so many ways shit ran down their legs for days?

God made the paint on the side of that house. God made his mother and his sisters and brothers and the trees lining the road and the rows of shotgun shacks and the ocean and the sky and the mansions he slinked behind to pull away their trash. God made the presidents and queens and the hos on the stroll and the wheels on the bus. God made it all. If God made him exactly how he was, with the urges he had, then he and God had a special deal. He understood that now.

Lucifer was God's favorite angel.

5

DETECTIVE MITZI ROBERTS

LAPD HEADQUARTERS, LOS ANGELES, CALIFORNIA
APRIL 2012

The elegant lines and windowed walls of LAPD Headquarters face due north, toward Los Angeles City Hall, rumored to be the most haunted building in a wicked town.

The elite Robbery Homicide Division, or RHD, is located on the fifth floor of LAPD Headquarters, not haunted by anything other than its storied past. RHD is composed of four sections (Robbery, Homicide, Gang Homicide, and Special Investigation), plus a Cold Case Homicide special section, and isn't limited by geographical divisions but rather tasked with investigating or providing support for high-profile crimes on any side of the freeways and boulevards that slice Los Angeles into racially divided islands. The triumphs and foibles of LAPD's crackerjack detective division have set fire to countless imaginations, inspiring iconic characters from *Dragnet*'s Joe Friday to Michael Connelly's Harry Bosch.

In 2012, one of the rising stars in Homicide even had a parrot named Joe Friday.

Five years before I interviewed her at Little Dom's, Detective II Mitzi Roberts, LAPD Robbery Homicide Division, left for work on the morning of April 26, 2012, knocking her elbow on the counter as she grabbed for her travel mug of black coffee.

"Fucker!"

"Fucker," echoed Joe Friday. It was the only word he said. She adopted yet another Doberman pinscher—four and counting—and named him Tucker so she could play it off for her mom.

The day before, she'd been to Davis and back, a seven-hour drive, with her partner, Rodrigo Amador, to interview the Klitschko brothers about the Exum Speight case, in which a boxer killed his manager. Roberts had a manner both straightforward and intimate that put suspects and victims alike at ease. She could (and did) easily charm a couple of boxers in Davis, Rick James, Phil Spector, and that guy who thought he was Haile Selassie and had his son's head in his freezer.

The truth was, horrors happened on a good day working homicide. The day-to-day slog was the bitch. Roberts and Amador were still pushing paper and organizing evidence from the task force on the murdered Giants fan at Dodger Stadium case.

The halls of RHD fizzed with another kind of case that day. You'd never have known it to look at the faces of the detectives hunched over countless screens and binders, banging out phone number after phone number, slagging over their cubicle walls.

Roberts worked in the Cold Case Special Section, or CCSS. Formerly the Cold Case Homicide Unit (CCHU), the CCSS was born when forensic advances in DNA science prompted the National Institute of Justice to offer grants to local law enforcement, enabling them to screen thousands of cold cases with the hope that trace DNA evidence might have been preserved. This DNA might then be matched with a suspect from the national DNA database called CODIS (Combined DNA Indexing System—both the software and the initiative).

The history and science of DNA identification both fascinated and confounded me.

The FBI piloted CODIS in 1990 with fourteen state and local laboratories. In 1994, Congress passed the DNA Identification Act, which authorized the FBI to create a national DNA database of convicted offenders as well as separate databases for missing persons and forensic samples collected from crime scenes. Cohesive national protocols developed for DNA analysis made forensic evidence collection simpler and enabled identification using smaller and sometimes degraded samples.

LAPD sex crimes and homicide detective David Lambkin and deputy district attorney Lisa Kahn shared a passion for solving cold cases, scheming behind overloaded filing cabinets about the developing forensic possibilities that might crack them open—and the nine thousand more behind them. The DOJ funded a unit, the CCHU, to screen old evidence, using fingerprint, ballistic, and DNA databases.

Located at the former Parker Center headquarters, the original seven members of the CCHU were squeezed into a windowless 250-square-foot utility closet in which there were one and a half computers that almost worked, one wall of telephone jacks that required the detectives to constantly pass headsets back and forth, and a door you couldn't open unless someone rolled their chair out of the way.

Lambkin and Khan recruited detectives Tim Marcia, Richard Bengtson, José Ramirez, Vivian Flores, and Cliff Shepard, with Rick Jackson as the assistant officer in charge. They screened for viable potential DNA evidence, uploading relevant results onto local, state, and federal databases to see if that particular DNA matched a genetic profile. If it did, they worked up their guy and tracked him down. DNA identification was so new, they played for time and used fingerprints and interviews while enough technicians were trained to handle the seemingly endless caseload. It sometimes took years to get screening results.

I hung out with Rick Jackson, the real-life Harry Bosch, who has a die-hard classic cop mustache, infectious confidence, and a knack for telling stories. He told me he'd bonded immediately with his new partner Tim Marcia. Marcia was witty, sometimes brooding, with hard ethics and a mouth to match. Together they juggled plates, incorporating emerging technologies into classic gumshoe work.

———

American biologist James Watson and English biophysicist Francis Crick unveiled their sea change discovery of the DNA helix in 1954, along with Maurice Wilkins and Rosalind Franklin.

DNA fingerprinting is a different animal—its current incarnation familiar to anyone who's been arrested and had their cheek swabbed or spit into a tube sent from 23 and Me. The process of determining an individual's unique DNA characteristics was developed only six years previous to the inception of CODIS in 1990. The forensic applications of DNA fingerprinting captured the attention of the public.

In 1984, Sir Alec Jeffreys of the Department of Genetics at the University of Leicester developed DNA fingerprinting, also known as DNA profiling. About 99.9 percent of DNA sequences, the building blocks that make us human, are the same in all human beings; the other 0.1 percent make us not just human but individuals. This 0.1

percent aids criminal investigations, enables medical advances, provokes legal battles, allows familial identifications, and holds limitless possibility.

The double helix itself contains clues to not just whodunnit but also who we are and why. A certain genetic profile combined with plasticity affected by activating environmental factors can indicate a propensity for aggression. For example, violent offenders and law enforcement officials alike often share the famed *MAOA* gene, or warrior gene.

DNA fingerprinting is based on the statistical calculation of the rarity of the produced profile of alleles within a population. A gene is a unit of hereditary information made up of that twisty beasty DNA, a complex molecule that codes genetic information. An allele is a rebel—a variant form of a gene that also codes for sequences. Copies of each gene cozy up together at a specific locus (location on a chromosome), one from each parent. The copies aren't necessarily twinsies.

Today's system of DNA profiling identifies short tandem repeats (STRs): simple repeating sequences of alleles. STRs vary in length, enabling scientists to distinguish one DNA sample from another. Genetic fingerprinting isolates these STRs and calculates the probability that the sample screened belongs to a specific individual. The FBI has identified thirteen core STR loci routinely used in the identification of individual offenders in the United States.

While the CCHU scrambled for properly trained analysts, they combed through fingerprints, talked to family members, and dug through databases like NamUs (the National Missing and Unidentified Persons System, established in 2007) and the Doe Network (the International Center for Unidentified and Missing Persons, founded in 1999).

As ancestry became a national obsession, Lambkin, Khan, Marcia, Jackson, and the rest of the intrepid CCHU Don Quixotes moved out of their closet and into a room with wide windows and a sweeping view of their city of bones. They became the CCSS. Detective Mitzi Roberts joined in 2010, and they took on the unofficial motto of Connelly's fictional Harry Bosch: Everyone matters or no one matters.

Cold cases were a long game, sometimes taking years for the screenings to cycle through the bogged-down system. On a bad day, bad weeks or months even, the endless rows of files could make the most seasoned detective flirt with hopelessness. Then, bam, a case-to-case hit and you were back full throttle.

Roberts and her then partner Amador first saw the name Samuel Little when the screening efforts of the CCSS connected DNA from two LA homicides in the late eighties to a man named Samuel Little, a.k.a. Samuel McDowell. The two four-inch-wide three-ring binders, known as murder books, carried all the hallmarks of a sexually motivated serial killer.

On May 6, 2009, a CCSS detective submitted evidence from the 1989 murder of Guadalupe Apodaca to the Serial Investigation Division, then on to Bode Technology lab for DNA analysis.

On March 1, 2010, epithelial cells extracted from the fingernail kit from the murder of Audrey Nelson were submitted for analysis.

On the morning of April 26, 2012, DNA fingerprinting confirmed a case-to-case match, linking two cold case homicides with a known criminal named Samuel Little through a national database. A case-to-case: the holy grail of homicide investigation. However, even the holy grail is only a start. High-risk lifestyles, including drugs and prostitution, can mean that multiple DNA profiles are present on a victim's body. DNA alone won't likely get you an arrest.

Roberts was still going to have to make a case corroborating the DNA evidence, at the same time tracking him and trying to get him into custody. He could have been out there stalking his next victim even as she reviewed the case files.

Roberts slid the first murder book toward her and opened a world. It was never laid out for you neat and nice like a mystery novel, but the story was in there somewhere if you knew how to work backward from the end.

6

GUADALUPE

The world of Guadalupe Apodaca, a.k.a. Isabela Luna, came to an end sometime in the days preceding September 3, 1989, when nine-year-old Alfredo Torres peered into the blown-out window of an abandoned warehouse near the corner of Ascot Avenue and East Forty-Third Street.

Roberts didn't know the corner offhand, but anyone working cold cases could make an educated guess. South Central LA was the most glamorous and vilified ghetto in the world. It had been over a decade since John Singleton's *Boyz n the Hood* made South Central the hood to define hood, and no one was over it yet.

During the 1940s, thousands of southern Blacks fled poverty and Jim Crow to the West Coast. Jim Crow or no, racial housing discrimination corralled the growing Black population into ghettos, subdivided by twist ties of freeways. Deindustrialization in the seventies further shook the community's already fragile economy.

The LAPD pioneered the country's first SWAT (Special Weapons and Tactics) team in the wake of the Watts Rebellion of 1965. For the first time in the nation's history, tanks equipped with battering rams rolled down urban streets, while behind the scenes, the FBI's COINTELPRO (Counterintelligence Program) aggressively targeted Black political organizations. By 1972, the Crips and Bloods fought over the same intersections the Black Panthers once patrolled.

In the mid-1980s, crack assaulted American urban centers, while the Reagan administration's War on Drugs imposed far steeper sentences for drugs predominantly abused in low-income and minority populations. While a generation of young men was slapped with unreasonably long stays in our increasingly for-profit prison system, a vulnerable population of women was left standing shell-shocked and bare-assed on Figueroa Street.

The unlucky turned up blue in the morning. No fewer than seven serial killers and rapists prowled the same killing fields during the eighties and nineties, picking through the wreckage of the splintered community of South Los Angeles. Most had MOs that included strangulation, including Chester Turner, "Southside Slayer" Michael Hughes, "Grim Sleeper" Lonnie Franklin, Louis Craine, Ivan Hill, and "Night Stalker" Richard Ramirez.

When Roberts came across the case of Guadalupe Apodaca, she knew in her bones she was looking at another serial killer.

Though only a few miles from the booming urban development of downtown, in 2012, South Los Angeles still looked much like it did in 1989. Along the wide boulevards stood rows of modest 1920s bungalows with stucco '60s apartments crowbarred between them. The main thoroughfares featured sewing machine shops, taquerias, and hair salons with colorful hand-painted signs. Gang graffiti delineated the territories unknown to Rand McNally.

No one sullied the myriad murals of Our Lady of Guadalupe floating above the sidewalks on walls of panaderías, carnicerías, and check-cashing places. Cloaked in cerulean blue, hands in prayer, the mother of God forgives you, protects you, cries your tears for you when you're fresh out. She's managed to be a virgin and still have nothing left to lose.

In 1989, half a block from a mural of her namesake, Guadalupe Apodaca's lifeless body was discovered in an abandoned garage on a cloudless morning in early September, still heavy with the heat of summer.

A few miles north in Hollywood, it was still the night before for an army of jaw-grinding wannabes and almost-weres with high waist-bands and wide shoulder pads. All that easy money was supposed to trickle down from Rodeo Drive to San Pedro Avenue. Instead, the money turned into snow drifts of Colombian hoovered off the backs of toilet tanks at the Roxy, the China Club.

As you drove south, the trickle slowed to a drip. Women desperate for a drink or a fix, or just plain desperate, combed the stroll. There was no free money. It trickled straight into your hand or not at all, and you worked for every cent. Six thousand miles away, the Berlin wall teetered.

Public schools were not yet back in session when, at about ten twenty in the morning, nine-year-old Alfredo Torres kicked a half-deflated soccer ball against the wall of an abandoned commercial garage in the debris-strewn alley off Ascot Avenue and East Forty-Third. A pink metallic streamer blew by his feet, freed from the con-certina wire atop the cinder-block walls of the church across the street.

Taking up an imaginary friend on a dare, Alfredo made himself keep both eyes open as he peered deeper into the banged-up shit shack, filled with food wrappers and an aluminum trash barrel on ash-strewn ground. He'd hoped to glean the shine of a nickel, a forgotten *Playboy* magazine, a dead rat. Instead, his eyes scanned the same familiar bags of rotting garbage, pizza boxes, lead paint peeling off the walls. He almost glanced right over the bare mattress wedged in a corner, but a flash of something pale and irregular caught his attention.

He rubbed his eyes with his sleeve before deciding it was not a trick of the light. He was definitely looking at a naked pair of women's legs, emerging from the space between where the mattress met the wall.

When the patrol unit showed up, they found the discarded, decomposing body of forty-three-year-old Guadalupe Apodaca, naked from the waist down, lying on her left side, hemorrhaged eyes open and staring at the scarred concrete floor. She wore only a buttercup-colored man's shirt half-torn from her body, one tarnished silver earring, and a silver ring on her middle finger, set with a large square of turquoise. Abrasions covered her back and rear thighs. When the coroner's investigator turned her, the curtain of dark hair that obscured her face in the first of the numbered photos fell back and revealed snow-white roots. Apodaca was no longer young, and she had the hard look of someone who probably never was. Flies alighted on her nose, mouth, and multiple contusions. Her body was a mottled canvas of injury, including a wide necklace of maroon bruising that nearly encircled her throat, crowned by a crosshatching of deep scratches.

Due to the bruising on the throat area and the fractures of the hyoid bone and thyroid cartilage, the LA County coroner's office attributed the cause of Apodaca's death to manual strangulation. Her body also showed signs of sexual assault. Homicide detectives with LAPD's Newton Division attempted to obtain additional insight into the murder of Apodaca, who had an arrest record that included narcotics possession, forgery, robbery, and attempted murder. Numerous witnesses were interviewed. Several plausible theories were developed. No viable suspect was identified. Within weeks, the case went cold.

Fifteen years prior, right around the corner, the kidnappers of white heiress Patty Hearst had been hunted down and shot in front of the hungry eyes of the entire nation. Guadalupe Apodaca's invisible killer slipped into the night like a ghost.

Roberts's approach to homicide was based on Occam's razor. It usually is what it looks like, once you figure out what you're looking at.

It was usually the husband.

If not, the boyfriend.

Or the wife's boyfriend killed the husband.

It was a guy who worked for a guy in the rival gang or thought he did.

Murderers are lousy arsonists.

People are terrible liars.

You meet a lot of dummies, pick through a lot of trash, push a ton of paper.

Everyone leaves a trace.

Roberts didn't make up that last one. Prescient French forensic scientist Edmond Locard (1877–1966) conceived of what he called "the exchange principle." According to Locard, every contact leaves a trace. We leave a piece of ourselves behind with everything we touch. We take something with us when we go.

Locard died after the discovery of the DNA double helix in 1953 but before witnessing its forensic applications. In Locard's day, the traces that unlocked the secrets of the dead included fingerprints, hair, clothing fibers, letters, receipts, whispers to spouses, gossip of neighbors, and vengeful lovers. The idea of DNA was still an embryo when Locard grasped that every cell of our beings carries a unique signature, and we always sign the guest book somehow. No one moves through the world like a haint.

Both DNA fingerprinting and digital tracking have transformed criminal investigations, but the exchange principle remains the same. DNA isn't a panacea, particularly with many cold cases, which number over 240,000 in the United States since 1980 alone. Much of the physical evidence has long since been swallowed by history, because it either never existed or has been degraded or destroyed. For those cases to be solved, the traces of contact can resemble a more traditional investigative model. A confession or strong denial can be the crucial tipping point.

Even if all the boxes are checked, a case-to-case DNA hit on two cold case prostitute murders from the eighties is not enough to indict. Even if it were, they had to catch the bastard first and get him off the street. Find the fucker. Get him someway, anyway, into custody. Get a confirmation cheek swab. Get a confession.

This one was slippery, transient. A glance at his record and Mitzi knew he'd be barely distinguishable from the shadows in which he lurked: a ghoul.

But there are no such things as monsters.

"Who the fuck is this guy?" she asked.

Is he dead?

Is he in custody?

Is he out and about? Does he have an address?

Does he have a driver's license? Does he have a car?

Is he still a threat?

How are we going to find him? How are we going to keep him?

The team around Roberts ran rap sheets and arrest records, pulled prison packages, and ran vehicle searches while she scanned the pages of the ever-growing stack of arrest records. The results flooding her desk shook even Roberts's unflappable cool.

The question wasn't where he'd been hiding all these years. He hadn't. He'd been killing in plain sight.

Samuel Little's arrest history began in 1956 (juvenile records being expunged), when he was first arrested for burglarizing a furniture warehouse. Over the next six decades, he was repeatedly arrested in Ohio, Maryland, Florida, Maine, Connecticut, Oregon, Colorado, Pennsylvania, New Jersey, Arizona, Georgia, Illinois, Missouri, California…the list went on.

The charges included burglary, breaking and entering, assault and battery, assault with the intent to rob, assault with a firearm, armed robbery, assault on a police officer, solicitation of prostitution, driving under the influence, shoplifting, theft, grand theft, possession of marijuana, unlawful flight to avoid prosecution, resisting arrest, battery, false imprisonment, assault with great bodily injury, robbery, rape, and sodomy.

She did the math. For all this, Sam had served just ten years altogether.

Roberts knew she had to start with the MO, look to the cases in Sam's history that most closely resembled the two murders in the white binders in front of her. Assault, rape, murder.

Roberts gave no fucks about this repeat offender robbing a ninety-nine-cent store, other than the fact that it placed him in a certain location on a certain date, especially if that place was behind bars. For patterns, she looked to the violence.

On September 11, 1976, Sam was arrested in Sunset Hills, Missouri, for the rape, sodomy, assault with great body injury, and robbery of Pamela K. Smith. Smith had shown up hysterical on a stranger's doorstep after escaping Sam's car and running nearly naked through the night, her face and throat bruised and beaten, her hands bound behind her with cloth and electrical cord. Sam had strangled, bitten, beaten, and sodomized her. He was convicted of the lesser charge of assault with attempt to ravish and served a total of three months.

Roberts read it again. Surely it was a typo and he had served three years, not three months. But no. This fucker truly served less time for rape and attempted murder than for his first offense, breaking and entering.

On September 12, 1982, the nude, strangled body of twenty-six-year-old Patricia Mount was found in a field in Alachua County, Florida. Eyewitnesses later identified Sam as the man last seen leaving a tavern in Gainesville with Mount, who had a mental disability and lived at a nearby assisted-care facility, in his brown Pinto station wagon with wood paneling. Hairs found on the victim were similar to Sam's. He was tried for Mount's murder, even admitted to being at the tavern at the night in question, but due to the lack of definitive physical evidence, the jury acquitted.

On October 4, 1982, the skeletal remains of twenty-two-year-old Melinda LaPree were found by a groundskeeper in the Gautier Family Cemetery near Pascagoula, Mississippi, a month after she had been reported missing by her boyfriend. A disarticulated hyoid bone and fractured cricoid cartilage indicated strangulation. Again, eyewitnesses identified Sam as the man with whom she had been seen getting into a brown Pinto station wagon. Two Black prostitutes by the names of Hilda Nelson and Leila McClain were interviewed in the course of the investigation, revealing that Sam had brutally assaulted and strangled each of the women the previous year, but they had miraculously escaped. Authorities had brazenly ignored the reports until young, white LaPree turned up. Sam was arrested, but the charges were ultimately dismissed by a grand jury for lack of evidence. The testimony of Nelson and McClain was never heard.

On October 25, 1984, in San Diego, California, Sam was caught by uniformed patrol officers in the act of beating and strangling Tonya Jackson in the back seat of his black Thunderbird. He was charged with rape, assault with great bodily injury, and sexual battery. Sam waived his rights, and the police report quoted him as saying to the arresting officers, "That bitch didn't give me my money's worth. She's going to give it to me or else." He'd met her at a downtown gay bar, offered her twenty dollars for sex, and driven her to the same deserted, trash-strewn overlook at which he'd assaulted Laurie Barros not a month before, on September 27, 1984.

"I told her I wanted more," he stated. "But she refused. I told her she wasn't going anywhere until I got my pussy. I grabbed her in self-defense. She deserved it. She tried to cheat me." He denied raping her and said he had just kicked the shit out of her. He also repeatedly asked the officers, "How's the bitch? Is she going to make it?"

The SDPD connected Jackson's attack with that of Barros, who had played dead and lived to tell the tale after being assaulted, strangled, and left by the side of the road. The cases were tried together, with the added charges of false imprisonment, assault with great bodily injury, and sexual battery. Sam pled guilty to two counts of assault with great bodily injury and one count of false imprisonment.

Barros identified him from a lineup, during which she asked him to say, "Swallow for me. I love it when you swallow." She later told police that she knew it was him immediately. She just wanted to make him say it.

From his prison package, Roberts learned that Sam received a four-year prison sentence. He served only eighteen months and was paroled on February 1, 1987. He traveled the one hundred and twenty-five miles north to his old stomping grounds of Los Angeles, where he shacked back up with his long-term girlfriend and continued his rampage of theft by day, murder by night.

She flipped through Sam's mug shots, watched his face turn from posturing child to dandy in a shark skin suit, to wilder and disheveled, to white-haired, scabrous, and transient. Every time, he got out.

How in the actual fuck could this have happened?

How this happened is that a judge in Missouri thought three months was an appropriate sentence for rape and assault. How it happened is that law enforcement officials in Mississippi in the eighties didn't believe it was possible to commit a crime against a Black prostitute. How it happened was, in a tradition of many serial killers before him, certainly the ones who had operated on Roberts's beat, he chose to dispose of victims society already thought were trash.

Roberts turned to the murder book on the case that had been linked to Guadalupe Apodaca through DNA. The second binder was that of Audrey Nelson, born August 27, 1953, found by a transient in a dumpster behind a Chinese restaurant on East Seventh Street on the morning of August 14, 1989. The high school photo of a beautiful if somewhat bewildered blond was unrecognizable as the emaciated, broken body curled in a fetal position on her left side in the dumpster, nude from the waist down, wearing only a red sweatshirt, pushed up around the top of her torso. Detectives had interviewed her boyfriend,

Jack West, a.k.a. Jack Winston, a.k.a. Preston Everett, who gave conflicting statements and was known to regularly beat Nelson. They'd
been together for many years, and he was responsible for the burn
scars covering half her body, which she told the doctors at Lenox Hill
Hospital had been an accident after they took her off the ventilator.
There wasn't enough evidence, and the case quickly went cold.

In the crime scene photos. Nelson's short brown hair was matted
to her face, her body a roadmap of beatings, burns, abrasions, drag
marks, and stark, black tattoos. On the knuckles of the left fist curled
next to her face were stamped the letters T-R-U-E. The next angle
revealed their counterpart: L-O-V-E. There was also a tarantula on
the side of her neck, a heart on her breastbone, and a cryptic symbol
on her hand, an arrow at its center.

Roberts saw hope buried in all this carnage: Audrey Nelson had
not made it, but there were living victims.

Prosecutors perform narrative somersaults to create empathy for
invisible victims, who are reduced to the two dimensions of photographs and microscopic epithelial cells in a marked tube. But nothing
told a story better than a warm human. Jurors turned their heads from
gruesome crime scene photographs, hands clasped over their mouths.
It's much harder to turn from eyes with light still behind them. The
living victims from Mississippi and San Diego could be Roberts's ace
in the hole: Hilda Nelson, Leila McClain, Laurie Barros, and Tonya
Jackson.

Roberts and Amador resubmitted the decades-old physical evidence for additional testing, flawless in their procedure, aware every
delicate thread of preserved evidence would be scrutinized. Roberts
spent days with a phone glued to her ear, talking to investigators in
Georgia, Mississippi, Texas, Florida, Ohio, Pennsylvania, Arizona,

and Louisiana, along with the LA Sheriff's Department, Long Beach Police Department, and San Diego Police Department. She tracked Samuel Little a.k.a. McDowell across the country, running near-constant offline searches with the National Crime Information Center, a catchall database of police record searches by name. Since he was a drifter and drug user, Sam's name was run by some cop or other every day it seemed. The problem was that the hits showed up a day or three or a week after Sam was ten miles down the road, who knew in which direction.

Sam was a phantom with no address, no registered car, no credit card. Roberts's urgency mounted daily as she pushed against her ass-chafing lieutenant's threat to release a wanted flyer. Her greased pig might see it and slide into the shadows forever. Or he'd have his story all cooked up when they did finally nab him, and they'd never get a confession.

One morning, same drill, she caught Sam's name in Calcasieu Parish, Louisiana, where a detective named Brett Young had run Sam after having seen him outside a local homeless shelter with some prostitutes and finding a crack pipe in his pocket.

Young hung up the phone without a goodbye to Roberts, strode straight to his car, and raced to the shelter. *Must have been the new guy*, she thought. That was a trick Rick Jackson had taught her: call and ask for whoever just made detective. You might just surf a wave of enthusiasm.

When Young called back, his tone was dejected, but only momentarily. He'd discovered the drifter had drifted again, two days before.

"I'm not done," he said. "If you'll allow me."

Young alerted law enforcement in the area. Detectives on the case gleaned Sam received disability benefits directly to a Walmart card.

Anything with numbers or magnetic stripes can be tracked.

Roberts called Walmart customer service. An automated message asked for a PIN.

Fuck.

"If you can't remember your PIN, enter your Social Security number and date of birth, followed by the pound sign," the automated voice told her.

Those, she had.

"For your last five transactions, press 1. You will be charged one dollar."

Roberts had him two days running in Louisville, Kentucky, same liquor store.

She checked again to make sure. Checked a third time, just to charge him the extra dollar for fun.

Within three hours, federal marshals in Louisville apprehended a bedraggled Sam, three steps from the door of Wayfair Homeless Shelter, a block from the liquor store where he'd last used the card. They took him into custody on an outstanding narcotics warrant.

They had him. The rub was they had a probable serial killer with a case-to-case match but not an indictment. They had actually only arrested and were holding him on a pissant narcotics warrant from when he'd skipped out on a drug diversion program in LA. They had him off the streets, but could they keep him?

Sam invoked his right to counsel, though not before he told officers he was a "braggadocio kingpin." They noted he never asked why they were there.

After a brief stay in Texas for yet another warrant, he limped out to meet LAPD's Fugitive Warrant Division detectives Chris Ratcliff and Jorge Morales, now missing one toe due to diabetes.

"Texas justice," said Ratcliff before calling Roberts from the TGI Fridays at the airport to say they had him in custody.

A curvy young woman hustled by.

"Look at that ass. I would like to get me some of that. Get in between those legs, and lick that pussy," Sam told the detectives.

"Bet she was thinking the same thing, buddy."

When they reached the gate, Sam crossed his arms, demanded peanut M&Ms, and refused to get on the plane. Ratcliff traded some candy for a scene in public.

When the plane touched down on California soil, Sam smiled as he finished the last of the candy, the corners of his lips crusted with green shards of sugar. They left him in jail in Wasco and handed the ball back to Roberts with condolences.

Sam staunchly maintained his innocence.

Roberts and Amador presented the case to deputy district attorney Beth Silverman with freshly screened evidence and the confirmation swab. Silverman is one of the country's most successful prosecutors of high-profile complex homicide cases, including notorious and egregious serial killers and rapists like the Grim Sleeper, the Southside Slayer, Chester Turner, and Latece Brown.

Silverman always closed wearing red. The evisceration of fools was game night for her. Her face only softened for the victims, when she was out of sight of the crowd. She'd gone to school for journalism, had once imagined herself a foreign correspondent in war zones. Instead, she became a soldier in a never-ending war against indomitable enemies—injustice, violence. Silverman dominated the battles at least.

"Not enough," said Silverman.

She ran a hand through her chestnut mane and dropped her palm to the paper stack.

"In twenty years, I've never seen a rap sheet like this—never. I want to file. I can't file with this. I can't. Get me more victims."

She paced.

"I need pattern evidence. Get me the living victims, see if they'll testify. Walking. Talking. People."

They'd all known the notoriously handsy head prosecutor Gary Hearnsberger would almost certainly need more than two hookers with matching DNA profiles on their corpses.

While Roberts doggedly built the case, her longtime partner and friend Amador held a slightly differing opinion on what constituted a hard day's work. Tall and handsome, with a charm school education, he was more of a skater. The mounting tension breached the divider separating their cubicles until they blew. Their shouting match in the records room rattled the shelves.

All parties thought a change of pace wise. Roberts's old buddy Rick Jackson got in the car for the next lap as she brought him up to speed while entering each case into the ViCAP (Violent Criminal Apprehension Program) system. They couldn't hang on to the monster forever. She'd exhausted the other options. She and Jackson were going to have to pound some pavement.

7

UNCLE SASHA

Humans adapt quickly. By the second weekend, I had gotten used to waking up at four and driving the hour and a half to the prison while the dawn broke over the desert. I blasted eighties pop music, nineties power ballads, ear junk food. One foot on the gas pedal, the other on the floorboard.

On the days I visited Sam, I did nothing but journal, organize my notes, and listen to music. No vicious text threads with my girlfriends, no guilty social media dalliances, no distractions. Mind in the game, but don't think too much.

I was willingly entering a situation I knew to be dangerous. It was not a scene from a horror movie. Norman Bates may have been his mother, and that was scary. Sam was something else. Sam was in Technicolor and could smell when I had my period. He knew if I was doing my push-ups from a hug hello. He smelled the garlic on my hair if I made spaghetti the night before. I willed the bile from the back of my throat.

There was no pure way of removing distractions, of course. My friend Sasha concerned me. Thoughts of his recent downward turn nudged at me. I listened to the Ramones, Depeche Mode. I was tired that morning. I opened the windows to the cool air. In an hour or two, the temperature would soar forty degrees in an hour, an express elevator to hell.

Sasha was a surrogate son. He met my husband, Scott, at a support group for men in recovery from drugs and alcohol (he was the one who told me about the quarters). For five years, he'd spent nearly every holiday with us, every birthday. My kids called him Uncle Sasha. He carried my son Jovi on his shoulders at my husband's concerts.

Sasha had grown up in a family that valued hardness in men above all. He was three inches shorter than me and a marshmallow. I found his compassion a rare and precious thing. He hated it. He liked mean girlfriends who called him a pussy to toughen him up. He took up bodybuilding, trying to turn himself into a fortress.

He showed up at our house with shaker cups of a vile smoothie that included grilled chicken and rice. He gagged as he choked them down. One day after a rainstorm, our driveway was blocked by palm fronds. He furiously tossed them aside to clear the way for my car, as if he was the Hulk. His mood had darkened exponentially.

I pulled off at Lancaster and took my place in the line of cars stacked along the shoulder of Avenue 60.

6:15 a.m. Eighth car in line. Not bad.

At 9:30 precisely, the line inched toward the guardhouse. A sheriff's deputy with a wide- brimmed hat and a face out of *Cool Hand Luke* approached my window. I fumbled for my ID.

"Don't be nervous, pretty lady." He checked my back seat. "You're not going to prison. You're just visiting." He handed me a slip with the number 13. "Don't worry. We'll get you back out again."

"I'll hold you to it."

"I won't be here," he replied. "Follow that red car."

The waiting room of the visitor's center was packed that Saturday. I filled out my paperwork on a shelf of children's books, signs around it hanging at haphazard angles:

NUMBERS!
TOGETHER WE CAN PREVENT CHILD ABUSE
LETTER SOUNDS!
WHEN TO CALL 911

The plug-in air-conditioning unit was no match for the 110 degree heat. We fanned ourselves with outdated copies of *Cosmo* and *Parenting* while a Paleolithic boom box played Eminem's "Lose Yourself."

Women who would probably never be in the same room for any other reason talked easily and lightly with each other. The only tacitly forbidden topic was why you were actually there. Some had forged unlikely friendships over the months or years they'd been visiting. A tall girl with a lank braid and an Eastern European accent traded recipes with a white-haired Black grandmother in a hot-pink tracksuit and matching Ugg boots.

A nervous newbie with a cherubic face and a swirl of blue and purple braids had brought a plastic baggie full of dollar bills instead of quarters. When she learned some of the vending machines only took quarters, she just about hyperventilated.

"I didn't know! I went to the bank to get all these singles. The teller asked me if I was going to a strip club and I was all, sure. I mean, which is worse?"

A middle-aged white woman with a voice like a lawn mower and flip-flops revealing poorly rendered toenail art offered to change some of her dollars. I had forgotten to pick up the rolls of quarters that week and had spent the night before digging through a mason jar full of coins, separating out any quarters from stray euros, yen, and Chuck E. Cheese tokens.

When in line to enter the cage, I met the deputy's eyes only briefly, answered what they asked, held up my hand to show my wedding ring. I pulled back my hair to show my earrings, showed the prescription for my glasses, turned around, emptied my pockets, ran my fingers along the lining of my waistband. I handed over my driver's license, got my wrist black-light-stamped.

Once inside the visiting room, I bought two Cokes, a container of honey-garlic wings, some chips for me. I checked in with the deputy at the front desk, learned his name. I said hello to the trustees, gave ol' Everett a little love. He was an ancient gangster who would smuggle me one of the pencils he kept for the kids for a wink. An enormous man named Calvin always wiped down my heavily guarded table and pulled out my chair with a limp and a kind smile. Turn on your bright eyes and let men help you. They grow three inches, glow like little boys.

I heated Sam's food and set it up for him. When Sam entered, I hugged him. I kept a bead on the guard, estimating the distance in yards. I popped the tab on Sam's Coke and served him. I sometimes wiped the corners of his mouth with a napkin.

Sam's stories flowed free-form, hypnotic. He followed bread crumbs of association rather than chronology. His eyes were either black holes or glittering disco balls. Around us, hard men with neck tattoos held babies as if they were made of glass and smiled down with the only unguarded facial expression of their week. Cans dropped from vending machines with a *thunk*. Microwaves beeped with every burrito.

"Five words you'd use to describe yourself?"

"Mad. Misunderstood. Unlikable. Angry. Hateful."

"But you weren't unlikable."

"What now?"

"Women devoted themselves to you. Jean. Ninah. They loved you. You had all the evidence in the world that you were lovable."

"Jean…"

Wrong move. Get him off syrupy sentimentality.

"How did it feel to kill them?"

"Oooeee, it felt like heaven. Felt like being in bed with Marilyn Monroe!"

A cartoon woman. Bed was not where he wanted to be with a woman, Marilyn or otherwise.

"It felt like being in love."

I wondered what he had for comparison.

Sam told me he loved women, worshipped them. Especially stuck-up white women. As a child, he didn't realize women ate and slept and shat. He thought they were angels.

"Must have been disappointing when you figured out the truth."

"I suppose it was."

"You wouldn't be the first man to be disappointed by the humanity of women."

"That's my smart baby. You got the psychology." He tapped a finger to his temple.

Sam told me about four more murders that day, in exquisite and haunting detail. He lit up like a child on Christmas. He hugged himself and made kissy-kissy noises. With one outstretched arm, he demonstrated how much force it took to crack a hyoid bone.

His face twisted into a grotesque mask of rage. Just as quickly, he went back to Perv Grandpa mode.

"I got only two things left now, my memories and my feelings."

Sam believed he owned the souls of every one of his "babies." Mine, he said, over and over. Mine, mine, mine. A deranged and diabolical toddler. He believed God was going to reunite his "family" in heaven.

"If I had a daughter, she'd be just like you." He brushed my leg with his hand. "You are my play daughter. My adopted daughter. I love you."

He told them all he loved them. He told them they were beautiful. He told them they were his, forever. Sometimes he made them say it back to him before he killed them.

Mirroring body language is a common interview technique. As he described the murders, I leaned forward, matching some version of what I thought was him lying in wait, ready to pounce: his words the apex of charm, his muscles coursing with threat. It probably never got better than that moment for him.

Maybe it would never get better than that moment for me either. After a lifetime of free-floating anxiety and sometimes paralyzing fear of the unknown, here was the real-life monster under the bed. He was neither spooky nor scary. Those words are far too twee. After a short time, I wasn't scared anymore for my safety. I willed myself to feel nothing. Give him nothing. When a tiny snarl, almost like a twitch, curled my left upper lip, I snapped back to my question list and my default sympathy/poker face. The more I did it, the easier it got for me. I wondered which was preferable—overwhelming fear for your safety or the inability to feel at all. I hoped I'd find something in-between.

"Why do you feel like you need to own women?"

"I wanted their helplessness. All I ever wanted was for them to cry in my arms."

"Denise cried. If it was all you wanted, why didn't you let her live?"

"Well, you got me there. Maybe it wasn't all I wanted."

"I had my own hard days, you know. I'm glad I never met up with somebody like you one dark night."

"But I never killed nobody like my smart baby here. I never killed no senators or governors or fancy New York journalists. Nothing like that. I killed you, it'd be all over the news the next day."

"How did it feel to finally get caught?"

Sam argued that the presence of his DNA didn't prove he killed those women. He said they railroaded him, lied and said he beat women. They got the three living witnesses who testified at his Los Angeles trial to come to town by promising them a free trip to Disneyland. Lying whores. He never beat women. He never raped women.

This last point was essential to him. He didn't box those women. He was no rapist. He didn't have to. They came to him.

"But you killed those women."

"You think you know me? You think you in here sparring with Mr. Sam now?"

He shadowboxed, throwing mock punches an inch from my cheekbone. I noticed he liked to scare me a little when I stepped out of line, reminding me he was in control of the conversation. I flinched.

"I like to think we know each other a little by now. I think you killed them."

"Well, you're right about that, little miss. They still set me up."

"What do you feel you deserve?"

"What's that question?"

"We live in a society that has rules. One of those rules is that you don't just go around killing people for fun. What I want to know is, what do you think you deserve for what you did?"

Sam lived in a world of wanting and taking, not a world of just deserts.

When I reached my car, I turned to the prison and instinctively spat three times on the ground—a tradition used by old Jewish ladies to ward off the evil eye.

I fumbled with my glasses, dug around for my key, before I remembered it was still in my bag of quarters. When I was safely down the road, I pulled to the side of the road and folded over the steering wheel, my chest collapsing with thoughts of Mary, the Norwegian blond, the barrel, the Everglades, the fresh grave, the bathtub. I looked around, making sure there was no one to hear, and screamed. Then I drove to the nearest Olive Garden, ordered myself a glass of crappy white wine and a salad, and wrote longhand for three hours, not wanting to lose a single detail.

As a civilian, it's impossible to bring a recording device into a maximum-security prison in California. You can't bring a writing implement. You can't take out anything you didn't bring in.

I did it all from memory. I use a popular and simple technique called a memory palace. I learned it from my father, who played decent chess, legit tournament bridge, and had a pretty vicious poker game, until my mother had it with his gambling and he took up the market instead. Early on, my father deemed me sharp, good on the fly, short-tempered, and short-sighted. Not worth the time for more than poker. Memory helps.

He taught me a simple technique of turning memories into images, the funnier and filthier the better (because that is what our minds seize on), and storing them in various places in a remembered or invented but familiar location. Most people start with a childhood home. When it's time to remember, you walk back through this location and retrieve each memory, one at a time. It works with cards and at social functions. It also allows me to remember up to about ninety minutes of conversation with remarkable accuracy, without recording or notes. After that, I can get a little hazy. It takes practice and concentration. Joshua Foer's excellent *Moonwalking with Einstein* discusses memory palaces at length.

In the case of Samuel Little, my memory palace involved populating my childhood home with the memories of a serial killer. It was a mind trick, not a metaphor. Sometimes a memory palace is just a memory palace. I cleaned the place with a power washer when I was done writing it all down so it would be ready for the following week.

I put down the pen and picked up the phone as I headed out to the parking lot.

"This is Detective Roberts."

"Hi, Mitzi. It's Jillian Lauren. I saw Little today. He's talking. I don't know what to do."

"Okay. Don't say another word. Hang up the phone. A Texas Ranger is the chief IO [investigating officer] on Little now. He'll be in touch. You'll do fine."

Shit. Talking to the LAPD was nerve-racking enough. The cowboy himself—Ranger Jimmy Holland—was gonna be in touch?

My husband called right after Roberts hung up without a good-bye to tell me he was still in the studio. A sitter was covering until I got home.

"Who's sitting? Sasha? I can't get Sasha on the phone."

"Honey. I didn't tell you this yesterday because I knew you had a long day today, but his messages have been green for two days."

"What does that mean? So?"

"It means...it means his phone is off."

"No, it doesn't. Lots of people have those green messages."

"That is what it means on Sasha's phone. I know him and he would never turn his phone off. I called the building manager this morning. He just notified the marshals, and they're going to the apartment. You need to prepare yourself."

A voice in my own head, as if watching from just above me, had to translate Scott's words as I pulled into my driveway and the last of the sun melted into the mountains.

He's saying be ready for the "Sasha killed himself" call.

I gathered my duffel bag from a day in prison and kicked the car door closed as I held the phone to my ear.

So dramatic. He's jumping to conclusions.

Except Scott never jumps to conclusions. He's methodical to a fault.

"No. Because his girlfriend is a bitch? He's in college. His girl-friend is supposed to be a bitch. No. This is ridiculous."

The other line buzzed. There it was: the Texas number.

"I'll call you back."

I picked it up.

"This is Texas Ranger James Holland," said a slightly accented voice, neither overly concerned nor overly friendly. The space cowboy himself. "I hear you've been talking to my boy Sammy."

I flopped onto the front steps. Jovi bounded out the front door, eyes alight, palm outstretched.

"Look, Mommy! Look! Try it!" Our first fig.

"Excuse me…" I said to the ranger and took a quick bite. "It's delicious. Can you go get me some more, please, honey?"

Jovi ran back to the yard.

"So. What did he say?" Holland asked.

"I mean, do you want me to just read from my notes? I could organize them better."

"Go ahead and read."

I paged through my still disorganized notes of murder after murder.

As I read, he said "Okay, okay…" or "Skip that one."

"Wait," Holland said after I told him about a victim in Omaha. "Read that one again."

"Um, okay. Well, I asked him who else knew about his secret life. If anyone else knew about the murders. He told me he thought his girlfriend Ninah knew. She was a Black prostitute. It was sometime in the mid-seventies. They were driving his white '69 T-bird through Omaha, and Ninah was fiddling with the radio. A story came on the news about a woman who had been strangled and left in a barrel behind an old factory. He said Ninah side-eyed him in a way that let him know she knew."

He cut me off. "You did the right thing. This is an open investigation, so…much appreciated if we could keep this to ourselves for the time being."

He hung up without a goodbye and without my getting a promise of an interview. Tough crowd.

Scott called twenty minutes later.

The kids had come in from the backyard and were downstairs rinsing the garden mud from their feet, the little-boy sweat from their hairlines, getting ready for their infuriating nightly argument over the remote control. The sky was a swirl of rose and deep gray, the trees silhouettes in the dying light.

I'd been right: Scott rarely jumped to conclusions. And he'd been right: Sasha had hung himself from his doorknob three days before.

For the second time in a day, I screamed. I couldn't remember the last time I'd screamed before that day.

We talked to a grief counselor. Scott and I decided we'd tell the kids immediately, each in developmentally appropriate ways, whatever that meant. I called my mother, who said a Hebrew prayer. I greeted my husband at the door, and together we sat on the couch. One at a time, we changed our children's lives forever.

I have a strong stomach. I'm not homicide-cop level, but I can look at crime scene photos and coroner's reports over lunch. I can study fly larvae in a nose cavity and eat a garbanzo bean salad.

I would love to have lived my life without ever having to see the expression on my older son's face when I told him his uncle Sasha hung himself.

8

TEXAS RANGER
JAMES B. HOLLAND, COMPANY B

CALIFORNIA STATE PRISON, LOS ANGELES COUNTY, CALIFORNIA
MAY 17, 2018

Eventually I heard about the day Sammy and Jimmy met from both of them, many times. It became codified into a kind of mythology: the day Sammy boy finally met his match. A moment of reckoning, witnessed only through staticky audio wire, by the FBI and the DOJ in the next room.

This is the story.

Three months before our first phone call, Texas Ranger James B. Holland, Company B, sat on one side of a metal table on top of which sat a family-sized bag of peanut M&Ms and a three-inch-wide black binder with every scrap of information he and his team had pulled together on Samuel Little, a.k.a. Samuel McDowell, the man sitting across from him. Next to the binder was a letter from Bobby Bland, the district attorney of Ector County, Texas, promising he would not seek the death penalty against Sam for the murder of Denise Brothers, which occurred on approximately January 12, 1994, in the city of Odessa.

Talking to serial killers was an unexpected specialty for this affable guy wearing tan Wranglers and a double rig belt. One might more readily picture a serial killer whisperer as a slick FBI agent out of *Mindhunter*, with troubled eyes, a secret sex addiction, and a snazzy gray suit. Holland was more like the only popular jock from your high school who wasn't a total douchebag. As far as I could glean from my conversations with Sam, Holland's method consisted of equal parts confidence, persistence, and Vulcan mind meld. He'd squeezed William Reece, Donald Wright, Anthony Shore, Charles Hicks…

Holland's neck tingled, right at the band of his hat. He knew he had a big fish in Sam. Maybe the biggest.

Holland had prepped the interview with the same rigor he applied to playing fullback at the University of Louisville, the same doggedness he brought to his master's degree in business administration, before he'd hopped on the first train headed for a more exciting destination. According to the Texas Rangers website, Holland instructed thousands of state and local police officers as well as whatever a "vast number of foreign law enforcement and military leaders" means. Holland has also provided instruction to U.S. Military Special Forces personnel in "firearms and interview techniques."

I boiled this down to a guy who liked adrenaline, uniforms, and the upper hand. He liked shady shit, secret clubs, shooting loud guns, and hiding in plain sight. You couldn't miss him, but you would anyway.

Holland had interviewed the LAPD extensively, and Roberts schooled him on the ins and outs of the man the LAPD had referred to as the Choke and Stroke Killer, because his MO was to strangle women as he jerked off on them.

Holland soon understood the world according to Sam: He was misunderstood. He'd been railroaded by detectives and lying bitches.

He loved women. He didn't beat them, didn't rape them. He didn't have to. There was just that inconvenient part about not being able to maintain an erection unless he was strangling a woman to death. Sex and strangulation were one and the same for Samuel Little. He papered his walls with drawings of long-necked women.

Innocent, innocent, innocent.

Holland knew sexual predators. He knew day after day the man in front of him lay in his cell and jerked off to the macabre quilt of faces of dead women on his walls. Strangulation is a slow and painful death. Sam had been sure to make it as slow and painful as possible, because to him, the killing itself was the sex, and his babies were worth more than a quickie.

Everyone wants a witness. This killer had kept no trophies to display. Holland suspected the drawings were the trophies.

"You're in control here," said Holland straight off. "You're never gonna do anything you don't want to do." He faced his palms outward in a gesture of surrender. "I'm just asking you for some help."

From the gate, Sam didn't even look down at the binder in front of him, opened to a blurry photograph of a shiny-cheeked, bright-eyed woman with Texas hair and sadness in the corners of her smile. Denise Brothers, murdered in Odessa, Texas, on January 12, 1994. Sam only wanted to rant about the trial that landed him in that dank cave in the first place. The same rant he repeated to his own wall a thousand times a day.

"Sure, yeah," said Holland. "I know all about that. I know all about you. I've been studying you. And you know what? I admire you. I think they got you all wrong, calling you a rapist. You're not a rapist, and I can prove it."

Sam's face came to life. He registered the tall hat, the shiny star.

"What in the hell is that on your head? You some kind of cowboy from Mars?"

Holland leaned his six-foot-three-inch frame back in his chair and crossed one ankle over a knee. Impatience was the enemy.

Texas Ranger James Holland first heard about Samuel Little at a homicide investigation conference in Florida. After Holland had delivered a lecture on how to interview psychopaths, a Florida cold case detective approached him about a murder he liked Sam for. Holland's interest was piqued, but he needed a Texas case to pursue. He reached out to DOJ senior forensic policy advisor Dr. Angela Williamson and ViCAP crime analyst Christie Palazzolo.

Palazzolo's first graduate degree was in criminology from the University of Pennsylvania. She pursued a second in strategic intelligence from the National Defense Intelligence College while working a day job as a federal police officer. She decided counterterrorism wasn't her bag. She liked facts, not lies. She also had an upcoming wedding to plan, kids to get busy having. When offered the ViCAP job as a data analyst, she jumped and in short order became one of the most widely respected in the field.

ViCAP—the Violent Criminal Apprehension Program—is both an FBI unit and an information-sharing database, begun in 1985. Prior to its inception, there was no central repository where state and local agencies could submit their violent crime cases and therefore no place they could go to search similar cases other than the library. The ViCAP database now enables local law enforcement to enter behaviorally focused data and search for potentially connected crimes across the country.

Advances in DNA science and corresponding federal and local databases have had phenomenal implications for the criminal justice also have limitations. To solve many cold cases, the ng the "traces of contact" can often resemble a more stigative model.

ViCAP's data focuses on serial killers, missing persons, and unidentified remains. Other offices in the FBI don't have jurisdiction to work these cases unless there's a federal crime involved, such as bank robbery or kidnapping across state lines. Behavior patterns are the sneak-around. The ViCAP division works under the umbrella of the Behavioral Science Unit (BSU), as depicted in *Mindhunter*, *Silence of the Lambs*, and *Criminal Minds*. The BSU's Robert Ressler came up with the term "serial killer."

The original idea of the ViCAP program was to collect data about offenders and identify behavioral signatures to link and resolve unsolved cases. For it to work, enough data had to be entered to make these connections possible. The current estimation indicates ViCAP contains less than 1 percent of the violent crimes committed in the United States each year.

In contrast, ViCLAS, Canada's Violent Crime Linkage Analysis System, was originally based on the ViCAP model, but its breadth has so far surpassed the U.S. database as to be nearly unrecognizable. It contains over half a million violent cases and has made connections between over seven thousand unsolved cases. The U.S. database would need to contain over four million cases to measure up on a per capita basis, but it has fewer than one hundred thousand.

Use of ViCLAS is mandatory. Participation in ViCAP, however, is voluntary. Data entry takes significant time and effort. Although ViCAP is considered the original model for linking unsolved cases, lack of engagement hinders its functionality.

Christie Palazzolo was in the dumps about it in December 2016, or maybe it was just the third pregnancy. She'd always carried well, but this one was already making her breathe hard.

Dr. Angela Williamson, the DOJ liaison, strode up to Palazzolo's cubicle. The two had hit it off talking about *The X-Files*, but this five-foot-two Scully in a cheeky outfit, hailing from the cane fields of rural Australia, was still more than a little intimidating. Williamson held PhDs in molecular biology and biochemistry from the University of Queensland and had considered work on vaccines but liked forensics better. As director of case work at Bode Technology, she'd worked DNA on the Hurricane Katrina missing and unidentified, JonBenét Ramsey, the West Memphis Three, and the National Center for Missing and Exploited Children.

Williamson liaised between ViCAP and the National Sexual Assault Kit Initiative (SAKI), a DOJ grant program that encourages large-scale reform of sexual assault investigations by funding a coordinated, multijurisdictional response, supporting increased testing of sexual assault kits. SAKI aims to link and close cold sexual assault cases.

Many in law enforcement would like to see both ViCAP and SAKI federally mandated, like CODIS and NamUs.

"Hey! Do you know anything about this guy Samuel Little?" Williamson asked.

The name was the quadruple espresso shot Palazzolo needed. "Do I?"

Williamson told her about a Texas Ranger—that's right, hat and all—who talked to psychos. "Dade County homicide showed him some cases he liked Little for. He needs a Texas nexus in order to look at them."

"A Texas nexus?" asked Palazzolo.

"A Texas nexus."

A Texas nexus would be a specific cold case in Texas that Palazzolo could identify Sam as a strong suspect for, strong enough to get a DA to send Ranger Holland all the way to California to question the suspect. Williamson told Palazzolo this guy had some kind of superpowers. There was gossip at a recent homicide investigation conference that this Holland might push things kind of far sometimes. He was unconventional, his confidence inspiring a blush here and there, a wink at Texas justice. Then again, he threw in things like hypnosis. The cops at the conference had gossiped later at the bar—he'd throw in anything.

"You almost don't want to talk to him," said a detective with a comb-over and a sweaty upper lip.

"Makes you fucking sure you did something wrong. Helluva cop."

"Helluva guy."

Williamson had heard the gossip and seen the panels. She needed to get Holland in a room with this Samuel Little. All they needed was one Texas cold case—one they were pretty sure he was good for. With that, Williamson would have bet good money he could open the floodgates and give them more. An Australian never takes a sucker's bet.

Palazzolo had done the original ViCAP workup on Sam for the LAPD during the manhunt that tracked him across the country. She turned to the computer without a word and went to the investigative leads matrix for Samuel Little: every arrest, every sentence served, every time his plate was run, known associates, known vehicles.

"Here he is."

Georgia, Ohio, Florida, Ohio, Florida, Maryland, DC, Florida, Ohio, Florida, Massachusetts, Connecticut, Florida, Maryland, Florida, Colorado, Ohio, Georgia, California, Oregon, Pennsylvania,

New Jersey, Nebraska, California, Louisiana, Florida, Mississippi, Louisiana, Florida, New York, Florida, Georgia, California, Michigan, Nevada, Florida, California, Arizona, Georgia, Florida, Illinois, Florida, Ohio, Georgia, California, Georgia, Tennessee, Florida, New Jersey, Missouri, Florida, Illinois, Texas, Florida, Mississippi, Florida, Mississippi, Georgia, Mississippi, South Carolina, Florida, Mississippi, Georgia, Alabama, South Carolina, Ohio, Florida, Alabama, Ohio, Florida, Alabama, Georgia, Ohio, Mississippi, Georgia, Louisiana, Ohio, Georgia, Mississippi, Kentucky, Mississippi, Ohio, Mississippi, Tennessee, Georgia, Arkansas, Florida, Georgia, Louisiana, Mississippi, Florida, Louisiana, Arkansas, Louisiana, Florida, Georgia, Florida, Georgia, Ohio, California, Ohio, Arkansas, Georgia, Kentucky, Florida, California, Georgia, Florida, California, Mississippi, Ohio, California, California…

Ford Mercury, Ford Fairlane, Pontiac Bonneville, Ford Fairlane, Ford Mercury, Ford, convertible Pontiac Bonneville, Buick Riviera, Buick Wildcat, Pontiac Bonneville, Oldsmobile Delta, Pontiac LeMans, Ford Thunderbird, Chrysler Imperial, Chevy Bel Air, Ford Galaxie, Ford Pinto, Lincoln Continental Mark III, Lincoln Continental Mark IV, Ford Thunderbird, Ford Mercury, Cadillac Eldorado, Ford F-150 bubble-top van, Cadillac Eldorado, Buick Riviera, Cadillac Fleetwood, Cadillac, Dodge motorhome, Chrysler, Cadillac, Nissan Maxima, Oldsmobile, Buick, Ford…

Even Williamson was taken aback by the mind-blowing pile of wreckage. There was arrest after arrest, and still he went free and killed again.

"How did this happen?"

"You can't start with that question. Look here."

Palazzolo pointed to an entry, buried deep in the initial investigative leads matrix she had worked up for Roberts. At the time, she had identified a baker's dozen of homicides across the country that smelled like Sam.

She'd always remembered this one for some reason.

Denise Brothers, Odessa, Texas, 38 years old, white female. January 12, 1994.

Smack-dab in the middle of Texas. It was what the Texas Ranger would need to go and interview Sam.

A Texas nexus.

No one had even tried to get Sam to confess since the original conviction. Texas Ranger James Holland seemed about the right kind of crazy to pull something like this off. Palazzolo and Williamson dove into the Samuel Little investigation, hoping it would be a dramatic and newsworthy demonstration of ViCAP's investigative potential.

Wouldn't you know it? It actually worked. The Brothers case landed Williamson and Palazzolo in a California men's maximum-security prison, fiddling with their recording equipment, while Holland interviewed a potentially prolific murderer. But how many, really? Would the old man in failing health remember anything useful? Would he agree to talk at all? It was a risky venture.

The two brainy, bookend brunettes leaned in, Palazzolo's hands paused over her keys, ready to start clickety-clacking the minute the monster talked. Photos and notebooks were scattered across the table in front of them.

"I didn't rape nobody. I never hit a woman with a closed fist in my life. I didn't hurt them."

"Nah, you didn't need to do that," Holland agreed.

"I never did that."

"You never did that. You don't need to take nothing from no one. Let me ask you something. How do you like it here?"

"Here?" Sam looked around. He laughed. "I fucking hate it here. I got things on my jacket I never even got arrested for. I should be a level three, and I'm a level four and I never did them things."

"Now, here I can help. But you're the captain of the boat. You're the pilot of this plane. I want to hear about your life because this is what I do. And you're important. I'll tell you what I could do. If you tell me about a Texas case, I'm going to go present that to a grand jury, and if we can corroborate the facts and you get indicted, I can get you out of here. I'm going to fly out there on a special plane. It's a really cool plane. I'm gonna pick you up, and you and me will go to Texas. But in order for that to happen, I would appreciate it if you would tell me about these things and that you tell me the truth."

"LAPD say I'm a rapist. It was all over the TV. What is her fucking name? I can never remember. The lying whore detective."

"Mitzi Roberts? Yeah…" Holland chewed an M&M and nodded thoughtfully. "She's a fucking cunt. You can set the record straight right now."

Sam threw his head back and laughed, then pointed at the cowboy. "What do they call you again?"

"People who don't know me call me James," said Holland. "People who know me a little call me Jim. My mom calls me Jimmy."

"I'll call you Jimmy."

"Okay. I'll call you Sammy."

"No one calls me Sammy."

"Well, no man calls me Jimmy."

It was settled. They would be Jimmy and Sammy.

"You know the thing about secrets," said Jimmy, "they feel pretty good. But you know what feels really good? Telling someone."

Sammy boy had done this remarkable thing, and no one had properly asked him about it. Jimmy knew no one wanted to die alone, unseen, forgotten. Especially not a serial killer.

"Say, you ever been to Odessa?" asked Jimmy. Sammy's eyes went poison green. Welcome to the show.

9

DENISE

ODESSA, TEXAS
JANUARY 1994

The outskirts of Odessa, Texas, are a moonscape of mile after dust-caked mile of oil derricks and drilling rigs. At night, the oil fields appear to be lit from within, casting an unearthly glow into the dark expanse of West Texas sky above them. The fields are neighbored by rows of slipshod shacks and trailers that serve as cheap housing for the oil industry's disposable labor force.

Follow the train tracks closer to the center of town and you wind through a barren maze of industrial warehouses, heavy machinery yards, and a handful of strip clubs that service their workers, with neglected letter boards outside:

T O TUESDY!! ALL LIVE GIR ZGRLZ RLZ!!
EVERY HOUR HAPPY HOU

Follow the tracks still farther into the city with one of the highest rates of violent crime in America, and you pass megachurch after megamall after megachurch to reach the world's largest jackrabbit, by the name of Jack Ben Rabbit, standing eight feet tall and firmly bolted to the ground to discourage thieves. Beyond that, you'll find rows of modest, well-tended brick houses, familiar to any watcher of *Friday Night Lights*, the television show famously based on the town's high school football team. These houses include the one in which Denise Christie Brothers, born Denise Doreen Powell, January 19, 1956, grew up.

In January 1994, Denise didn't live in her childhood home anymore, but her two middle boys, Dustin and Damien, still resided there with her parents. That night, they were probably tucked into their beds, Damien reading a comic book under the covers with a flashlight, waiting up, listening, to see if she was going to try to break in again, like she did on Christmas. Because he wanted to bust her. Or because he just wanted to see her face.

She'd felt guilty, sure, but you can't think about it too much. As she'd told Damien, "You get hungry enough and you do what you need to do. As long as there's a tomorrow, there's always another chance."

She would get back those gifts and more. She usually did. They always forgave her, especially Dustin, with his liquid chocolate eyes. Just the other day, her boys rode their bikes through a storm to visit her. She held their wet faces in her hands, kissed their velvety cheeks. They smelled like grass and sweat and rain. They arrived at a bad time, when a mean jones started to gnaw at the back of her throat, and her delight wore off quickly. She sent them out for a loaf of bread and a pack of cigarettes.

"You're supposed to be taking care of us, you know, not the other way around," Damien said, his arm around his little brother. The boys returned to a locked door.

The drawer of the nightstand was open an inch. Inside, Denise could see the glint of a spoon's edge, the bright orange of a syringe cap, several creased packs of matches, and a few scattered Polaroids: her second wedding, she and her mom getting their hair styled. Her favorite was her and the three boys at the Monahans Sandhills, a state park where she used to rent red plastic disks and take them sand surfing. Her boys posed on either side of her, squinting into the sun: Damien and Dustin, always joined at the hip, Dennis to the other side, practicing his handsome glower. She hadn't seen Derreck since he was born. She had been too far gone by then.

Damien was the angriest at her, the angriest, period. She worried. All that anger can get twisted up inside, make you do stupid things. He had once asked her, shortly after Derreck, why she kept having babies she couldn't take care of. She'd tried explaining to him that every single time, she knew, *knew*, it was finally going to be the love that saved her.

From the window of her second-floor motel room, on the corner of Royal and Second Street, Denise looked out at a no-man's-land of body shops, industrial warehouses, and cheap but never cheap enough motels. The yellow arrow was the only part of the motel sign that still lit up.

Below it, the words receded into darkness:

LOW WKLY AND MONTHLY RATES
DIRECTDIALPHONES
HBO AND CABLE TV FRIENDLY
KING AND QUE...

She buttoned the waistband of her newly lifted Gitanos, ran her hands over her sharp hips. She hadn't been eating much. Her boyfriend Elton gave her shit about it.

"Have a Waffle House. Treat yourself, baby. Skinny-legged women ain't got no soul."

On the twelve-inch screen in front of her, some bouncy Jewish kid with poseur dreads was singing about what? Something about *Sha-la-la-la-la*.

Something about *we all wanna be big, big stars.*

Something about *I want to be someone who believes.*

She gave consecutive handies to six sensitive assholes who sounded just like that when they came around slumming last week. They wanted to sit and talk about the government. They wanted to cry about their mean mommies. They wanted to tell you about the one who got away. If they gave you a fifty, one dollar was for the pussy. The remaining forty-nine dollars were for the rest of you. In the end, they found a way to feel cheated somehow. Usually because you only pretended. To love them? To come? Such fake-ass bitches.

Denise wiped a water mark off the nightstand with a thin square of toilet paper. She sometimes even got down on her hands and knees and tidied the brick-red syringe blood spatter from the grout between the tiles with a threadbare towel and a sliver of soap. She always liked things to be tidy, and needles are messy business.

She pulled a bedazzled *D* T-shirt over her head. D for Dennis, Damien, Dustin, Derreck.

D for Denise.

Denise had been a head turner. Her academic performance had been spotty, but she had the talent of simply being herself: popular, bright-eyed, a little bit wild, a lot beautiful. She was fashionable, creative. She made her own too-short dresses, paired with go-go boots and sparkly blue eye shadow shoplifted from the pharmacy.

She married at fifteen to a vain and violent man who believed himself entitled to many more prizes than he had won in life and blamed her for the injustice. She was stumbling out of that marriage when her second husband, Ron, caught her.

Ron was square jawed and broad shouldered, with a theatrical mustache and a defiant glint in his eye. He was a roofer—a respectable trade. He loved her. For a moment, it felt like all their jagged edges had come together to make something whole. It was another illusion. She found him shooting up heroin in the bathroom. She packed a bag. She came back.

She remembered the night he tenderly tied a blue bandanna around her bicep, felt for a vein in the crook of her elbow, and pulled her into the endless sea of forgetting. Heroin wasn't the crazy cosmic orgasm she'd expected. It simply and irresistibly softened the edges of an unfairly sharp world. Who is invulnerable to something that feels so much like mercy? Until "mercy" hits you like a two-by-four and becomes nothing more than a cruel joke.

Denise pulled on another T-shirt, another pair of socks. At least the rain had stopped, and it was a dry, cold, clear January night, with a sliver of moon hanging over the sad industrial stretch. Need gnawed her nerve endings. Her skin crawled, and her body shuddered with waves of profound unease, as if all her organs were in the wrong place. She'd had a fix earlier, but not nearly enough. Half a hit was worse than none.

She took one last look in the mirror, finger-combed her blond bangs, and half-heartedly applied a dab of concealer to the bruise-colored circles under her stormy eyes. She remembered the first time she'd stepped a toe onto the stroll. She could almost laugh. She had worn white patent leather pumps, a pair of matching hot pants. She had put a swing into her hips. This wasn't really her life. It couldn't possibly be. She was a character in a movie, with Richard Gere in his silver Lotus waiting right around the next corner to save her.

Denise headed toward Elton, four blocks down. She only made it half a block before an engine grumbled behind her. A boxy white Cadillac with a blue fabric top and a shiny steel grill idled.

She used to try not to look eager so they didn't lowball her. She was thirty-eight years old now and shivering inside her coat. There was little call to pretend anything else.

The driver slouched in his seat, partially in shadow. From what she could tell, he was a light-skinned Black guy, heavy browed, broad shouldered. She had a rule that she never went with a trick if she didn't like the look in his eye, but she couldn't see him well enough. Elton didn't like her to go with Black dudes, period. Misgiving fluttered in her gut, but a biting wind kicked up behind her, and she yanked open the passenger-side door against it.

"Just pull up here," she said in a girlish voice, resonant of her years as a soprano in the church choir. "A little farther up. I gotta get me and my man our fix first, then I'll take care of you, big daddy. Look at you! You a tall, strong one."

"Yeah? You like that? I used to be a prizefighter."

A little mischievous, maybe, but seemed kind enough. Maybe her luck was changing.

"Now that's something. I love a good fight. Just up here."

They pulled up to another fleabag motel that reeked of despair. Denise got out, gifting the man in the car with a little hip wiggle as she gave him the one-minute sign, and took the steps to the breezeway two at a time. When Elton emerged shortly after, he stormed toward the Cadillac.

"Who the fuck that? That ain't your nigger. I'm your nigger."

The man in the Cadillac was easy, unconcerned by the man's size or disposition. "No, no, no, brother. You her nigger. I'm just a friend."

When the three returned an hour later, they were thick as thieves and high as fuck. Denise kissed Elton goodbye. He gave her a pat on the ass as she slid shotgun.

Denise had been surprised when the guy, what was his name? Sam...when Sam had shelled out so generously. Plenty of dope to last her all night, plus some crack thrown in just for fun.

"What do you do for work?" she asked.

"I'm a traveler."

"The fuck kind of job is that?" She was always playing. What else could you do?

"Like to see new places, meet new people. I'm also an artist. Ooooh, I could draw you so pretty. Just like van Gogh." He cracked himself up. "You're beautiful. I love you."

It seemed a little strange and sad, but also sweet—a man who actually told her he loved her when he wasn't coming.

"We can go to my place up here."

"Nah, I got somewhere else I like."

He rolled his shoulders snugly back into his motorcycle jacket. His worn T-shirt read HUG ME, I'M HAIRY! He was sort of funny.

"Sure, whatever."

A few miles northeast of that corner, she'd once cartwheeled all the way down the block. She held the neighborhood record to this day. She still remembered what it felt like for her body to be strong. Strong and hers.

Sam swung into an alley. His teeth were sharper and longer than she'd noticed. The big bad wolf. The crack could do that sometimes— make the world into a scary fairy tale. Especially when it was wearing off.

"Cross those legs for me."

He stroked her thigh. She noticed his hands were abnormally large, smooth, and hairless as a woman's. A man who hadn't done an honest day's work.

"God, you're gorgeous. And you're mine forever."

"Right, baby. I'm all yours."

She looked down and spit into her palm. Give 'em a fast handy, and you might be spared a degrading negotiation, where you tell some married cheapskate it'll be an extra twenty-five dollars to stick his dick up your ass, and he says twenty.

Before the saliva even hit, a hand grabbed her by the throat and tossed her over the seat like a doll. The pain in her twisted legs brought her back to the surface of consciousness.

Shoes? Shoes. Find your shoes. She reached. Gone.

Jeans, tights, underwear tangled around her ankles. D T-shirt shoved up over her bra. The world was out of focus, stained with floating blotches of color that almost obscured the boxer straddling her with his dick in his hand.

With the hand that he wasn't using to jack off, he fondled her neck.

Trust me. I'm not going to hurt you. I love you…

Her arms sprang to life. She thrashed, clawed. His arm was solid as a tree trunk. She grabbed for his face.

"Wildcat!"

He dropped his cock, delivered four blows to her head in rapid succession. The Mad Daddy. The Machine Gun. Her hands went instinctively to protect her face. He pressed down harder, and her arms went numb and dropped to her sides. She was almost disappointed when the world appeared above her again.

She still had some hope. She had been raped and tossed out of a car alive. This guy surely knew there was no danger in leaving a junkie ho as your only witness. No one would believe her anyway. If they did believe her, no one would care.

She tried, "*Please*."

No sound came out. She cried, and he softened, kissed the tears off her face.

Maybe he would let her live after all.

He sat her up in the seat beside him, legs still immobilized by the tangle of clothes. He put his arms around her and she leaned into him, shaking with soundless sobs. He stroked her hair.

"All I ever wanted was you," he said. He laid her down gently in his lap and tilted her head back, her hair spilling over the seat onto the floor of the car. "Look at your eyes. Like two big marbles," he chuckled. "Like you looking at the devil himself."

She could feel his erection growing again. He wrapped both hands around her throat, thumbs resting on the indentation between her collarbones.

"Swallow for me. I love it when you swallow."

She heard a low sound like a train whistle. Or was it hooting? An owl. The owl that had nested close by to her childhood window for years, who had spoken to her in the night, promising that it understood the things that haunted her. Telling her it would be okay. It had left when she was eleven, but she'd always known it would mean good things when it returned.

Blood and mucus filled her mouth.

She was so sorry. So sorry, sons.

She should have seen it coming.

———

Three weeks later, a truck driver making a turn into a vacant lot at 2700 South Van Street, adjacent to the Coca-Cola plant, spotted a department store mannequin discarded among the blowing plastic bags, fast-food wrappers, used condoms. He shifted gears, but something told him to stop and look twice. As he approached the mannequin, it became clear it was not a doll at all. It was a half-naked, half-green dead girl, concealed by underbrush at the other side of a guardrail. He stopped about ten feet away. He looked one direction up the deserted street, then the other, hoping to see a pay phone.

Dogs barked. He looked back, almost reluctant to leave her alone. Wasn't like she was going anywhere. From the looks of it, she'd been alone a while. The man went in search of a phone.

When Odessa Detective Sergeant Snow Robertson pulled up in an unmarked blue Chevy Lumina, uniformed patrol officers had already secured the yellow-taped perimeter, and the crime scene photographers were snapping away. Like a hawk surveying a field, his eyes scanned the large picture, then zeroed in on the object with the strongest gravitational pull. The wind cut through his suit. He folded his arms across his chest and approached what was left of a female body, lying half on her side, face to the sky, arm wedged under her.

This cold streak had been a lucky break, because she was still basically intact. Her skin had begun to slip from its contours, looking more like crumpled silk than skin, her lips were cracked and dry as tree bark, and her nose and mouth crawled with fly larvae. Still, he recognized her. He shook his head. They'd identify her with fingerprints, but they wouldn't need to. Denise was familiar to local law enforcement. Hard time, that one. Rough friends.

The medical examiner's van pulled in behind him, scattering

pebbles. He held out a hand for them to stop. Dead hookers are dogs for cases. Something stirred in him for Denise. He wanted to make absolutely sure it was done right, so he did this one himself. He walked the scene, photographing what needed to be photographed, tagging what needed to be bagged. He crouched beside her, breathing through his mouth, and ran a hand through his white-blond hair.

"Okay, honey," he said. "What happened to you?"

He reached into his pocket and snapped on a pair of rubber gloves before carefully bagging her hands, then lifting first her upper body, then lower, into a black body bag and zipping it up. He lifted the scant hundred pounds of her and placed her in the coroner's van.

The medical examiner did a thorough and meticulous job with the autopsy, noting the clean break in the hyoid bone, a horseshoe-shaped bone situated in the anterior midline of the neck between the chin and thyroid cartilage. The hyoid is anchored by muscles from the anterior, posterior, and inferior directions, and it aids in tongue movement and swallowing. It's also essential to breathing and speaking.

"Hyoid" is derived from the Greek *hyoeides*, meaning "shaped like the letter upsilon or the Latin Y." Upsilon is known as Pythagoras's letter, because Pythagoras used it as an emblem of the path of virtue or vice. The fork in the road. The crossroads.

"This woman was strangled to death," the medical examiner concluded. "Manual, with tremendous force."

The investigation wore on. From the vaginal swabs, police identified two likely suspects, including Elton, for whom there was both DNA and circumstantial evidence. There was also the fact that not one but both of the suspects were utter scumbags. Many detectives would play eeny, meeny, miny, moe, and call it a day. Robertson didn't roll that way. His Spidey sense told him it wasn't right. It wasn't scumbag number one or scumbag number two. Someone more nefarious had met Denise at this particular crossroads.

Denise fell somewhere in between "more dead" and "less dead," but unlike many of Sam's other less dead victims, she did not suffer the indignity of being ignored. Robertson put his back into it. He called in the Texas Rangers. He questioned every single prostitute arrested. He sniffed out all known associates and hit wall after wall.

Odessa is a city full of transients, truckers, and careless domestic violence. It could have been anyone. In his gut, he felt a sexually motivated serial killer murdered Denise. It had all the hallmarks. Serial killers are notoriously hard to catch, because the connections with their victims are fleeting, the traces left behind hard to locate.

A week after the body was found, Robertson arrived home an hour and a half late for what would have once been dinner in the years before his divorce. There was no longer a lasagna under foil. He shoved a Marie Callender's frozen dinner in the microwave and dove for the phone, desperate to hear the voice of his nine-year-old son. It rang and rang. So many moving pieces you can't control. He tossed his briefcase under the desk off the kitchen that served as an office in his two-bedroom apartment and settled in to fill out a ViCAP entry on Denise.

A couple of nights a week, he generally spent an hour or two inputting his homicide cases, past and present, into the ViCAP system, because he believed in its still underused and underrecognized capabilities. He imagined a U.S. law enforcement system that was more than a scattered network of haphazardly connected jurisdictions but rather a single organism working toward a common purpose: getting the bad guys.

He pulled out a ViCAP booklet and began to manually enter the information in block letters.

Someone in the future will see the pattern. Someone will find the missing piece.

DATE: FEBRUARY 2, 1994
AGENCY: ODESSA POLICE DEPARTMENT
VICTIM: DENISE CHRISTIE BROTHERS
CASE TYPE: HOMICIDE
OFFENDER: UNKNOWN

10

DR. JAMES FALLON

UNIVERSITY OF CALIFORNIA, IRVINE, CALIFORNIA
NOVEMBER 2018

I spent my days researching the brain science behind criminal deviance, and my nights transcribing my interviews with Sam. I couldn't tell up from down, right from wrong, night from morning. It was fascinating and felt legitimately dangerous. I get a tic in my left eye when I'm exhausted or inordinately stressed. The tic increased both in frequency and intensity. My nightmares escalated.

I was relieved to be interviewing a scientist and not a killer on the day Dr. James Fallon greeted my research assistant Amaia and I with teddy-bear hugs at his home on the UC Irvine campus over a doormat that read *COME BACK WITH A WARRANT*. He ushered us to his kitchen table, set with a decadent charcuterie plate, from which he ate with abandon before he even sat down as he told gossipy stories. He didn't bother to wait for questions.

Fallon is one of the world's leading neuroscientists examining the potential neurological and genetic correlates of psychopathy. He talked about science in a way that made you feel smart. There was something both paternal and wild about him. I could have listened to him build castles in the air for days.

Fallon is not just a neuroscientist who studies deviance. While doing his graduate research, he discovered his PET scan was nearly identical to those of the violent offenders he'd been studying. After further inquiry, Fallon concluded he is indeed a dyed-in-the-wool psychopath. He chronicles this discovery and its aftermath in his excellent book *The Psychopath Inside* and his corresponding TED Talk.

Fallon is not a violent psychopath. Not all are.

He's a brilliant, mesmerizing, and manipulative psycho just the same. He talked freely about it over wild boar sausage and bloodred sliced tomatoes, fresh from the garden.

We discussed the difference between a narcissistic personality disorder (NPD) and the colloquial use of "narcissism." The colloquial use is the Kardashian selfie.

"A personality disorder is different. Somebody with NPD doesn't know they're narcissistic. Somebody narcissistic, just full of themselves, they kinda know it. Then there are narcissists like Muhammad Ali, who really are the best. So it's just a fact. With any of these personality disorders, you have to find out this difference between having the trait and having the personality disorder."

Fallon explained his famous three-legged stool analogy for the development of the adult psyche in relationship to psychopathy. I've cribbed this from his momentous book *The Psychopath Inside*. He continues to challenge and advance the field of neuroscience.

1. GENETICS
Essentially set in stone at birth. Big subject, but from the perspective of psychopathology, the *MAOA* or "warrior" gene

is almost always present, often combined with predilections for addiction. Not everyone who has this gene will go on to kill. Environmental factors impact individual genes, changing and affecting how those genes are expressed. By modifying the activity of these genes, DNA itself is modified, although the DNA sequence remains unchanged. These are epigenetic changes, and they can be passed to future generations.

Genes are the basic function of heredity carved in stone, but epigenetic influences can be caused by a variety of environmental factors, including pollution, physical environment, diet, traumatic experiences. Unpredictable factors determine whether a gene is activated or not, thereby affecting the proteins produced in each cell. Shadowy genetic issues can lie in wait for generations.

2. NEUROLOGICAL

In the brains of psychopaths, Fallon's neurological imaging showed deactivation in the anterior cingulate cortex, the orbitofrontal cortex, and the amygdala—regions of the brain associated with many things, including serotonin and dopamine production.

There are two main types of neuroimaging: structural, which looks at the architecture of the brain and larger scale issues such as injuries or tumors, and functional, which looks at the way the information is processed and can reveal deficits in cognitive processing, or diagnose metabolic diseases.

The most prominent test, with the most exciting forensic possibilities, is the positron emission tomography (PET) scan, which uses a radioactive tracer drug to reveal the activity in brain tissue. The tracer is injected and then observed as it moves through the brain. It gathers in areas where chemical activity is occurring and shows up as bright spots on the imaging, helping to identify regions where disease may be present.

3. TRAUMA

Trauma, most specifically childhood abuse, affects the expression of genes linked to psychopathic behavior, as can a positive childhood environment. Someone like Fallon, with the genetic and even neurological predispositions for psychopathy, can go on to lead a relatively harmless life if they have a nurturing and supportive upbringing. Conversely, a person who suffers abuse from an early age—and was born with damage to the first two legs of the stool—is set up for a life of violent, psychopathic behaviors. Extra points for traumatic brain injury.

Fallon was not abused as a child. He claims that is why he is a scientist and not a murderer.

"But you know, I am related to Lizzie Borden," he said. He clapped his hands together. "So now, epigenetics. You have cells in your nose and your teeth, and all these cells have basically the same genes but they look different. How does that happen? Some of the genes are turned off, some of the genes are turned on. There's a selective turning on and off of the genes, by turning off and on the regulators called promoters. There are also insulators, and when they're the regulators—we don't have to jump there immediately… You are what your epigenome is. It's all of those genes and a bunch are turned off and a bunch are really turned on and what comes out: the genes that are being expressed."

Fallon's adult daughter breezed into the kitchen from the garden, kissed her father on the forehead, and cleared a couple of dishes.

"Can we talk about the amygdala?" I asked.

"Ooh, I love the amygdala," she said.

"I know you do!" he replied.

"Hang on," she said. "I have some fig jam I just canned. I want to grab you a jar."

Fallon turned to me.

"You too. I can tell. You and I have similar reactions to things. We tend to be addictive. We tend to be a little over the top. You inherited really high executive memory and genes. But then along with that, you got the traits of being highly anxious. Then you got knocked around. Right?"

Had I said that?

"Look," Fallon said. He held out his hand. It trembled slightly. "Now yours."

I dared to reach mine out for a New York minute. I summoned all the will I had to keep it steady.

"See?" he said with a mischievous glint. "See how you shake? You're smart as hell, and you're a nervous wreck, and you're going to stay that way."

With a shaking hand, he poured one cute little dish that said vinegar into one that said oil and dipped in a chunk of mozzarella.

"Would you like some cheese?"

"I would."

I ate it from his hand.

The amygdala is one of two almond-shaped clusters of nuclei located within the temporal lobes of the brain, close to the brain stem. Reach behind your head and feel the ridges at the bottom of your skull. Buried somewhere under there lives your fear. I like to think of the amygdala as the basement into which no one wants to climb. At its best, the amygdala kicks into gear if you're facing a lion on the savannah.

Research suggests the amygdala is overactive in people with anxiety disorders and underactive in psychopaths. Violent offenders often have severely diminished activity in both the temporal and frontal lobes of the brain—the centers of basic human emotion, empathy, and impulse control. But along with psychopathy, Fallon has a side dish of bipolar disorder. While his frontal lobe takes a nap, his amygdala hops all day. This, we shared.

I asked him what he thought about my aunt's description of what it would feel like to be with Sam: he's stealing the shirt off your back, you know he's stealing the shirt off your back, he's *telling* you he's stealing the shirt off your back, and yet you feel inexplicably compelled to give him the shirt off your back.

Fallon went further. "He sees what you're thinking before you do, because he doesn't project, he barters. He's not looking for his answer. He's looking for an opening. He doesn't get crushes. He covets."

The amygdala is the seat of memory, decision-making, and emotional responses. It is the home of the familiar fight-or-flight response. This part of your brain is subject to fear conditioning, which occurs when a neural stimulus gives you a big enough scare that the reptile in you decides it's safer to stay under a rock for good. Or at least always be checking your six.

In other words, get hit enough times, and you flinch at a hummingbird. In that way, my anxious brain functioned in the opposite way from Sam's or Fallon's. The parts of the brain do not function independently but are connected by an elaborate network of freeways.

I've learned that when I become paralyzed by anxiety, I can coax my thoughts forward, out of the roadside ditches carved by trauma. Start with always forward. Look back and you're in the limbic brain. Look back and you're a pile of salt.

I play a game to engage my frontal lobe (reasoning, planning, speech). I make myself think of five movies that start with the letter W, five words with five syllables in them, or, if I need something easy, I do serial killers:

Five serial killers whose names start with D…

Dahmer
Dr. Death
David Berkowitz
DeAngelo
Dennis Rader

The point of the exercise is to pivot from lizard to logic brain.

Fallon was right. I was a nervous wreck. Five foods that start with the letter R. The first five American presidents.

"My purpose isn't to psychoanalyze you," said Fallon. "You need to understand this if you're talking to a psychopath. I may analyze you, but it's not my point."

He paused. I didn't bother to fill the silence. I felt sure he was about to answer the obvious question.

"My point is *always* to own you."

There it was.

"Even if it's for an hour or two. Everyone wants to talk scans, scans, scans. First thing you do is not get scans. You ask, 'Why are they this way?' That's when the scans and the genetics come together.

I get tired of saying you got it upside down. What we try to do first is a psychiatric analysis. But they don't want that."

"They want the fast answer," I said.

"Right. Fast. And free."

We both reached for the last mozzarella ball.

———

Robert Kennedy is quoted as saying, "Every society gets the kind of criminal it deserves. What is equally true is that every community gets the kind of law enforcement it insists on."

I live in a deeply divided city. I do not know if Samuel Little was the criminal we deserved.

I know he was the criminal we allowed.

11

MAMA

Reynolds, Georgia, is a rural town bisected by train tracks, about sixty miles south of Atlanta as the crow flies. In 1940, it had a largely African American population of 871 people, many employed by its rail yard. On the seventh of June, the last of the white blossoms littered the ground beneath the magnolia trees, their delicate white edges curling in on themselves, turning transparent and brown, the air around them redolent with the sweet smell of rot.

Malcolm X's father, Earl Little Sr., was famously born in Reynolds in 1890 but had long since fled by the time his young cousin Bessie Mae Little lay dying in an unpainted shotgun shack on the south side of town as twilight turned the sky to bruised shades of purple. Bessie Mae's grandmother Josephine Little stood at the foot of the same four-poster bed in which sixteen years before, she had watched the blood drain from her own beloved teenage daughter. At the time, she had cradled newborn Bessie Mae in her arms and promised her dying daughter that this baby girl would not suffer her same fate.

There she stood. For yet another in the countless times in her life as a midwife, blood was smeared across Josephine's forearms, her face, the kerchief that covered her hair. In spite of her impassioned nightly prayers; in spite of the sense of purpose that had buoyed her through the many years of toil, poverty, and hardship; in spite of the strict upbringing she had visited upon the girl: the admonishments, the curfews, the warnings. Still, she found herself again between the shaking, bloodied legs of a teenager in labor.

Josephine blamed her own ice-blue eyes—she'd always been told they were a curse on her family. A white devil's eyes, a slaveowner's eyes, an ocean of rape and pain. The sins of the father visited upon the sons. Except it wasn't the sons, was it? They got cut down like so much sugarcane. Or they ran. It was the daughters who lived to take the brunt of it.

Josephine was in her late fifties and had been midwifing consistently since she was just a girl herself and her aunts had taught her to use her delicate nine-year-old hands for the tricky work. All that time, she had never seen a baby the size of the one inside her granddaughter. It would take nothing short of a miracle to save the girl. Josephine made a split-second decision. She would bring this thing into the light of day if it killed all of them.

"One more try, child."

Bessie Mae lay there bleeding out, her skin ashen, her eyes fluttering closed.

Josephine reached both arms into her granddaughter's birth canal, seized the baby by the shoulders, braced her foot on the bed frame, and leaned backward.

Moments later, she had toweled the blood and slime off the twelve-pound infant and looked down at him. He was white as paper, the largest newborn she had ever laid eyes on. Staring up at her were the wolf-blue eyes she hated in her own face, and in a boy, no less.

"Eatin' chalk," Josephine said, meaning Bessie Mae had been eating the chalk found in the ground in those parts. It was what they said about Black babies born looking white.

For this thing, Bessie Mae had ruined her grandmother's carefully laid plans for her young life.

Josephine leaned her face in close to the chalk boy, looked into those familiar eyes, and whispered, "I curse you."

She then laid him on her dying granddaughter's breast for what she imagined would be the last time. Maybe Josephine would be lucky and poor Bessie Mae would at least take him with her into the next life.

It was not to be. The boy suckled immediately.

"Greedy bastard," said Josephine. "He had a twin up in there and he gobbled him up what happened."

But Bessie Mae eventually recovered, and the baby boy grew strong. Josephine did not recover. She would not allow the boy to be named, would not touch him, rarely looked at him.

About six months later, Josephine returned home late from her job as a maid. It was a rainy night with barely a sliver of moon in the sky. She found Bessie Mae with her head lolled back on the couch, the monstrous little beast on her breast, as he always was, looking like some kind of vampire, sucking the life from her. As he thrived, Bessie Mae grew weaker and more shriveled. She was only sixteen but looked forty-five.

Josephine and her sisters had tried to kill the child when he was still unborn, but Bessie Mae had been weak. They'd tied a rope around her belly and pulled until she screamed for them to stop. They'd knocked her down the stairs as a last-ditch effort before they let go of the rope. The next day, they had sat her down at the kitchen table and placed a glass of turpentine in front of her, but she hadn't been able to drink it. She gagged and complained until they finally gave up. No sense in that girl. It would only be harder now.

Though it pained Josephine to do it, it was time. Maybe there was still a chance.

"You are a disgrace, Bessie Mae Little. You are no longer welcome in this house."

"But, Mama…"

"I am no such thing to you. You *killed* your own mama. And for what?"

"What am I going to do?"

"It's a rainy night, child. It's a quick kind of thing. Just lie him down peaceful, eyes to God. Take no effort at all."

"I can't."

"You want to act like a slut, go walk the streets like one. And take that chalk-eating beast with you."

"What, now? We'll die out there."

"If you're lucky. Now get. You have a bed to come back to. If you come back alone."

Josephine turned and walked toward the kitchen, limping slightly on her arthritic hip. She shoveled coal into the stove, the rattle not quite drowning out Bessie Mae's pitiful sobs.

"Hush your mouth," she called. "Or I'll put you out with no shoes on."

It wasn't long before she heard the front door shut with a quiet click that might as well have been a gunshot. Josephine sank to her knees.

———

Old witch, thought Bessie Mae. *Vicious cow. She's just jealous. No man would touch her dried-up pussy with someone else's dick.*

Bessie Mae carried no bag. She wore her one good wool coat, half covering the boy, but it was soaked through. She had stuffed her pockets with extra swaddling cloths, little more than wet rags. She wore thick stockings, a green dress that had been mended too many times, and a pair of men's shoes inherited from some other uncle or other.

She had exhausted her tears. They felt extraneous next to the rivulets of rainwater running down her face. She made slow progress in her ill-fitting shoes that stuck to the mud with every step, like a mouse trying to escape a glue trap.

She thought about Paul. Paul with eyes that flashed green-blue fire, cheekbones that could have cut stone, smooth carney patter. You were the star of a movie when he took your face in his hands. It had happened in a cemetery in Reynolds, on a little bench, next to the chapel. When it was over, she looked into the darkness and realized there were no cameras after all.

She learned later she had been part of a game. Paul and his friend had a contest going—how many of the local girls they could seduce. There were actual scorecards, bets placed. She wondered how much she had won him. When he saw her again, he looked through her like a glass figurine.

She trudged on. She might not have been clever or beautiful or serious—or any of the things her grandmother had wanted for her—but she knew one thing. Whether or not she had been a fool, she loved this baby with a white-hot passion. He needed her like no one ever had, and the depth of his need was a thing to behold. She was finally special to someone, and she knew this was a formidable someone.

He was a strange baby. He rarely slept, was the size of some two-year-olds, had grown-up eyes, like he was about to recite the Declaration of Independence, and ate with the ferocity of a starving tiger. There was not enough milk in all of Georgia to sate this baby. She was shriveling into a rotten lemon even trying.

Bessie Mae had no particular destination. No one wanted another mouth to feed, much less two. Her uncle Otis had already tried to kill the boy. She caught him holding a pillow over his face. Why everyone was so intent on murdering her son, she didn't know. But she knew she couldn't protect him from her family. She couldn't even protect him from the rain.

The dense foliage of the oak trees obscured what little moonlight illuminated Bessie Mae's path. When she turned a corner and saw a row of houses on stilts, she had reached the river. She could walk no longer. With one arm, she held the boy, and with the other, she supported them as she dropped to her knees and crawled under the first house in the row.

The cold from the ground soaked into her back. Her body trembled.

She lay there for what felt like three minutes, or a day, or a life, waiting for the river to take them both. She drifted off, and when she woke, a different kind of chill rose slowly from her toes. She had gone plenty cold in this life but had felt this particular sensation only once before, when the baby now at her breast had been wedged in her pelvis. She was dying.

"Jesus," she said. "I can't protect this child. I give him to you. If it be your will to let him live, Lord, save him. Or take us both home."

With her last ounce of strength, Bessie Mae crawled to the side of the road, lay her baby down in the mud, eyes to God, and crawled back under the house. She didn't bother to roll onto her back. She had prayed, sure. How many prayers went unanswered? There were those who had prayed for her, even, and look at her now. She fell asleep with her face on the wet ground, not wanting to watch.

An hour later, in a modest but well-kept white A-frame on the west side of the railroad tracks, Fanny McDowell served a late dinner of biscuits and gravy to her husband, Henry, whom she called Big 'Un, because he was. He'd come home later than usual, what with the rail yards mired in mud. Usually there were more people around the house, but that night was quiet, with her friend Mrs. Ballard drinking a sweet tea at the counter and her daughter, Jeminah, already tucked into her attic bedroom, looking at magazines she and her friends probably boosted from the drugstore. They weren't bad girls, but you got to worry when they're that pretty. Henry Jr. was holed up somewhere, wondering whether to check his ass or scratch his watch, no sense at all.

Who knew where Paul was running around. He was the prettiest of them all, but you don't worry about boys in that way. The both of them getting ready to ship off. Days now.

Mrs. Ballard called from the pantry, "Want I should make a batch of cornbread for tomorrow?"

"Nah, you go ahead and rest now. Better warm anyway," said Fanny. She poured a finger of whiskey each into two rose-patterned teacups and handed one to her behind Big 'Un's back with a wink.

"You got the devil in you sometimes, Fanny."

"Devil never did come and offer me a thing. I'm still waiting."

"Bite your tongue. The mouth on you."

A knock interrupted.

Mrs. Ballard opened the door and didn't see anything. She squinted into the darkness.

Must have been the storm.

"Ma'am…" A voice startled her. She looked down and was surprised to see Mr. Quint, a familiar face around Reynolds. Quint was a peddler of pretty much anything you could want or need. He had no legs and shuffled himself around on muscled arms and calloused knuckles. He swung himself up every day onto a cart pulled by a goat. The cart had tall wheels that navigated the dirt roads of Reynolds, mud or no mud.

"Mr. Quint!"

The legless peddler held an infant in his arms. She called for Fanny, who found herself in a rare condition of speechlessness.

"Mrs. Fanny, this is Paul's boy. Take one look at him, you'll know that to be true. I found him by the side of the road."

Fanny took that one look at the boy and knew he was right. No way to prove such a thing though. She weighed her options.

Her own children were grown. Who needed another mouth to feed? Mrs. Ballard waited. Even Big 'Un stood up from his biscuits and hovered in the kitchen doorway, the shadow of his frame darkening the room.

Fanny held out her arms and took the child. She gave Mr. Quint a biscuit, a sip of whiskey, and sent him back out to his cart. They cleaned and dried the baby, wrapped him in a blanket, found him some milk.

"He's a gift from God. We'll call him Samuel," said Mrs. Ballard. "Samuel the prophet. I just learned in my Bible study. It means 'heard by God.'"

"Samuel," said Big 'Un. He gave the boy's head a stroke with one thumb. Loved him straight off. "I'll call him Sam."

Fanny stared down into the boy's eyes.

"He's lucky he's a boy and not a girl. Girl—I would have had the cripple throw him in the river."

"Of course." Mrs. Ballard patted her friend's shoulder. "No one needs that."

12

THE MCDOWELLS

LORAIN, OHIO
1942–1953

There are a couple of different stories about why Henry went to the rail yard one day not to go to work but instead to hop on the first and fastest train, headed true north for the steel factories of the Midwest. Maybe he killed a white man, and they were going to come lynch him. Maybe he messed around with a white girl and they were going to come lynch him. In any case, they were coming for him, and he was not about to sit around and wait.

He wasn't alone. By 1942, millions of Black Americans had flocked toward the industry and relative lack of segregation in the Northeast and Midwest during the First Great Migration. Henry had even heard of folk who went as far as California. They migrated north in droves from the impoverished southern rural communities that offered them little opportunity other than wage slavery, even if actual slavery had technically been abolished eighty years earlier. Henry heard rumors the war had created good jobs in steel, and steel was due north, in

Ohio. He'd heard tell they were so desperate for workers, they'd give good jobs to Negroes and even women.

"I'll send for you," he told Fanny. "And bring our Sam."

Their unexpected treasure. He was so hungry all the time, a bottomless pit of need, but adorable. And the eyes—you looked at that baby and it was like he could see your soul. They loved the wild little thing, brought to them by God's grace.

You never know, when a man gets on a train...

Two years later, Henry made good and sent for Fanny. She packed a suitcase and a box of her famous biscuits, put the toddler on her back, and walked two miles to the rail yard.

She had anticipated a tougher trip, but Sam seemed unusually content, watching the landscape change from minute to minute. He gazed at the dense foliage, ramshackle piles of houses, redbrick factories spewing smoke, covered bridges, towering spires of silvery cities in the distance. The movement calmed the fussy child. When they arrived in Lorain by morning, a barely budding spring greeted them, fresh and full of promise, even if it was covered by a steel-gray sky and the air held the whiff of something sharp and metallic, belched from the rows of factory smokestacks.

Henry met them at the station. He had secured them a house at 223 East Thirty-Third Street on a predominately white, middle-class block, surrounded by families who would have little truck with them. He was ambitious and determined to bring his family up. He assured Fanny a short walk down the alley to Thirty-Second Street would bring young Sam to a neighborhood where he would find Black friends.

In 1942, the sidewalks outside the Victorian-style houses in the McDowells' neighborhood were largely bereft of young men, mostly off at war. Those left behind found plentiful work at the steel plants.

Jeminah and Henry Jr. soon followed. Paul was still over in Germany. Fanny prayed on her knees every morning and again at night, begging God for his safe return. Jeminah's husband was over there somewhere too, but Fanny thought less of that one.

In a matter of years, the McDowell family was firmly planted in the Rust Belt town on Lake Erie, with a picturesque lighthouse on the sound and a sparkling river flanked by the factories whose workers prowled its colorful, bumping main drag, Broadway, on Friday nights, looking for an escape from the grind of their days.

When men came home from the war in 1945, there was essentially a game of musical chairs, a rearranging of gender and color lines, but Henry managed to keep his job. Sam grew up believing he was the youngest son of Henry and Fanny rather than the bastard progeny of their youngest. When Paul returned from the war in 1945, there was a tacit agreement not to correct the error. Paul quickly scooped up a young wife named Betty. He was a brickmason by trade, and he built a house around the corner from Henry and Fanny, where he would eventually father seven children, who Sam believed were his nieces and nephews rather than his half siblings.

Another man who came home from the war that fall was Jeminah's husband, James, Navy veteran and soon-to-be father.

Fanny and Henry loved Sam, but they were well past child-rearing years. Sam was more of an indulgence than a responsibility. Paul didn't want him. What new wife wants a constant daily reminder of her husband's sordid past? Fanny and Henry resigned themselves to raise Paul's child as their own. Fanny fed Sam when she remembered. She changed out his too-small shoes when she could, dressed him in whatever ill-fitting clothes fell on their porch from one relative or another.

One twilight, in early June, a handful of neighborhood families gathered in the backyard of a very pregnant Jeminah's house. They chatted as Betty bounced a baby on her knee and their kids chased the fireflies dancing through the darkening sky. Five-year-old Sam had said he was going to the bathroom. He peered around the corner of the kitchen door, weighing his options. He had been hungry for hours, had asked for food several times and been ignored. He wasn't allowed to rummage in the icebox in Jeminah's house. They would eat when they ate. Unlike her own children, he hadn't eaten all day. He could hear her lilting laughter and that of the children playing in the backyard floating on the wind through the kitchen window.

Behind him, the light switched off in the hallway. He froze. He'd always been scared of the dark. He turned to see Uncle Jimmy, silhouetted by the porch light coming through the back door. The man grabbed the boy by the arms and pulled him into a corner of the darkened kitchen. A few feet away was the door to the basement few of the children would even go down to on a dare, because that was where the monsters were supposed to live. Maybe they were wrong about the monsters, because they weren't in the basement at all, but there was Uncle Jimmy, unzipping his fly.

"You're hungry?" asked Uncle Jimmy. "I have something for you to eat."

He stroked his dick, hanging out of his sharply tailored pants, and it hardened. Sam hadn't properly seen a grown man's penis before. It was a mystifying thing, a piece of the human body that changed in front of your eyes. A milky white substance lined the ridge behind the tip.

"It's cheese," said Uncle Jimmy. "You're hungry? Have some."

Sam hesitated.

"I won't tell anyone that you've been stealing food." Uncle Jimmy held out a shiny silver coin. "And you can even take this and go get some candy."

Uncle Jimmy instructed him to suck and held the back of the boy's head until Sam sputtered and choked, arms flailing, unable to breathe. When Uncle Jimmy abruptly stopped, Sam gulped in air, only to find his throat was coated with some salty glue that only closed it further. He gagged.

"Hold that down now. And you won't have to go hungry."

Sam rinsed his mouth in the sink and put his hand into his pocket. Uncle Jimmy had never given him the coin.

———

Three years later, Sam had the run of the neighborhood. He'd walked down the alleyway to Thirty-Second Street, and they were like the Little Rascals. They built houses out of cardboard and played pretend family. Other parents tolerated Sam, but behind Fanny's back, they called him bad news. When the lights shut off at the baseball park at sundown and all the other children ran home for dinner, Sam wandered off toward nowhere, pushing a handcart. Why would an eight-year-old have a handcart?

A few blocks away, the factories were booming. It wasn't like it had been in Georgia, when there had been a real chance of going hungry. Fanny was a hell of a cook, with famous biscuits and cobblers and fried chicken to die for, but she cooked for Henry, and he worked erratic hours. Dinner was as likely to be served at 10 p.m. as at 6 p.m. No one cared if Sam came home anyway, and the streets were far more interesting.

Sam was hungry plenty. If you get hungry enough, you begin to hunt. Sam took to it naturally. He was a lousy student, he'd quit trumpet, he had dreams of playing baseball, but he could never keep track of where to show up for a game or when. Here, finally, was something he was good at. He loved the thrill of the hustle, the bittersweet taste of adrenaline in his mouth when he was getting away with something.

Sam had boosted the handcart from a hardware store. He learned to make himself invisible, stopping to peep in the lit windows of houses and watch the picture show that was other people's lives. When he was sure they were occupied, he popped the hoods of their shiny, bulbous cars, and silently lifted the batteries. Sam slid through the shadows of the leaves on the moonlit sidewalks as he'd wheel them to the dump, where a white man with six teeth would give him seventy-five cents for each one.

"Got paws like a Saint Bernard puppy," he said to Sam, placing the quarters in his palm. "You missed a quarter."

He never once got caught.

Somewhere inside, he knew that despite what people said, it wasn't for lack of intelligence that he failed at school. Though he wouldn't argue with their assertions of his laziness and insolence. Why try if you were just going to fail and no one cared either way?

At least that was what he thought until he saw Carol Messenger. Carol was a thing you might try for.

They'd been in school together since kindergarten, but in the fall of third grade, she was something totally new. He couldn't explain the difference. From clear across the schoolyard, anyone could see that Carol glowed, with nearly transparent skin and a spray of freckles over her nose. Her red hair fell in ringlets around her face that seemed to annoy her, as she spent half the school day adjusting them. Sam sat behind her and to the left. She'd pull her hair to the side as she chewed her pencil, exposing the delicate knobs of her spine, turning once in a while to glance back at him.

When Mrs. Harris faced the board and wrote THEY'RE THERE THEIR, Sam's gaze never wavered. Carol put her thumbs in her ears, stuck her tongue out, and wagged her fingers at Sam. Sam turned hot. Stuck his tongue out right back at her, but Carol was already facing the front of the room, wide green eyes trained on their teacher.

Mrs. Harris, who Sam had often noted had a lovely neck also, smiled at the peach of a girl and turned on the class clown with holes in his shoes, the discipline problem.

"Samuel McDowell, you may stand and face the back of the room until you can control your gaze."

Sam stood. Bitches. He faced the back wall, studying the posters of maps of the United States, the Founding Fathers with their creamy skin and strange hair that looked like rolls of toilet paper, the letters swimming together.

Just thinking about Carol, Sam's penis was erect. He didn't know how he was going to turn around when the bell rang, and he certainly had no idea what to do with the erection. No one had talked to him about masturbation or anatomy. No one talked about anything, really. But he knew one thing, even if he didn't understand what it meant yet. He knew necks gave him that same feeling he got when he browsed the candy aisle at the five-and-dime.

In the reflection in the back, Sam saw Mrs. Harris adjust her scarf, clear her throat, and continue with the lesson.

THEY'RE THERE THEIR

I don't know about all that, thought Sam as the letters swam in the shifting light of the reflection.

MINE, he thought. *I like that word better. MINE.*

13

BOYS' INDUSTRIAL SCHOOL

LANCASTER, OHIO
FEBRUARY 1954

The plan hatched over three whole weeks of whispered conversations in the dugout of the neighborhood baseball field, cemented by a secret handshake.

They would run away to Oberlin College. It was only a short bus ride from Lorain, and though Sam had wasted plenty on candy and the ten-cent cinema, he'd made enough money with his battery business to pay for one-way tickets for all three of them. From there: freedom. No more teachers, no more books.

In the spring of 1953, the three boys entered the Greyhound station in Lorain, hands in pockets, shifting their eyeballs like amateurs. They bought the tickets without question, Sam already being nearly the size of a fifteen-year-old. The air-conditioning in the bus raised goose bumps on their arms, the boys' toes tapping the floorboards with anticipation.

Their first glimpse of the college dazzled them. The buildings looked like stone castles they'd only ever imagined somewhere in

Europe, with arched doorways, spires reaching toward the clouds. White coeds peppered the rolling lawns, laughing and flirting, lying on blankets.

Did people live like this? People for whom their mothers had worked as house cleaners, maybe. People for whom they could one day hope to wash dishes.

In front of one of the castles was a row of bicycles, manufactured with the steel forged by their own fathers and grandfathers not a hundred miles north. The bicycles looked like a shiny row of Porsches, candy colored, with sleek lines and fat, whitewall tires.

Coveting, they called it in church. Sam went once in a blue moon, even though he mostly blew off Sundays at Lorain Gospel Tabernacle and went with his cousins Jimmy, Johnny, Joe, and Joe Dale to spend their dimes for the collection plates to see westerns. In the larger-than-life world on the screen, Gene Autry, Roy Rogers, and John Wayne would head toward a western horizon, fight for what they believed, kill without a twitch of the eye, get the girl in the end, sure, but not because they needed the girl. Sam was a cowboy like that.

"Which one do you want?" asked Sam as the boys surveyed the bicycles.

He wanted to hop on and pedal until the tip of the wheel met the edge of the Pacific Ocean. Sam had spent enough time facing the back of the room and staring at a uniform blotch of true blue, meant to represent water on the map. He would see the real thing one day, if his lungs burst from pedaling.

The three boys exchanged looks. Jimmy wordlessly picked a black number with red racing stripes. Sam picked a sparkling green Schwinn with streamers hanging from the handlebars. Billy picked a solid red. They adjusted the seats and handlebars, and in a shot, they were off. The wind dried the rivulets of sweat running down their temples before they could even reach their cheeks.

These bicycles were shiny things, prized possessions. The surge of fear Sam experienced when stealing his was followed by a lingering feeling of power, of ownership, of being above the rules. He didn't so much ride as fly the twelve blocks they managed to travel before the strange sight of two ragtag Black boys and one white boy, riding bicycles too big for them, prompted a gas station attendant to call the local police, who apprehended the burgeoning criminals within ten minutes.

When the sirens began to wail and the lights spun on top of the black-and-white behind them, Sam's eyes scanned the road ahead for avenues of escape. It wasn't a western movie set after all. It was a flat, midwestern suburb. There was nowhere to go.

Sam wouldn't see his home on Thirty-Third Street for almost two years.

———

Parents used the Boys' Industrial School, or BIS, as a threat.

Keep sassing me like that, you'll wind up at BIS.

In 1857, the Ohio government established the Ohio Reform School, predecessor to the BIS. The Ohio Reform School was a reformatory for boys between eight and eighteen years of age. Located approximately five miles south of Lancaster, in Fairfield County, Ohio, the institution accepted its first inmate in 1858. Thirty-five miles southeast of Columbus, the BIS was located on 1,210 acres of land. By the time Sam was driven through its stately gates on February 8, 1954, the original log cabins had long been replaced by handsome brick Victorian buildings, accented by white columns and built by the residents themselves with hand-hewn bricks. The sprawling campus housed gazebos and gardens and chapels and even mansions, reserved for the administration. It didn't look half-bad at first glance.

Sam was herded into what looked to him like a castle, arranged on the floor next to his fellow students, and given a warm welcome by the superintendent.

He had to keep pinching his own thigh to keep himself awake during the lecture that followed. He kept himself occupied by staring at the superintendent's wife. Kind of plain, but a lovely slim neck on that one.

The superintendent was on about the history. BIS was founded around the concept of the "open system." The boys lived in dormitory-style cottages rather than cells. The cottages were named after rivers in Ohio. BIS was a "family model," open, semi-military, almost entirely self-sufficient farm school. They grew and cooked their own food, made their own clothes. There was even an electric light and power station.

Sam learned he'd spend half of the day in school and the other half on the farm or in one of the vocational education buildings. The school offered training in blacksmithing, tailoring, baking, carpentry, stenography, brick making, butchering, shoemaking, horticulture, cattle raising, farming, carpentry, chair caning, and brush making, among numerous other professions.

They also boasted a forty-two-member band and mandatory military training. They marched everywhere.

"You'll learn what it means to have a sense of pride. You'll learn to respect yourselves and others," said the superintendent.

"You just missed the Christmas lights but you'll love Chestnut Day," said his wife, standing a pace behind him. "And French Toast Sundays. We're a family here. We don't have guards or wardens. We have house parents. Elder brothers. Trustees. People who can help get you back on God's right path in life. You can even turn out like one of the BIS boys we're very proud of: Mr. Bob Hope!"

The boys ate a quick supper, were separated by race, and walked through a processing center, where each was handed a uniform and card with a certain number of demerits, based on the severity of their crime. The cards hung around their necks. For good behavior, students lost demerits. Once they reached zero demerits, they'd be freed and returned to their families.

Demerits were also added for bad behavior.

In 1954, BIS was at its height, with eight hundred boys between eight and sixteen years of age. The first four dormitories housed the white boys, and the last four—Herrick, Hawking, Harris, and Patterson—housed the Black ones. Sam was placed in Herrick House.

The Black boys were assigned a trustee who led them to the back cabins.

"Might as well start your sorry asses marching now," said the trustee when they were out of sight of the main house.

A small group of white boys marched by them, stiff as nutcrackers.

"That ain't how we do it, case you're wondering. How we do it, Wilbert? Step up in front here. You back so soon?"

The boy directly behind Sam clicked his heels together, turned his hat at a jaunty angle, and sauntered to the front of the line.

"We do it like this, sir," shouted Wilbert, breaking into a cool kind of shuffle as the trustee called out, "To the *left*. To the *left*. To the *left, right, left*."

Upon reaching their new home, the boys broke formation. Sam caught up to Wilbert. He noted a sign for the cemetery.

"Boot Hill," said Wilbert. "You'll want to stay away from there.

Stay away from shoveling coal too. Try to go pick beans on the farm. Name's Wilbert Taylor."

"Sam McDowell."

When the boys reached the doorway of Herrick House, the forest beyond the grounds swallowed the last of the sun. As each boy entered, a trustee handed him a long white shift. They were led to a dormitory-style room and told to choose their bunks.

"You stronger than me," Wilbert said to Sam. He was soft spoken, with limpid brown eyes and long lashes like a girl. "I don't mind taking the top bunk if you want the bottom."

"How'd you wind up back here anyway?"

"I'm incorrigible."

"Not sure I know what that means," said Sam as he unfolded the stiff linen garment, unevenly sewn in the residents' tailor shop. Looked like his mama's nightgown. Not good.

Wilbert dropped his eyes and, as if psychic, said, "Not good at all."

Sam soon learned the meaning of incorrigible. He talked back, hustled, fought, shucked, and jived. He had so many demerits they had to give him a new card and then another after that. When they realized he responded to neither incentives nor consequences, they began giving him the strop. When that didn't work, they stood him in the lunch room facing the wall, along with the other tough cases who held thirty-pound iron balls, chained and shackled to their ankles. The rule was if you dropped the ball, your time started over. The trustees walked down the line of boys, smacking the backs of their heads at random, causing them to pitch forward into the wall and drop their ball.

Each day, the boys marched and worked, marched and worked.

Each night, the younger boys kept their eyes shut tight and prayed, listening to the footsteps of the trustees. They knew the next sound would be screams from the coatroom. If on some nights, the screams sounded suspiciously like Sam's, almost as if coming out of his own mouth, he knew it was never him. Some other child was being hurt, having his ass stretched, over and over. If it was you, you never admitted it. It was never him.

Wilbert got a bad deal, being so pretty, but he was no little thing, and both Sam and Wilbert shared a love of the fights.

Wilbert and Sam began to bob and weave between the trees, shadowboxing, getting stronger, learning to fight back. Be the punisher rather than the punished.

Based on the demerit system, the average stay at BIS was twelve months. Samuel McDowell entered the gates of BIS at age thirteen, on February 8, 1954. He walked out again at fifteen years of age, nineteen months later. His file read "especially incorrigible." Even the superintendent was glad to be rid of the headache.

———

No one picked him up at the gate. The precept put him on a bus with a pat on the back and a sack lunch.

Sam moved back in with Mama and Big 'Un, but the whole family had started looking at him sideways, cracking down harder on his mischief. They hadn't come all this way, from the plantations of Georgia, to start acting like no accounts now. Sam always wondered why Fanny called his older brother Paul when it was time to whup him. He mentioned it to his cousins one Sunday afternoon, and Paul Jr. fell out laughing.

"You ain't figured this out yet? Paul is your daddy, you idjit. Not your brother."

No one seemed surprised. Had they all known the whole time? Mama confirmed the devastating revelation, and Sam exploded.

"Liars!"

Big 'Un was on him in a flash. He grabbed the poker from the coal stove and swung it at his grandson, catching him on the temple. Sam caught him in a headlock.

Mama begged for Big 'Un's life until Sam dropped to the floor and wrapped his arms around Mama's knees.

"Don't blame us. This badness in you, it ain't us. It's them Little niggers."

Sam had no idea what she was talking about. Little niggers? He pictured a bunch of tiny Black people running around, and him gigantic, like that Gulliver movie.

He and Mama wept at the kitchen table as she told him the story that turned his world upside down and then just as quickly righted it again. He was free of all this guilt and obligation and trying to do the right thing by his family. Free to be who he truly was.

He lay his head on the pillow that night with an uncharacteristic sense of peace and a new sense of purpose. He knew exactly what he wanted to do. He'd known since he left BIS, but at that time, his nuts hadn't dropped yet. Now there would be no stopping him.

He had come from all that marching and bean picking even more convinced he loved the sparkly things in life. Like he had wanted the bicycle. He wanted things so powerfully it felt his whole body would fold in on itself like a dying star. He just hadn't figured out how to get those things without getting caught yet.

He had only recently even figured out what to do with his teenage erections. Until a few months before, he'd gotten hard and wound up just sitting there staring at his dick, like it was some kind of puzzle.

On a whim, he'd started stealing pulp detective magazines from the drug store: *True Detective, True Crime, Master Detective, Inside*

Detective… He'd shoved them down his pants, hid them under his mattress. Opening them was unwrapping the world's best Christmas gift. He couldn't believe what he was looking at.

The photos between the covers were real women, and they were really dead.

Women with chunks blown from the front of their skull, heads lolled over a bathtub, limbs twisted and broken on the concrete after having been pushed from a height, their glassy dead eyes staring at nothing.

It wasn't until Gloria Ferry that his interest blossomed into true passion. Dare he say it, true love.

Gloria Ferry.

Gloria Ferry had been buried on page 38 of the March 1956 issue of *Inside Detective*.

Glorious Gloria, graceful Gloria, the most beautiful woman he had ever seen. He read the story and learned how she had left a bum-fuck town in the Ozarks where they tied corn sacks to their feet for shoes and ran off with an old buzzard thirty years her senior when she was sixteen. When she had tried to leave him, he had strangled her and left her naked body in Brookside Park in Cleveland.

The headline read "If You Play House With a Fiend."

Poor Gloria.

In the photograph, Gloria was a bottle blond with an unusually long, slender neck, around which she wore a black choker necklace. She reminded Sam of Barbara Stanwyck in that movie where she plays the lying bitch. Humphrey Bogart strangles her as she writhes on the bed, blond hair shimmering like a waterfall on the satin sheets. In Sam's opinion, Gloria was even prettier than the Stanwyck woman. Maybe because movie stars belong to everyone, but Gloria was his secret. His alone.

If you looked at the very, very, very fine print, you would see the photograph of Gloria in the magazine was a postmortem reconstruction. No one had bothered to photograph Gloria when she was alive. Sam skimmed over that part.

In the reconstruction, her saucer eyes were laden with some elemental sadness. She had left her controlling, older lover, fled to Columbus, obtained a job in a laundromat. Her body had been found by a search party, her eyes shot through with petechial hemorrhaging, her hyoid bone cleanly cracked, her throat stained with a necklace of maroon bruises. Her boyfriend, Robert West, was arrested and convicted for the crime.

A young woman caught in a cycle of poverty had latched onto a jealous older boyfriend in a desperate bid to escape. For the sin of changing her mind, he squeezed the life out of her.

A commonplace story, but for Sam, it was the moment the needle hit the vein. He crept downstairs and grabbed a pair of sewing scissors and two thumbtacks, carefully clipped Gloria's picture, and pinned it on the wall over his bed. He jerked off to it over and over, finally understanding what a dick was for, what pleasure felt like.

What was it about necks? Slender like wrists, but so much more vulnerable. A liminal body part, a bridge between body and mind. The gateway for oxygen, the passageway for sustenance, the place from which your voice emerged. Necks were everything.

Necks were his private world, but in the real world, he needed money.

There had been only one person left he was trying to front like a good boy for. It was his mama. But Mama had lied to him. There was nothing left to stop him.

14

THE DRIVER

PASCAGOULA, MISSISSIPPI
NOVEMBER 1982

Danny hadn't seen it, but he'd heard the man talk about it. Sometimes the man would slip into Danny's room and not the old lady's when he came back from his drives. He'd promise him things in his ear, tell him stories.

The man took the Pinto those nights, but only until they got the Lincoln. Almost always had two cars. One for the man and one for the old lady. Danny chauffeured the old lady on her boosting expeditions while the man slept all day, gathering his strength.

The man said he was a lion who had just eaten. Sleeping in the sun. Digesting, until he got hungry again.

Danny was somewhere he didn't want to be. Someone was asking him questions. He got confused like that. His thoughts bounced around like foosball. He'd bounced around the country just the same, with the man and the old lady. How was he supposed to remember?

"Okay, let's just start again, young man," said the suit and tie with flossy strands of hair superglued to his pate. Cop #2 looked so similar to cop #1 that Danny wondered if he was seeing double.

The white cop sipped from a white cup. "Want one of these?"

"No, sir."

"You sure?"

"Come on, son. Just your name."

The other one said, "It's not hard." Sounded a little angry. Sounded like he wanted to go home.

"See, we already know. It's like a little test."

"Name's Danny."

"Anyone call you Dan?"

"Nah, just Danny."

"Okay, Danny, let's try another easy one. When were you born?"

"My birthday?"

"Son, you are being about as useful as a steering wheel on a mule, and I promise you, you are going to want to be helpful if you'd like to ever go home."

"Home?"

He was in Mississippi now, he guessed. They moved so fast and so sudden. Arkansas was where the old lady and the man picked him up. The old lady traded his mama some clothes for him. Had a banged-up face been smacked around six ways from Sunday. Probably started out ugly too, but now she was straight hard to look at. Won you over so you hardly noticed after a while.

"I got this bad eye," she'd told his mother.

Danny remembered thinking it looked like an asshole, puckered up. He'd right away felt bad for thinking it, nice lady like that. His mama had barely had enough money to feed them, plus she had his sister to worry about, coming home knees scraped to shit like some five-dollar whore.

"She sold me to them for some clothing and a vodka drink," he said. He thought it was in his head. Maybe it was out loud. "Born November 28, 1963." Felt proud of himself for that one.

"And it is now November 24 of 1982, so that makes you, what, Danny? Nineteen?"

"I only drove. I drove the old lady."

"You talking about Orelia Dorsey? The woman they call Jean? Jean? We have her down the hall, and she told us you didn't treat women right, Danny. Told us you'd been up to no good. Said you had the urge to put the hurt on ladies."

"Who? That wasn't me!"

"It's okay, son. We understand. We all want to do it sometimes. Heck, I told Detective Harrison here just the other day my wife deserved a smack in the kisser, didn't I?"

"Don't piss on our leg and tell us it's raining, son."

"God's honest, it wasn't me!"

"Who was it then?"

He'd been nice to the old lady, tried to protect her, because that was what a gentleman does. That's what he was taught. She turned nasty as a rattlesnake.

Don't you talk about my Sam that way. You ain't fit to wash his feet.

Danny drove while she crocheted, with tissues wadded into her bloodied nose.

Everyone knew when Jean came to town. She had the top-shelf boosted goods, a wink and a hug, a mouth on her that made people fall out cackling. She'd have Danny pull over by projects and set up shop in the trunk.

They called him the Driver. He knew he'd started as Danny. He was a little slow—not plum crazy. Somewhere on the road, he became what they called him.

The man and Jean conspired over a map of the country. They made notes and drew ballpoint lines for routes. The man called him son. The man hadn't hurt him much. The man had maybe thought he was in the wrong bed now and again, but that was nothing new and a small price to pay for a family.

Danny got them where they wanted to go, checked them into the motels under his name. The man told Danny he liked to smack the ladies around. Told him he liked to choke 'em. They loved it.

"You ever pick up a prostitute, Danny?"

"Not me, sir!"

The man was an artist. The man and the old lady both had skills. The man even showed him an article about a painting he once did on a wall. Was that what's-her-name Betsy Ross and some other Black folk, and it was big as a whole city block, and they put it in the *Miami Herald* in 1976. He was an important man.

Danny drove.

"You help this man Samuel procure prostitutes? Was this part of your job? Some kind of a scout? Set the bait in the trap?"

"I never did like how he treated ladies. Never did go in for any of it. You got a nice lady at home who taking care of you, why you gotta go act like that?"

"Act like what?"

"Get mad."

"Mad at what?"

"Mad at ladies. Like when they didn't treat him right. Turned their noses up. He called 'em stuck-up bitches. Said their noses were turned up so high they'd drown in a rainstorm. He like it here though."

Carver Village in Pascagoula was Candyland to the man. He'd say, "Ooooooooweeeeee, here we go."

One side of the road was the village—the projects—and the other was the stroll. The man would stick around for longer than usual, crawl the Jump Club, the King William Hotel, the juke joints and pool halls with rooms for rent by the hour round back. People came from miles around to get anything and everything they wanted: Ts and blues, guns and hos.

The man had told him it was because of the shipyards. World War II brought all kinds of crazy business to the yards, making warships and stuff. The man could talk a blue streak when he was high. He told Danny cops in Mississippi didn't care nothing for Black folk, so they pretty much just gave up and left them to handle their own business, long as it didn't start spilling over to the proper citizens.

Carver Village was a world unto itself. The man had brought Danny inside, and he had been proud to be called son in front of a bunch of ladies wearing hot pants and tube tops. Disco music blasted and light swirled around their heads. Girls named Moon Pie spun around poles for pimps named Pretty James.

"What did he do when he got mad?" asked the detective, who fiddled with a loose thread on the cuff of his sleeve.

"He'd yell. Like at the juke joints and bars and what not. He'd yell right in their faces. *You nothing but trash. I got bitches you ain't fit to lick their shoe, sorry ass ho. You bitches ain't shit.* Like that."

"But you never picked up a ho for him."

"I never did that."

"But he told you he did that."

"He told me things."

"You know what a punk is, Danny?"

"I heard it before."

"You a punk, Danny? You like a little girl to him?"

"No! He was with them hos. He told me he liked to slap 'em around and choke 'em. Told me they liked it. He liked to talk about it. See, I wasn't no punk."

"Sure, sure, not you. We won't tell your mama…if you can help us. What else did he tell you?"

Get me a bottle of vodka, you sad piece of pussy.

"Told me if they made him mad, he leave 'em out in the middle of nowhere. Made him laugh real hard."

"He was getting arrested all over the place."

"Sure was!"

"But still no one asked about the ladies?"

"Huh?"

Every arrest just made the man hungry in the eyes, and he'd go out crawling. The next morning, Danny had to hose down the car with the old lady. The man and the lady would have a good old tussle about the earrings, the odd shoe, the chones, the shit. She cleaned it spick-and-span though.

Wanna know how to get a woman sexually excited, you retarded little girl? Offer 'em money.

There was the one he told him about, the scrappy bitch who tried to run his car into a wall, then had run across the freeway with her titties in the wind.

Offer 'em money. Just make sure you take it back.

The men placed newspaper articles on the table in front of him. Danny remembered Jean with her careful scissors, stuffing the clipping into her knitting bag. Danny was never much of a reader.

"You know what these are?"

You know what these fools think of me? They think I'm just a petty criminal.

"They from the newspapers?"

"They're articles about dead women, Danny. Did you save these?"

Rough 'em up. They like it. Made a mistake of tying up that one cunt in Florida and we was just having fun. She was ashamed for herself and lied like the lying ho she was born to be. Did three months for that. Done more time for stealing a straw hat. Nobody cares a damn about a lying whore.

"Danny? Where are you right now? Oh, fuck this. He's half a retard," said the second guy, the one without pit stains.

Retard.

Danny remembered. "The one girl was a retard and a freak and loved it. That's what the man said."

The cop man stopped fiddling with his cuff. "Which one was that?"

You snitch and you'll get yours.

It was as if Danny was watching himself talk from a corner of the ceiling. He couldn't stop.

"The retard in Florida. The one who bit him."

Danny told them about the bite mark on the man's hand. The fight with the old lady. The shit in the car.

"You know this girl?"

The men put a photo in front of him. A white girl playing a flute with those white girl feathers in her hair. Someone plain and pretty. This wasn't the Florida girl, he was sure of it.

"No, sir. I don't know that kind of girl."

"You never saw her?"

"I swear to Jesus I never did."

"Name's Mindy."

"Pretty name."

"Your daddy there killed her."

The men put down another photo in front of him. It looked like a costume skull, the body below it like melted rubber.

"Is that from Halloween?"

"That was a girl," said the detective. He tossed his cup, missed the trash. "Get this mongoloid out of here, and put him on a bus to his mother."

On the bus out of town, Danny was no longer the driver. He had told the cops he'd never had enough money to escape from the man and the old lady, but the truth was he'd never tried. He wondered if he would ever feel needed again.

15

HILDA

The first time I drove through Biloxi was pre-Katrina. Scott and I got engaged in New Orleans and decided to drive the Gulf Coast, seeing road signs for Mobile and singing "Stuck Inside of Mobile with the Memphis Blues Again." Miles of green rolled out on one side of us and miles of navy sea on the other. Famished and nearly out of gas, we stumbled upon a gas station where the owner's mom fed us fried chicken she'd happened to just cook up, and when it was gone, it was gone.

"Is this chicken or is this cake?" asked Scott.

"Chicken cake!" I said.

"Chicken cake, baby!" the owner's mom echoed. "That's what we call it now! Next time y'all come visit, I'll make you my famous chicken cake!"

I was love-drunk, and it all sparkled: the gulf, the chicken cake, the ring on my finger throwing points of light on the rental car's ceiling like a disco ball.

I was the opposite of love-drunk the night I navigated the same stretch of I-90 Sam had driven hundreds of times: the thirty-two miles between Biloxi and Pascagoula. Malls turned to marshland. I saw road signs for Mobile, New Orleans.

Ohio, Maryland, Florida, Maine, Connecticut, Oregon, Colorado, Pennsylvania, New Jersey, Arizona, Georgia, Illinois, Missouri, California...

Burglary, breaking and entering, assault and battery, assault with the intent to rob, assault with a firearm, armed robbery, assault on a police officer, solicitation of prostitution, driving under the influence, shoplifting, theft, grand theft, possession of marijuana, unlawful flight to avoid prosecution, resisting arrest, battery, false imprisonment, assault with great bodily injury, robbery, rape, sodomy, murder, murder, murder...

I contemplated the string of events surrounding the bewildering dismissal of Sam's crimes in the eighties. Hurricane Katrina had wiped out not just human beings, homes, businesses, and communities but also warehouses of evidence. Instead of hunting down nonexistent case files, I talked to detectives, family members. I ran the timeline in my head. It never failed to baffle.

On July 31, 1980, Samuel Little assaulted Hilda Nelson, a twenty-six-year-old Black woman. He drowned and strangled Nelson in her apartment in Carver Village. She survived due to the intervention of her best friend, Delores Hester. She was hospitalized at the Singing River Hospital for three days for her injuries. Because her mother didn't know she was a prostitute and she was ashamed, she called it breaking and entering. The cops wouldn't do anything either way, so why bother?

Nelson made a formal report about a year and a half later when detectives came to question her about the strangulation of a young white woman named Melinda LaPree. Her mother already knew by then.

On November 19, 1981, Leila McClain, a nineteen-year-old Black woman, known in the neighborhood as Bowlegs, was offered fifty dollars for sex and picked up by Sam Little in a brown, wood-paneled Pinto station wagon. She had a room at the village, but he insisted on going to the Shamrock Motel up the street, then passed it and turned off on a side road instead. Sam had oddly chosen poorly. That little bowlegged five-foot-two monument to survival reached over, turned the wheel, shoved her foot down on top of Sam's on the gas pedal, and tried to drive the car into a brick wall. When that didn't work, she boxed him. Of ninety-three, eighty-six, or eighty-four victims, she was the only one who fought her way out.

On August 16, 1982, the naked, badly decomposed body of Rosie Hill, a twenty-one-year-old Black woman, was found in a field near a hog pen in Marion County, Florida. Only a navy terry-cloth slipper was found in a tree nearby. The Pinto and the man last seen offering Rosie $100 for sex were both identified by eyewitnesses.

On September 12, 1982, the nude, strangled body of Patricia Mount, a twenty-six-year-old white woman, was found in a field in Alachua County, Florida. Eyewitnesses later identified Sam Little as the man last seen leaving Willie Mae's Beer Tavern in Gainesville with her in his brown Pinto station wagon with wood paneling.

On October 4, 1982, the skeletal remains of twenty-two-year-old Melinda LaPree were found by a groundskeeper in the Gautier Family Cemetery, nearly a month after she had been reported missing by her boyfriend on September 17. A disarticulated hyoid bone and fractured cricoid cartilage indicated strangulation. Again, eyewitnesses identified Sam as the man with whom she had been seen getting into a brown Pinto station wagon.

When detectives from Marion and Alachua Counties had gotten together and figured out they had eyewitnesses on both the Hill and Mount cases with the same vehicle description, same description of the man last seen with the victims, and same MO, they put out a widely distributed BOLO (be on the lookout) with a composite sketch of the suspect and the vehicle. Detectives in Jackson County, Mississippi, recognized these descriptions as the same man seen picking up LaPree in front of the King William Hotel.

On November 24, 1982, Sam was arrested with Jean and Danny in the Pinto for shoplifting. The arresting officers recognized the car from the BOLO. The Pascagoula PD and the Jackson County Sheriff's Department arrested Sam for murder.

Hilda Nelson and Leila McClain were both subpoenaed to the grand jury hearing for the murder of Melinda LaPree. Neither had a car at the time, so they walked to the courthouse. Nelson was eight months pregnant, and the minute she saw Sam, she peed herself with fear. She was asked to leave, and the two women walked home without testifying.

The grand jury failed to indict due to lack of evidence.

Sam was almost on the loose again, but not quite. They extradited him from Jackson County, Mississippi, to Alachua County, Florida, where he was arrested for the murder of Patricia Mount on July 19, 1983. Hairs found on the victim were similar to Sam's, and eyewitnesses identified both the car and Sam.

He admitted to being at the tavern at the night in question. A six-person jury found Sam not guilty due to the lack of definitive physical evidence.

It had almost happened again in Los Angeles in 2012. Cold case veteran Rick Jackson and Mitzi Roberts had built a methodical case, with strong pattern evidence. This time, they had secured powerful living witnesses. Hilda Nelson, Leila McClain, and Laurie Barros had all reluctantly agreed to testify. Solid as it may have been, they were left with the same problem: the only physical evidence was that one case-to-case hit. It wasn't enough for the DA to indict.

Roberts had been one step behind Sam for months, and now she worried he was gaining ground. Armed with a DNA profile, a distinctive MO, an incomprehensible rap sheet, and Christie Palazzolo's investigative leads matrix, Roberts and Jackson set off on a cross-country fact-finding mission. They planned to interview Sam's living victims, meet with detectives across the country, and build their own case with pattern evidence while generating momentum for what they hoped would become a nationwide effort.

Jackson was known for solving complex homicides, but few knew his first job was working for AAA—employee of the month three times. He loved the veins and arteries of maps, treasures of invisible history buried between the lines. The partners drove from Memphis to Mobile, from Alachua to Pascagoula, from Pamela K. Smith to Melinda LaPree, in late October 2012.

On the morning of November 26, after seven months of playing a wild, half-blind game of Marco Polo, Roberts rubbed her chlorine-stung eyes.

She had gotten a third case-to-case hit on her suspect.

Through the CCSS screenings, Sam's genetic material had been detected on the bra and shirt of forty-one-year-old Carol Alford, who'd been found strangled in a residential South Central LA alley-way in July 1987.

It was what they needed.

On January 7, 2013, assistant district attorney Beth Silverman filed three charges of murder with special circumstances against Samuel Little.

I followed in their footsteps, going to Pascagoula to interview two of the key trial witnesses, Hilda Nelson and Detective Lieutenant Darren Versiga, and to see the place for myself.

———

A river ran beside the road the Pascagoula, with small boats anchored to battered docks and seafood shacks with twinkle lights. I opened the window. It smelled like the end of summer.

A landlocked lighthouse caught my attention. Was it a theme restaurant? Why would a patch of grass next to a two-lane highway need a lighthouse? A sign beside it read:

WELCOME TO PASCAGOULA

A smaller plaque informed me this was the birthplace of Jimmy Buffett: singer, songwriter, and author.

Detective Darren Versiga worked the 10 p.m. to 4 a.m. shift. He preferred the quiet. Hard with a kid but less headache in general, and more time to work on his cold cases. Leila McClain had died of cancer six months before. I would be meeting with Versiga at the station that night around midnight and Hilda Nelson the following day.

Versiga was a husky, white-haired, ruddy-complected cop who greeted me with a handshake and an avuncular smile in the otherwise empty reception area. I followed him down a hall lined with vintage photos. I caught glimpses of what I think was a word processor? A fax machine? A picture of Jesus hung over Versiga's desk, surrounded by those of a bazillion kids and grandkids.

Versiga was a cold case devotee who spent any blink of spare time pursuing leads. He'd been integral to the 2012 investigation that led to Sam Little's conviction, finally, for the strangulation of three women in Los Angeles in 2014. I recognized a familiar obsessive intensity in him. What else would propel you through horror toward a solution?

Now, he was an inch from long-sought justice for Mindy LaPree. He passed me a photo of a feather-haired, apple-cheeked flower child playing the flute. Showed me another of Billy Hampton, LaPree's boyfriend, who reported her missing in the morning, at least. Hampton was white, blue-eyed, long-haired, holding their one-year-old in his arms. He looked a lot like a Billy I once knew. He told his baby mama to go sit on the wall until she brought back money and drugs. "Would if I could, babe, but y'know, equal distribution of labor. It's feminism." Her skeletal remains were found nearly a month later.

"I was a reserve when it happened. Stood watch over the crime scene," said Versiga.

LaPree's remains were curious to me. She looked burned somehow, encased in a melted black garbage bag.

"She's not exactly a skeleton."

"Skeletal just means all that remains are bones, teeth, and hair for identification. I have one Jane Doe right now I'm looking at with a gold tooth. Also cracks and fractures. Childhood injuries. Signs of trauma. But no soft tissue."

Only LaPree's skull was clean bone.

"Is that because areas of trauma decompose faster?"

"Exactly. Head trauma. The bugs go to the open wounds first. Not just wounds, wet spots. Mouths, nostrils, vaginas…"

I stayed for another couple of hours before the jet lag hit me like a plank. As I headed back to the hotel, I repeated what I'd learned, obvious as it might have seemed.

Bugs go to the open wounds first.

I sat next to Hilda Nelson in one of the padded office chairs of the Hilton conference room, my recorder between us on the kidney-shaped table. Nelson pulled a pamphlet out of her purse and placed it on the table in front of Versiga. It was the program from Leila McClain's funeral.

On the cover, McClain was all dolled up in a hot-pink dress, mink lashes, and a feather boa.

"Can I get a copy of this?" Versiga asked.

"Oh, that's for you, honey."

Nelson was sixty-four years old and going through her fourth round of chemo. She was nearly bald, but for a dusting of salt-and-pepper hair. She wore leggings and an oversize bedazzled T-shirt that read THINGS ARE HAPPENIN' IN ATLANTA over an airbrushed Atlanta skyline. She wore a gold cross and chunky gold earrings.

She was game to talk, as long as she got out in time to take her granddaughter to get her nails done for homecoming.

"Used to always have my nails done. They're too thin now with the chemo. They hurt."

I asked Nelson about her background.

"I grew up middle class. We lived right there on Live Oak. My grandparents raised me. My grandfather worked on the railroad. My grandma, she worked for the Veneer Men... It's one of these Pathco..."

Versiga said, "...with the milling."

"Yeah, they still going. I got one brother, and it was just us. We grew up good. But then there was just this mystery about the Village. That was the name of the apartment complex, and across the street from the Village was nothing but clubs, juke joint, hit houses. And when we were kids, if anybody told my grandma they saw us down there, you know what that was, but as soon as I got grown, that's the first place I went."

"Must have sounded intriguing."

"I was working at the shipyard, and I had two girls at the time. I started hustling, but like I said, the things I was doing, I didn't have to do."

"And what did you like to do when you were a kid? What were you into?"

"Booooys." First hint of a gap-toothed smile. "How you think I got into this mess? I had my own car. Most of the boys, they didn't have nothing. But I liked to read. I used to like to read and dress real sharp."

Nelson placed one peeling fingernail on the photo of McClain on the table in front of us. "See how she dressed? We probably was on our way to the club that night because that's how we lived in that glamour life. Or so I thought. Because it was good as well as bad. Then, after this thing happened with this man, I backed up a little bit."

"When you say backed up a little bit, you mean..."

"Yeah, with the prostitution and the hustling and the men. I kind of got back. But Bowlegs? That's what we called her. Bowlegs—even from the time we was in LA, it was three men called on her in one weekend! I said, 'Girl, you still?' She said, 'Oh yeah!'"

Versiga shook his head. "She was something else. Y'all were alike in ways, but you're definitely more laid-back."

"I wanted to be a writer. I got two years of college. I went to JC, but like I said, once I got that twenty-one and I could leave my grandma's house, I went. It's just that I'm nosy, honey, and I like that fast life."

"Tell me about the Village."

"When I first moved there, I was still at the shipyard. I would walk on the Village side. I hadn't moved over to the Front side yet. The people that I knew that would be over there, they be, 'Hey, come over. Oh, you think you're too good.' You know how people are. And sooner or later, going in that shipyard cold, going in there hot. I had seen other ways to get money other than working in the shipyard. So that's what I did."

"What were the clubs like? Bars? Dancing? Gambling?"

"E-ve-ry-thing. We wouldn't wake up until about maybe about this time because we would have been up all night. Get a shower. Get dressed. Eat. Between four and five, we hit the track and would just be out there drinking beer, dancing, turning tricks, doing whatever. You partied. Just getting down in the Highway Club, the Jump Club. We just, that was an average day and then we'd get out there to like I say four, five, or six when it's cool. Jumping in and out cars and running around corners, going across the street and back, just handling business."

"How many dates would you have a night?"

"Well, like, I'd say like from Thursday to Saturday, those were the good, good nights. You know, maybe seven or eight because I just sat there. If you came to me, good. If you didn't, good. I wasn't for all that hopping in cars and all that because I lived right across the street."

"Leila would be the one," said Versiga. "She would, as many as she could get under her belt."

"I mean from sun down to sun up!"

They laughed.

"Her own words, I mean that's her words. She just..." Versiga couldn't say it.

"How'd she say it? I'm a whore!" laughed Nelson. "When she came to the Village, she was driving an Oldsmobile or something. She came from right over there in Franklin Creek, but she was a nice—to the day she died—she was a nice, nice, nice person. She didn't know nothing about no prostituting then...or so she led us to believe. She was selling shoes out the trunk of her car. I'm nosy. What's up? What's going on over here? She say, 'What size you wear?' I said, 'Girl, you ain't got nothing in there that fit me. I'm a ten.' She say, 'Yes, I do,' and she gave me a pair of shoes. And she started calling me her sister."

"Do you remember your first date?"

"My friend Lois said, 'Girl, you could make you some money.' She say, 'You look good, you dress nice, and you don't fool with that riffraff.' The first time I did was in Lois house. We walked across the street. They was fisherman and they gave us fifty dollars apiece then. And I said, 'Damn, that was easy.' As long as you don't be fooling with no fools. Nobody want to act like they do with they wife. All that foreplay, ain't none of that. You know what you want. Do it and get out of my house."

We talked about our first times falling in love, how she met her oldest girl's daddy at a record shop.

She told me about her seventeen-year-old granddaughter: cheerleader, volleyball, debate team, homecoming court, student council.

"She sounds like a good girl," I said.

"Yeeeah. Right now, she is. But I see you know how that go."

"Was the city pretty segregated at the time?"

Nelson laughed in my face.

"Were you addicted to drugs?"

"I used to smoke a little reefer during that time, but no, nothing heavy after I stopped turning tricks. I dibble and dabble a little bit in cocaine, crack, rock, whatever. Then when I got tired of doing that, what happened, I went to jail. I caught two cases. Possession with intent."

"I actually worked the case. I worked it when we had an under-cover unit!" said Versiga.

"Mm-hmm. That night I told them, I said, 'It's somebody in them bushes.' They thinking I'm high and paranoid!"

"You remember where that was at?"

"On the dog pound."

"That's exactly where it was at. There *was* a guy in the bushes! Makes you feel any better, we had ticks. We were in them woods and there were so many ticks on us. When we got out of them woods, I kept saying, 'What's that crawling on us?' Never went back."

We talked about blackjack, chemo, Jesus.

"If you were going to pick five words to describe yourself, what would they be?"

"First one would be loving…fun. Sometimes mysterious. I don't know. I'm not no bad person. I'm a darer.

"I didn't want to go to no Los Angeles for no trial. I was about through with it, because I got to have closure somewhere. I felt sorry for that little old man in the wheelchair. I couldn't believe he had done all that to me, but I knew what he had done. He looked up and I looked him in his face. Oh, I knew that was him. I had to just hold my mule, you know, get it over with. Everything we say he did, every-thing police say he did, his low-down ass did it. And for what? For what? He ain't even rob us. He ain't take our money or nothing. And the people he killed. What for?"

———

After the interview, Versiga gave me a tour of the town.

"Here we have what they call the Singing River," he told me. "The story is, one of the Pascagoula Indians was sweet on a Biloxi Indian and they were warriors. We were bread makers. The bread maker Indians here and the warriors over there, and one of the bread makers decided to marry a warrior, and that did not go well. Story is, the Biloxi Indians were setting up for war, and instead, cowards that Pascagoula Indians were, they went into the river singing a chant and drowned theirselves. That was the end of the Pascagoula people. That's why it's called the Singing River. I never heard it, but there's stories out there that you can hear like a chant or a hum. I guess it's a folklore kind of thing."

We stared out at the shipyard. It was a massive and baffling Erector Set of cranes and half-built aircraft carriers, framed by an expanse of deep blue sky, decorated with dollops of clouds that looked like roses on a wedding cake.

The town was a mix of neat suburban boxes, charming Victorians, and massive colonial beachfront houses, most rebuilt after the hurricane. What passion drives a person to keep sinking roots in land that faces inevitable catastrophic flooding? Versiga himself had decided to wait out Katrina and wound up with the roof blown off his house and eight family members, including two infants, clinging to a single Jet Ski.

We visited the Longfellow House, one of the few left standing after the hurricane. All I could remember of Henry Wadsworth Longfellow was the Paul Revere poem:

One if by land, and two if by sea;
And I on the opposite shore will be.

Longfellow's greatest achievement, however, is considered to be his translation of Dante's *Divine Comedy*, divided into three parts: *Inferno*, *Purgatorio*, and *Paradiso*. Over seven centuries later, *Inferno* remains ubiquitous in popular culture. Hell.

"It's about an author who gets a VIP tour of hell from a poet in a toga," I told Versiga.

"Coincidoinks!" he replied. He swung around the corner. "There was the old Steak and Eggs, where we'd all go after the night shift."

I imagined early mornings decades before when off-duty cops scarfed down greasy after-work breakfast plates, sitting on counter stools next to whores equally as famished and exhausted.

"This was the old entrance to Carver Village," he said and turned right onto a seemingly endless two-lane blacktop that stretched as far as the eye could see.

On either side of the road was pretty much nothing.

To the left, the Village side, were wide manicured fields, a few saplings planted ten feet apart. A circular driveway led to a lone assisted-care facility.

It was hard to imagine the operation that had razed all those buildings to the ground, grinding a storied Black neighborhood from history, leaving only saplings and a nursing home.

To the right, where the Front had been, there were still meager remnants. The one standing structure was an abandoned cinder-block church with no windows. Weeds and brush had mostly obscured the hints of the wall the girls used to wait on, but you could still see the footprint of the King William Hotel.

"All the way back then, it was as punishment," Versiga said.

"What was as punishment?"

"A rookie would get in trouble with the department, if we wrecked the car or anything, you had to walk Carver Village. They would throw things at you and holler, 'blue, blue, blue, blue, blue.' Lucky in the old days, I could run pretty fast!"

A tour of a ghost town.

"Let me bring the picture up. Okay. We're on this road. Here's the railroad. That foundation? This is the King William Hotel right here. Club after club after club all the way down as far as you could go both directions. This was called Liberty Street. Dunbar. Carver. That's gonna bring back memories."

Versiga pointed out where Leila McClain had been picked up as well as the location of the old Shamrock Motel. We drove the route Sam had taken with her.

"Up here, Auto Zone was not there. Grass growing up. And there was a trail that you could walk all the way down to the back of King William. Here's where she got attacked. She ran this way right across that busy highway, fell down in the bushes, and that's where Smokey Joe was taking a pee."

"Wait. Here to…" I looked back to the aerial. "It's so far."

"Oh yeah, it's far."

"That's a really busy road."

"Oh yeah, it is."

You don't get that from the maps. I stood there and looked at the route, the nonstop traffic. It was such a long way to run.

"I wasn't messing," said Versiga. "She was something."

Our final stop was the historic Gautier cemetery, dating back to 1847, where Sam had dumped the body of Melinda LaPree. I'd heard the story of LaPree's murder several times from Sam. He'd carried her down a small slope, laid her on the flowers atop a fresh grave. He described the proximity from the street. Something wasn't right.

"Was this fence here then?"

"No."

I saw it. Exactly as Sam had described. I placed a stone, as Jews do for remembrance.

My final night in Pascagoula, cicadas haunted my dreams. A man fished by the river in surgical gloves. I hadn't slept much and was ready to put my purse under my head and curl up in a corner of the Biloxi airport while rain pelted the windows—the tail end of Hurricane Florence. I settled in for what I imagined would be a delayed flight, another drive in the dark to another motel. Next stop: Sam's hometown of Lorain, Ohio.

I was nearly asleep when the phone in the bag under my head buzzed. I fumbled to grab it. The space cowboy. Really now?

"What should I call you, sir?" I asked Texas Ranger James Holland, casting about for a rapport with him. "What do your friends call you?"

Names are important, as Jimmy had demonstrated by cementing his rapport with Sammy. I didn't have the key to unlock the ranger on my particular key ring.

"You can call me Jim."

"Well, Jim…"

I wheedled, cajoled, cited precedents of famous embedded journalists. I asked him to let me come to Wise County for the confessions. There are only so many ways you can beg. I'm not proud; I'll invent a few more, but he was a wash. There would be no mixing it up gonzo style with the cowboy.

"Yell at ya soon. Gotta jump for my kid's game."

I still want an interview, I texted him.

Talk to the DA. I'm just the guy with the gun, was his response.

On the plane, I scribbled pages of notes of stories filled with characters with names like Dinky and Stanky and Sea Dog and Big Rob. It turned out the landlocked lighthouse that puzzled me upon arrival in Pascagoula is a restoration of the historic Round Island Lighthouse, built in 1859, ravaged by hurricanes, brought to the mainland, and restored in 2010.

One if by land, and two if by sea;
And I on the opposite shore will be,
Ready to ride and spread the alarm…

Lighthouses warn of rocky shores but also promise harbor, somewhere beyond the edges of the floodlight.

16

OHIO STATE REFORMATORY

MANSFIELD, OHIO
SEPTEMBER 1956

The pimps on Broadway in Lorain looked so sharp, with their conk haircuts, sharkskin suits, straw fedoras, pinky rings, and gold teeth. They had hos hanging off them like they were made of Velcro. They drove Coupe de Villes and Lincoln Continentals, with whitewall tires and shiny grills. They didn't have to work the line at the steel mill or lay bricks in the sun twelve hours a day just to get by.

Sam Little knew he was a player at heart, but he didn't know the rules of the game—he could only covet its spoils. He crawled the streets at night, but it was as if he was at an aquarium, peering through the glass at the life he wanted. He couldn't figure out how to dive in. He thought he saw his opportunity one day when he walked by a closed dry cleaner and spied all the neat suits hanging in bags, the freshly cleaned and shaped hats standing in rows, with their tickets stuck in the brims.

He scanned the deserted street before wrapping his fist in his shirt and knocking it straight through the window. No alarm sounded. No dogs barked. He turned the doorknob from the inside and walked into the quiet of these things that belonged to someone else. The smell of cleaning chemicals and the delicious adrenaline of the moment surged through him like a crazy hit of heroin. His eyes adjusted to the light, and he took two suits that looked like they'd fit his already six-foot frame and one straw fedora. Then he ran.

The next afternoon, when Big 'Un was at work and Mama was at the market, Sam dared to throw on his new duds and hit the stroll. A friend clocked him immediately.

"No one ever going to believe those are your rags, Sam McDowell. You're gonna get cuffed and stuffed again before you know it."

The immovable confidence he'd felt while putting the suit on drained out of him like water through a sieve. The friend had a point. Sam had turned sixteen a few months before, so if he got convicted, he would be going to the Ohio State Reformatory at Mansfield, and rumor had it, OSR made BIS look like a day at the ballpark.

"Just give it back," the friend advised. "They won't do nothing to you if you give it back."

For the crime of stealing two suits and a hat that he returned two days later, on May 27, 1957, sixteen-year-old Sam McDowell, a.k.a. Samuel Little, was arrested, charged with breaking and entering, and sentenced to seventeen months in the Ohio State Reformatory. He even saw his birth certificate for the first time. Indeed, it read Samuel Little. He was a Little nigger after all. It was right there in black and white.

The Ohio State Reformatory opened its doors in 1896, and it was meant to be a halfway point between BIS and the Ohio State

Penitentiary in Columbus. Construction hadn't yet been completed, and the first inmates were immediately put to work building the sewer system and the twenty-five-foot stone wall surrounding the Victorian stone structure, with its six-story windows and Gothic towers. It was designed in the era of prison reform, and its architecture was meant to facilitate the prisoners' connection to their spiritual lives.

By the time Sam walked through its doors, OSR housed over three thousand men. In his well-appointed home attached to the facility by a tunnel, Warden Glattke talked to all the new prisoners personally about God this and God that before handing them over to the guards to be checked into a penthouse, which was what they called the cells on the sixth and top floor of the largest freestanding steel cellblock in the world.

That first walk to Sam's cell, his head swam with the vertigo of the height while the humid air redolent of that many bodies hit him like a wall. He knew much about his future in the stinking, strange palace of punishment would be found at the end of that walk. The guard grabbed the bars of his future home and slid them open, and Sam stepped inside the nine-by-six-foot cell. In spite of the unmistakable sound of the iron gate closing behind him, his face lit up. The guard barked a brief schedule—line up, meal, lights out—but Sam wasn't listening. Would you look at that? Of all the things.

"Well, Wilbert Taylor!"

"Hello, cellie."

Wilbert had changed in that brief period between their release from BIS and their present accommodations. He was broad as a bulldog now, his muscles visible even beneath the shapeless prison garment. His hair was straightened with lye and long like a girl's. He'd lined his eyes with smears of coal.

"You really let your hair down, girl."

"Make no mistake. They don't fuck with me no more."

Sam learned Wilbert had become what was known as a Boxing Betty. A Betty was a particular kind of girl in prison culture—one who would kick your ass.

When Wilbert had entered OSR, he'd been gang-raped by four men. He was strong but no match for four. Wilbert became Betty, and she had gotten stronger until she was a match for that many or more. She exacted a uniquely humiliating retribution on each, one by one, beating them to a pulp before sucking their dicks in public.

"Wait," said Sam. "You made *them* let *you* suck their dicks. You something else, girl."

"Yes. I am. Now they're girls too. And it ain't even natural to *them*."

They fell out laughing.

"I can't believe you here."

"I thought about you. Out there."

"I'm not gonna call you Betty. I'll call you Wilbert. But you can still be my girl. And, Wilbert, you're gonna teach me to fight."

With Wilbert's guidance, Sam negotiated the gauntlet of OSR and integrated seamlessly into prison life. He soon realized that while he had never found the direction he needed on the outside, he had hit the jackpot in the prison, where all the fun and games began.

The prisons were segregated and merciless. The Black inmates shoveled coal while the white inmates worked administrative jobs. The sissies worked in the mattress factory. Sam thought that was pretty funny.

There were few ways to garner favor, but Sam managed. He understood in his bones every human exchange was a transaction—every hello, every goodbye, every threat, and especially every favor. His natural predilection toward wheeling and dealing served him well on the inside.

Sam was also fast and strong. He showed startling promise as a boxer. Wilbert wasn't allowed to fight in the proper prison ring because he was a sissy, but he saw something special in Sam, even if it was a bit frightening and unhinged. He trained him.

"You got to be a little bit wild in the eyes to win, Big Daddy."

Together, they turned their mattresses to the wall and used them as heavy bags.

Sam rose through the ranks of the boxers in the prison with a fury few had seen before. Most stepped out of his way when they turned the cavernous prison chapel into a basketball court every Friday. They even turned it into a proper boxing ring once a year. It was a big event: anticipated eagerly and bet on by both guards and prisoners. Several famous real-life boxers had been funneled from the prison system. Sam was a favorite with the guards. They even outfitted him with proper shoes and shiny shorts.

The Mad Daddy. The Machine. The Machine Gun.

He was born for the dance between control and explosion—unapologetically defensive, relentlessly aggressive.

In 1960, the Mad Daddy defeated a man named Bubba by KO to become the middleweight champion of the Ohio State Reformatory.

Just a few cells down, Don Draper, a very different kind of inmate, spent most of his day hiding out, head down, scribbling on any loose scrap of paper. Other inmates left Don alone, because he'd draw pictures to send to their wives and kids and grandmas. Every day, Sam passed by his cell, and damn, it fascinated him. The man could make something look like that with just paper and a pencil, like magic?

Drawing something was almost like stealing something. Don said he would teach Sam to draw if Sam would teach him to fight. It was hard for Sam to believe he could achieve such a thing, but then, as Mama had told him, anything any human being had the ability to do, Sam could do if he put his mind to it. He just hadn't put his mind to much yet.

By the time Sam walked out of the gates of the Ohio State Reformatory in early 1961, he was an accomplished hustler, an up-and-coming fighter, and a promising artist. He even had dreams and goals. He wanted to be a prizefighter. Or a pimp. Or both.

There was one essential piece of his education that was still missing...not getting caught.

He was back inside by June. He'd attempted to steal money from a furniture store by breaking in the skylight. They'd gotten him on the roof and tossed him right back.

He was the middleweight champion again, in both 1963 and 1964. Would have won in 1962 also if the warden hadn't banned the fights when Benny Paret died in the ring.

In the meantime, Sam was mocked for another essential piece of his missing education. He'd yet to have a sexual experience with an actual woman. He was a celebrity on the inside, valued for his boxing and art skills alike, but that didn't stop the other inmates from guessing his secret.

"Of course I've seen a pussy"

"So draw one, van Gogh."

Even he'd laughed at his attempt.

17

JACKIE

LORAIN, OHIO
MAY 1965

The third time Sam was paroled, in 1965, he considered himself a twenty-five-year-old virgin, as far as that went, and he didn't plan to be one at twenty-six. He also knew he didn't want to go back to the pen.

Though visions of pimpdom still danced in his head, he got a job at the steel plant back home with Henry, fitting pipe. They drove silently to work that first humid morning, the spring blossoms starting to wilt. No sooner had they crossed the bridge when Sam knew it wasn't for him. This kind of job was its own prison.

He wanted to drive with the windows down, music loud, three decked-out hos beside him, giggling and whispering in his ear. Instead, he trudged beside his grandfather, face impassive. He fitted pipe, bit his tongue, did his time.

He went to the local YMCA, expecting a staircase made of gold. He'd ascend to his rightful place at last. A pimp, a king, a pharaoh, served by an army of servants and fans bearing biscuits and gravy and filthy magazines.

He trained there for a while a few days a week after work, but it wasn't what he'd hoped. He fought for a space, jostled amateurs in the locker room. Everyone was jealous and jockeying for position. He couldn't understand why they weren't giving him the respect he deserved. Even the guards in the prison had given him proper shoes. Here, he was fighting in threadbare Converse and too-small gym shorts.

He didn't have shit for a corner. When his ragtag gym went to Columbus to fight, a treacherous teammate gave him bad advice. Sam was a knockout kind of fighter, powerful and animalistic. He was the fighter who came out of nowhere with a deadly and unstoppable body combination. Or with such a right cross you might never stand up again if it connected just right.

"Hang back," said his Judas. "Let him tire himself out."

Sam's lip split. It stunned him. Before he knew it, the fight was over and he had never even taken a proper shot.

Another thing he'd never learned during his prodigious prison education was how to lose with grace. He only knew voracious wanting and getting at any cost. Losing takes a different kind of character. Losing feels like shit, but quitting feels ecstatic.

The team stopped at a hamburger stand on the way home. He drank four chocolate milkshakes, and with each sweet mouthful, he swore off boxing—the only thing he had ever loved. He put his gloves in the trash on the way out. He knew as sure as he knew his grandmother's face, he would never step into a boxing ring again. It was a victory of sorts. If you don't care, they can't touch you.

After he took a few days to recover, Mama running up and down the stairs with a cold compress for his mangled lip, he decided maybe he'd try the normal life thing. Four days after he lost his last match, six months after his release from OSR, Sam walked into the medical clinic of U.S. Steel with a wart on the middle finger of his left hand. The receptionist was a big, red girl, easy 275, with a warm smile, a spray of freckles, face pretty as an angel, ass the size of France.

Sam married Jackie Pellerin that August in a small ceremony with immediate family. The rumpus room of Jackie's mother's house was nothing more than a furnished basement with forest-green stained carpet and a plaid couch they had pushed into the corner for the event. They'd borrowed folding chairs from the neighbors, heaped the kitchen table with platters full of Mama's biscuits and ribs. Jackie wore her cousin's snow-white, too-tight gown. Sam wore Stacy Adams shoes and a suit with pegged pants. He imagined he was starring in a movie. The kind with a happily ever after.

After his sour-faced mother-in-law retired upstairs, Sam beheld his first genuine naked woman. On the pullout couch in the same basement in which he had been married hours earlier, he fumbled his way through. In prison, he had heard enough about sex that he understood the general mechanics. What he didn't understand was why, unlike the jailhouse braggadocios, in order to climax, Sam didn't need to think of boobs or asses or pussies or nurses or whores or schoolgirls or beauty queens. He only needed to look at Jackie's neck and imagine his hand around it.

He felt ashamed. You shouldn't imagine strangling the good woman who cooked you jambalaya and crawfish pie, folded your clothes, followed you around like a puppy. That wasn't right.

That first night, he'd run straight out the front door, jumped in Jackie's robin's-egg blue '59 Ford, gunned it, and crashed it into a pole three blocks later. That had been a hell of a thing to explain to his mother-in-law, who looked like she'd sucked a bag of lemons on a good day.

Wasn't this love? They got a puppy and named him Buttons. They danced barefoot in the kitchen to her mother's radio. Eventually, he stopped having sex with her entirely, because he no longer wanted to kill her.

Sam catted about, crawling the city's underbelly after work, drifting from bar to bar looking for weed and women, preferably both. One or two days a week, he didn't make it to work the next day. He sometimes kept the pink Mercury convertible he and Jackie shared out all night. Her mother drove her to work in the morning.

Jackie's mom told her again and again, "That man been hit in the head one too many times. Some men just no good. No matter how nice they are to you. No matter how handsome he is. That man is a snake."

Sam knew Jackie loved the snake in him. He made her laugh and let her mother's evil eye bounce off his broad shoulders as if they were Teflon. Jackie worked her receptionist job, kept house, hoped for children, though there seemed little likelihood of that, given the infrequency of their sexual relations and the increasing frequency of his all-nighters. When she dared challenge him, he reared like a cobra, his hair-trigger anger a fearsome thing.

One night around Christmas, he slipped out of her grasp and passed under a set of blinking lights, strung across the doorway of a brick box bar called the Pink Elephant, with blacked-out windows. The barmaid, Diane, was known for turning tricks on the side and famous for her fondness for black dick. She lived in an unpainted duplex on Thirty-Sixth, one of only two white women on the street. The other one lived on the opposite side of the duplex, with Sam's friend Freddy. They called it the country, because that was where the roads turned dirt.

Sam pulled the door against the wind. Four inches of fresh snow had just fallen, and it was already beginning to ice over and crackle under his feet. The bar smelled like Lysol, perfume, beer, and pee.

Diane wore two sets of false eyelashes and was a stout thing, thick calves, around forty-five, with a bottle-blond bob she teased at the crown. Still, she wore her miniskirts and heels with brash confidence and was a popular local character.

Sam hadn't come there looking for Diane, but the pickings were slim that night with all that snow. Only the diehards were out. Diane handed Sam a beer with one hand while twirling the gold sailboat pendant around her neck with the other. The light spilling from the pool table glinted off the chain, and though this particular neck wasn't the long, slender stalk of Sam's fantasies, she knew how to work it.

Sam had a sixth sense about bitches, like he was wearing X-ray goggles from a cereal box and could see through to their souls. He knew that by twirling that necklace, Diane was issuing an invitation to close his hand around the most fragile part of her neck and squeeze.

He wasn't going to kill her. He'd never do that. Of course. He just wanted to play with her a little bit.

You could find plenty of freaks who wanted you to throttle them, show them who's boss, straighten them out. Sometimes they don't even know they want a man to take charge, but that was where the X-ray goggles came in. He could see what a woman really wanted, regardless of what verbiage poured out of her mouth.

X-ray goggles or not, all the really pretty ones—the Carol Messengers, Gloria Ferrys—snubbed him like he was a smelly old dog. The ugly ones needed him too much. If he thought about it long enough, he could start feeling sorry for himself. That night, there was Diane and her necklace, so maybe there was a Christmas angel or two looking out for him.

"You ever been on a sailboat?" He gazed straight at the necklace.

"Nah, but I like looking at 'em out on the lake."

She cocked her head toward the door, and he returned her gesture. She went to gather her things. When she leaned in as he followed her to the parking lot, he could smell her spearmint gum breath starting to sour, the sweat from a night's work overpowering her drugstore deodorant.

She smelled easy.

He pulled into Diane's driveway and prowled behind her as she plucked her high heels gingerly from iced-over snow, making neat tracks that looked to Sam like hoof prints. She hugged her red wool coat tightly to her body and fumbled for the keys in her purse before wrestling the door open and beckoning him inside. They clunked in, half-drunk and giggling. Sam collided with the kitchen table, more drunk from the hunt than the liquor. She dropped her coat over the back of a chair and headed up the stairs without a word. He followed so closely he could see straight up her skirt, could smell the pussy that had been sweating into that turquoise rayon all night.

Her bedroom had a scarf over the lampshade, a wig head on the dresser in the corner next to a bridal magazine, a double bed with a grandma quilt tucked neatly into its sides. She hiked up her skirt, grabbed her stockings around the waistband, and tugged them off, tossing them into a corner.

"Twenty," she said. "On the dresser."

Even with the scarf over the lamp, he could now see the alcohol bloat under her eyes, the marionette lines around her mouth. Been nice to her all night, telling her she looked real good. He was only there as an act of charity. Did this old skag really just ask him for money?

"What did you say?"

She watched the charming young man from the bar disappear in a puff of smoke and understood two things. First, he had not asked a real question. Second, she had made a big mistake.

Diane stood, willed the quiver from her voice, and told him to get out.

Wrong answer.

Sam's hand shot out, propelled her through the air, and slammed the back of her skull firmly against the headboard. She lay stunned as he crawled on top of her and knelt over her chest, clasping both hands around her throat. He could feel the pulse of blood, the sinew and muscle and bone. He was finally doing it.

The panic of being unable to breathe shot through her like a current, and she brought her arms up to scratch him, but they found nothing. He pressed harder. She stopped fighting, her limbs turning to oatmeal. He wished she knew how beautiful she looked at that moment.

He got a hold of himself. He wasn't a killer. He released her, stood at the foot of the bed, and tucked in his shirt. Diane's skirt was hiked up and she was naked from the waist down, her shirt pushed up over her breasts. He couldn't remember when either of those things had happened. He watched as her eyes regained their focus and trained on him with fear so pure he could smell it. He breathed it in.

Diane silently lay back and spread her legs, turning her face to the wall.

"You think I want the clap for Christmas?" he said, his lip curling. "I don't want that old pussy."

Driving home, he sang along with the radio.

Come a little bit closer, you're my kind of man, so big and so strong.
Come a little bit closer, I'm all alone, and the night is so long.

Window open to the freezing wind, he felt deliciously alive. He had finally done it. He had watched as if from somewhere near the ceiling as his body accomplished what up until then, his mind had only dared. He closed his hand around a woman's throat and took the very breath from her body. He could have crushed her as easily as the stem of a flower. It was stealing, but a hundred million times better. Made his cock hard as a length of pipe. Maybe he'd even fuck his wife with it, just to make the heifer feel good.

He walked in hard and high to find Jackie pacing the living room in her flannel nightgown. Sam's friend Freddy had called twice already. The police had been by Freddy's. Diane had reported a rape. She told the police Sam broke in through her window.

Vindictive, lying whore.

"Pack your stuff up, baby. Grab Buttons, and get in the car."

18

BESSIE MAE

Buttons was a cute, fat motherfucker. He nestled in Jackie's lap as Sam peeled the Lincoln out of the driveway at 2:00 a.m. It was a crapshoot if it would carry them the roughly thirteen hundred miles due south to a place called Coconut Grove in Miami. Last time he was in OSR, the mother who birthed him had written to him out of the blue about this mystical place, edged with white sand beaches and sparkling turquoise ocean.

Sam hadn't seen Bessie Mae since he was four, but she had learned her only son was in the pen somehow and wrote to say she had the magic beans. Money. She'd gotten a little inheritance and could put him up at the rooming house she managed.

"I wonder what a coconut looks like," ventured Jackie.

"Like a big, hairy nut."

Sam and Jackie drove as far as the hills of North Carolina before the transmission gave out. They sold the Lincoln for Greyhound fares, tearfully surrendering Buttons to the ticket seller. Sam consoled

Jackie by managing to get it up long enough to fuck her in the back of the bus. Pussy was somehow more palatable in motion.

In January 1966, Sam and Jackie McDowell saw their first coconut. Sam also saw his mother for the first time he could remember. Though it had been twenty-odd years, Bessie Mae knew it was Paul's eyes in her doorway.

Bessie Mae melted into the arms of the strong son, come back for her at last, with a wide-eyed, yellow heifer standing behind him, shoulders bowed forward. Bessie Mae was a little red thing, just north of forty. She smiled, revealing a gold-streaked grill, missing four lower front teeth.

"My baby!" she screamed loud enough that the neighbors stood up from their dinners and appeared behind screen doors.

Jackie stood on the porch, her straightened hair already starting to frizz in the Miami heat, while Bessie Mae dragged Sam around the neighborhood, knocking on doors, introducing him to the neighbors.

"My son! My boy!"

In 1966, Coconut Grove was a historically Black neighborhood turning bohemian enclave. White, long-haired kids brought the beginnings of gentrification along with their flower petals and shake weed. It was a steamy stew of bars and corner stores, slipshod apartment complexes, and shotgun shacks, all infused with the sulfurous, briny smell of the neighboring bay.

Black and white residents alike knew Bessie Mae. They'd all heard about this mythical son she now offered up like a prize pie at the county fair.

Sam and Jackie moved into the room recently abandoned by a grass dealer. Bessie Mae wanted one thing: a grandchild.

A week passed, and then another and another, and still no sign of a pregnancy. Sam came home one night to discover a pencil-eraser-sized hole in the door of their room. When he confronted Bessie Mae, she admitted to having drilled it but insisted she had the right to monitor what was going on. It was her house after all. Bessie Mae glued her eye to that hole every night, looking to get to the bottom of it.

A few months later, Sam came home late after prowling the local bars and saw Bessie Mae in her doorframe, backlit by the bare light bulb in the corner. Without a word, he dropped his coat on her floor as he followed his mother into her bed. She wrapped him in her arms, and he breathed in the scent he had missed for so long.

"Mama," he said, rubbing his tears into her neck. It was a word he had previously only used for Fannie. Until then, he'd called Bessie Mae by her Christian name. "Can I call you Mama?"

"You always were a greedy little son of a bitch," she said. "It's okay, baby. Mama's here."

"You're my wife and mama and everything else."

"I know, baby, I know."

The loose, lazy folds of her skin, its clammy texture, the thick yellowing in the corners of her eyes—all a giveaway of her overtaxed liver—disgusted him. Yet his mouth found her breast and suckled the fruitless nipple. Could have bitten the thin skin clean off if he'd wanted. Hallucinatory visions of devouring her flesh pulsed through his body.

He woke up in the bed he shared with Jackie but didn't remember getting there.

The next night, Jackie cooked up some gumbo while Sam lurked in the doorway, itching to pick a fight, storm by her, and get the fuck out. His body ached to careen through the nighttime streets, the pool halls and juke joints. His thoughts turned and burned.

One of his Mama's skinny-legged, foul-mouthed friends, half-drunk on Mad Dog, leaned in the doorway.

"Handsome devil, ain't you," she said and gave fat Jackie a look. "That must be a hell of a gumbo."

Jackie's shoulders slumped.

Sam upended the gumbo, scalding the front of a screaming Jackie's thighs. He seized the butcher's knife off the chopping block, spun, pinned the disrespectful hag to the doorframe, and plunged the blunt end of the knife into her stomach over and over.

He dropped the knife and savored the look on her face. He loved the moment they realized they'd underestimated him.

Aw hell, he had only been kidding around, only used the knife's handle. Still, she was so terrified it nearly made him come.

Bessie Mae walked in the door as the drama queen blew by hollering for the police. Jackie dabbed her burned legs with a wet towel.

"Mama's here now, sugar," Sam said to Jackie. "She'll finish cleaning up. Pack our stuff."

Sam knew better than to hang around and let some lying whore call the cops on him again. Jackie's aunt had been writing from Cleveland, begging her to come home. He'd had a recent craving for the road. He missed the way the world rolled by like movie scenery. The keys to his stepfather's blue '64 Bonneville rattled in his pocket. Jackie tugged their two suitcases behind him.

Bessie Mae kneeled at the doorway, clinging to Sam's knees.

"Don't leave me again, baby!"

"I'll come back, Mama."

He shook her off his leg and headed due north.

Ohio was colder than Miami and bereft of coconuts, but it was home. Jackie's aunt tearfully greeted the crumpled couple. She fed them and put them to bed on the living room floor. The cops woke them up.

Jackie's aunt had called them the minute the sun rose over the river.

Cleveland PD arrested and charged Samuel Little with Diane's rape, but in the end, her statements to the police didn't match the evidence. She told them he broke in through her window, but the snow on her ledge was undisturbed. Male footprints clearly indicated a walk to the back door and back out again. The charges were dismissed.

Sam knew no one listened to a nigger-loving hooker, which was why she'd lied in the first place. After all, he *hadn't* raped the vindictive bitch. He'd only strangled her.

The problem was Jackie's mother had engineered a divorce in the meantime. In return, though, Sam learned a valuable lesson.

If you choose victims no one believes, you get your car keys handed back to you.

19

MARYLAND STATE PENITENTIARY

BALTIMORE, MARYLAND
MARCH 1966

It might have been the fact that he ran a red light and got away with it. Getting away with stuff made him hard.

In front of him was the open road, behind him the same old thing.

He had some cash in his pocket and the clothes on his back. This was God telling him he was invincible. This was how he and God talked: through signs and secret messages. He ran another red light, just to test his theory.

This time, the world exploded with a crunch of metal, a sparkling shower of glass, spinning streetlights. A van had T-boned the car. He didn't count bad signs from God.

He wrenched open the driver's side door and stood to his full six foot two inches. A hysterical jackrabbit of a redhead was crying, apologizing.

He looked down. Limbs intact, a scratch here and there. His coat was made of glitter now, dusted with glass fine as sand. He brushed off the bigger chunks as he walked in the direction of the Greyhound station.

He didn't mind the bus. He was happy as long as he was moving through the night, watching the hypnotic broken white line. The one that pulls your thoughts back, even as it guides your vehicle forward.

Sam stopped over in Baltimore. Never takes long to find the stroll, get by on petty theft and the kindness of women. But even in March, the wind off the harbor was cold as a dead hooker's pussy. Sam had a hankering for the lush humidity of Miami. He'd need enough pocket cash to get there.

Sam walked into a liquor store on the south side of town one night with visions of a sunset over the Miami ocean, a layer cake of blues and yellows and pinks, the silhouettes of palm trees. He sported his favorite leather trench coat, a pair of Stetsons. He ran his hand over his slicked-back hair. Some of the kids in the big cities were letting their hair grow wild. Black power, all that. Sam watched the news with interest, but it was more for entertainment than anything. For his purposes, he preferred Blackness as invisibility.

Facing him from behind the counter was a clammy old Jew with a comb-over and a shirt yellowed at the armpits. Spur of the moment, half a goof, Sam put his hand in his pocket as if it were a gun.

"Give me all your money!"

The lackluster store owner sprang to life and pulled a .38 from behind the counter. Sam should have realized no Jew was unprepared for an attack. The first bullet caught Sam in the side, the next two passed through either arm, and the final two lodged in his back. He thought for a moment he was being hit by bricks. It took five shots to drop him.

———

Handcuffed to the bed in the hospital, Sam watched as his roommate coded and was toe-tagged. The poor sap had only been stabbed in the leg, but he developed sepsis. Sam took five bullets and was still strong as an ox. It was only a matter of time until he was free again. Another little greeting card from God, though he did catch a four-year armed robbery sentence.

He was a model prisoner, painting pictures for the inmates and guards, sending cheerful letters to his family in Ohio.

On the morning of April 5, 1968, he was looking forward to road detail. That was where you got to see girls. No sooner had they piled out of the bus than they turned back around as the block around them erupted in shouts and sobs. Martin Luther King Jr. had been assassinated the day before in Memphis. In the halls of the penitentiary, the men roiled with grief and anger, their howls bouncing off one another like bubbles in a boiling pot.

Sam never met his cousin Malcolm X, but he knew the famous man had spent time in prison too. Malcolm went a whole different way with it. Look at him now. Dead.

Sam slouched beside the bus and snuck a cig. Why would you get into a fight you're sure to lose? Sam saw racial inequality as not a social ill but a reason for the rest of the sheep to be distracted while he slid through the shadows like a wolf.

———

In 1969, he was paroled, having served nearly two years of his four-year sentence. Next thing, he was on a Greyhound to Coconut Grove, back to Bessie Mae. Sam's hair was already growing long and wild. He was ready for coconuts and brown-eyed girls…brown-eyed *squirrels*. Ha!

You, my brown-eyed squirrel.

So many fucking squirrels. What was one, more or less?

Later that night, Bessie Mae cried whiskey-infused tears as she shoved plate after plate of ribs in front of her son. Sammy was a rolling stone, but Bessie Mae launched right in—she wanted a grandchild.

A big gal in a gray maid's uniform with a white apron shuffled past, offered a half-hearted hello toward the kitchen with her eyes locked on the floorboards.

"Yvonne, honey! Yvonne, baby," cried Bessie Mae with a gusto that startled the girl. "Meet my son."

"Didn't know you had no son."

She caught Sam's eye, looked down again.

"Don't be a fool. Told you a million times, this is my one true boy," said Bessie Mae. She cradled Sam's cheeks in her palms and loudly kissed his face. "Don't be shy, honey lamb," said Bessie Mae. "You afraid of them eyes? Could fall into those eyes and get lost forever, huh? Has his rapscallion of a daddy's cheekbones too. Indian blood, what fault that is."

Bessie Mae's husband, Robert Lee, disappeared to the kitchen to fix Yvonne a bowl of leftover dirty rice and a finger of whiskey.

The Littles had been from the wrong side of the tracks in Reynolds. Bessie Mae told Sam the Guices on Paul's side weren't exactly pastors either—ask anyone in Reynolds. Look what that smooth-talking son of a bitch had done to the both of them.

"You know what, Mama?"

"Yes, baby?"

"I think I'm gonna be Sam Little now. I ain't no McDowell."

"Mr. Sam Little," said Yvonne as Bessie Mae cried with joy. "It's a handsome name."

He shacked up with Yvonne in two days, in the same room he had shared with Jackie, with the same hole in the wall. After a failed gig digging graves, Sam landed a job with the Dade County Sanitation

Department. By day, he ferried other people's trash. By night, he trolled the stroll, stalking the boulevards of Miami's Overtown. Day and night, it crawled with whores and homosexuals and wannabes.

Thoughts of necks permeated his days of drudgery. Necks—so weak. Faulty engineering, really. He looked around and saw weakness in bar crawlers. Weakness in the white folk Yvonne happily served. Weakness in his girlfriend. Weakness in his own mama. Weakness everywhere. Opportunity.

20

MARIANNE

As she entered the Pool Palace, Marianne linked arms with two of her girlfriends and wiggled her knees together in a move she had invented herself for when her tuck had started to slide sideways in her gaff—popped the li'l beast right back into place. Gisele and Penny were real girls far as that went, but she was the prettiest. In Overtown, they didn't care too much anyway. Marianne could pass. She was yellow and soft as butter. She had what her meemaw would have called *natural class*. It was easy enough if you were Grace Kelly with all that silky hair, bathtubs full of hundred-dollar bills, princes, and palaces. But it was a whole other game to be a class act if you were a lady who happened to be born Curtis Lee.

Oh well, she had the Pool Palace that night, and she would be the queen of the Palace, real girl or no.

Gisele's shorts were wedged so far up her crack you could see Christmas. Marianne never went in for that cheap kind of display. That night, she had rimmed her wide hazel eyes in smoky gray, carefully tweezed and penciled her eyebrows into two delicate arches, and circled her neck in the gold chain that rat bastard Wes had given her, back when he was less of a rat bastard. Or he was probably already a rat bastard but she just hadn't figured it out yet. She wore a delicate pair of nude hose with a seam up the back. Out of vogue, true, but they made her feel like an old-timey movie star—Princess Grace herself. She had a cream-and-red-checked skirt and a top that pulled just slightly over her chicken cutlet boobs, underneath which her real boobs were just starting to bud, with the black-market injections Wes had scored for her. He was good for something anyway. She wore her hair loose and wavy, pushed off her delicate face with a kerchief.

"You deserve better!" said Gisele, tripping over nothing but her own shoes.

"Girl, we don't get what we deserve. We get what we get. Don't you know that by now?"

The bar was populated with townies, stragglers, hippies, gamblers. Used to be that Muhammad Ali walked shadowboxing down this same stroll, the patrons of the diners and barbershops and juke joints pressing their faces to the glass. Anytime you got too blue, even thinking about the Champ out there could bring you back.

Lady Day stayed two doors down after she'd performed for the adoring audiences of Miami Beach. The swanky hotel guests rested their blown minds—could you imagine such grit and gorgeousness at the same moment in time? Pay for her cab to Overtown. Truly a lady.

If anyone deserved better than what she got, it was Lady Day. Marianne loved the old stuff. Sang "God Bless the Child" to herself in the shower. Her two roommates in Liberty City told her she wasn't half-bad. They weren't ladies like her; they were pretty boys and hustlers. All of them in Overtown and Liberty City doing what they gotta do to get by.

Marianne left the girls at the bar and did a quick scan as she unsnapped her purse. She wasn't especially looking for a paid date that night, just a drink or two and a little company. A night to take her mind off Wes and the empty coffers and the mama who wouldn't love her no more no matter how hard she tried. Meemaw would still take her calls now and again, but even she still called her Curtis. Mama was a God-fearing woman, and the last time they talked, she had called Marianne an aberration. Mama had beat her breast and told Marianne she was glad, *glad*, her poor father was in heaven with Jesus rather than having to see his son become Satan's minion.

"You. You could have done anything! You could have been anything!"

"I still can, Ma. Anything but a lie."

Mama's parting words had been, "Curtis, your demons will follow you all the days of your life. Don't come around here no more. You are dead to me. Do you hear me, son? Dead."

Marianne wasn't alone. The Pool Palace was a haven for night crawlers as good as dead to their people. But what were you gonna do? Lie your whole life? Clutch your threadbare housedress, wring your hands, call everything that scared you a sin, pretend you never dared to dream of anything bigger than winning the casserole contest at another church picnic, like her ma had?

Marianne had a purse full of change at least. She sauntered over to the jukebox and picked not just one but five songs. She sang with one hand twirling in the air as she wound her way back to the bar.

It was two more of her songs and one drink in (bought by Gisele, who was straight haired and practically white and sure to get a date by night's end) when Marianne caught the eye of a hulk of a guy she hadn't seen before. He moved a foot at a time down the length of the bar toward her. Marianne positioned herself on the outside edge of her girl gaggle to make herself more available, the antelope on the fringe of the herd.

The man's hand nearly eclipsed the glass of amber liquid it held. He wore his flowered collar wide, his suit sharp, his hair a little bit wild, his mustache trimmed unevenly. He bowed his head to his beer and looked up at her, almost shyly, then looked away. She felt in her bones there was something unusual about this one. Something surprising.

She let one corner of her mouth turn up just slightly and shot him a sideways glance, a subtle bat of her eyelashes. He responded immediately, sidling up beside her.

"You are about the most beautiful thing I've ever seen. You like something on a movie screen."

"Oh, stop it now, big boy. You playing me."

"You shine so bright, I'm half-blind looking at you."

"You dance?"

"I do with you."

Marianne had been slight, even as a boy. In her heels, as he pulled her onto the makeshift dance floor, she folded into the handsome stranger's chest, her head resting neatly on his shoulder, like they were born to dance together. The man wrapped her in his arms in a bear hug and nuzzled her neck with his nose, taking a deep drag of her scent.

"You smell like apricots and cotton candy," he said. "You smell like dessert." Glued together, they swayed. *I know a place. Ain't nobody crying...*

The man himself smelled oddly like nothing. A tinge of BO maybe, a hint of pomade.

She took his hand at one point when they were dancing and noticed it was hairless, smooth, with long, square, manicured fingernails. *Like a woman*, she thought. Strange.

Some inexplicable wave of emotion rose from the tips of her toes crunched into her too-tight heels up the back of her spine. Marianne usually felt she had lived a hundred lifetimes in her eighteen years, but something about the night—the moon, her mother, the rat bastard she had left behind, the stranger who found her beautiful—caught in her throat. She cried into the stranger's neck.

"I'm sorry." She hastily drew her arm back and wiped her eyes, giving her head a little shake. "I never do this."

He drew her back in.

"It's okay. Cry for me. All I ever wanted was for you to cry."

Marianne stiffened for a moment before surrendering. She cried into the man's shirt, not caring about her mascara, finally letting herself weep for all of it. For how goddamn unfair life was. Across town, all along the beach, rich white folks were clinking glasses and eating steaks and throwing around $100 bills like confetti, later weaving through the streets of Overtown in their shiny cars when they got drunk enough and wanted to sample some ghetto pussy. Two weeks ago, one of them had been sweet as a peach until he finished up, then he had spit on her. Spit on another human being who had three seconds before been sucking on his measly cocktail wiener without once laughing.

Pasty-ass, white, spoiled, cruel, rich shitbirds like that would always come out on top.

Those hippie kids could march through the streets of Overtown all day, hang out smoking weed and playing guitar in the park, holler about love and equality and revolution until they were blue in the face. Marianne knew that she would forever be confined to the shadows. Maybe a magical *Star Trek* day would come, bringing with it a safe world for people like her, who lived in an in-between space—not a boy or a girl, not an angel or a whore. Just Marianne. A child of God like any other. Maybe on Mars.

Bravo to the protestors and everything. *Hell no, we won't go* and all that. Have a ball.

Marianne knew that nothing they were hollering about was going to change what it was like for her to walk down the street every night, hoping no one caught the telltale Adam's apple, the wide wrists, the man-size feet that had once carried Curtis Lee flying over hurdle after hurdle to win the gold in the all-state track meet three years running, the four-hundred-meter hurdle champion. Running had been the only time Curtis had felt like he wasn't living in the wrong body. Muscles pumping, blood coursing through his veins, buoyed by adrenaline, sucking in deep breaths of the clean country air, he had flown. He had been barely a body at all, just a heart in motion.

Curtis had given his final medal to his father in the hospital. He'd been buried with it.

Marianne kept the other two golds in the bottom of a drawer. She never took them out to look at them, but occasionally she'd reach in to grab a sweater and one would catch the light. She was a winner.

Marianne may have been jaded, but she believed in love. She didn't need the world to understand her. All she needed was one right person to know and love her. She had thought for a moment it would be Wes, but she could see now that was just her telling herself stories. That was the problem with having what her teachers had always called a vivid imagination: you invent people rather than really seeing them.

"That's all right," the man said. "There you go."

He kissed her tears away. With one hand, he held the back of her head, and with the other, he gently stroked her neck.

"Take me home," Marianne said.

"Let's go somewhere else. You want to take a drive in the country?"

Marianne hesitated. She wasn't sure he knew the little secret. Sometimes they surprised you with their stupidity and then blindsided you with anger. You don't want to be in the "country" with a man who felt duped and emasculated.

"Okay," she said. "But let's stop at home first. I want to change my clothes." It would buy her a little time at least. She'd get a better bead on him.

He shifted, suddenly restless. His eyes wandered as if he was losing interest. She wasn't ready to lose this one yet, and she didn't want to be alone.

"I have some grass," she offered. With that, he was back.

Marianne bid goodbye to her girlfriends with a cursory wave. They raised their eyebrows.

Gisele gave her a little hip shimmy, a tacit gesture of approval for the date she'd scored.

Once they reached the street, the man's posture changed. He hunched forward, hands in pockets, eyes scanning the area around them. Wouldn't be the first time she got in a car with a dodgy and paranoid man, but it was a marked change from the sensitive guy she had met at the bar less than an hour before.

"Hey, what did you say your name was?"

"Name's Sam."

He didn't bother to open the door to his red Pontiac LeMans for her. Marianne nursed a sinking suspicion she'd be facing yet another disappointment. Still, she slid into the white leather bench seat.

When they reached the cramped, concrete-block apartment she shared in Liberty City, he trudged silently up the stairs behind her. She turned and jutted a defiant hip forward, resting a hand on it.

"You got somewhere else to be?"

His smile snapped back like a rubber band.

"No, baby. No, no, no. I only want to be with you."

The clacking of her heels on the concrete was swallowed by the shag carpet when she opened the door. A strong waft of grass, cigarette smoke, and cheap Chinese food hit them like a wall.

Two of her roommates, one Black, one white, both bare chested and clad in blue jeans, sprawled on the brown velour couch, personal ads spread out in front of them on the coffee table Marianne had scavenged and painted herself. Sam posted himself in a corner of the room, arms crossed over his chest. Marianne trotted into her room to get changed. She was wiggling into a pair of silk black bell-bottoms when he opened the door without knocking.

"Wait," she said, pulling up the pants in a panic.

"I don't care what's between your legs, sugar," he said.

She breathed a sigh of relief. She caught a glimpse of herself in the mirror and was embarrassed to notice she needed a shave. She popped her head out of the room and locked eyes with her Black roommate.

"You got Magic Shave?"

"Girl, we been out of Magic Shave for days. Have big handsome there take you for some. Hey, big handsome! You want to take Princess here to get her Magic Shave, or you want to kiss a hedgehog?"

"Let's get out of here," Sam said. "I'll buy it for you myself." In the car, he shook his head and said, "Those homosexuals you live with. I don't cast judgment. That's for God, not me. But I personally do not care for it."

The comment caught her off guard, but she shook it off when he pulled over to the five-and-dime and bought her the Magic Shave, like a proper gentleman.

Except he didn't turn around and drive back toward Overtown. He swung onto the 27 instead, which led to a whole lot of green nowhere.

"Where we going?"

"We going for a nice romantic drive in the country. Find somewhere quiet we can get our freak on!"

"Nah, I don't think so. Let's go back to my place. I got grass. We can party."

"Trust me," he said. He put his arm around her shoulder and she snuggled closer to him, mostly because the insistence of his grasp gave her little other choice. "I'm not going to hurt you."

Marianne drummed her long nails on the can of Magic Shave as the foliage flanking the road grew denser, seemed ready to swallow the highway entirely. His arm around her neck tightened yet further, and a chill ran up the back of Marianne's spine. Cold sweat pooled in her armpits and under her bra. Lord knows she had developed a preternatural sense for when things were turning wrong. The problem was they often turned so quickly it was hard to keep ahead of it.

"I'm not feeling so good. Let's turn around."

"What's wrong, sugar?"

"Little bit too much to drink, I guess. I feel like I'm gonna throw up."

"You want me to pull over?" He ran his tongue over his left incisor. It was pitch-black around them, with half a pale moon caught in a web of clouds. Only the headlights coming the other direction illuminated the world for a heartbeat, then turned the dust on the windshield into a white screen, blinding her.

"Turn around."

"Where you want to do that? Look. There's nowhere to turn. C'mon, let's just pull over and relax for a minute. I'll take care of you."

There was a wide swath of grass between the north and southbound lanes of the 27. There was, indeed, no visible place to turn around. Marianne felt her panic mounting, climbing toward her throat. Maybe she was actually going to vomit after all.

The headlights of the Pontiac illuminated what looked like a perpendicular road up in the distance.

"There!" she cried too enthusiastically.

"Okay, okay," he said, taking the one hand that was on the wheel off it and holding it up in a gesture of surrender. The car began to veer toward the shoulder. Marianne shrieked and grabbed for the wheel, but he tightened his grasp around her neck and held her back.

Sam laughed, and the temperature in the car dropped twenty degrees. He put his hand back on the wheel.

"Oh hey, hey, now, beautiful. I was just playing. It's just me here. Your friend Sam. See, I'm turning around right here, just like you want. Any way you like it, okay? Look," he said, noticing a wide, U-shaped driveway in bad repair encircling a battered barn and some old farm equipment. "Let's pull over right here and talk a little."

Stupid, stupid, stupid. How had she been so blind?

Blind. Blind him. That was it. It was her only hope.

Magic Shave was a bitch to open. It was like a tiny can of house paint. You needed a screwdriver or a nail file to pry off the metal top, and she had neither. She gripped the can tightly in her left hand.

She hooked a toe into the back of her left heel and nudged it onto the floor of the car. But she had broken out in a sticky panic sweat, and the right shoe had been tight to begin with. She couldn't get it off.

As Sam slowed to a stop, Marianne turned to him and smiled sweetly as a debutante.

"I love you," he said.

Loved her?

With desperate strength, Marianne both crushed the can in her palm and dug her fingernails into its metal rim. The top popped off and her nails came with it with a spurt of blood she barely felt. She tossed the white powder into his face, and he screamed, batting the cloud around him like a wounded animal.

Marianne kicked open the door with the heel that wouldn't come off and hit the ground running. Run toward the light she might have seen in the doorway? Run for the road?

Just run.

She heard her teammates, her father. A small crowd.

Run, Curtis! Run, son!

Marianne blasted through the cooling night air, heavy with the smell of spring grass, the tang of stagnant water, a faint whiff of fertilizer from a farm nearby. She ran chest first, arms pumping. For a brief moment, she was back again. She was winning, fast and light as the wind on her face.

Her one heel lodged in a crack in the pavement and her ankle turned. She wrenched her foot free, took her mark, and started again, just like her coach had taught her. Everyone catches their foot on a hurdle once in a while. What you don't do is sit there.

It was one hurdle too many. With the instinct of a runner who knows never to look back, she felt he was on her.

The man was big, but he was also swift and powerful as a hound from hell.

Was this the dark, vengeful thing her mother had spoken of, gnawing at her heels all along?

Sam fell upon Curtis from behind, but Marianne ran on. As she ran, she rose, off the ground, above the trees.

She looked back for a moment to watch the demon named Sam tackle Curtis, wrap his forearm around Curtis's neck from behind. Marianne watched the boy thrash, then grow limp.

Marianne noticed the light in the barn turn off. Someone had heard the tussle but hadn't wanted trouble. She watched as each last hope for Curtis's survival receded one by one into the shadowy recesses of the Everglades.

Marianne watched as Sam locked an arm bar around the boy's neck and dragged him back to the Pontiac. Curtis's bloodied heels, stockings shredded to a thread, tried to find purchase on the concrete, but there was no strength left in his legs.

Sam hoisted the back door open and tossed Curtis inside like a doll.

The boy shook his head, sucked air into his aching lungs, wordlessly pulled down his bell-bottom pants, and kneeled on the back seat, facedown, his body offered in one last gesture of surrender.

Sam laughed.

"You think that's what I want?"

Marianne felt an itching between her shoulder blades, a brief sharp pain. Hardly hurt a bit as a pair of glorious wings, the same she had always imagined when she was on the track, unfurled from between her shoulder blades.

Sam flattened the boy, pants around his knees, to the seat. He wrapped his thick forearm around the boy's neck and pressed his hard cock, still in his pants, to the boy's back. When Curtis stopped struggling, Sam flipped him over and wedged the boy's body to the floor of the back seat. Sam unzipped his fly, freed his cock, grabbed hold of it, and stroked. It didn't take long.

The boy was weak already and long done fighting. Sam ejaculated on Curtis's sweater as the boy drew his last breath, with only Sam's two fingers pressing on his windpipe.

Below Marianne, the deep green trees and silent black water shifted and blurred until all that remained was the dark firmament on every side, studded with sparkling pinpoints of light.

She knew she was home.

She'd always had faith love was possible and here it was: bold, warm, and bright as the stars all around. She had made it. She was Marianne. Whole, perfect, and loved for who she was at last.

Her wings beat furiously at first like the thrum of a heart, until the rhythm slowed and there was only silence. Marianne drew breath deep and full as the sky.

21

THE JEWEL OF THE PORT

LORAIN, OHIO
SEPTEMBER 2019

"You listen," Betty McDowell, Sam's niece, said on our first call. "Don't you go bothering my mama. She has had enough trouble with this. Don't you go bothering my family. They ain't going to talk to you. If you're having compassion, you have it for those poor women."

"No, no, I want to hear what you—"

"He is a blood stain on our beautiful family tree. I speak what I think. Ten years old, he was my favorite uncle. He always showed up with backpacks and school supplies and crayons and shoes for us kids. I found out later he was boosting them. Anytime Sammy showed up, the cops would be three days behind him. We had cops hanging around at family funerals. We are good people and we been bothered long enough. I was ten years old when he showed up at the house. I ran out to greet him. He grabbed my vajayjay and stuck his tongue down my throat. That's what I call a pervert."

"I'm sorry that happened to you."

"You ain't need to be sorry. You know why? Because I told my mama, who took me by the hand and walked me straight to my grand-dad, Sam's dad, and told him what had happened. My granddad went to his closet, took his shotgun, and run Sammy off the property. He said, 'Go on now and don't come back, Sammy. You family and we love you, but there are too many kids around here, and you ain't right.'"

I was far more accustomed to hearing stories of abuse disbelieved, denied, ignored, gaslit. I told her I was planning to visit Lorain and would love to meet her. I got a hard maybe and never heard back when I called. If I couldn't get Betty, I'd make friends with the research librarian, see Lake Erie, take photos of the Palace Theater. I planned a coffee with Carolyn Sipkovsky, who ran the Lighthouse Foundation, as a backup.

I drove first to U.S. Steel, where Henry, Sam's grandfather, had worked as a pipe fitter, and watched it from across the river. It was one of the two great steel factories that stood side by side on the banks of the Black River, the mouth of which meets Lake Erie. Republic Steel closed a decade before, but these monolithic *Mad Max* half-empty remains of an empire were majestic, even in ruin. I viewed it from the strip on the other side of the bridge, lined with clubs and bars and liquor stores. Shadows of something once bumping and alive floated behind the boarded windows.

Some had survived as fell-off-the-back-of-a-truck lingerie stores; some had turned into barbershops with hand-lettered signs. There was one functioning go-go bar, with two pickups parked at odd angles in front, in what seemed to me to be the middle of the street. Catty-corner on the same intersection stood an abandoned Mexican restaurant with faded murals and turrets shaped like cacti. Beyond that, it got residential quickly.

Few had cars in 1942. Most walked to work. Sam had followed

Henry over the bridge to U.S. Steel for months after he got out of OSR, after he married Jackie and thought maybe a life was the thing. It had only taken weeks before he started stalking the nighttime Broadway crawl.

I crossed the bridge, and a security guard was on me in two minutes. I'd been calling U.S. Steel with no answer, asking for a tour, for two days. The guard slammed his car door and came at me, chest squared. Even as he led me by my arm to the car, I trusted my instinct, sharpened on a whetstone of hypervigilance—not always fun but pretty sharp. This guy was no threat. Furthermore, he was a non-threat with no health or insurance benefits—they'd cut him off before the hours that would make him eligible. That's how it works now, if it works at all.

I drove toward the gentrifying waterfront, where the Black River looked different, according to the Welcome to Lorain website. I'd texted Betty twice already that morning. It took a number of tries to find a bottle of wine that wasn't in a jug. It took even more to find a delightful florist who traveled the few blocks to her closed shop to whip me up a special bouquet for Betty. She even held out a bowl of smooth stones on which were printed inspirational words. I closed my eyes, picked one, and bought that too.

The stone is in my pocket as I write this—the word is for me and the woman who made the bouquet. Choose your own word, picked with eyes closed, from a bowl in the city's only flower shop.

I looked for the library while I shoved a Taco Bell quesadilla in my mouth and was reminded of why I don't generally do that. I waited for Betty's call as I passed soaring bridges, a bandshell by the water. I arrived at Broadway—the charming "main street," with proper columns in front of the closed-down bank. A cool marquee atop the

closed-down theater. A cute hotel, wrapped in tarps, was being reno-
vated. This was a town struggling to build something new on an old
blueprint.

I wasn't sure what odds I'd have given it.

The simple sadness of walking a street of empty midwestern storefronts was almost a relief by then—something shared and human.
One ideal dying, another rising. A social contract rewritten again and
again throughout history. It is hard to bear witness to what we don't
yet understand and harder still to ask the questions that might point
us in the right direction.

I sat on the steps of Lakeview Park under a crescent of iron that
read East Beach as I watched my phone and lost the battle to keep
my hair out of my lip gloss. Ripples in the water caught knife edges
of light.

There was no way to be simply sad facing the Sam Little story. It
was a puzzle and a war.

I looked out at the lighthouse, about ready to cash it in and go
bring my flowers to Carolyn instead, when I got a text from Betty:
yeah sure.

I pulled up to a 1970s bi-level in a neighborhood of well-manicured
lawns, about the same size and era of the house in which I grew up. A
gardener cleared a path under the crab apple tree with a leaf blower as
I approached with my flowers and wine.

"You looking for Betty? She left!"

"She what?!"

"She left!"

He turned the leaf blower off.

"She'll be back. Garage door still open and she ain't paid me."

The gardener continued blowing as I rang the bell a few times just to confirm that she had indeed left. He weed-wacked as I sat on her stoop like a jilted prom date for about half an hour before he took pity on me.

"How you know Betty? You a friend of Hollywood?"

Trick question? Inevitable irony? I took a shot in the dark. "Hollywood her boyfriend?"

He fell out laughing, and I noticed he wore a halo cast on his left leg with visible screws.

He got Hollywood on speaker.

"No, she right here. She looking for Betty. Her name is Jillian, like that secretary at my doctor. Jillian. With a G though I bet."

"Um, no, it's a J. Jillian. Hi. Nice to meet you."

"She nice looking?"

He took me off speaker.

"She pretty enough, if you like that kind of figure. Hurry over if you want to see."

"Hey! Hey, can you ask Hollywood, does he know where Betty is?"

On cue, a Betty I did not expect pulled into her driveway and walked straight by me to her front door, waving her hand. She wore sweats with stripes up the side and a sports bra. Multicolor sister locks hung to her waist, and she was pierced and tatted to the teeth.

"I apologize for the delay," she said. "My baby ran out of gas. She's fine. She's barely weepin', but anyway. I apologize. That won't happen no more." She opened the door. "You can see I like plants."

The walls dripped with spider plants and philodendrons and lilies. A black rock fireplace mantle that would have made the fanciest interior designer in LA swoon dominated a living room full of nothing but plants, blocked off by upended chairs—because they had a new puppy.

"Such a pain, right?" I said. "I had, like, nine baby gates around every rug in the house."

"Right? We hang in the kitchen and den anyway. But this here is my own beautiful little world."

"You like green things."

"I like plants, flowers, anything that got life. That why it crushed me. I knew my uncle wasn't good. I mean he's still my uncle, but I would never let my daughter around him or anything like that. You can't pick your family. It just… He was shady. I learned when I was a little girl, he wasn't right. And it wasn't a big deal, because I told."

"It sounds like your family listened."

I trotted behind her into a house at once alien and familiar.

"Oh yeah. Oh yeah. My mama said, 'You okay? Do I got to take you to the doctor?' He probably won't never say that because I know he cared for me. Or he would have never gave you my number. Li'l Scooby."

"Is that what he called you?"

"When I was born, I looked like Scooby-Doo. That is what my mama said. My mom still call me that. It's a term of endearment. And he was like a good uncle because he always had gifts. I was a little kid. He always had stuff."

Betty pulled a tray of salmon out of the oven. She tidied as she went, wiped down every counter.

She was touched by the flowers, put them in a vase.

"I'm a Capricorn. I'm of the earth. Hey, what you writing down over there?"

"I wrote 'Capricorn.' Would you prefer I not take notes?"

She put the wine in the fridge, grabbed a Colt 45, sat down smack in the middle of the couch, and pulled out a pack of Marlboro Lights.

"Sure, write. So what? This is the end of my day. I do elderly care and I'm doing the night shift and she's a hundred and three years old for real. I love her. So this is my after work. I clean too. Like deep crazy clean. Hoarders and shit. I have a bit of that OCD, and I love to clean."

She showed me a few photographs, and she had transformed some scary hoarder shacks into sparkling, hygienic homes. I hovered behind her and bummed my first cigarette in about ten years, took a sip of her beer.

"You know, write your thing. I'm a straightforward kind of person. My family, I don't want to hurt them."

I invited myself to sit at the dining room table and faced her. It was hot as hell. She apologized for the air-conditioning being broken. I rolled up my sleeves.

"I usually hide my tattoos, but I think I'm good here," I said.

"My mom drove a Harley! I'm *still* trying to be that MILF. Don't you write that down now. I had the blue glitter helmet and the blue glitter boots. I was the coolest thing in my Catholic school."

She led me to a picture of her mother on the wall. They were a family of lookers.

"She was the coolest thing in the world. Wasn't until I got older I learned she was dead broke and it was cheaper. Had to fill up the tank. Had to get you to school. Had to get to work. Six dollars. Yep. Oh my goodness. If I could be a third of her, I would be... I would be..."

"She sounds like a neat lady."

"Brilliant. I was gonna say brilliant. Not too many you come across. Not like her."

Vintage family photos lined the walls. Betty gave me the tour: this one was mean as a rattlesnake, this one was beautiful as a porcelain doll until her last day, this one was a saint with a genius IQ, this one was my little homey, this one had fantastic gams—all the women had fantastic gams, ran in the family—this one got run out of town for supposedly messing with a white lady, these had the cheekbones, these had the famous lion eyes. The blue-green-gold slaveowner's eyes.

"This one right here, see. She has the eyes. The hateful eyes. You've seen the eyes?"

"Yes."

"They change, right? Like with the blood pressure, with the liquor, with the rage or whatever. I was an only child like my daughter, and I only hope I have traits like my mother, not like those niggers. Oh shit. I'm sorry." Betty doubled over laughing.

"It's really okay."

"No, some things ain't proper. And that's offensive."

"I'm not here to judge."

"I don't think you judge me. I'm in my own home, so I have a different comfort level. That's why I'm glad I invited you here."

Betty's eighteen-year-old daughter, named for Sam's sister Inez, walked in, looking remarkably fresh, considering she was wearing a McDonald's uniform after what I could only assume was a long day. She took her name tag off and put it in a dish on the counter.

I hadn't been prepared for her arrival and didn't know how much she knew about her uncle, if anything. She looked at me like I was from another galaxy, but she was far more excited about a makeup palette she'd gotten in the mail from a blog giveaway. Betty told her to eat some salmon, please, next time, instead of the garbage at work.

"Who is this?" asked Inez.

"She writing about your uncle."

"Oh."

Inez sat and opened her palette. We oohed and aahed over the colors.

Betty took her daughter's chin in both hands, tilted her face to the light.

"We got everything in my family—Choctaw, Italians, Spanish, Jewish, Black. We got no racial tensions here. But me? I found a silverback. Because all my family members look like Sammy."

"Mom! You cannot *say* that."

"He's a good dad, a good man. I'm saying he had calluses on his hands. You seen that on your green-eyed uncles? They hands softer than a baby's bootie. They can't even take out the garbage, eyes like that. I don't want no pretty Ricky up in my hair products. We got enough of those I'm related to. We were married for a long time. We were just better as friends. Look at her. She's Black as the ace of spades, Black as train smoke in the wintertime. I did it on purpose. Look at this beauty."

"Are you writing about what goes through a man's mind when he does something like this?" asked Inez.

"Oh, honey, if we understood, we'd be as nutty as he is," said Betty, smoothing an invisible bit of frizz from her forehead. "I paid a therapist one hundred twenty dollars an hour for a year to tell me that. But I can tell you what my cousins say. They say his great uncle smacked him around. They say he was never right again after he came back from that reform school."

"What's reform school?"

"Where you got to go when you ain't acting right and they didn't care back in the day. You got your ass beat, molested, teeth knocked out, mentally, anything went. There was no regulations and he was never right again. They also say he was already acting a fool before that anyway, and he was nothing but trouble, trouble, trouble. Every time Sammy was around, someone went to jail. Oh, he broke my mom, skipped out on her bond. Three thousand dollars or something. Couldn't pay her mortgage. We wound up here, and she's in Kentucky."

I asked to see a painting Betty had mentioned to me on the phone. Sam painted it for her when she was a little girl, and it had hung over the bed in her childhood room. Before.

"That's going to stir up memories right there, because that's when I loved him. He didn't do that then. I realized my finger was broke when I was born, so it's always been like this, and in that picture, he captured this little crooked pinky. You very nosy. You're going to send me into rapid heartbeat."

She left and reentered, holding a framed acrylic painting on canvas.

"There's that crooked little finger. I look at this now, the little braid come out, my little ponytail, and I had the pink barrettes. But was he thinking nasty then? That's what I think now. That was an Easter picture."

"I don't know."

"My baby and her friends, I had to tell them the other night, 'All, y'all are the shit.' Because all four of them are in college and then working. I said, 'Y'all over here in my house, doing homework all crinkle face. Y'all the shit! Y'all want some pizza? I'll order y'all some pizza, because you are the shit!' I blow the girls' heads up. I gas them up. I give them that. I'm telling you, 'You perfect. I don't care what you feel, what the world say. Look at you!'"

"Scary to have a girl," I said.

"Period. And especially a pretty, dumb girl. I told my daughter, 'You are not going to be that.' There's too many thumbs-up, beautiful women that became victims because they're not smart."

"Remember when that coach got handsy with me in my junior year?" Inez said.

The two busted up laughing.

"What did I say?"

Inez side-eyed Betty for smoking and I bummed another. I'd forgotten how much I like to smoke.

"I said, 'We are going back there right now, and if they won't lay him out, I'll do it myself. Like my mama did for me.' See, this is what I mean when I said I learned. I told my baby she could tell me anything and I would always believe her and always have her back. I *would* have laid that man out. I don't give a shit. I'd be mad cute in prison."

"And she did! Laid him out! Fired him. It was in the papers and everything."

"No one is touching my child."

"Tell me about your tattoos."

"You don't plant bad seeds. If me and her dad would've never got married, we might still be together, because he was like, 'We married now. You my wife.' It was more like a possession thing. Like if you get your man's name tattooed on you. You get what I'm saying? I seen people got their husband's name, they went ziggity boom. I'm not marked like that."

"Here we go," said Inez.

"So instead they're all peaceful flowers, butterflies, hummingbirds, leopard spots. But they're all also pussies and dicks and tits. If you don't know me, it's a flower. If you know me, that's a clit on my arm."

"He got them funny eyes too, Sammy?" asked Inez. "I'm mad I didn't get them genes. Everybody's got blue eyes except me."

"Girl, you might have children with blue eyes. You better love Boston baked beans. There are more girls, aren't there?"

"I think so."

"I just blacked it out, I think," said Betty. "He's like two completely different people. He loved his family. My mom, he was trying to get to her, right before he got locked up. That's where he got caught. She's like, 'Uh-uh, no. You on the run, aren't you?' She wouldn't give him her address, and they ended up getting his old ass, diabetes, half a foot, seventy-something years old."

"Like how many more?" asked Inez, still looking down at her makeup palette.

"I'm not sure."

"Oh, shit. Oh, my poor mom," said Betty. "I'm glad my grand-dad's dead."

She showed me the door.

"I admire you because you're moving and shaking. We strong and we be fine here." She put her arms around me, then turned her back and began straightening the already-immaculate house. "You tell that motherfucker to call me. I have a few things to say to him. You be careful in your travels. I bet your mom's a nervous wreck, you running all over the place like this."

 . As I let myself out, I heard Inez say, "Yah, her mom probably got over it."

———

The Sipkovskys' living room had freshly vacuumed stripes on the beige living room carpet, seasonal fall decorations, a La-Z-Boy recliner and matching flowered sofa upholstery in dusty rose and blue, a rocking chair, and a dark wood hutch with commemorative plates.

And lighthouses. Tiny wooden lighthouses. A shelf over the couch with a mini village of the town of Lorain—like my mother-in-law's

Christmas village, but year-round. Lighthouse-embroidered pillows. Brass candlesticks with candles that looked like lighthouses so adorable I noted: *check etsy lighths cndls CUTE.*

About my notes—I don't look at the page when I'm writing them. I look people in the eye until they forget my hand is moving. It takes decoding later. I never did find those candles.

Carolyn welcomed me with warmth and a hint of *wtf are you doing here?* Not many Los Angeles journalists knocked on their door at three o'clock in the afternoon asking about the Jewel of the Port. She ushered me through the kitchen, back to the garden to meet Frank. No matter how lighthouse tchotchke–stuffed your living room, you don't live to have a hallway packed with generations of family photos and not know when something is up.

Frank held court at a café table in the middle of a backyard garden. It was the tail end of summer but still hot as a greenhouse, regardless of the fall decorations, and there were still tomatoes. The Sipkovskys were starkly white haired, and both wore khakis and sensible layers. We talked kids and grandkids. There were a lot—a bunch lived just around the corner this way and a bunch more just around the corner the other way. They gushed about the Lorain Lighthouse, the Jewel of the Port, in use from 1918 to 1938. It was so decrepit it was about to be torn down, and then someone bought it for a dollar. For the last ten years or so, they'd been restoring it, detail by agonizing detail. They'd even gotten a historical plaque.

"Oh, and Admiral King and General Gilmore and the tornado of 1924. The fifties and sixties, the steel plant hustle and bustle. We were an American crucible, U.S. Steel, Lorain products," said Frank. "My wife is the real historian. She's the expert. You tell her about it, Cookie."

"Dear, what did you say your book was about exactly?"

I could have said I was writing about the current state of industry in the Midwest and made a quick exit. I decided not to sit in the backyard of these generous people, have them show me their handmade book about their lighthouse, and lie to their faces.

"Ooooh, a killer!" said Carolyn. "Finally, someone exciting came over. Tell us all about it, dear. Maybe we can help you. Of course, you'll be visiting the library and looking through all the old phone books. We have a wonderful collection! Oh, Frank, let's just show her. There are only two areas of town a Black person could have lived in at that time. Drive."

We pulled over next to a gray-clapboard two-story house, neat but could have used a coat of paint, with a peaked roof, a white-fenced front porch, and a satellite dish. No paved walk to the door, just grass worn to dirt.

"2245 Elyria Street," said Carolyn. She clapped her hands together. "At Twenty-Third?"

Was I supposed to know where I was?

"It's the house where Toni Morrison grew up!"

Well, take me to church.

The first Toni Morrison book I'd read had been *The Bluest Eye*, her first novel, set where I was sitting, in 1941. It's about a Black girl consistently regarded as ugly and confronted with poverty, abuse, incest. She wishes for the blue eyes she believes will solve her problems. The eyes to which Betty said, "Hell no, not me. Not if I can help it."

Morrison would have been ashamed by the wave of sentimentality that hit me like blunt-force trauma.

"There is no time for despair," she is quoted as saying. "No place for self-pity, no need for silence, no room for fear. We speak, we write, we do language. That is how civilizations heal."

We drove past closed storefronts, empty lots. Frank pointed out clubs: the Campdale, the Republic, the Shell, the Bop Shop, the Shovel.

We drove through the center of town on our way to the lighthouse, past a cluster of enthusiastic new shops, a microbrewery. A soaring bridge spanned the Black River. A still-green park with a bandshell waited for the inevitable decay of winter.

"We're looking at concerts, small businesses, the lighthouse. We're looking forward. Ain't that right, Cookie?"

We reached the pier. The Ohio Historical Marker dedication plaque was all Cookie's doing—print on both sides. One of the fun facts: part of the renovation in 1990 was funded by pennies collected by kids in the public schools in town.

I only saw the Jewel of the Port from the shore. It was way out on a jetty and looked intrepid and windblown. It was too late in the day to call the one guy they knew who might have a boat to make it there, and even so, I had missed the season by two days, and rules are rules.

The Sipkovskys made hope out of kindling with sunset wine tastings, concerts, and cruises to the Jewel of the Port all summer long.

I spent my last hours in Lorain on the floor of the public library, making friends with the research librarian and getting addresses from directories dating back to 1940. I already knew the structures had been knocked down, but I drove by them on my way out of town all the same.

When I got home, I sent Betty a card with a Georgia O'Keeffe orchid on it.

Thank you for your generosity and kindness. It was a pleasure to meet you. This was my grandmother's favorite artist. She also painted clits in flowers! Love, Jillian

22

LUCY AND JEAN

CUYAHOGA COUNTY COURTHOUSE, CLEVELAND, OHIO
JULY 1972

Diane, Sarah, Carolyn, Mary, Sarah, Emily, Linda, Norwegian baby...

Sam slid through the night on the 98 north toward Lorain. Couldn't ever stay away from home too long.

Yvonne would be fine. Wouldn't be the first time he slid away. He always came back bearing gifts. She was ungrateful anyway. He'd given Yvonne the Eastern Star ring the green-eyed girl from the motel pool hall had given him before he killed her. Yvonne turned around and gave it to the white bitch she worked for. No taste. No class.

All that receded behind him as he sped through the twists and turns of the Tennessee mountains before sleeping at a truck stop, scarfing a burger at the neighboring diner just after dawn, and hulking back out the door, not exactly refreshed. You had to sleep with one eye open in that kind of place. These degenerates would steal your car out from under you and put a cock in your mouth for good measure while they were doing it.

Somewhere, two days behind him, the sun was sinking into the Atlantic, and Bessie Mae was likely crying into a jelly jar full of wine. She hated when he left, liked to throw histrionic tantrums that never worked to keep him.

The screen door at the house in Lorain had a trick latch, easy to trip. "Mama!" he bellowed to Fanny, his voice catching. This mama thing was trickier than it was supposed to be.

From the kitchen came a shriek of alarm that turned into joy. Fanny limped out of the kitchen on swollen, diabetic ankles. She and Sam clung to each other and wept. He smelled the lavender water in her hair, the liver and onions on the stove.

"You sit down. Almost never cook since Big 'Un died, but I made liver tonight. Must have had a premonition."

"You always did have the sight."

"Don't talk witchcraft in my home. Talk truth to your mama for once. Why you here, Sam?"

"Seeing my mama. Is that a crime?"

"Anyone can make it one, it'd be you, son."

She put the liver on the table.

"Sam," ventured Fanny as he shoveled in bite after bite, barely stopping to breathe. "None of those no-account friends of yours around here this time. And none of them around Paul's. We got babies around here now to think of."

"Who popped 'em out this time?"

Fanny swatted Sam's head. "You just stay away from Broadway and those floozies. They never caused you anything but heartache."

"I promise, Mama," said Sam with a grin that never reached his eyes.

Sam slept for nearly a day. It was funny—he either slept ten, twelve, even fourteen hours at a time or barely at all. There was no in-between. He went to church with Mama Sunday morning and hit the stroll that night. What are you supposed to do when there's an animal trapped in your chest, clawing to get out? Sit and knit?

He swung around the corner, and the lights of Broadway swirled in the metallic paint of his car hood. It was late May 1972, and clothes were falling from the women piece by piece all along the stroll as the lake sucked up the winter winds and returned them north. The stroll was seedier with every passing year, the flow of money from the steel industry grinding to a near halt after the ten-year boom that followed World War II.

Sam rolled down the window just as a delicious-looking little Puerto Rican ho stepped onto the street in front him, her curly black hair ringed with a halo of pink neon. She walked to the car on two thick bow legs, unsteady on her feet, already a few drinks into the night.

Sam swung his car around and pulled up next to Lucy Madero. Might not even be a one-night baby. Needed some cleaning up, but this could be a proper ho.

Sam was leaning toward killing Lucy when she tried to pick his pocket playing pool. He gave her a sharp backhand to the side of the head that dropped her.

"Don't never steal from me again. You steal *for* me, you understand?"

She stood, wiped the grit from the bar floor from her knees, and agreed.

Something about how quickly and completely she bent to his will made him like her. They got a fifth of whiskey and went back to her hotel room, where they passed out talking on top of the bedspread.

Less than a week later, Lucy waited uncomfortably on the green-and-yellow-flowered couch in Fanny's living room, wearing a pair of sunglasses. She grabbed her minidress by the hem and attempted to wiggle it down. Sam climbed the stairs to say goodbye to Mama. The house was quiet that day, the grandkids and great-grandkids giving Fanny a chance to recover after emergency surgery for a blood clot in her leg. Henry Jr., with whom she shared the house now, was working his job at the steel plant.

"Don't leave me, Sam," Fanny cried, writhing in pain.

"I'm sorry, Mama," he said. He lay on the bed beside her, his arms around her thighs, her leg below wrapped in bandages, her foot turning a strange shade of gray. He felt the warmth of her, the woman who had loved him, had changed his diapers and fed him and made sure there were shoes on his feet, even when they'd had holes in them. A wave of tears rose and broke.

"Forgive me, Mama. I disappointed you."

"I forgive you. You a rolling stone, Sammy, but you're my good boy and I love you."

Sam wept into the thighs of her housedress while she stroked his hair until she dropped off to sleep.

An hour later, Sam and Lucy were on the road to Cleveland, twenty dollars in Sam's pocket, stolen from Mama's nightstand. They drove a '68 blue Pontiac Bonneville Sam had traded the Wildcat for. Didn't like to keep anything for too long. In the glove box was Lucy's .45. Guns were a magnet for trouble, but she insisted.

She'd been wrong, and they got popped for armed robbery outside Cleveland.

Jean and Lucy were cellies on the fifth floor of the Cuyahoga County Courthouse. Male prisoners were locked up on the floor below. Jean didn't think much of Lucy, with those shifty eyes and too little fabric covering too much skin. Serve her right when night fell. The stones of the drafty old edifice held a chill that was no match for regulation blankets.

On the night Lucy showed up in her cell, Jean wore a pair of maroon slacks and a shapeless shift over a body she preferred not to think much about. It had carried her through fifty-seven hard years. Even the very first year she'd spent on this planet, they'd called her ugly. When you start out an ugly baby and are then orphaned at a young age, you learn to use your wits. Jean had supported her brothers and sisters all throughout their teenage years in east Arkansas by shoplifting from the Goodwill and reselling the merchandise.

Jean's real name was Orelia Dorsey. Back in Arkansas, they called her the Black Mare, because she was blue-black and carried a mare's leg pistol. It was the same pistol she used to shoot a handsy sheriff's deputy in the ass, landing her on a chain gang when she was twenty.

People liked Jean straight off, even with that unfortunate head of short, matted hair and a scrunched-up face like an apple doll. She exuded a natural warmth, swore like a sailor. No one had ever bought Jean a doll in her life. Maybe that was why she had taken up her hobby of crocheting bottle cozies that looked like dolls. No chance of getting a crochet hook or yarn in her current cell. Supposed she had nothing better to do than talk to the sneaky slut in the next bunk.

Jean told Lucy about how she'd dressed as a man and ridden the rails to St. Louis, where she had stepped up her shoplifting game and began to steal from Dillard's and other snooty department stores, selling the goods at half price. She couldn't resist bragging she knew everyone from Tina Turner to Bo Diddley. She'd even met Josephine Baker once.

Jean told Lucy that she'd joined the circus, just for kicks. She tap-danced with a group of Black girls called the Brown Dots, a take-off on the singing group the Ink Spots. When they were in towns where Black people weren't allowed to perform, the Brown Dots did the laundry. She got tired of it after a while and set up shop in St. Louis before moving to Cleveland, after she caught her jazz musician boyfriend fooling around with some Indian and shot at them both through the screen door with her Smith & Wesson Lemon Squeezer.

"You sure like to shoot people," said Lucy.

Lucy told Jean she'd been arrested with a guy she called Mr. Sam. They held up a liquor store in Westlake on their way to town from Lorain.

"What the hell were you doing working in a white neighborhood like that?" asked Jean.

"Coincidence," Lucy replied.

So many cases of being in the wrong place at the wrong time.

In the morning, when dawn lit the sky the palest shade of blue, Jean heard a man's voice singing "Just My Imagination."

Both Jean and Lucy sat up in their bunks. They listened at the walls, pressed their faces to the bars to see if they could hear footsteps in the hall, but there was nothing but the creaking and stirring from the other cells. Jean finally noticed a small hole in the floor where the old stones were crumbling. Emerging through the hole was the tip of a funnel. She got down on her knees. It was the end of a newspaper rolled into a cone.

The song was coming from the cell below. "Lucy?" said the cone.

Lucy scuttled over and looked as confused as if the floor itself really had talked.

"He's under us, you ding-a-ling," Jean said.

Through the cone, Jean heard chuckling.

"Lucy," the voice called again, softer this time.

Lucy maneuvered herself down onto the cold floor and put her ear to the cone. Jean cozied up beside her.

"Whatchu ladies wearing up there?"

Lucy giggled and talked to this Mr. Sam nearly all day. Why anyone wanted to talk to that wet-brain hooker was a mystery to Jean. Jean had loved a handful of men and a few women during her five decades plus, but it never seemed to matter how well she cared for them, how much she cooked for them, the cars and clothes she bought or stole. They always left in the end for a moron like this bowlegged kitten, purring into a hole in a jailhouse floor.

A dense loneliness settled over Jean. Why had this man's voice pressed that bruise? That was a poisoned well, and no good would come of it. Keep your chin up, keep food on the table, keep sharp, and you won't wind up begging on the corner or worse.

A couple of hours later, a deputy escorted Lucy from the cell. The voice in the floor called to Jean. "Who are *you*, now?"

She should pretend to be asleep.

"What's your name? Come on. Come talk to me."

"Ain't you all talked out yet?"

"Tell me your name."

"Name's Jean."

"That's a pretty name."

"Came up with it myself."

"Did you now? Why'd you do that? Did your mama name you something terrible?"

Jean giggled. "Yes she did, bless her soul in heaven. Named me Orelia. Now who can say that? I named myself Jean after the film star Jean Harlow. You know who that is?"

"Ooooooeeee, yes I do. Pretty blond hair, mouth like a heart, neck like a swan. You telling me you look like Jean Harlow and I'm trucking with that bowlegged, beady-eyed bird?"

Jean knew that whatever happened between her and this man from that point on, he would never love her more than he did now—porcelain skin, satin robe, platinum waves. Jean in black and white, larger than life.

"No. My own mother used to say I was ugly as a bucket of home-made sand, and that's the truth. I'm Jean on the inside."

"That's who I'm meeting. I'll picture you that way."

———

Lucy later confided to Jean in a whisper, "They're pressing charges. No way around it. But they're not gonna stick me with this."

"Can't say I blame you," said Jean. "We gotta look out for number one, right?"

"I'm not going down for him, no, ma'am. I'm not going down for no man, and this one I barely know."

"Seems about right," said Jean.

"Does it?"

"Oh yeah, honey. Don't go down for no man. Not if you can help yourself."

———

Jean was released. So was Lucy. Sam was left to face the armed robbery and assault charges.

When Sam saw Jean sitting on the other side of the visitor's glass for the first time, he almost jumped. She knew what he saw. She wore a pair of slacks, orthopedic shoes, and a shapeless flowered blouse.

He picked up the phone.

"I'm Jean," she said.

"*You* Jean Harlow? You…are a sight for sore eyes."

Jean laughed, showing wide, Chiclet teeth.

"Listen, I got to tell you something That girl you got is no good. She's planning to turn state's evidence on you."

"Lucy Madero? On me?"

"Of course. Why she out there and you in here? I'm a good woman, Sam. When you get out of here, I'll wait. I want to take care of you. I can teach you how to take care of yourself."

"I don't need no woman to teach me how to take care of nothing."

"You get your ass popped right and left. You're doing something wrong. I'm the best booster in all these United States."

He hesitated.

"I'll get you a car to get you started. You can drive me around. Can't hardly see, so I hate to drive."

"You are a real pip."

If not for the fact that she could see her own reflection in the bulletproof glass, superimposed over this handsome man's face, she could almost believe she was Jean Harlow. This man was her future.

———

Jean wore the one dress she owned and sat demurely in the courtroom during Sam's trial. Lucy showed up to testify on behalf of the state, but her character came into question. The jury voted to acquit.

Jean lived in a red, doll-sized house in town. There was a knock on the top half of the door she had roughly sawn through the middle in order to act as a makeshift store for her boosted goods. She pushed her face out into the darkness and squinted up to where Sam stood, framed by a light swirl of snowflakes and a gray-white sky, wearing only the summer suit in which he'd been arrested.

She threw the bottom half of the door open and wrapped her arms around his waist.

"Don't just stand there, woman. I'm freezing to death."

He looked around the strange living room, barely bigger than a closet, packed floor to ceiling with clothes and shoes and purses. Nice stuff, not Goodwill garbage.

"This my shop right here. I sawed the door so no one can come busting in."

Jean dug through pile after pile until she found what she was looking for—a tan wool men's coat with a black fur collar.

"This should do."

Jean fed and bathed Sam and led him to her bed.

She knew she wasn't his cup of tea, but she also knew a man had to choose between treacherous whores and smothering mothers. Smothering mothers don't turn state's evidence, and treacherous whores can't cook for shit.

He kissed her wrinkled neck, hugged her. She closed one hand around his cock with a kung fu grip as he closed his eyes and imagined that they were somewhere on a savannah in Africa, surrounded by the night sounds of the jungle. He imagined she was a princess and he went to her hut and sneaked her out. Together they found a grassy knoll next to a creek, where they made love under the stars, and he held her head under the shallow water until she stopped thrashing.

In the real world, he managed to ejaculate and not actually kill her. A minor victory. He'd have to do it again if he wanted to stay.

That wasn't all. Within days, she was schooling him on the tricks of her shoplifting trade. She didn't want him getting popped, so he only had to drive. She walked into department stores with an empty garment bag and waltzed out with it full of stolen merchandise. She belly crawled behind a counter and scooped shelves full of jewelry into her bag with the hidden pocket.

The world had pegged him as a petty thief, the commonest of common criminals. What idiot would get arrested every three days for penny-ante possession, assault, or theft and secretly be committing the most heinous of crimes? No one would suspect such a rube to be capable of murder after unsolved murder. These cops and their derision. These snotty cunts and their turned-up noses. This whole damn world that never gave him what he deserved. He was showing them all. He held his secret in his heart. He held his babies in his soul, and they were his, his, his. Each one of them the most delicious piece of candy, except they never dissolved, never left him, never went away.

Jean trotted him around town and showed him off, much like Bessie Mae had when he had first arrived in Miami. She protected him, and for a moment, he allowed her to fold him to her breast and rock him like a baby into the night. It was almost enough. She didn't even complain when he stopped fucking her because he couldn't stomach it.

What was it about pussies? He liked thighs just fine, liked faces, liked necks above all. But he wasn't a pussy man, or a titty man for that matter. He was unapologetic for his absences, reckless with his promises, disastrous with follow-through. She forgave and forgot.

"We should open a restaurant," he told Jean while amped and riffing one night. "You're the best cook this side of the Mississippi. We could have a life right near Mama in Coconut Grove."

"I've never seen a coconut!"

Why were all these bitches so interested in coconuts?

In the car, Jean snored in the passenger seat, her head lolling on its hinge. He glanced at her and turned away in disgust. No neck at all to speak of. Lucky for her, he supposed.

Sam breathed deeply and plunged south, south, south. Back to the deep, lush cover of the Everglades, which ate human bodies like air.

23

—

MOTHER DIED TODAY

There was Mama and then there was Mama. There was Mama Fanny, who he thought was his mama but was really his grandmama, and then there was the mama who birthed him. The mama whose titties he had sucked so dry they never came back. The mama who he had only really just met.

Now she was gone? Gone, Lord, gone!

"Why, God?" asked Sam as he threw back his head and bellowed at the roof of his 1970 gold Pontiac LeMans with the whitewall tires. Jean had bought it for him with the meager proceeds from Samuel Little's Southern Kitchen, the restaurant they had started up in Miami in her attempt to go straight.

Jean cleaned out the car every morning. An earring here, a shoe there. He called her a nosy old nag, a sniveling dog. She kept them for herself if there was still a pair.

"Why?" Sam asked again.

Left hand on the wheel, he beat his breast with the right as he sped toward Coconut Grove. Sam let up on the gas, not wanting to get arrested for some pissant traffic violation. Not yet thirty-four years old and already he had a jacket so long it could keep the rain off half of Miami.

His poor mama had been just forty-nine, and the drink had taken her fast. Only weeks before, her eyes had gone yellow and her stomach swelled so that she thought she might be having a miracle baby. She was gone, and now he'd never really know her. She had loved him. Oh, how she'd loved him.

He'd shown up after she was already dead, took one look at her tree-bark corpse lips, and turned tail. Never did like a dead body. Dying he loved. Dead creeped him out.

He pulled up and dropped his forehead to the steering wheel. Neighbors gathered on their porches, waiting for news. Sam trudged up the walk. He expected Jean's outstretched arms.

Instead, she cocked her hip and dropped a hand to it.

"She's gone," said Sam, hands at his sides. "Mama's gone."

His shoulders heaved, and the neighbors turned their heads away in respect. No shame to cry when your mama dies. Women as far as two blocks down blotted tears from the corners of their eyes.

"I got to get back to the restaurant when you're done with this squalling," said Jean. "Those half-wits can't cook a proper chicken."

"Woman. My mama just went to meet Jesus. You're talking about chicken?"

"Did you crawl back up in that womb one last time?" asked Jean. "Everyone knows you were fucking her instead of me anyway."

Since the neighbors had averted their eyes to give a crying man some privacy, no one saw Sam grab Jean by the collar. She was on her back in the middle of the street before anyone thought to grab a shotgun. Sam kneeled above Jean's prone body. Their German shepherd, Buster, broke through the screen door and ran around them in circles, barking. The neighbors pressed to the edges of their porches.

Sam raised one powerful fist and wordlessly brought it down onto Jean's face and chest again and again. He punched her square in the tits, dead in the sternum, cracked a rib with two knuckles alone.

He remembered how they'd gone absolutely wild for the beach, running from the car while it was practically still moving and gathering every coconut she could fit in her arms, like a child gathering daffodils.

He softened and switched from a closed fist to an open hand, slapping her face back and forth until she was good and bloodied.

"Sam!"

Sam looked up straight into a double barrel, his neighbor behind it.

"Back away, Sam. I don't want to shoot you, but I'm not going to let you kill Jean."

The pavement below him swam, like heat waves rising from Georgia asphalt in summer. He looked down and saw an immobile pile of bloody laundry beneath him.

"You take care of my dog?"

"I got Buster. Get the fuck out of here."

Sam loped toward the Pontiac. The neighbor's wife ran to Jean's side.

"Why you gotta do this?" she cried, cradling Jean's head. "What demon lives in you? You ain't right."

Sam took one step toward the woman, and the man racked the shotgun. "Start driving. Keep going."

———

Diane, Sarah, Carolyn, Mary, Sarah, Emily, Linda, Norwegian baby, Air Force baby, Marianne, Maryland baby, Prince George baby, Cuban baby…

No one could take the road from him. Every mile erased the mile before it, unlimited possibility. He wondered if he had killed Jean, but the thought left his mind as quickly as it entered. Probably not. Tough old bird.

Florida, Alabama, Mississippi, Louisiana…

He'd taken the money from the smock pockets on Jean's blouse. It would get him through a couple of days if he slept in the car. He'd boost a few steaks in Mobile, maybe see Memphis. Mobile to Memphis, how 'bout that? Just like that white boy with a cold sang about on the radio.

Always wanted to see Biloxi. New Orleans…

His thoughts trailed behind the Pontiac, littering the freeway. Ideas and memories and plans whirled into the night sky, spiraled down the drains of truck stop showers.

The last time he'd left, Jean had pitched a hissy with a tail on it, accusing him of flirting with the lunch crowd of secretaries at their restaurant. He'd upended the deep fryer, a tidal wave of boiling grease pouring across the floor. That time, he'd headed to the Bahamas with a suitcase full of men's suits, a round-trip ticket, and $200 from the register in his pocket. Thought maybe the island life would be paradise. Maybe he'd stay forever.

Inside of two weeks, he'd sold every suit plus the one on his back and couldn't find shit for a stroll. What was he gonna do?

Dress a palm tree in a little black dress, put some lipstick on it, and call it a ho?

He'd returned to Samuel Little's Southern Kitchen to find Jean hunched over an industrial-sized steel pot. Can't expect a man to take talk like that lying down. Best lady he ever met, except for Mama. Even if she could piss off the pope with the mouth on her.

This time, Sam arrived in a city decorated like a damn wedding cake, crawling with drunks leaking dollar bills onto the piss-soaked cobblestones of Bourbon Street.

A gypsy who looked more like a Mexican read his palm in front of a cathedral. She predicted long life, trouble with the ladies, the soul of an artist. He had a haint on his tail, and for another five dollars, she could do some hocus-pocus and shoo it away. He didn't give her the extra fiver or even the fiver he'd offered to begin with. Something told the woman not to signal her cousins on the next corner. Let this one go—far and fast.

You didn't need the sight to know that.

24

NINAH

TRENTON, NEW JERSEY
MAY 1973

Diane, Sarah, Carolyn, Mary, Sarah, Emily, Linda, Norwegian baby, Air Force baby, Marianne, Maryland baby, Prince George baby, Sarah Brown…

In a workhouse in Trenton for the assault of a police officer, Sam played his whole movie back as if projecting it on the wall of his cell.

Florida, Louisiana, Mississippi, Alabama, Georgia, Arkansas, Texas, New Mexico, Arizona, Nevada, California, Oregon, Idaho, Wyoming, Nebraska, Iowa, Illinois, Indiana, Ohio, Pennsylvania, New York, New Jersey…

He'd hightailed it out of the Big Easy after Miss Sarah Brown gave him a run for his money, or tried at least. Maybe he was toying with them too much first, should get it done faster. She had said she needed to pee and had taken off running across that damn field. Burrs ripped the seam out of his hem before he got to her. The full moon shined on her ass as she ran, naked as the day she was born. A porch light glowed in the distance, beyond the edge of the high grass.

She'd almost made it. He tackled her and did her from behind. He folded her last breath into his palm and locked it in his heart before he flipped her over and laid her arms out in the shape of a cross. That was a nice touch.

New Jersey wasn't much to look at, but he couldn't see beyond the walls of the workhouse anyway, and he knew he wouldn't be there long. Doing time was easy, a rest from the road. His new girlfriend, Ninah, was waiting for him on the outside. He'd picked her up off the street in Macon, Georgia. She was big, pretty, and yellow, how he liked them, and she'd flagged him down. He told her to meet him around the corner. He'd planned to do her quick, a junk-food meal. He'd learned his lesson and didn't want to give another one a chance to run. He took her to a salvage yard. They passed a hulking pile of crushed steel. She clung to him and yelped.

"What, kitten?" He stroked the back of her neck while yearning for the front.

"I'm afraid of the dark," she said.

They'd found a pile of junk so compacted it was practically a park bench and sat down.

Sam had leaned in for his first scent of the peppermint-laced breath he'd soon be stealing. She stopped him with a palm to his chest.

"If you want me to be yours, I already am."

She'd uttered the magic words. *You own me.* He let her live. She never asked a question as they traversed the country, east to west on the southern route and back again west to east through the north. Along the way, he'd gotten a stiletto blade in his side in a pool hall in Detroit, a face full of brass knuckles at a bar in Vegas, an ice pick smack in the middle of his sternum outside Bakersfield. Would have liked to have picked up another baby along the way, but he'd been too busy narrowly escaping death at every turn.

"Yes, Daddy," she said to his cockamamie ideas. "Yes, Mr. Sam. Yes."

He survived all these brushes with death, stunned faces of doctors telling him how lucky he was they hadn't hit any major organs. He emerged from each hospital with a prescription for antibiotics, a bandage he'd forget to change, and a bonus painkiller prescription they could hock at their next stop.

Sam kept his bargain with God. He hadn't told anyone that he was His avenging angel. Working for His sanitation department, dumping society's trash. As long as it was their little secret, Sam remained impervious to injury.

While Ninah had been sucking cock around the side of a gas station in lousy New Jersey, some police officers tackled him, and one of the officers dropped his gun in Sam's reach. His partner trained his service revolver on a spitting mad Sam. Ninah practically flew around that corner, still stuffing a tit into her top, and threw herself on top of him until the cops grudgingly lowered their weapons and cuffed him.

Ninah was a good girl even if she wasn't all there—staring off into the distance for hours, sometimes crying one minute and cackling the next. She would always be waiting for him on the other side of the wall.

———

New York looked like someone put Magic Grow on Miami, strung the whole thing with Christmas lights, and then ground about a billion pounds of soot into it. He and Ninah swung off the highway and slowed immediately to a crawl in a sea of cars moving like molasses in the snow. Catcalls echoed through the concrete canyon, intermingling with music from the doorways of juke joints. Looked more like a carnival than a city. He pulled over after just a few blocks, sent Ninah to make some cash money, and ducked into the first bar that took him out of the wind whipping down Fifth Avenue.

Grass mellowed other people out, but it made the Mad Daddy even madder. The lights behind his eyes came to life, and he got to looking at throats.

A jukebox played the Righteous Brothers' "Soul and Inspiration." Men and women danced like they were practically fucking, dresses so short you got a beaver show. Women danced with women, men with men, everyone slick with sweat. It was a wild scene.

Sam slid into an empty seat at the bar, and a Black man approached him with a slow smile, holding out a lit joint. His tie was loosened under a stiff wool military jacket emblazoned with medals and ribbons.

"You a doorman?" asked Sam.

"I'm a sergeant in the United States Army." Sam reached for the joint, and the sergeant pulled it back again and put it to his lips. "You could say I'm the doorman who stops the enemies of democracy."

The corners of Sam's lips danced as he took a hit. The sergeant was pretty, neck slim like a woman. Sam was high as fuck when he followed the man to his hotel room for a steak dinner. He'd find Ninah again. Or he wouldn't. The two men bellowed with back-slapping laughter as they stumbled into a closet-sized room in a Harlem flophouse. The neon of the streetlights flickered as the sergeant moved in to kiss him.

Sam, being Sam, wrapped his hands around the man's throat.

Before the killer knew what was happening, he was flat on his back, a pair of strong hands encircling his own neck this time.

"You out of your goddamn mind, you piece of shit?" said the combat veteran above him.

Sam struggled for air as the world around him pixelated. Was he being beat at his own game?

Were these his last breaths?

Shadows pressed at the corners of his eyes. He remembered. Back, back, back...

This wasn't the first time he was strangled.

Someone had smothered him, robbed him of oxygen. Someone had tried to take him out this way before. His uncle. Someone. Someone was about to do it again.

He remembered what Wilbert used to say: fight like a girl. Faster, smarter, and for your life.

Sam lashed out with his fists, throwing haymakers into the darkness, thrashing like some kind of fish, as they used to call the new prisoners.

He remembered that he used to take Big 'Un's tie and loop it over a nail in the basement, then around his own neck, pushing against it while stroking his cock, halfway in between worlds. Was it someone else who gave him the idea, or was it him all along?

The soldier above Sam caught an index finger between his teeth and bit it clean off. He then hoisted a bleeding, howling Sam by the waistband and kicked him hard enough in the ass that he hit the opposite wall before slamming the door behind him.

Goddamn, lesson learned. Mess around in New York, you lose a finger. Sam preferred warmer climes anyway—secret worlds tucked behind curtains of trees and trash where you could glide silently through the dark waters like a shark. Always sniffing for blood in the water. Always moving, lest you die.

———

The gates of the Trenton workhouse opened to reveal Ninah shifting from foot to foot, arms at her sides like a child. She'd known when to be there. Clever in her own way, he supposed, when she wasn't spinning batshit crazy talking nonstop or going silent for hours.

Ninah broke into a run and he swung her around. He was alive with freedom and propelled by the hunger he'd nurtured with fantasy after fantasy, night after night in his cell. Over Ninah's shoulder, the white T-bird waited.

25

THE PEOPLE OF THE STATE OF CALIFORNIA V. SAMUEL MCDOWELL

SAN DIEGO, CALIFORNIA
MARCH 1985

Diane, Sarah, Carolyn, Mary, Sarah, Emily, Linda, Norwegian baby, Air Force baby, Marianne, Maryland baby, Prince George baby, Sarah Brown, Agatha White Buffalo, Cuban Donna, Cincinnati baby, Savannah baby, Martha, the other Knoxville baby, Pamela, Mary-Anne, Bobbie, Jo, cowgirl, Angela, pipefitting baby, Macon baby, Carver Village baby, Carver Village baby, Plant City baby, Charleston baby, Clearwater baby, Evelyn, Julia, Cleveland baby, Hilda, Leila, Brenda, billboard baby, Chattanooga Choo Choo baby, Gulfport baby, Jackson ladyboy baby, Tennessee baby, Linda Sue, Atlanta baby, Anna, Rosie, Fredonia, Ohio baby, Nawlins baby, Little Woods baby, Dorothy, Patricia, Melinda, Atlanta stripper baby, college baby, Mary Jo, Fort Myers baby, Tampa Bay baby, Savannah baby, Kentucky Vegas baby, San Berdu baby, Memphis blues baby, Laurie, Tonya…

Pick the ones no one will notice are gone. Don't leave a witness. Don't get caught. If one of the above fails, demand a lawyer. There is no such thing as a jury of your peers. You have no peers. It's not your fault. You were born this way. They asked for it.

Samuel Little sat at the defense table in a courtroom that smelled faintly of wood rot and disinfectant. He tumbled back through the previous eight months in his mind while they droned on.

A smart man learns from his mistakes. The other two, the what's her name Melinda and the freaky-deaky Patricia, had inconvenienced him, and now this. He'd rotted in one shithole jail cell after another for over a year on the last one, waiting for the world to confirm that no one cared about them in the first place.

Melinda LaPree: failure to indict by grand jury.

Patricia Mount: acquitted by a jury of his peers after less than half an hour of deliberation.

Those other two lying whores couldn't even keep from peeing themselves.

No convictions and he'd had to do the bogus waiting time. He was the victim of an unfair system. All that stuff and nonsense about hair, eyewitnesses. A hair could get caught up in a breeze and blow clear across the state. All the eyewitnesses within a ten-mile radius of Sam were hopheads and whores, like the bitch yapping on the stand.

REMPEL: How old are you, Miss Barros?

BARROS: Twenty-two.

REMPEL: Have you ever been married?

BARROS: Yes, I have.

REMPEL: Did you become separated in 1984?

BARROS: Yes, I did.

Oh right. This was the one who whined for her mommy. Laurie Barros was her name. That was the thanks he got for leaving her alive, even if it had been an accident. It was up to God, not him.

REMPEL: How are you employed?

BARROS: I'm currently working at San Diego Medical Foundation, and I am a claims examiner.

REMPEL: Is that like an insurance company, commercial insurance, or something?

BARROS: Yes, it is. It's medical, major medical, basic health insurance.

Snore. When would they get to the part about Sam already? Wasn't it his trial?

REMPEL: Now I want to direct your attention to September 27, 1984. At this time were you separated from your husband?

BARROS: Yes, I was.

Was it already 1984? Where had the time gone. Lost behind him on the 90, the 75, the 10, the 20, the 40...

Jean sat behind him in her one good dress. He'd be out by Friday and make all this mess up to her. They'd go to LA. Sam winked. Jean kept her head bowed, humble as a pastor's wife, Bible in her lap.

He'd done her wrong. He'd done a lot of them wrong. Take his old girlfriend Ninah. Jean had been staying in LA for a while in '74 and had sent word to him in the workhouse in Trenton to get his ass to LA immediately, with Ninah or without her. Sam had made it to

LA and checked Ninah into the Cecil Hotel downtown before heading straight out to see Jean.

Jean had a party waiting for him. She kissed his face a thousand times, treated him like a king, didn't take her eyes off him for two weeks. He almost forgot about Ninah. When he went back for her, no one could remember seeing her in the first place. Years later, Ninah's mother's mother told him the poor wretch had gone batshit crazy. She'd flown out to LA and found Ninah rocking in the corner, talking nonsense about dead girls. Ninah was in Midgeville now, the local loony bin.

The next time they'd passed through Macon, he'd taken a detour, sauntered into Midgeville, and checked Ninah out then and there. Once he bundled her into the car, he noticed she was altered, touched or something.

Maybe she'd been listening when they'd been driving out of Omaha that night and the news story had come on the radio, about the Indian girl he'd left naked, head down, in a fifty-five-gallon barrel behind some dismal hide plant that smelled like the mouth of hell. He'd always thought she was just staring out the window.

No one would believe her anyway. He gave her a tenner and dropped her at the movie theater, told her to get them a couple of tickets. It wasn't without sadness that he left her there. He even circled the block for one last look at her, clutching the matinee tickets, craning her neck around for him. Poor crazy-ass ho. Someone would notice her eventually.

He prayed to God that if he got off this one last time, he'd treat Jean right and make up for every hurt he caused Ninah and the rest of them. He'd change his ways. He already felt like a better man just thinking about it.

REMPEL: And were you downtown on that evening?

BARROS: Yes.

REMPEL: Did you drive down there?

BARROS: Yes, I did.

REMPEL: Park your car?

BARROS: Yes.

REMPEL: Approximately where did you park your car, if you recall?

BARROS: Tenth Avenue and "C" Street.

REMPEL: Did you get out of your car?

BARROS: Yes, I did.

REMPEL: Did you commence walking?

BARROS: Yes.

REMPEL: And before anything else happened, about how far did you get?

BARROS: Tenth and "B." Close to "A" Street.

REMPEL: Were you headed toward some buildings or something there?

BARROS: Going north, toward Ash Street.

REMPEL: Getting towards that location, could you tell us what the lighting was like in that area?

BARROS: It was very dark.

REMPEL: Okay, and as you go to that location, what happened?

BARROS: I was approached from behind and grabbed around the—waist, the neck, and the chin area and pulled—dragged into a car.

REMPEL: How far was the car from you?

BARROS: It was about 25 feet. 20 to 25.

REMPEL: Was the door open or closed?

BARROS: It was open.

REMPEL: Did you struggle?

BARROS: Yes, I did.

REMPEL: Were you able to scream?

BARROS: I didn't dare.

REMPEL: Why was that?

BARROS: I guess I was so taken and shocked. I didn't
know if I should scream or not—there was nobody
around to hear me—for fear I would have been hurt
worse. I had a good knowledge that I was going to be
hurt, beaten.

SPENCER: Your honor, objection.

Good man. Object! They always made it so easy. Same with the
bitch from Missouri. They had just been playing around. No one
believed her either. Did three months for that.

THE COURT: The question was, why did she not scream.
For that purpose, I'll allow her answer to come in.

REMPEL: Now, when you got in the car, was the door of
the car open or closed?

BARROS: It was open.

REMPEL: What happened when you got in the car?

BARROS: I was nudged into the—from the driver's side,
into the middle position of the seat.

REMPEL: Were there any keys in the car?

BARROS: Yes, they were in the ignition.

REMPEL: And what happened next?

BARROS: He took off driving. I was still cuffed around the
neck.

REMPEL: Describe for us how it was that he was holding
you while he was driving.

BARROS: It was in a headlock-type position, with his hand
over my mouth and neck. Like this, over my mouth, so
that I could not speak, and—

Lies. Wasn't no headlock. It was a billfold of twenties.

REMPEL: It was a headlock, then, with his arms going
around behind your—the back of your neck and then
around your face.

BARROS: Yes.

REMPEL: Was this with his right arm?

BARROS: Yes, it was.

REMPEL: Did he do all the driving with his left?

BARROS: Yes.

REMPEL: And was this an automatic transmission car?

BARROS: Yes, it was.

REMPEL: What happened when he had to shift?

BARROS: He stuck his hand through the steering wheel to
shift it, like that.

REMPEL: Now, describe where you went.

BARROS: Took off toward Market Street driving east, 'til we
got to a location of 3600 block of Market Street, drove
up a gravel dirt road, up on—which was an incline, up
to a deserted area, which appeared to be an illegal dump
site.

REMPEL: Have you since gone back to that area?

BARROS: Yes, I have.

Yes, yes, yes, he remembered now. She'd been dressed like something out of a music video from that new MTV nonsense, in a black dress with white polka dots, a red belt, big white plastic jewelry Jean could have sold to the youngsters. She'd worn shiny white heels he'd tossed straight off when he'd slid her stockings down. His penis started getting erect thinking about it. He was almost looking forward to the next part of her testimony. What was she on about? It was a lover's lane. Of course it was dark.

REMPEL: After he stopped the car, what happened next?

BARROS: He turned it off. He got out of his car door, out of the car, in a quick fashion, and pushed the driver's seat forward to jump into the back seat, and still had me cuffed. He had to release me for a minute to open the door and get into the back seat, but then he grabbed me through the console in the front seat, just kind of threw me right into the back seat, and from there he proceeded to try and kiss me. I fought him off and when I did that, immediately he clamped right down on my—clamped right down on my neck and started choking me.

REMPEL: Okay, describe what this person did to choke you.

BARROS: He took his hand, his right hand, and just clamped right down on this portion of my neck and started applying pressure so that my air, my breath, was completely cut off. I could not breathe and he threw me into a lying position on the seat.

The lawyer puppet asked the whore to identify Sam, and she pointed. He didn't meet her gaze. The whole thing was making his dick too hard. The moment she pointed, he knew in his very soul that he loved her and always had and she was his forever, drawing breath or not.

Why was it everyone who loved him he couldn't love, and everyone he loved he needed to kill? How can sex and hate and love and death get twisted up inside a person?

> REMPEL: After the defendant commenced choking you in the back seat of that vehicle, describe what happened next.
>
> BARROS: He let up after about two minutes of doing this and I had the chance to speak. I asked him not to hurt me, that I was willing to cooperate with whatever his intentions were. I just didn't want him to hurt me. And he proceeded to reply that he wouldn't, and he said, "Trust me, I'm not going to hurt you." He says, "I love you." And that's when he started taking my nylons off and my underwear. They got stuck in my shoes, and so he just ripped them off, and took the nylons—and took the nylons and flipped me over onto my knees and tied my hands together very tight.

Maybe he did, maybe he didn't. If he had, it was only because she freaked on it.

> REMPEL: Okay. After the defendant had you on your knees there in the car in the back seat and he tied your hands behind you, what did the defendant do next?

BARROS: He flipped me back over on my back and I was laying on my hands. He kind of just put a lot of pressure on me from laying on me and started choking me again.

REMPEL: As he choked you, did he say anything to you?

BARROS: Yeah. He said, "Swallow for me. I love when you swallow."

REMPEL: When he was saying that: "Swallow, swallow for me," was his hand actually on your neck at the time he would say that?

BARROS: Yes, it was.

REMPEL: What is the next act he performed?

BARROS: Pardon?

REMPEL: What is the next thing he did?

BARROS: He let go of my neck and took his pants down, and then lifted me from my lower back, since I was on my back, and he held me up so he could start rubbing against me with his genital area, and then I guess he was trying to perform sexual intercourse. He wasn't able to. His penis was flaccid...

REMPEL: Now, did he ever perform any other sex acts on you?

BARROS: ...He performed oral copulation on me.

REMPEL: Is this while you were in the same position?

BARROS: Yes.

REMPEL: Was this against your will?

BARROS: It certainly was.

REMPEL: Were you still tied up?

BARROS: Yes, I was.

REMPEL: Approximately how long, just roughly, was it that he performed oral copulation?

BARROS: Four minutes.

REMPEL: Is that just an estimate on your part?

BARROS: Yes.

REMPEL: Now, what else did he do or say at that time, as you recall? What else was happening after he did that?

BARROS: He just came back over behind my neck and started choking me again, playing a little game and applying a lot of pressure on my neck, and then easing up for a moment for me, enough so I wouldn't pass out, and then applying a lot of pressure again. And this just kept going on.

Over and over again, she described it. How he took her breath, then gave it back.

Sam scissored his thighs to feel the equivalent of the retinal afterimage of a tingle. Like when you rub your eyes and see spots. Wasn't quite as good as the real thing, but reliving it was better than nothing. Doing it with an audience had its own special charm.

REMPEL: Did you fight as hard as you could at that point?

BARROS: Yes, I did. There wasn't a lot of energy that I could do so. It was a very, very short period of time and then I just gave up…

REMPEL: Did the defendant give any reason why he continued choking you after he had done the sex acts which you've described?

BARROS: None whatsoever, other than the fact that he

liked seeing me swallow and having total control of my
life, whether I breathed from one moment to the next.

Coached bullshit. The thing about choking people out—their mind is the first thing that goes. They start talking nonsense, eyes rolling around. They're half-awake, half-asleep once you start taking their breath away. In all his years, maybe only one or two of them ever even regained the sense enough to beg.

She didn't remember, but he did. The last time he'd choked her out, he had pressed his lips to hers and said, "Take my breath."

She described stumbling down the road, calling some whore of a friend. She hadn't called the cops, just sat in a bathtub crying—handed him a hall pass.

The green police officers on the stand sounded like boy scouts vying for their next badge. The next whore was drunk as a skunk on the stand.

Got lazy. He'd make sure they were good and dead from now on.

In the end, he sat back and watched his lawyer take every last one of them apart. He pled to lesser charges: assault with a deadly weapon and false imprisonment. A four-year sentence.

If he were smarter, he'd have done it like Manson: all those girls serving and worshipping and killing for him. But then again, Charlie had never felt the ear-ringing, mind-scrambling, toe-curling climax of death. More importantly, Sam would rather be free than famous. He would be exactly that in about eighteen months if he played his cards right.

Full name of child: Samuel Little
Sex: Male
Place of birth — County: Taylor, City or town: Reynolds
Date of birth: June 7, 1940
Full maiden name of mother: Bessie Mae Little
Race: Colored — Age at time of this birth: 16
Father of child — Full name: Unknown

Samuel Little's birth certificate

OFFICIAL FBI TIMELINE, SAMUEL LITTLE, 1970-2005

1978

1975

1973

1967

1977

1974

1972

1966

Little had a rap sheet over 100 pages long, with a criminal history spanning twenty-four states and nearly six decades

1985

1990

1994

1984

1988

1993

1995

Muskingum Building, B. I. S., Lancaster, Ohio.

Boys Industrial School

Ohio State Reformatory

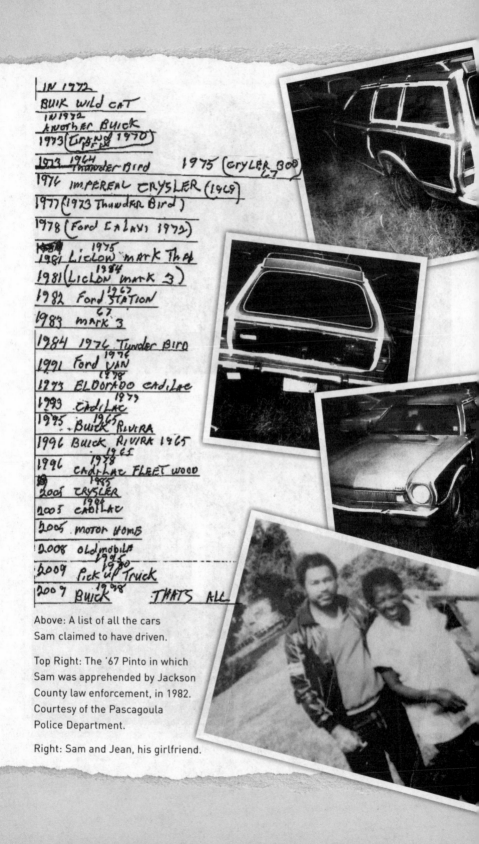

IN 1972
BUIK WILD CAT
IN 1972
ANOTHER BUICK
1973 (GRAND 1970)
1973 1964 Thunder Bird   1975 (CRYLER 800)
            67
1976 IMPEREAL CRYSLER (1969)
1977 (1973 ThundER Bird)
1978 (Ford GALAXY 1972)
            1975
1981 LICLOW MARK THR
            1984
1981 (LICLON mark 3)
            1967
1982 Ford STATION
        67
1983 mark 3
1984 1976 Tunder Bird
            1976
1991 Ford VAN
        1978
1993 ELDORADO CADILAC
            1979
1993 CADILAC
            1965
1995 Buick RIVERA
1996 Buick RIVIRA 1965
            1965
1996   1978
        CADILAC FLEET WOOD
        1985
2001 CRYSLER
        1994
2005 CADILAC
2005 motor Home
                1995
2008 oldmobile
                1980
2009 Pick up Truick
            1998
2009 Buick   :THATS ALL

Above: A list of all the cars
Sam claimed to have driven.

Top Right: The '67 Pinto in which
Sam was apprehended by Jackson
County law enforcement, in 1982.
Courtesy of the Pascagoula
Police Department.

Right: Sam and Jean, his girlfriend.

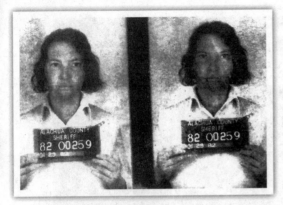

Patricia Mount

Sarah Brown

Patricia Mount crime scene

Below: A November 17, 1973 article in The Omaha World-Herald reported the murder of Agatha White Buffalo at the age of 34. The back of the abandoned tannery, where White Buffalo was found in a barrel.

Agatha White Buffalo

Map of the route traveled by Little and Mary Brosley. DOD January, 1971. Miami, FL.

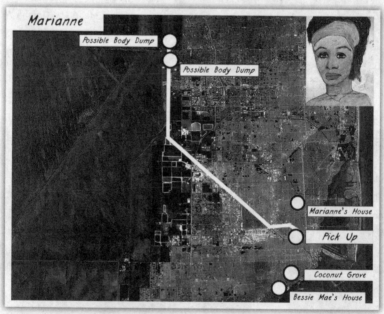

Map of the route possibly traveled by Little and a transgender woman possibly named "Marianne." DOD 1971-1972, Miami, FL. Drawing by Samuel Little.

Top: Carver Village
Left: Melinda Lapree
Bottom: Darren Versiga

The eight pack from which Leila McClain and Hilda Nelson identified
Little after he was arrested for the murder of Melinda LaPree.
Courtesy of the Alachua County Police Department.

Denise Brothers

Denise Brothers' children

Top: Hilda Nelson, one of five known surviving victims

Right: Leila Mae (Mclain) Johnson, one of five known surviving victims

Bottom: Laurie Barros, one of five known surviving victims

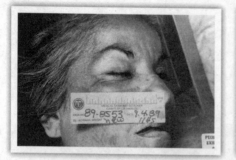

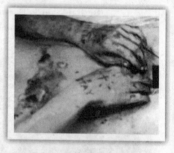
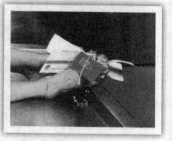

Top: Guadalupe Apodaca

Middle Left: Carol Alford

Middle Right: Site of Alice Duvall's body dump

Bottom: Audrey Nelson

Top: Alice Duvall

Bottom Left: Audrey Nelson
pictured as a child

Bottom Right: Alice Duvall

Above: Detective Rick Jackson (aka Harry Bosch)

Left: Dr. Angela Williamson, FBI Crime Analyst Christie Palazzolo, and Texas Ranger James Holland awarded for their meticulous and groundbreaking work

Robbery Homicide Division Cold Case Special Section Detective Mitzi Roberts and LAPD Detective Tim Marcia

August 23, 2019. Little pleads guilty: two counts first degree murder in Cleveland, and one count of murder in Cincinnati

(Left to right) Juror, Juror, Laurie Kerridge, Pearl "Unique" Nelson, Robbery Homicide Division Cold Case Special Section Detective Mitzi Roberts, Sherri "Buela" Nelson, Beth Silverman District Attorney Los Angeles County Major Crimes Division, Tony Zambrano, Diana Flores

COUNTY OF LOS ANGELES
REGISTRAR-RECORDER/COUNTY CLERK

3052020320630

CERTIFICATE OF DEATH
STATE OF CALIFORNIA
USE BLACK INK ONLY / NO WHITE-OUT, WHITE-OUTS OR ALTERATIONS
VS-11 (REV 3/96)

STATE FILE NUMBER

3202019077162

LOCAL REGISTRATION NUMBER

DECEDENT'S PERSONAL DATA

1. NAME OF DECEDENT- FIRST (Given) SAMUEL	2. MIDDLE	3. LAST (Family) LITTLE

AKA, ALSO KNOWN AS – Include full AKA (FIRST MIDDLE LAST) SAMUEL - MCDOWELL	4. DATE OF BIRTH mm/dd/ccyy 06/07/1940	5. AGE Yrs. 80	IF UNDER ONE YEAR Months / Days	IF UNDER 24 HOURS Hours / Minutes	6. SEX M

7. BIRTH STATE/FOREIGN COUNTRY GA	10. SOCIAL SECURITY NUMBER 297-54-8662	11. EVER IN U.S. ARMED FORCES? YES / X NO / UNK	12. MARITAL STATUS/SRDP at time of Death NEVER MARRIED	7. DATE OF DEATH mm/dd/ccyy 12/30/2020	8. HOUR (24 Hour) 0503

9. EDUCATION – Higher Level/Degree UNKNOWN	14/15. WAS DECEDENT HISPANIC/LATINO/A/SPANISH? (if yes, see instructions on back) YES / X NO BLACK	16. DECEDENT'S RACE – Up to 3 races may be listed (see worksheet on back)

17. USUAL OCCUPATION – Type of work for most of life. DO NOT USE RETIRED UNKNOWN	18. KIND OF BUSINESS OR INDUSTRY (e.g., grocery store, road construction, employment agency, etc.) UNKNOWN	19. YEARS IN OCCUPATION UNK

USUAL RESIDENCE

20. DECEDENT'S RESIDENCE (Street and number, or location) 44750 60TH STREET WEST

21. CITY LANCASTER	22. COUNTY/PROVINCE LOS ANGELES	23. ZIP CODE 93536	24. YEARS IN COUNTY UNK	25. STATE/FOREIGN COUNTRY CALIFORNIA

INFORMANT

26. INFORMANT'S NAME, RELATIONSHIP INEZ MCDOWELL, SISTER	27. INFORMANT'S MAILING ADDRESS (Street and number, or rural route number, city or town, state, zip) 12402 ALFRED BERRY COURT, LOUISVILLE, KY 40223

SPOUSE/SRDP AND PARENT INFORMATION

28. NAME OF SURVIVING SPOUSE/SRDP–FIRST -	29. MIDDLE -	30. LAST (BIRTH NAME) -

31. NAME OF FATHER/PARENT–FIRST PAUL	32. MIDDLE	33. LAST MCDOWELL SR.	34. BIRTH STATE GA

35. NAME OF MOTHER/PARENT–FIRST BESSIE	36. MIDDLE MAE	37. LAST (BIRTH NAME) LITTLE	38. BIRTH STATE GA

FUNERAL DIRECTOR/ LOCAL REGISTRAR

39. DISPOSITION DATE mm/dd/ccyy 04/22/2021	40. PLACE OF FINAL DISPOSITION LOS ANGELES CO. CREM. CEMETERY 3301 EAST 1ST STREET, LOS ANGELES, CA 90063

41. TYPE OF DISPOSITION(S) CR/BU	42. SIGNATURE OF EMBALMER ▶ NOT EMBALMED	43. LICENSE NUMBER -

44. NAME OF FUNERAL ESTABLISHMENT LA. CO. DEPT. OF CORONER	45. LICENSE NUMBER NONE	46. SIGNATURE OF LOCAL REGISTRAR ▶ MUNTU DAVIS, M.D. 50	47. DATE mm/dd/ccyy 04/20/2021

PLACE OF DEATH

101. PLACE OF DEATH ANTELOPE VALLEY HOSPITAL MEDICAL CENTER	102. IF HOSPITAL, SPECIFY ONE X IP / ER/OP / DOA	103. IF OTHER THAN HOSPITAL, SPECIFY ONE Hospice / Nursing Home/LTC / Decedent's Home / Other

104. COUNTY LOS ANGELES	105. FACILITY ADDRESS OR LOCATION WHERE FOUND (Street and number, or location) 1600 WEST AVENUE J	106. CITY LANCASTER

CAUSE OF DEATH

107. CAUSE OF DEATH		Time interval between Onset and Death	108. DEATH REPORTED TO CORONER?
IMMEDIATE CAUSE (Final disease or condition resulting in death) → (A) PNEUMONIA	Enter the chain of events — diseases, injuries, or complications — that directly caused death. DO NOT enter terminal events such as cardiac arrest, respiratory arrest, or ventricular fibrillation without showing the etiology. DO NOT ABBREVIATE.	DAYS	X YES / NO
Sequentially list conditions, if any, leading to cause on Line A. Enter UNDERLYING CAUSE (disease or injury that initiated the events resulting in death) LAST (B) COVID-19		DAYS	CORONER'S CASE NUMBER 2020-12488
(C)			109. BIOPSY PERFORMED? YES / X NO
(D)			110. AUTOPSY PERFORMED? YES / X NO
			111. USED IN DETERMINING CAUSE? YES / NO

112. OTHER SIGNIFICANT CONDITIONS CONTRIBUTING TO DEATH BUT NOT RESULTING IN THE UNDERLYING CAUSE GIVEN IN 107 ARTERIOSCLEROTIC CARDIOVASCULAR DISEASE, DIABETES

113. WAS OPERATION PERFORMED FOR ANY CONDITION IN ITEM 107 OR 112? (If yes, list type of operation and date.) NO	113A. IF FEMALE, PREGNANT IN LAST YEAR? YES / NO / N/A

PHYSICIAN'S CERTIFICATION

114. I CERTIFY THAT TO THE BEST OF MY KNOWLEDGE DEATH OCCURRED AT THE HOUR, DATE, AND PLACE STATED FROM THE CAUSES STATED. Decedent Attended Since ___ mm/dd/ccyy / Decedent Last Seen Alive ___ mm/dd/ccyy	115. SIGNATURE AND TITLE OF CERTIFIER ▶	116. LICENSE NUMBER	117. DATE mm/dd/ccyy

118. TYPE ATTENDING PHYSICIAN'S NAME, MAILING ADDRESS, ZIP CODE

CORONER'S USE ONLY

119. I CERTIFY THAT IN MY OPINION DEATH OCCURRED AT THE HOUR, DATE, AND PLACE STATED FROM THE CAUSES STATED. MANNER OF DEATH X Natural / Accident / Homicide / Suicide / Pending Investigation / Could not be determined	120. INJURED AT WORK? YES / NO / UNK	121. INJURY DATE mm/dd/ccyy	122. HOUR (24 Hours)

123. PLACE OF INJURY (e.g., home, construction site, wooded area, etc.)

124. DESCRIBE HOW INJURY OCCURRED (Events which resulted in injury)

125. LOCATION OF INJURY (Street and number, or location, and city, and zip)

126. SIGNATURE OF CORONER / DEPUTY CORONER ISRAEL BARNETTE 50	127. DATE mm/dd/ccyy 04/20/2021	128. TYPE NAME, TITLE OF CORONER / DEPUTY CORONER ISRAEL BARNETTE, DEP CORONER

STATE REGISTRAR

A	B	C	D	E		FAX AUTH.#	CENSUS TRACT

010001004932870

Samuel Little's death certificate

HI ANGELE,

YES you ArE AN ANGLE WEATHER you KNOW IT or NOT, I LOVE YOU, IS IT A crime To LOVE AN ANGLE. THEN I HAVE COMMITTED A crime bigger THEN MY murbERS, which I ALLSO had THE SAME FEELINGS for my Girls EACH ANd EVERY ONE of THEM. MURDER IS NOT IN MY LOVE. I DONT HAVE THE SLIDEST MOTIVE of To KILL. WHEN I ride down THE STREET of LONE SOME IN SOME TOWN or OTHER WITH THE Tugging hope of MAY bE This IS THE ONE THAT Will bE MY DrEAM Girl, ANd WHEN SHE GETS her FEMINITY IN THE CAr SuddENLY THE CAr FEELS LIKE A DrEAM JUST ENTEREd MY, LiFE. I DrIvE ANd SHE SAYS with her VOICE sounding like MUSIC oh so SWEET, DON'T DRIVE So FAST, bE ZAREFUL, I FEEL likE THAT IS MY WOMAN MY DrEAM WOMAN A LONE WITH ME. THEN SHE LAYS her HEAD ow MY Shoulder AWd I CANT EVEN SEE THE ROAD. bE CAREFULL BEFore you KILL ME. I SAY CAN I GET you A BLACK PRESS. SURE you CAN. I forGET EVERY thing buT hEN A LIVEINg DrEAM I AM going To WALK down THE STREET, So I CAN show her off AND ShouT Look world I have A WOMAN ALL MINE, I OONT FEEL MY FEET Touch THE ground. I AM ow HEAVEN. I PLAN To drESS her I PLAN To FEEd her AWd I SMELL her Body IN MY NOSE AND IT IS LIKE INTOXTATION. WHEN SuddENLY THE buETIfuLL GoddESS SAYS I COST TWENTY DOLLArs for MY LOVE. THErE goS MY dream of TruE LOVE. I SAY To MY VIOCE you Fool SHE DON'T ZARE for you SHE NEVER INTENDED To LOVE you, To cook for you To CRY with you To LET you IN To hER HEART. But WAIT THErE IS ANOTHEr WAY you ZAN HAVE her For EVER. KILL her SLOW WATCH HER STRANGLE SLOWLLY, beg LIKE SHE MADE you FEEL WHEN you ThougT SHE WAS THE ONE GoddESS. Look IN To her EYES AS SHE dIEd AND WAS gowE. Oh God WHAT dId I do To her SHE hAd THE right To SELL her LOVE To THE highEST bidder. I goT To gET out of here. <u>MURDER for LOVE</u> WHO ME!!

The STREET is full of PREETY WOMAN There
oVer There Look here She come Hi Honey She SAYS
CAN I get in. Help me God i CAN'T STOP STOP
i LoVe you. MAd DADY PLEASE for give me.

      Mr SAM

HONEY BOY you ARE LooKiNg IN The wrong PLACE
~~for LoVe GiVe me my money~~
JUST beCAuse A woman Looks buetiful iT
doS NOT MEAN You CAN have her
YOU ARE NOT A baby ANY MORE ChiLd!!

    i LoVe JiLLiAN my BUETiful friend

CAN you understand This madness

   FOR YOU JiLLiAN

26

ALL SINS ARE EQUAL

CALIFORNIA STATE PRISON, LOS ANGELES COUNTY, CALIFORNIA
DECEMBER 2018

In Sam's version of the world, he loves.

When he wanted to feel human during our interviews, he'd wax sentimental about the girlfriends he'd kept alive: Ninah, Lucy, Barbara.

He circled back again and again to Jean, the best woman he ever knew. Everyone had loved Jean. Tina Turner came over when she was in town to shoot the shit and see if Jean had that Sergio Valente jumpsuit in a size eight.

Jean was also the only woman Sam admitted to beating within an inch of her life, over and over, during their over fifteen years together.

Jean gave Sam Little an airtight alibi for the evening Patricia Mount was murdered. During his San Diego trial, she sat behind him prim as a Sunday school teacher, Bible in her lap. Jean told Sam she'd die and go to hell with him. She didn't just take him back every time; she tracked him down. When he left her, she'd have him arrested for stealing her car, then go bail him out. She'd call his parents or his cousins and leave word where to find her.

Jean was a sharp and industrious woman, accustomed to extreme violence. Jean had girlfriends too. It didn't seem to matter—she supported them, dressed them, cooked for them, bought their cars, protected them. She did it all.

There was an oddly feminine quality about Sam, although it wasn't immediately apparent. Maybe both he and Jean hated the femininity in themselves, the weakness it represented. When Sam went on the hunt, Jean stayed in the motel and crocheted doll cozies for empty bottles—Coke, Pepsi, vodka, whiskey, didn't matter. For Easter, she crocheted bunny ears on the dolls. She displayed them next to the victims' earrings in the trunk of her car when she pulled over in Anytown, USA, to shill her wares. Once in a blue moon, she even sold one.

I believe she knew.

Pure speculation. Most detectives I talk to disagree. Sam disagreed with me. No way she knew. I could be wrong.

Jean was invisible to a world she scammed too easily. Sam was the shadow who did the dirty work of killing her symbolically while she slithered across the floor of Saks to support them. It wasn't her shit in the car. It was left there by a filthy whore in hot pants: the thing she could neither have nor be. She scrubbed the back floorboard so often, the smell of bleach in the car never went away, always made their eyes water.

I asked Sam if he felt bad, walking out of the hospital after she died and leaving her remains for her family in St Louis.

"About that? Oh, no. Not about anything, really. The minute you ask for forgiveness, you are forgiven. I asked God for forgiveness and I was forgiven. You know about the apostle Paul?"

"Betwixt the stirrup and the ground, he something lost and something found?"

"How you know that, Jew?"

"What if your babies didn't see the ground coming?"

"If they didn't forgive, I'd hate to see where they went."

I could have strangled him myself sometimes. I could have strangled God himself.

"All sins are equal in the eyes of Jesus," he said to me. "Stealing a cookie from the cookie jar is no worse or better than murder."

"I don't agree with that."

"Because you're a sinner. It's okay. I don't hold it against you." He held everything against me, but especially this.

"I'm a sinner, sure. I just don't agree all sins are equal."

"That is the Bible. That is Jesus. That is truth."

"I think even in the Bible, there's kind of a hierarchy, right?" I held up a finger. "One. Come on. We can do this. I'll start: One, I am the Lord your God. You shall have no"—*Fuckity fuck. Could I really not even get the first one? Okay, I got it*—"other gods before me. Two? No? Two, you shall not take the name of the Lord your God in vain."

I was on a roll. I could have gone on. I knew not to embarrass any man, but most importantly, this one. God was not his shepherd. God was his apologist.

Jimmy called him Sammy. I called him Mr. Sam. That was what his girls called him.

"Mr. Sam," I said, laying my palm on his forearm, hairless from being burned in a pile of hot ash as a child. "Which commandment is don't steal the cookie from the cookie jar?"

27

AGATHA WHITE BUFFALO

OMAHA, NEBRASKA
NOVEMBER 1973

Aggie slept the whole six-hour bus ride from the Rosebud Reservation in South Dakota to the Greyhound station in the center of Omaha and could have easily slept six more if the bus driver hadn't shaken her shoulder. She donned the red coat she'd been using as a blanket, grabbed her overnight bag, and wound her way through the cavernous station out into a clear fall day.

She had closed her eyes amid rolling plains and pine groves and opened them onto a bustling city. The air threatened winter. She flattened her back against the wall of the bus depot and pulled out a wrinkled piece of paper. Denise. A friend of a friend. Back home, almost no one was a stranger. But she was personable, bright-eyed, and generous with her smiles. She'd be okay.

Aggie straightened her spine and followed the directions that would take her the three miles to Denise's address. She stopped every few blocks to catch her breath. The gasping was why the doctor had given her the X-ray. When he first saw the spot, it had looked like nothing more than a white smear, no bigger than a thumbprint. He had told her she'd need to have it looked at, and the closest facility was Omaha.

Aggie found Diane's address as the tall buildings of downtown trailed off to bungalows shadowed by the last of the blood-colored foliage of the maples. Diane worked odd hours as a nurse and had left a key under an empty terra-cotta flower pot on the front porch.

Aggie slipped off her shoes, stepped through the ribbons of amber afternoon sunlight unfurling across the hardwood floors, and sat on a couch in yet another empty house.

Her Patrick had taken just one step too many outside the lines, and now he was gone to prison for a good long time. She had been good at loving him, reveled in the noise and clutter of being a mother, even when seven kids seemed impossible on a cop's salary and in a tiny clapboard house. She and the girls had smelled the pillowcases dried on the line in the morning sun before folding. Pat had been proud when he bought her the washer.

How can a person be opposite things at the same time? That was what messed her up. He was funny and wild and romantic. And he damn near beat her to death. Too many times. Then he really did kill someone and got put away in Valentine.

She had thought about telling him about the lung spot, but why? The kids were farmed out one by one as she tried and failed to get a position as a maid two hours south, attempted to get a job mucking stalls, a job anywhere. Half her babies had gone off to boarding school. The others were with relatives or in foster homes on the res.

Joyce, Pattee, Peter, Ernest, Mona Lisa, naughty Billy, baby Jack...

Someone else getting a paycheck to feed them. Someone else

kissing their feverish foreheads. Someone else telling them bedtime stories. Someone else making the food stretch—extra sauce and extra rice did the trick. Just until she got back on her feet, got stronger.

Except when you didn't have breakfast to cook and hair to braid and a line of little shoes by the door, why would you even get out of bed? You do it because you have to do it, and then you figure out a way to stretch a dollar and smile through. Not the other way around.

How had she wound up in room after room alone? She pulled her good coat around her diminutive frame. She was barely five feet to begin with and hadn't been eating much since there had been no one else to cook for. A plaque above the front door read BLESS THIS HOME AND ALL WHO ENTER. She'd take a blessing.

Aggie lay her head on the forest-green velour, reciting the same prayer she always did when her eyelids grew heavy. The same she'd recite the following day when they inserted a needle through her rib cage and extracted a sample of lung tissue.

> *Hail Mary,*
> *Full of grace,*
> *The Lord is with thee.*
> *Blessed art thou among women,*
> *And blessed is the fruit of thy womb, Jesus.*
> *Holy Mary, Mother of God,*
> *Pray for us sinners, now and at the hour of our death.*
> *Amen.*

Aggie had no right to feel sorry for herself in the shadow of the pain of the Virgin Mother, but hers was somehow still so acute it doubled her over. The stain wasn't on her lungs; it was on her heart.

———

"Here's a pick-me-up!"

Aggie opened her eyes. A white lady with blue-red lips, teased blond hair the texture of cotton candy, and a midnight-blue velveteen jumpsuit held a fat tumbler of whiskey under her nose.

"Are you...?" Aggie searched for the name, pulling herself out of a swamp of dreams.

"Denise? I'm Phyllis, the roommate. Denise won't be home for hours. Got the night shift, poor thing. Don't worry. I'm way more fun," she said with a flowery laugh. "You must be the Buffalo Gal."

Not the first time Aggie had heard that one, but she liked the woman and was happy to have the warmth of the whiskey in her belly.

"You know that song was about a bunch of old-timey hookers? My grandma used to sing it to me, bless her heart. I don't think she knew, but you never know the secrets those old biddies keep. Hey, I'm part something or other Indian too, y'know. Chippewa I think."

Phyllis clacked across the floor.

"I'm starving, you? Jesus, you look like you haven't eaten in a year. Come on in here and sit down."

Agatha stood and followed her, leaning in the doorway and watching as Phyllis pulled containers out of the fridge and sang, "Buffalo Gals, won't you come out tonight and dance by the light of the moon?"

Was this how single women lived?

"When's your thing?" asked Phyllis.

"Biopsy?"

Phyllis covered her ears with her hands. "I don't like that word. Just say they're checking you out."

"Okay. Then they're checking me out tomorrow."

"You'll need a drink after that. I work for the phone company, but I get off at five. Wanna meet me and go grab a drink? If Denise is off, she can come meet us too."

Phyllis put a yellow-flowered plate with a couple of cold chicken thighs and some potato salad down on the trestle table.

"Siddown, would ya?"

Aggie ate like a convict and washed it down with the whiskey.

"We'll give you a proper adventure tomorrow. White Buffalo really your name?"

"Married name," said Aggie through her chicken.

"That's a mouthful."

"It was even longer. It was White Buffalo Chief, but Pat's parents shortened it."

"What were you, some kind of chiefs or kings?"

"Back when."

"Neato."

"It's a famous story too. The White Buffalo woman brought the peace pipe. White buffalos are sacred. We're Catholic, you know. The kids like the old stories though."

"Right, sure," said Phyllis. She looked up at the orange plastic owl clock on the wall. "I could use a peace pipe right about now. Oh shit, we're missing *Columbo*."

———

Aggie approached the Happy Bar the next night. Its glowing yellow sign with a line drawing of a foamy mug of beer was a beacon in the bruised twilight. Phyllis and Denise perched on bar stools. A few stragglers milled around.

Aggie eased herself onto a stool. The numbing shot they'd stuck in her side was wearing off, and so was the Valium they'd given her when she freaked out.

Surely goodness and mercy shall follow me all the days of my life and I will dwell in the house of the Lord forever.

She popped a painkiller and sucked down two drinks while Phyllis and Diane gossiped about mutual friends. The words washed over Aggie. She was happy to not be alone. A few guys in flannels and work boots huddled in the corner of the bar, where a small TV played a grainy UNO football game. The after-work crowd from both the downtown businesses and the warehouses nearby began to trickle in.

Phyllis clocked the door. "Never seen that face before. I'm sure I'd remember."

The man surveyed the bar with cat eyes that reminded Aggie of the swirly marbles she'd liked best as a kid.

"Lipstick on your teeth, babe," Diane said to Phyllis. Phyllis ran an index finger over them and straightened her skirt.

Diane rolled her eyes. "Three, two, one, and…"

Phyllis approached the man with a flip of her hair but turned around fast.

"He asked if you were a real Indian. Whaddaya look like, a wooden one? Says he wants to meet you. Never met a real Indian before."

"He buying?"

"Not for me, but he's buying."

"He seem okay?"

"A little pushy. Asked me all manner of shit right up front. Where did I work. Did I have family around."

Aggie was out of money, and every time she breathed, the soft hollow between her jutting ribs hurt like she was being stabbed. She wanted another drink like she wanted air. She stood and her knees nearly buckled. The neon beer signs on the wall swam and blurred.

She walked over to the stranger. He studied her through the cat's-eye marbles.

"You a real Indian? Where your feathers?"

They should put her behind glass in a museum. "Left them at home," she said.

The man stroked the front of Aggie's neck.

She flinched. Look what had become of her. Some days, she wished she hadn't woken up at all.

"What did you say?"

Had she spoken out loud? She was confused. Must be the medication.

"You don't want to wake up?" He bellowed with laughter. "Is that what you said? Hell, you came to the right place. I'll kill you right here!"

"I didn't mean it like that."

"You ain't no buffalo. You look like a pretty little brown kitten to me. Where's your whatchacallit...*tribe* at?"

"Oh, way up there. South Dakota. Where I live. I got no people here. Going back on the bus tomorrow."

Her tongue sounded thick and far away.

"Tomorrow's a long time from now. I got a nice warm room. I'll drive you to the station in the morning."

"I don't gotta do anything I don't want to."

"No, no. No, ma'am. You just need to relax and let Mr. Sam do all the work. You deserve a little rest. Plus, I got a bottle of good stuff. We don't need this overpriced well swill."

She weighed her options. Another lonely night on Denise's couch, another walk to the bus station. She was out of money. For all she knew, she might be out of time. What the hell.

Aggie let her friends know she was going with the guy. Phyllis shot her a sharp look.

Denise said, "Oh, don't be all sour grapes."

"It's not that. It's...something."

Phyllis trotted to Aggie, caught her by the arm at the door.

"You have our address on you, right? You have our number? In case you need it."

"She don't need nothing," said Sam. "I got her from here."

Sam opened the door of his white T-Bird and practically tossed Aggie inside. The car was moving before she could lift a hand to wave goodbye.

28

EVERYDAY SADISM

HOLLYWOOD, CALIFORNIA
MAY 2018

"Nice to meet you. *Norman IS his mother*."

That was how my pissed-off aunt greeted my father's hot date to see *Psycho*, when not spoiling the ending was all the rage. Hitchcock had nurses stationed at theaters across the country, in case the ladies fainted at the sight of a knife, or a mummified mother.

The iconic split personality of Norman Bates has remained an incestuous Freudian trope so culturally impactful that its next incarnation in Sally Field's *Sybil* made Sybil not just a name, but slang for nutso female. The Urban Dictionary includes a definition of "sybill" as "A girl that is hot, yet crazy. Might have several different personalities and may use all of them on you."

The clinical name for the largely cinematic trope of "multiple personality disorder," is dissociative identity Disorder. DID is both a fun idea to kick around and a powerful metaphor for the compartmentalized lives of even the most "normal" among us. In the movie version of this shattered self, distinct characters named Brad, Sunshine, Bruce

Lee, Miss Toyah, and Uncle Morty hang out playing Yahtzee in the green room of your shattered subconscious until their number gets called. This extreme iteration is quite rare, if extant.

Still, the fragmented mind, the classic *Dr. Jekyll and Mr. Hyde* scenario, speaks to fundamental questions about how even the most "normal" among us organize and integrate a sense of self. Compartmentalization, at its most extreme, enabled many notable serial killers to commit grotesque and sadistic acts for pleasure, only to return home to their wife and kids and apologize for being a little late for dinner. It's difficult to imagine the pathological cognitive dissonance of those who torture and kill someone else's child for a fuck, then go home to kiss their own family good night.

Is serial killing somewhere on the spectrum of DID? Or is it a cruder process of wanting, taking, and justifying? I'm not a diagnostician and can only explain what it felt like to talk to Samuel Little over a span of years.

I experienced Sam as three different people. Call it a metaphor. Drop me a line if you figure it out. In my notes, I alternately called him:

Three-Card Monte
Snake Monster
Perv Grandpa

I learned the actual game of three-card monte from a world-class carny—magician Penn Jillette.

Three-card monte, to be specific, is a trick, not a game. You play, you lose. Yet some version of it has been played all over the world for centuries. We know we're being fooled, but we will pay handsomely to watch it done well or to think that we're going to be the one special person with the hawk eye who catches the huckster mid con. We're all going to game the game.

We're all vulnerable. We're all greedy. We're all marks. We're all hustlers.

Snake Monster was the killer. I only met him a few times, when he reared in anger at me, like a cobra. I will not soon forget it.

Perv Grandpa was his go-to. He was that endearing, mischievous old codger with terrific stories…but you had to sit on his lap to hear them.

I give everyone nicknames. If I know you, you have one. That's how I code information. The nicknames are organic, the first thing that comes to me. Sam is the only person I've ever known who had more than one.

All three of these shady characters knew me. They all had similar if not identical memories but different ways of articulating them. Were they distinct personalities, or was it more like a braid you couldn't quite tease apart? I don't have the answer.

Swiss psychiatrist and psychoanalyst Carl Gustav Jung transformed the field of psychoanalysis in the early part of the twentieth century by shifting the focus off Freud's libido-driven model of consciousness (see: Norman is his mother). He favored the concept of a core personality informed by the collective unconscious—a level of consciousness we share as part of the organism of humanity, including memories and ideas inherited from our ancestral and evolutionary past.

Jung organized his ideas into a set of symbolic imagery called archetypes. The main twelve are ruler, artist, innocent, sage, explorer, outlaw, magician, hero, lover, jester, everyman, and caregiver.

The heavyweights are the four archetypes to rule them all.

The persona is the mask we use to face the outside world. It's our public self. The one we show.

The anima/animus is the mirror opposite of our gender identity. If one identifies largely as female, it's the unconscious masculine and vice versa.

The shadow.

So much to say about the shadow.

The shadow is the enemy of the persona. It is akin to Freud's id, everything we keep hidden...the dark side of the moon. The shadow is the source of both our deepest creative and destructive energies and is neither inherently negative or positive.

The shadow is irrational, impulsive, prone to projection. Projection is the process by which we take a perceived inferiority or an unconscious desire or unfulfilled need—or desire to confess—and smear it all over another person until we can't see them. We see only our shadow.

We all have a shadow. Samuel Little, while obscene and monstrous, has no monopoly on the shadow. Nor does he absolve yours, however banal.

You may protest, "Monsters go berserk."

You probably don't go berserk and hang little girls, bludgeon coeds in their beds, strangle women and let them regain consciousness over and over. Are you fucking kidding? Incomprehensible.

We like our monsters unrecognizable.

The self is the unification of these four archetypes into an ecosystem of a core personality.

In Jungian terms, Sam wasn't all shadow, but his shadow was definitely in the driver's seat. He did a lot of driving. He hated his anima with such passion it became his life's work to kill it. His persona was why it confounded people that he was such a nice guy, essentially not violent with women, except for that little strangling-to-death thing. He might have even believed it himself. I'm not sure. I know it was what he wanted others to see, and to really sell a story, you have to believe it, at least in the moment.

What he did not have, as far as I could tell, was a self.

Talking to an absence was an extraordinary experience. I thought of Sam telling me drawing gave him the same rush as stealing. I looked at his art and saw emptiness.

When I saw him in person, he pointed at the drawings and pantomimed going down on these dolled-up Venus de Milos. He dug his nails into the skin of his arms until white crescents appeared beneath them. The tone of every woman he mimicked—even when he quoted their pleas for their lives—sounded like vicious bitchery.

I warmed Sam up with stories of my humdrum life. I told him about my cousin Jill, who lived across the street when I was a kid and had two sons around my age, both close friends. When I was small, the family called me Little Jill, and she was Big Jill. Big Jill is barely five feet tall, so by the time I was eleven, I was Big Jill, and she was Little Jill. We remain so to this day.

I made a throwaway joke—no girl likes to be called Big Jill.

Three-Card Monte called me Big Jill after that.

He said, "Some of them, I licked their pussy for hours. They died in sexual pleasure, not hate, you understand? I'm not like these, what did you call it? Homicidal sexual maniacs."

"That's one thing I'd call it."

"What else you call me?"

"Which time?"

"Ooooh, that's right. A pervert. Well, you a ho, Big Jill."

———

Sometimes Sam was boring and rambling with the endless phone calls. When he was really annoying, in the background, I did my homework and watched brain dissections:

the occipital lobe for visual processing
the parietal lobe for sensation
the temporal lobe for memory
the frontal lobe: the last gift from the fairies...

You don't grow a frontal lobe properly until you're twenty-seven: impulse control, language, judgment, sexual behaviors. The right hemisphere of the frontal lobe controls the left part of the body and vice versa. The frontal lobe is also the most common place for brain injury to occur. Damage to the frontal lobe can create significant changes in personality.

With their Fibonacci sequences, double helixes, and inseparable dualities, I'm pretty sure the gods were tripping balls...

"Okay, that's so messed up already, but wait for it—let's split it in half!"

Like the mother and the whore, the hemispheres of the brain are opposite as can be, but if the corpus callosum (tough body) nerve path between them is severed, the body they govern loses an essential piece of perception, and the world fragments. The left brain is for words, the right brain for pictures. If you show a person with split-brain syndrome an orchid on the left side of their visual field, they can't recognize it. They name it only by feel, as if blind. Put it in their right visual field, they recognize it's a...something, but they can't find the word.

There are many types of strangulation, all of which involve increasing hypoxia, or the deprivation of oxygen to the brain, sometimes to the point of death. Manual strangulation is achieved with the hands or a blunt object and can either interfere with the flow of blood in the neck, the airway, or both. Depending on the amount of pressure applied, it may also damage the larynx and fracture the hyoid and other bones in the neck. It can take as long as you want it to, if you know what you're doing. Sam loved the sound of a snapping hyoid.

"Ever played the wishbone game? Sounds like that."

It was always refreshing to interview a scientist and get a break from hearing from a murderer yet again about the pleasurable sound of a hyoid bone cracking.

I interviewed Dr. Del Paulhus, professor of psychology at the University of British Columbia. Paulhus is one of the world's leading experts on half of the iconic duality that trumps even the Madonna and the whore: evil.

Paulhus's research has done much to explore and elucidate the dark triad, or malevolent personality. As defined by the gold standard if ever-shifting *Diagnostic and Statistical Manual of Mental Disorders*, now in its fifth edition, the malevolent personality is made up of a cluster of personality disorders that, put simply, make you a really, really bad person. These are antisocial personality disorder, Machiavellianism, and narcissistic personality disorder.

Paulhus's innovation to the dark triad is a sneaky little sister, sidling up to make it a tetrad: everyday sadism.

I intuitively understood everyday sadism to be exactly as it sounded. Unless we're shockingly abhorrent, like Sam, cruelty works on a spectrum. With Sam as a yardstick, most of us are the Dalai Lama.

I stared out at the same square of yard I did every morning—the half-painted fence with thorny bougainvillea crawling over the top. I fought not to wonder when the darkness would swallow it all.

Dr. Del Paulhus was witty, whip-smart, and a delightful conversationalist. It takes a hearty, essentially optimistic nature to make a career of juggling the dark triad like so many bowling pins. Paulhus had been drawn to the dark triad by his mentor, Dr. Richard Christie, who conceived of Machiavellianism as a distinct constellation of personality traits.

Paulhus took Christie's research a step further and examined the connective tissue—the figurative corpus callosum—between what is human and what is monstrous without disconnecting it and leaving us lopsided.

"Maybe people are good in the same way but can be bad in a variety of ways. They could have an ordinary character, except for some extreme variable. We started creating a taxonomy to separate the bad characteristics and narrowed it down to the triad. We added everyday sadism later, which turned out to be our most novel contribution."

"What distinguishes everyday sadism from plain old sadism?"

"Until now, people isolated sadism as something not normal, the epitome of evil. Instead, we looked at examples of sadism in everyday life: the enjoyment of violent sports, violent media. Sadism is not always the Marquis de Sade–type sexual sadism. We tried to cleave away the different aspects of it. It was exciting to reinterpret what was accepted."

"I get spectrums," I told Paulhus. "The intersection of strangulation and violent video games is a tough one for me. I want to understand the connective tissue. Tell me about the bugs."

I was referring to a famous research experiment Paulhus devised in which the participants could choose from several different unpleasant tasks: cleaning dirty toilets, submerging their hands in ice water for sixty seconds, or grinding three roaches, named Muffin, Tootsie, and Ike, in a coffee grinder specially designed to drop the roaches first (don't worry—Muffin, Tootsie, and Ike survived every torturous decision). Or you could be Igor and help an experimenter grind.

The number of people who chose to grind—with a dramatic slot-machine lever, not just a button—surprised the research team. Overall, 33.8 percent of those studied chose toilet cleaning, 12.7 percent chose pain tolerance, 26.8 percent chose to kill bugs, and 26.8 percent chose to help kill bugs.

The bug slayers had the highest scores on the sadism scale and reported having the most fun.

"We tried to anthropomorphize the roaches by giving them cute little names. It's always a trade-off. It's not that we want to hurt people's self-concepts, but we need to push this as far as it can go to get people to reveal their dark side."

"Are people's self-concepts generally wildly different from their actions?"

"There's a link between self-concept and actual behavior, but there's also a general tendency to try to maintain a positive view of yourself. People get defensive when we use labels. We beat around the bush, ask people the extent to which they agree with statements or are willing to do things or even empathize with characters who do such things. That's an indirect way of revealing their dark side."

Scott yelled up the stairs while I was on the phone. The car had been there for twenty minutes already.

"Can we not with the murder tonight?" asked Scott as we pulled up to the Staples Center for some music awards show. Was it the

VMAs, the Grammys? I'd been so preoccupied I couldn't remember. It was definitely too late to ask.

"People don't want to hear this poison," he said.

"People want to hear nothing but this poison."

"Edited. With a soundtrack."

"How nice for them."

Scott disappeared into the camera flashes while I was herded up a ramp like the one Temple Grandin designed to make cows less panicky when led to slaughter. There were band wives, hangers-on, a few moms of some artists either really rap or really country, and K-pop girl band boyfriends, who I suspected were actually the K-pop boy band boyfriends. I had a smaller notebook for evening bags.

It was the Grammys. Demented or decadent as the scene around me may have been, it was also worthy of close attention. But I had a hoard of impatient murdered sex workers lurking over my shoulder, and I didn't have a thousand pairs of eyes. I had to choose. I chose to take notes on sadism, not K-pop. Anyone who made a run for the bar faced the wrath of the wife wranglers. I scoped the exits.

"OMG, Zendaya!"

Every head turned. I couldn't believe people still fell for that one. In five minutes, I was at the bar. A friend of a friend put a glass of wine in my hand and asked what I was writing down.

"Observations about everyday sadism. Not sexual sadism, not serial killer sadism. You know what I mean? Like, casual sadism. What does that mean to you?"

"We met before at Mark's party. You're that writer. I invented *The Bachelor*."

I laughed.

"What? I did."

I could think of almost nothing as casually sadistic as treating our fundamental desire to be loved and seen as a competitive sport. I was just surprised the creator didn't get the joke.

I crossed to the other side of the room to say hi to a "crossover" porn star, a cultural icon with an empire of her own. I asked her what she thought about everyday sadism.

"*Which* kind of sadism?"

"Okay, say, would you want your daughter in porn?"

"I'd kill myself."

I was headed to our seats when my phone buzzed. It was Holland. I ducked behind a column.

"We found her," he said. "Her name was Agatha White Buffalo. Omaha. 1974. Naked and upside down in a barrel, behind a tannery. Like you said."

"You really got her?"

"Yes, Jillian," he said, letting it land slowly, with what I like to think of as the patience of a guy who still remembered what it was like to hear those words for the first time. "We really did."

29

THE PEOPLE OF THE STATE OF CALIFORNIA V. SAMUEL LITTLE: PATTERN EVIDENCE

LOS ANGELES, CALIFORNIA
AUGUST 18, 2014

In the weeks before the trial, Mitzi Roberts's essential witnesses lobbed question after question at her, sometimes at midnight, punctuated with sobs.

In Pascagoula, Hilda Nelson and Leila McClain tried on hats. Nelson wondered what was proper in a Los Angeles courthouse, in a Los Angeles anywhere.

McClain said, "I am the queen of Antarctica if that's where I got to go. I ain't changing."

In Portland, Laurie Barros practiced chin up, don't cry. She practiced looking that piece of human garbage in the eye, practiced the mind scripts suggested by her therapist to banish the thought loops.

Don't think about the attack. Don't think about the heart attack, the drugs, the getting clean, the loves who were terrible at love. The kids, the kids, the kids.

Barros told Roberts she had superglued her tears down this time.

Prepping a trial was like running a bucket brigade of meticulously labeled chains of evidence while juggling witnesses with your feet. Trials were a bitch.

The prosecution's solid team had completed their homework. Opposing counsel usually trembled at the paperwork deputy district attorney Beth Silverman hurled at them, but Michael Pentz was a good lawyer, worthy adversary, all that, no love lost between them. She'd win with what she had. He'd just make it a pain in her ass.

The real hurdle, the only thing she'd been truly worried about, had been the admission of the pattern evidence. The court had excluded four cases, but she had her three living, breathing, talking survivors who would take the stand and the cops who caught Sam in the act with Tonya Jackson.

Mike Pentz defended capital cases from the Los Angeles County Public Defender's Office on the eighth floor of the Clara Shortridge Foltz Criminal Justice Center on West Temple Street. It overlooked a patch of green where the pastel multicolored benches and chairs now mostly provided brief respite for what the cops liked to call urban campers. The staggering numbers of LA's homeless community grew in proportion and pace with the live/work lofts going up all around.

Pentz had once been a kid who struggled—an urban camper himself—decades before. It gave him the kind of supercharged compassion it took to sit next to a lot of shitbirds and know even the worst shitbird had a story. Pentz was handsome, with careworn blue eyes and a beard showing the first hints of gray. He was a surfing, sun-kissed sharp dresser.

Pentz was a true believer. When the presumption of innocence is your motivating belief, you're in for a ride.

On the morning of August 18, 2014, twenty-five years and four days from when Audrey Nelson's body was found in a dumpster, Pentz sat in the Superior Court of California, Los Angeles County, next to a wheelchair-ridden Samuel Little, who faced multiple murder charges with special circumstances. As Judge George G. Lomeli had said during the pretrial hearings, the *People of the State of California v. Samuel Little, a.k.a. Samuel McDowell* was an important case but straightforward.

Across the aisle sat Silverman. Pentz didn't think her vitriol belonged in a courtroom.

Silverman's world was one of good guys and bad guys. Anyone at the other table was the bad guy, even the lawyers. Especially the lawyers.

Silverman had gotten her witnesses admitted, with limitations, to establish a behavioral pattern. Pentz had the admission of third-party culpability evidence—a mark on Audrey Nelson's neck that could have been made by a ring or a belt buckle. Nelson' boyfriend, Jack West, had regularly beaten the shit out of her, lied to the police, and wore a ring. A shoe print found next to Guadalupe Apodaca's body matched a scumbag named McLaughlin she ran around with and with whom she was last seen alive. His brother told the police he did it. It was what Pentz had to work with.

White-haired, in a wrinkled light-blue shirt. Sam showed up nonchalant, glassy-eyed. Pentz found him surprisingly personable when they'd met before the trial, different from this dissociated flat stare. Sam perked up when Silverman opened, leaning in to comment not on her statement but on her ass.

"Don't stare," said Pentz.

Sam leaned in again to complain about the detective sitting at the prosecution table, arms crossed, pressed gray suit. Bitch—she was the one who called him a rapist. A bowl of peanut M&Ms sat next to the stacks of paper in front of Mitzi Roberts.

"Don't engage. She'll try and get to you."

"This going to feel like forever no matter what. This Jew slut here just getting going."

SILVERMAN: These three cases, you're going to hear them
referred to as cold cases. They're the cold case murders
of Carol Alford, who was 41 years old at the time of her
death; Audrey Nelson, who was 35 years old when she
was murdered; and Guadalupe Apodaca, who was 46
years old at the time of her death.

You're going to learn throughout the course of this
trial that the victims in this case were women who had
lost their way. They were women who were troubled,
women who perhaps had drug addictions, women who
resorted perhaps to prostitution in order to support their
drug habits. You're going to hear that because of these
things, because of the lifestyle that they were engaged in,
that it made them particularly vulnerable, that it made
them easy targets for a calculated killer who was looking
to prey on easy targets.

Silverman always led with the sticky stuff. She gave it to the jury
straight. Let the years of judgments and assumptions cycle through
them for a bit—those very judgments meant to be somehow magi-
cally set aside the minute a person stepped into a jury box. As if wood
paneling walled out bias.

Present in the audience were a few reporters, scattered clusters of
family members.

Silverman laid out the blueprint of Sam's killings, broke down the

DNA science, and talked about the Cold Case Special Section. She addressed the importance of evolving DNA science to cold cases in general.

Silverman talked with her hands as if already physically pushing the case to its conclusion from the starting line. She wove together story and science.

DNA was Silverman's magic bullet, the great equalizer. As a prosecutor, she was taught to represent not the victims but the community. Silverman knew differently. She was there for the victims. Sometimes she was the only one, with DNA her only eyewitness.

> SILVERMAN: What you're going to hear is DNA revolutionized police work in this country.

Silverman broke down the three murders sequentially, explained the witnesses who would be called, demystified the DNA analysts. She didn't want the jury getting the thousand-yard stare. She established an MO. A pattern. A story.

> SILVERMAN: The first victim is Carol Alford. Her body was found on July 13 of 1987, in an alley that you can see here in this photograph to the rear of 848 East 27th Street, in South Los Angeles. She was nude except for a blue t-shirt that was pulled up over her bra.
>
>   And here is where the circumstances are going to repeat themselves:

1. She's not wearing any type of underwear, and no underwear was found at the crime scene or in the vicinity.

2. She's not wearing any pants or skirt or shorts, no undergarments at all, and none of those were found anywhere in the vicinity of this crime scene.

3. There was no identification or personal belongings.

4. There were drag marks in the dirt that were leading up to her body, indicating that this is what is referred to sometimes as a "body dump." What that means is that she was likely murdered at one location, and then transported and dumped at a second location.

Sam yawned as Silverman talked about chains and stains and wet brains. He perked up at the mention of strangulation but just as quickly slumped back into a snarl when Silverman said "blunt-force trauma."

> SILVERMAN: You'll also learn about the strangulation process, in terms of the amount of force that has to be applied to the neck; the fact that the pressure to the neck has to be kept constant, otherwise the person will regain consciousness; and how long it takes for someone to lose consciousness with constant pressure to the neck; as well as how long you have to apply constant pressure of a certain amount to the neck before the person will expire. It's not a quick dying process.

She then went on to establish the pattern she'd repeat over and over again throughout the trial:

SILVERMAN: All of the victims, as I mentioned, were vulnerable targets.

1. All of them, as you can see from the photographs, were left undressed from the waist down, which is, of course, suggestive of sexual assault.

2. No identification was found at the crime scene for any of these victims.

3. No pants or underwear was left, a skirt, bottom, anything of the sort.

4. All of them were strangled to death. All of them appeared to be manual strangulation.

5. All of them had cocaine in their system at the time of autopsy.

6. All of them appeared to be body dumps, in isolated locations.

Silverman told the jury what to expect from the surviving victims. The dead victims could not talk, but the living ones could testify to Samuel Little's violent behavior. Roberts had told the victims day after day they'd be taking their power back, using their voices for the voiceless.

SILVERMAN: Now, the charges in this case. This won't be complicated. It's the charge of murder.

While DNA was admittedly a sea change for the criminal justice system, Pentz didn't believe in magic bullets. DNA fingerprinting was a profound forensic tool but not a substitute for critical thinking or an excuse to stop thinking, period. He acknowledged the horrors of the crimes, the emotions and anger they provoked, but brought it back to the evidence being circumstantial, brought it back to the possible third parties.

PENTZ: You're going to hear an instruction, and by now
        you probably know, the statements that I make to you,
        and all of the statements that the prosecutor just made to
        you, are simply not evidence.
            The only thing that you're asked to do as jurors is to
        hear what is said on that witness stand, and to review the
        documents that are actually placed in your hands as part
        of the evidence.
            Much of the evidence you're going to hear in this
        case, just like the bulk of the statement that you just
        heard from counsel, will be about incidents that have
        nothing to do with the charges Mr. Little faces.

Roberts stepped out to take a call from Tim Marcia. Leila McClain sobbed into his phone. From what Roberts could discern, a black-and-white had arrived for them at the airport.

McClain had pitched a hissy. She wasn't getting in that fucking thing, no way. They out of their damn minds? Marcia had gone to meet them at the airport to do damage control.

Turned out the orca had been the least of it. While the cops and professional witnesses were at the Doubletree getting a complimentary warm cookie, the DA had drop-kicked McClain, Nelson, and Barros into a shithole meth den hotel called the Kawada. The hallways smelled of stale smoke, the bedspreads were stained, the carpets blackened with burns.

"I have not been a whore for years, and I have never felt more like a whore."

"Bowlegs," said Roberts. "Take a breath, and put Tim on the fucking phone."

Roberts told him to take them to the Doubletree with everyone else, and then she called Gary Hearnsberger, the head deputy at the district attorney's office, himself and swore to almost beat Bowlegs.

"You're making my Black victims stay at the fucking Kawada? This is fucking bullshit!"

He finally conceded when she put it that way.

The next day, when McClain went in for her pretrial interview, Hearnsberger popped in to say he was real sorry. He didn't know the Kawada was a dump.

"You ever heard that saying birds of a feather?" McClain asked him. "That sure the hell ain't my nest."

30

THE SPACE COWBOY

DECATUR, TEXAS
OCTOBER 2018

Sam sometimes called Texas Ranger James Holland the space cowboy, which I thought was funny, because Holland didn't conform to my Steve Miller Band karaoke idea of that image: he was not a joker or a smoker, and he was certainly not a midnight toker. I know, because I asked him. By the time I was taking his calls at midnight, I was almost always high.

"You on that grass again?" he asked. "Why not be high on life, sister?"

"Why do you talk like a fed at Woodstock?"

The space cowboy surprised me. I never trusted him nor fooled myself into thinking he had my best interests at heart. He called once in a while to confirm an odd detail with my notes, and sometimes that detail would be the missing puzzle piece or simply corroboration.

"Did Little mention what kind of job Sarah Brown had?"

"She was in a white uniform, too short for a nurse."

"Roger that."

I trudged along with my research. Two weeks later, there she was on the news: Sarah Brown from New Orleans, in a waitress uniform, smudged as if she had gotten off work. Sarah, who had almost made it to the porchlight on the other side of the field.

My feelings about the space cowboy fluctuated by the day. He didn't want me around, which made him hard to like. Nevertheless, I was intrigued by this bold enterprise. He played it straight, but it was a wild idea, and why go through the trouble? Was he an adrenaline junkie hung up on polishing the Cinco Peso iconic Texas Ranger badge?

"I would rather you accept my thank-you and go away," he said one night.

"I want a story, not a thank-you. Are those mother-of-pearl handles on your pistol?"

I can usually distract a man by asking about his gun.

Holland replied, "I'll quote the great General George Patton, who thrashed a reporter in public for the same question..."

We both waited out the pause. Was I supposed to set myself up for the forthcoming burn?

"What did the Great Patton say?"

"'Son, only a pimp in a Louisiana whorehouse carries pearl-handled revolvers.'"

"So that's a yes?"

"Ivory. 1911."

"Roger that."

I was a reporter who had basically been sworn to secrecy by the FBI, the DOJ, the Texas Rangers, and the LAPD about a huge story I was sitting on. No pressure. Was I doing the right thing?

They promised me the first interviews. When the story broke, it would be all over the place. I had the jump, but I also agreed to keep a sock in it, and that's a gamble. The possibility of seeing justice done was worth both the risk and the wait, no matter how agonizing.

On September 23, 2018, the Texas Ranger jet took off from Lancaster Airport, extraditing Sam to be tried for the 1994 murder of Denise Brothers, for which he had been indicted by a grand jury in Odessa, Texas. The Wise County Detention Center would be his home, where he would await his hearing while hopefully (you never really know with a psychopath) giving a series of historic confessions.

I followed from afar as Holland methodically reached out to detectives with promising cold cases from far-flung jurisdictions that could potentially match Sam's confessions. Many jumped on the opportunity and began scouring case files and planning their trips.

I thought Sam was gone forever, which was both a frustration and a relief. There went my primary story source. I had hundreds of hours of interviews, stacks of paintings and letters, and interviews with original detectives, DAs, living victims, family members, and his niece. I just needed a thorough interview with Holland, Angela Williamson, and Christie Palazzolo, and I would have everything I needed for the *New York* magazine article.

I knew LAPD Detectives Mitzi Roberts and Tim Marcia, along with DDA Beth Silverman, had been promised first crack at Sam in Wise County. They were already on their way with binders of cold cases they had long thought might be Sam's. They were only the first in the long line of detectives and DAs who would queue up over the next month and a half. Drawing materials were stacked in the middle of the interview room table.

Some of the drawings Sam sent me were of his victims. Others were Tupac, Madonna, Condoleezza Rice (under which he wrote: MY DREAM), Toni Braxton, a drooling baby surrounded by aliens, a blue dead girl, Cleopatra, a skeleton in a soldier's helmet. Some were on legal paper, some on blank paper, some painted on fabric. Some featured text like *I OWN HER* or *MARTHA KNOXVILLE* or even a date, but the date was when he drew them, not when he killed them.

Palazzolo and Williamson would be in Wise County for the first week, returning promptly to Quantico to launch a nationwide media campaign that included Sam's drawings. The federal government rolled their eyes when my name came up. I talked in a kitten voice to a killer, sang him lullabies, wore fishnets. What kind of reporter does that?

I do almost only wear Capezio professional fishnets for dancers, with a reinforced toe and back seam. I've been wearing the same ones, different sizes, since I started tap class at the age of seven. They cost twenty-five dollars, are made of rubber, and work better than Spanx. I've owned my lucky set for over ten years. Also, you only ever need Aqua Net—expensive cosmetics are made in the same factories in China as the ones at Rite Aid. Don't wear high heels on a soggy lawn. Never pay retail. Keep your good jewelry sewn into a coat lining in case you ever have to grab the coat and run. Survivors have a million tips.

Tension between law enforcement and media is a classic, and my exchanges with federal and local law enforcement officials varied widely. The tight group circling their wagons around Sam were a tough crowd. We all had personal and career stakes. We were all true believers. We all had kids and mortgages. I did the Big Daddy talk, they did the DNA. I asked the odd questions, they analyzed data to which I had no access. The FBI classically thought of the free press as a bullhorn for their scripts. I believed myself to be a witness, not a propaganda slinger. Journalists liaise between the cloistered law enforcement community and the public they're sworn to protect and serve, whether in fishnets or fatigues. I picked at the bones they threw me for any bit of information.

Detective Tim Marcia was ready to take his first crack at Sam in

Wise County, except he never got in the room. Holland told Sam the LAPD was there to talk to him. Sam faced the camera. He pounded a fist on the table, reared up, and spat.

"Those dogs. I ain't saying shit. This is bullshit. Those lying bastards. Fucking cops. Lying whores. They think I did it so they set me up. They know I did it so they set me up. It was the Mexican Mafia killed that bitch. I can't even pronounce her name."

Holland shifted in his chair, the ivory handle of his pistol a few inches farther from the grandpa who turned on a dime into a cobra.

Sam demanded letters from each DA, ensuring him they wouldn't seek death if he confessed. Los Angeles hadn't brought one. Sam sent them scrambling and went back to his cell. Los Angeles was the centerpiece of Sam's murderous career. If Holland lost LA, he lost double digits.

Sam sulked until Holland coaxed him back into the windowless white box with fluorescent lights, dropped ceilings, cameras in the corners, a table pushed against the wall.

"You better, brother? You okay now?"

Holland told him the LA detectives had gotten so pissed they'd gone home.

"They gone home?" Sam sounded disappointed.

Back in his cell, he asked for an eraser. The deputy thought he said a razor.

"I need an eraser because I'm trying to draw that little girl in the bathtub for them."

In the end, Sam calmed down, or got ramped up, hard to tell. In any case, he started talking, but by that time, Holland had already told him LA had gone home.

The map of Los Angeles is an expansive puzzle, broken into

jagged bites. There are intersections in South LA with a separate jurisdiction for each corner. This is not a system that works well for solving serial murders. ViCAP was a start, but without some kind of comprehensive, mandated, multijurisdictional database with federal resources allocated for support, it was hit or miss.

There is no perfect interview, but with patience, you can usually get a basic understanding of what most people are about and what they're hiding. Psychopaths are different. Everything is out there; everything is hiding. You will always be the pinball, never the lever. If you're any good at it, you go in knowing you're the one being played, but that doesn't mean you can't get your answers. If you excel at it, you may find you have a higher score than most on the Hare Psychopathy Checklist.

Establishing the ratio of truth to lies is an electric kind of tight-rope. You get a patter going: nicknames, code words, special songs, in-jokes, secrets. This shared language keeps you connected to a person essentially incapable of connection. It's easy to get locked inside your own invention before you fully understand it. The LAPD and DA's office didn't share the space cowboy's ethos.

Holland back-slapped Sam in the interview room. Holland hugged him.

No, shit? You did, man?

Who's the fattest bitch you ever killed? Who was the ugliest?

I love you, brother.

You're the boss. You're in charge. None of this happens without you.

I did the same, in my way. I didn't judge it. You can't understand a transactional dynamic from the other room. The silences are darker than the slurs and slags.

Silverman did not share my sympathy for role-play. She'd spent too much time with autopsy photos of broken bodies and didn't appreciate Holland's rough rapport. She fought every day for victims dismissed because of these exact bro tropes. How do you come back from the bro zone? How do you humanize victims you've torn apart?

I knew the Rangers took Sam for joy rides in their trucks, to "look for victims." They stopped at every traffic light to comment on every ass on every corner. They fed him McDonald's pancake breakfasts.

I knew Sam a little by then. What's the point of living a movie no one gets to see? His moment had arrived.

Did Holland and Roberts and the FBI and the rest of them really think he was going to give up a lifetime of secrets for a lousy milkshake and a plane ride? I pulled over a bucket of popcorn and waited for the inevitable drama when detective ego, cowboy ego, federal government ego, lawyer ego, and serial killer ego started playing bumper cars. I hoped the victims wouldn't wind up under the wheels.

When I got calls from Sam from Texas, he was babbling, paranoid, lucid, elated, annoyed, confused, angry, docile. He asked after my kids' soccer games, my dogs, my meatloaf. He told me he was going to eat my lips off my face, described murder with giggling glee. He demanded kissy noises and songs and supplications, all while I was on speaker phone with the Texas Rangers.

Night after night, I talked an agitated psychopath down from a paranoid rant. I flattered, cajoled, and calmed him. I gave him a positive self-concept, let him know he was not abandoned or alone. I shot all my own ego straight down into my reinforced fishnet heels and sang "Misty" for the Texas Rangers.

"You're a little flat on the bridge," Scott noted as he passed the door of my office. The man in the background on the other end laughed. It's a tough bridge.

"Mr. Sam? I am so proud of you. You are doing amazing! You are so important. It means so much to me that you're being honest. You're a hero. You're doing God's work. I love, love, love you, mwah, mwah, mwah."

At the end of the second day of watching the cowboy interview the monster, Silverman snapped.

"I can't stand here and watch you talk about victims like this. *You* sound like a monster. These girls deserve this? Cheering him on? What about when their families have to watch this? Is this some numbers game to you?"

When Marcia, Roberts, and Silverman boarded the plane, they held a stack of Sam's Los Angeles confessions, but Holland had done all the interviews, and he didn't know the twists and turns of LA. In all, they had six hours of recordings, possibly seventeen murder confessions, and several drawings.

Cold cases in major urban centers are especially challenging. LAPD detectives were looking not for one murder in a small town in Georgia but between fifteen and twenty in a five-to-ten-year time frame in a city where hundreds of women were murdered with a similar MO. These were going to be difficult confessions to match with their famously strict investigative standards and few concrete, verifiable facts.

———

During the confessions, Holland told me, "Don't ask Sammy about the murders right now. Keep it positive. Don't contaminate the investigation. Trust the law, trust the FBI, trust me."

In exchange, I got cursory, general reports.

I called Holland as I approached the donut store one Saturday morning. My children would not eat eggs because it was donut

Saturday. I'd been up until 2:00 writing the night before. I was so far behind, exhausted, and I hated every ungrateful asshole with a Y chromosome I'd ever encountered.

I tapped my fingers on the steering wheel. "Just thinking..."

"You? Never *just* anything."

"Who else am I supposed to talk to about this?"

I'd told him the week before I planned to visit Odessa to research the Denise Brothers case and interview her family.

"You still planning to come to Texas?" he asked.

"Yes."

"If you do come, would you want to see Sammy?"

"Of course."

Dallas was about five hours from Odessa. I'd already booked my tickets to Dallas.

I suspected Holland would be sick to death of Sam by then. All those hours? It seemed about time for Sam to start throwing fits, wanting more, wanting better, demanding his journalist. If not, I had a long drive to Odessa.

I asked Holland how it was going.

He said, "What's that quote? 'People sleep peaceably in their beds at night only because rough men stand ready to do violence on their behalf.' Sumpin' like that."

"Sorkin?"

"Orwell."

I looked it up later. The quote is loosely associated with Orwell but generally attributed to a film reviewer, though no one can say for sure. It's often misquoted and misattributed, but the sentiment—crystal.

31

THIS IS IT

Drive about forty-five miles north of Dallas as the crow flies, and the city flattens to suburbs before opening onto rolling fields on either side of Highway 380, red-tailed hawks circling above.

Decatur, Texas, established in 1856, is the seat of Wise County, location of its sheriff's department, home of the famed Petrified Wood Gas Station, and namesake of the "Eighter from Decatur," a hard eight roll in craps and a song by western swing legend Bob Wills. In 1949, a Decatur mayor named Sly Hardwick put up two swell midcentury welcome signs with a picture of a hard eight.

THIS IS IT
EIGHTER FROM DECATUR
COUNTY SEAT OF WISE
SURE IT'S IN TEXAS

The day I drove to Wise County in mid-October, I only knew

this from what I'd seen on the town's website, because a freezing rain turned the world around me into a white screen.

I planned to write my article, get some heat going under the story, and be done. I went to Texas for what I thought was my last visit with Sam Little and my only glimpse of the space cowboy in his natural habitat. Sam's future remained a mystery, dependent on the intentions of dozens of district attorneys across the country.

Denise, Rosie, Patricia, Hilda, Audrey, Laurie, Leila, Carol, Lupe, Dorothy, Melissa, Nancy, Melinda, Fredonia…

I fumbled for the windshield wipers, couldn't find shit on the radio, settled on whatever was playing the closest thing to "Dream On," and drove like my grandma toward Decatur with eighteen-wheelers plowing through inches of water on either side of me.

The history of the Texas Rangers was dodgy, if fascinating, and they seemed more of a concept than anything until I talked to detectives in various towns who had been helped by their multijurisdictional capabilities and access to state-of-the-art technology, air support, and serial killer whisperers. As far as I could tell, these days, the Texas Rangers were cowboy cops who rode into town at high noon with a saddlebag full of access to innovative DNA profiling technology and the ability to get your evidence pushed through fast. Public opinion split as to whether they started out as thugs or heroes, largely based on one's ideas about the expansion of the American West. I tried to go in with none of that. Switzerland. I was a witness, not a judge.

I knew the Texas Rangers had a fancy plane. I knew they most definitely did not carry pistols with mother-of-pearl handles. I knew they had Sam. I relished the opportunity to see a world to which I wouldn't normally be granted access.

I couldn't make blanket assumptions based on the fact that the Ranger drove me batshit crazy, with the "no comments" and/or long nonanswers that made you forget your question in the first place. Not that it mattered. Whatever the question, the nonanswer was usually some version of, "Because I'm the best and I do what I want."

Or, "You can't handle the truth." From *A Few Good Men*.

Holland told me he'd only be at the sheriff's station until about five. I'd texted about the weather.

Might still be here at 6. Yell at me.

The lobby of the Marriott was empty at 6:00 p.m. exactly. I called out several times before a woman with a polo shirt and a lazy smile wandered out from the back room.

"Hello. I have a reservation. I'm late. I need a key right away, and I need the jail."

"Mmkaaaay. We'll get that taken care of for you right now, ma'am."

Her long nails clacked as she entered my credit card and ID.

"Oh, and that's the jail," she said, indicating a one-story slumped stone building across the highway with a lower fence than my local high school. "Careful crossing the street though."

Just got here! There in 10?

I rolled on a pair of fishnets, noticed dead moths silhouetted in the light fixtures. I shook my hair, powdered my nose, applied true-blue red, and was out the door in twelve.

Holland had told me a thing or two about his routine with Sammy. I knew he warmed him up every day, spending an hour talking about girls, football, the news, Trump, the Kavanaugh hearings, whatever was on the cover of the *National Enquirer* or *People*. Every day was exactly the same routine. Structure was key.

Holland had learned from the mistakes of a retired ranger named Phil Ryan, three-time Wise County sheriff and something of a friend. Ryan had been the linchpin of serial killer Henry Lee Lucas's false confession debacle. Lucas had also liked to draw.

From what I'd read, Ryan was a craggy, intelligent, retired eccentric who spoke thoughtfully about the case and took responsibility for his errors. If those egregious mistakes hadn't been made and eventually brought to light by journalist Hugh Aynesworth, there would be less scrutiny and reconsideration of the interrogation techniques that encourage confession at any cost, with few checks and balances. The most familiar of these is the Reid technique.

It is perfectly legal for sworn officers of the law in the United States to lie during the course of an interview. The Reid interrogation technique is the one you recognize from TV, and it is still popular in real life. It opens with an accusation of guilt, provides no chance for a response, and references real or imagined evidence while minimizing the seriousness of the crime through sympathy, normalization, and possible moral justifications. It has been known to elicit high numbers of false confessions from people who believe confession is in their best interest and would rather go home already.

Those white Ranger shirts had cycled through a couple of different collar styles since Lucas's famed false confessions. Holland picked up the baton with a new set of forensic tools at his disposal amid a rapidly evolving world of law enforcement and different ideas about checkable facts. I was curious to witness the hybrid that had emerged.

My houndstooth jacket was no match for the freezing sleet. I wiped my nose on my sleeve and made a run for it across the four-lane highway, which Sam no doubt had once driven. An American flag and a Texas flag stood at either side of a sign that read:

WISE COUNTY

LAW ENFORCEMENT CENTER

DECATUR TEXAS

Don't apologize with your body. Don't apologize with your language. It's one of the mental scripts I use before interviews, usually with men. I was five minutes late though. I would apologize for that.

Behind two sets of double doors stood Texas Ranger James B. Holland, Company B, straight backed, hands folded in front of him, tall hat, boots made from some endangered species he'd no doubt wrestled and skinned himself.

I waited, not some city mouse who goes and opens a door for herself.

I also knew the strangeness and possibility of that moment was as good as it was going to get for Holland and me. The glass would melt away, and we'd be just two people who, in an odd bit of synchronicity, had stumbled onto the same monster at the same time.

Different as we may have appeared, we still ran into each other at the dark end of the street. We were in good company at least. Many brilliant minds had been innovators in the field of the psychological aspects of criminal behavior and the value in eliciting an understanding of it. Some of the more celebrated of these include the original "profiler," Dr. Thomas Bond, who gave us Jack the Ripper. William Marston and his wife, Elizabeth Holloway, invented an early prototype of the lie detector and, incidentally, created Wonder Woman. Dr. Dorothy Lewis, a pioneering forensic psychologist, believed sexually motivated serial criminals all suffered a version of dissociative identity disorder. John Douglas and Robert Ressler helped start the FBI's Behavioral Science Unit, which now houses ViCAP. Before Sam Little came along, the two special agents were credited with nailing the nation's most prolific serial killer: Gary Ridgway, the Green River Killer.

Ridgway strangled forty-nine prostitutes, manually or with ligatures. Ted Bundy suggested to Ressler that Ridgway would likely return to the bodies. The FBI should find a fresh one and stake it out. That was how they caught him.

Stephen Michaud and Hugh Aynesworth conducted a brilliant series of interviews with Bundy in which they got him to talk about his murders in the third person.

As I stepped forward, hailstones crunched under my heels. Holland opened the door and removed his hat.

———

I was used to the prison industrial complex, not a county jail. There was a wall of vending machines that made me crave a Dr Pepper on either side of something that looked like an ATM but was there to put money on the inmates' books. Above it, a TV played Fox News. Living plants were scattered about, and a table with a tasteful seasonal centerpiece displayed pamphlets for meth and opioid addiction, domestic violence, an annual pancake breakfast, a hog contest. A framed cowboy painting hung over the water fountain. From behind bulletproof plexiglass, two women regarded me with bafflement.

Ranger Holland and I stood between the empty rows of plastic chairs. His eyes were shattered navy, his face Hemingway stoic. He filled me in in the most not-filling-me-in way possible.

"Look, he's behind glass because he wants to kill you, and I'm not comfortable with that."

The cowboy was *so* the guy who started sentences with "Look."

"Fair enough."

"Hey," he said. "What do you talk to him about?"

He must have known the answer to this. All my calls from the prison were recorded. I wondered if he wanted to see what I'd say.

"Boxing. His life. My life. My kids. What do you talk to him about?"

"Football, boxing, life. He's someone that you can actually carry on a conversation with. Not like a William Reece or a Shore or someone like that, with the kids and all. Reece. Pure evil. I wanted to kill him myself."

Anthony Shore was responsible for the murder of one woman and three girls between 1986 to 2000, and he became known as the "Tourniquet Killer" because of his use of a ligature with either a toothbrush or bamboo stick to tighten or loosen it. The instrument was similar to a twitch, a tool used to control horses.

Holland told me the confessions were going great, and he'd catch me tomorrow.

"You're not staying?" I asked.

"Me? No."

If it had been me, I'd have stayed and watched for at least a little while. I showed the wide-eyed woman behind the glass my ID.

Holland made a shooing movement toward a green door a few feet away. "Go ahead."

"In here?"

"Keep it upbeat," he said with a double thumbs-up. "Okay? Up. Beat."

I was used to metal detectors, concertina wire, four-story-tall guard towers. In Wise County, I faced a door I could apparently just open.

On the other side of the door was a wall of five windows, each with a telephone beside it and a red stool bolted to the floor. On the far right was the handicapped station, with no stool but space for a wheelchair on both sides. Except I didn't have a wheelchair—or any chair. The phone cord didn't reach, so I had to double over, causing my notebook and photos to spill across the linoleum. Someone made a mistake and cast Lucille Ball in *Silence of the Lambs*. I crouched and gathered my things as a deputy wheeled Sam to the wheelchair window. I did the hand on the glass thing. He drummed his fingernails on it, then pointed at me, pressing the LEGO-sized buttons on his phone over and over. He began to cuss and get frustrated. You don't want that.

I wrote on my pad and held it to the glass.

Hang on. I'll get someone.

I walked out, hollered for the deputy, grabbed a chair on my way back in. I was practically a local.

While we waited, we sat in silence and looked at each other. It was like one of those acting exercises designed to make you uncomfortable, except no one was acting. I smiled and silently prayed—any old prayer I could think of. I even made up one of my own. Sam couldn't hurt me. He was behind glass.

I wrote in my notebook and held it to the glass.

arraignment?

He nodded.

no more milkshakes?

He laughed. Holland brought him milkshakes. Sam sometimes called me his milkshake.

I took out the McDowell family photos I'd gathered from the linoleum floor and held them to the glass one by one. Fanny and Henry. Paul, Sylvia, Jeminah.

He was shocked and delighted. I showed him photos I'd taken of the main drag and lakefront of Lorain. I didn't show him the photos of Betty and Inez and me. He didn't get to see those.

A deputy with forehead acne helped Sam figure out again how to enter the PIN as my beta blocker wore off.

Perv Grandpa, Three-Card Monte, Snake Monster.

He was in Perv Grandpa mode. He wanted to talk all about me and him, him and me, him and Jimmy, me and Jimmy, his new friend Detective Kelly from Cincinnati, the detectives from Miami who brought him oranges. The detectives from Kentucky who brought him BBQ. He wanted me to be sure to understand they were all so thankful to him. Everyone told him how great his art was. They wouldn't know any of this if it hadn't been for him.

He'd been having a ball talking about himself, expressing remorse, being right with his creator, being an artist, being a star. Sam's genuine empathy was only for himself. He lamented that God and the world conspired to give him these desires, but what could he do?

"God gave me a twisted understanding. The basic reason for sex is life, so I got hurt or changed one way or another, and it got tangled with death. No one has the right to judge me but God."

"You Tupac now?"

The call dropped mid joke.

A Hebrew prayer floated somewhere in the back of my memory like a half-remembered nursery rhyme.

Baruch dayan torat ehmet.

God is the one true judge.

"I'm trying to tell you something," he yelled. I could hear him, but just barely. "I don't get angry at girls. Unless they have a very poor disposition on life."

Who do you get angry at? I wrote on my pad.

"Bullies," he yelled, his eyes cartoon pinwheels.

He figured the phone out, picked up the handle, and dialed.

I held my final photo to the glass. "Do you know who this is?"

"Is it? Is that *Gloria Ferry*? How did you get this?"

"*Inside Detective*, 1954. Tell me about Denise."

"Who?"

"Denise. Odessa."

"It wasn't the strangling. It was the helplessness in the face, the desperation. Let loose and cry in my arms. That's all I wanted. Cry with me."

"That sounds like you must have been lonely."

"Hungry. I didn't ask to be born liking cake."

32

EIGHTER FROM DECATUR

WISE COUNTY LAW ENFORCEMENT CENTER, DECATUR, TEXAS
OCTOBER 2018, DAY 2

At the center of the town square in Decatur, Texas, population 6,482, stands a red granite Victorian courthouse with terra-cotta ornamentation, a spire, and a bell tower.

On the surrounding streets, clusters of Victorians gave way to neat seventies brick boxes or gated communities of matching stone McMansions. The usual big-box chains and drive-throughs hugged the edges of the highway. Just a few blocks south, horses grazed in bucolic fields, turned their heads toward the wind, and tossed their manes.

My best trick in a strange town: buy something. Walk into any shop, let someone help you, and then spend money. You might leave with not just a new throw pillow but also town gossip, ghost stories, the best restaurant around, the number of someone to call if you need an emergency manicure on a Sunday.

In Decatur, the cowboy hat shop seemed a logical place to start. I'd grab some cute hats for the boys. Biggar Hat Store wasn't exactly a store full of cute hats. It was more like Coco Chanel collided with the mayor of Deadwood an hour north of Dallas. Biggar's was a family business that custom-made felt and straw hats by hand. They were out of my price range at that exact moment, but the one in turquoise felt is still on my birthday wish list. The guys working there were sympathetic to my plight and proud of the shop. They not only scrounged up a couple of kid hats but also gave me a tour of where they hand-made the good stuff, with brass steampunk equipment that looked like if you turned the dial the right way, you got a beautiful hat, but the wrong way, you conjured an ancient demon. A shop called 287 down the street had great jewelry, A-game throw pillows, and an owner who used to live an hour away from my house in LA.

I spend money in places I'm trying to understand not just as a conversation starter but because money is a big piece of understanding. I also know you don't get anything for free. If you want to understand the cash value of our time on this planet, spend months on end hearing about the final breaths of prostitute after prostitute.

By the time I got to the coffee shop, I was so hungry I practically chopped and snorted the signature grilled cheese while I locked eyes with a mounted deer head in a baseball cap above the espresso machine. Whimsical hand-painted western murals covered the walls. The bearded barista could have been from Williamsburg. I did the last of my local research, counting the minutes until I'd have to cut bait on getting the Holland interview, stop reading about the Great Hanging at Gainesville in 1871, and head back to DFW.

I spent my last few minutes studying the entrance requirements for the Wise County Hog Contest on the corkboard by the bathrooms. It ran throughout the month of February and had an elaborate list of rules, including the following highlights:

DO NOT GUT THE HOGS! WEIGHT WILL BE HOG AS A WHOLE!

  $20 Side Pot on the Longest Cutter—Winner Takes All

Polygraph will be given in order to receive prize money. The polygraph fee will come out of the winnings! If there is any discrepancy in the polygraph, there will be a vote between the 2 coordinators of the contest, a local game warden, and an outside party of what will be done.

  NO BS!!! We don't want to hear drama about other teams and bickering back and forth.

  If you have legitimate proof a team is cheating or a possibility, please let us know, but no need to keep calling every day.

  All late sign ups will be online unless you are not computer savy [sic]!!!

I hadn't come to Decatur to ponder the relative benefits of a polygraph test for a hog contest, though that was an unexpected perk. I'd worked hard prepping the Ranger interview. I was disappointed.

He texted when I was already a mile down the road.

Have 10 minutes now.

OMW.

———

The second time I walked into the Wise County Law Enforcement Center, they were used to me. A woman in leggings and Reeboks led me to a conference room where Holland sat at the head of a long table, back to the door. I'd never known a detective, criminal, or gambler other than Holland who sat with their back to the door.

Holland joined the Texas Department of Public Safety in 1995, worked as a highway patrol trooper, served as a security detail for

Texas governor George W. Bush during his campaign for president, and was the state criminal interdiction coordinator and El Paso Intelligence Center instructor for the DEA.

The list alone made me need an edible.

He'd told me he was the one who had made sure all that grass I smoked wasn't soaked in gasoline.

You're welcome, young lady.

Along the way, with all the work with the TX DPS, he'd also met Beyoncé, Chuck Norris, and Destiny's Child before pulling on his Ranger boots in 2007.

Dazzle camouflage was used on certain battleships during both world wars, vessels painted with complex patterns of geometric shapes in contrasting colors, the art of war. By making no attempt to blend into the sea and sky around them, dazzle-painted ships strategically challenged the enemy's ability to estimate a target's range, speed, and direction, causing them to take a poor firing position.

While you were being dazzled by the hat, this cowboy would out-draw you, seize your narcotics, get you to confess, and then make you sell your mother up the river. The last part was just for fun.

Furthermore, he'd figured out how to get away with doing all that and still manage to be a respectable member of society. *Helluva guy* was what nearly everyone I talked to said about him. Holland was collecting a gallery wall of award plaques, including the 2017 Texas Department of Public Safety Officers Association Peace Officer of the Year Award and the Governor Clements Award for Career Excellence.

I thanked him for giving me some time.

"Not a problem. I find the way you think entertaining."

That was probably true. He was anything but a boring guy. But he was a former DEA agent who talked like a square. His enjoyment of extreme sports didn't necessarily make him a fan of "entertaining" thinkers.

Holland worked with the Texas Ranger Unsolved Crimes Investigation Program. Created in 2001, according to the Texas DPS website, "The program's primary objective is to provide Texas law enforcement agencies with a process for investigating unsolved murders or what appear to be serial or linked criminal transactions. Since there is no statute of limitations on the offense of murder, the state has the moral and statutory obligation to pursue these cases to a successful resolution; or until no other lead is viable."

Holland was the lead investigator or assisted the detectives on cases that screamed "psycho." Extra credit for sexually motivated serial killers, ritual murder, strangulation, and dismemberment. The sick, sexual, gruesome, unimaginable shit that gives you nightmares is his wheelhouse. How many people do you meet in life with the same niche interests?

Some of Holland's more notable cases include the following:

- Wallace Bowman Jr., convicted of murder/arson for the deaths of a couple he robbed and set on fire.
- William Lewis Reece, who killed four teenage girls. It took two backhoes to dig their bodies from the Texas killing fields. On the news clips, you can spot Holland next to the not-so-shallow graves.
- Donald Wright, who confessed to three murders but was probably good for more. He killed both alone and in tandem with his incestuous male cousin.
- Richard Keiper, a murderer to whom Holland lied about

DNA evidence in the process of obtaining his confession. This forty-seven-year-old Pennsylvania case was the second oldest adjudicated cold case in the United States.

- Charles Bryant, who dismembered a college student and carved out her heart.
- White supremacist gang members who conspired to kill a prison chief in Colorado.
- Charles Hicks, who kept hands in his walls.
- The North Texas serial killer, who killed old ladies for their necklaces.

Holland closed the binder in front of him. Beyond the binder was a drawing for me from Sam. Audrey Nelson.

"Sammy said he was hoping you'd wear a black dress, so I was sure it was going to go well last night. Oh, and he wants those family pictures."

I took the photos out of my purse and placed them on the table.

"Look, I'm sorry. I've been working around the clock for a month. I told you I'd talk to you, and I keep my promises. I gotta bounce soon because my kid has a game." He pushed the drawing toward me, commenting offhandedly, "I look at these drawings or the confessions, and when we match them, I notice the same thing about them he does. The odd detail."

Holland had grown up just west of Chicago. After he'd graduated from the University of Louisville with his master's in business administration, he got a tech job and wound up doing some work for the governor's Fugitive Task Force in Austin. They goaded him, telling him he should quit that boring shit and come be a trooper.

The pay was ridiculously low, but he applied for the heck of it... and didn't get the job.

A good fight flipped his switch. He applied again, made state trooper, and asked where he could get into the worst stuff. They sent him to Houston, and that hit the spot. He'd moved to Wise County when it was time to start a family.

We talked about the possibilities and fallibilities of new forensic technologies. He walked me through the Brothers case. I asked about DNA.

"None."

"You don't have any on Brothers?"

"Nothing. Nothing on most of these cases. DNA degrades. There were no rape kits. Old evidence gets lost or damaged or destroyed. Without proving up these confessions, we got nothing. Brothers was a ViCAP match, not DNA."

I was speechless—a rare occurrence. I'd assumed many of these cases had been connected to Sam through CODIS in the same way he'd been connected to the three confirmed Los Angeles cases. It was the other way around—the confessions might point to DNA, if there even was any.

Holland had gone into the first interview with a strong-looking Texas case, an indulgent major, and FBI support behind him. No one does this work alone, but he had spearheaded and implemented the effort on sheer will. Never have I been as grateful for a loquacious mansplain about how to talk to criminals. I recalibrated as he spoke. It was an entirely new approach to cold cases.

"So many investigators fail before they start. You warm people up, take your time. It'd be like sex without foreplay. How long would it take for you to tell your darkest secret?"

"Me? However long it takes to write a book about it."

Note: *the ranger does not appreciate jokes.*

"Christie said you told them to set their watches for an hour and a half to get Sam to start talking. That doesn't seem like much foreplay for serial murder."

Holland was also *so* that guy who asks questions, then answers them.

"So when you're warming him up, how does that look? Someone with this personality, you can't force them; you can't drive them; you can't step on them; you can't push them, because they're going to push back. So you can ask, and then let it be. I gave him time. I said to him, 'Man, secrets are cool. But they're only really cool when you get to tell someone.'"

He leaned back, crossed one brown boot over a khaki knee, and tented his fingers in front of his chest, like he was planning a takeover of Gotham City.

"What makes you good at this?" I asked.

"Trial and error. Tenacity. Rapport. Normal interviewing techniques don't work. I come up with a way to communicate. Why am I good at it? I don't know. I guess it's who I am. It's easy with him, I don't hate Sammy. Reece, Shore…"

Shore was sentenced to death in 2004 and executed by lethal injection on January 18, 2018.

"Did you attend his execution?"

"I was going to, but my son had a game. Couldn't justify it. By state law, a Ranger has to be at every execution. Good friend of mine stationed in Huntsville was there. Been to over a hundred. You should talk to him. I wanted to see Shore die, if that gives you any indication of who he was. If you went to some of these scenes or met some of these perps, you'd have no issue with the death penalty."

"What makes you think I have an issue with the death penalty?"

He tilted his head and waited for the next question.

I asked about the first confessions.

"So day one is truth, day two is *pow*: states, towns, numbers of victims. We left there with thirty or something!"

"Did you believe him?"

"Oh yeah, oh yeah. We'd already hit some that were dead on. I went way out into left field to keep Odessa alive."

Ector County DA Bobby Bland told Holland he wanted absolutely everything before he would decide whether to convene a grand jury. Holland ran it up the flagpole and fast to get the evidence to a Lubbock lab for an M-Vac, or wet vacuum, a DNA collection tool that allows for more DNA to be collected, such as touch DNA or from porous surfaces. It's a valuable tool for giving cold cases a second chance. Just not Denise's.

"Lubbock lab, end of the day, we didn't get shit: fingernails, panties, nothing. DA still not sold—doesn't mean shit until we prove it up. The whole area is totally different today. I got a Texas Ranger in Odessa to find the original VCR tape of the crime scene. We found this rail—this rail he perfectly describes in the confession. The DA goes for it. I'm getting ready to head to Odessa in my own truck, and my dad is going through this chemo. He's sitting there looking a little depressed. I said, 'You want to come to Odessa?' Now, that's a shit drive. He's a quiet guy, hasn't been feeling well. He thinks about it, nods his head. He rides with me and waits around the corner, reading at a diner."

Holland described watching a woman on the grand jury cry when faced with the Brothers crime scene photos and being struck for the first time by the emotional impact of the case.

"I'm black and white, logical, task oriented. By the time I meet the victims, they're inanimate. If it's your family member? You want the cold-hearted SOB who has a task at the end of the day. You're doing them no service by praying with them and crying over the grave. They want the guy, or gal, who's going to go out there and work with blinders. Who's not affected by this horrible crime or the pain the families go through. To be effective, to continue to do what homicide investigators do, you have to wall it off."

"How does it affect your relationships?"

"I try not to let it affect anything. I'm the garbage man. I'm the one who deals with what other people don't want to deal with. People can read about it in generalities and know about it, but do they ever understand it? No. I don't think you want them to. It's not for them. Are you going to go home and tell your kids about how Sam talks about killing someone? It's not a conversation piece, y'know. It's not healthy."

A silver fox of a cowboy with a pressed pink shirt and checked tie stood by the water cooler outside the windows of the conference room and gave me a hard once-over. I guessed he was the boss.

"After they indicted, I talked the whole time in the car. I got to Abilene; I couldn't even eat. Warrant, extradition, California timeline. Let's go. There's the yin and yang—here's my dad sick, and here's Little on the horizon." He clapped his hands together, "Okay, I really gotta go."

I didn't know the guy's dad, but I know as a parent, you give so many speeches about the importance of losing gracefully. It is important. Winning is more fun. I bet it was cool for Holland's dad to see his kid win.

"So what do you think about families seeing the recordings later? When you ask him, who's the ugliest bitch he ever killed? Who's the girl with the fattest ass? When you write their profession down as ho and go all 'no shit? no way!' and all that?"

"I think they'll be grateful it got solved. I'm an athlete. I know how to talk like that. He wants me to talk like that. People who talk to him straight, he's bored. Next? I tell these investigators, don't go in there all thinking he's doing it for the families or he has remorse. He isn't and he doesn't. He's having fun."

"He said you think I talk too much, and you prefer girls with great big knockers."

"Got ya thinking, didn't it? Got you a little bit mad. You've been sitting here the whole time waiting to bring up the great big knockers. He got ya."

"He got me, but you said it."

"What's that quote about rough men?" he asked.

"People sleep peaceably in their beds at night only because rough men stand ready to do violence on their behalf? That one?"

"Close."

I shook hands with the watercooler silver fox on my way out.

"It's a pleasure to meet you, ma'am. Lane Akin, sheriff of Wise County."

Hey now, I was a ma'am, not a young lady. The sheriff gave me a wink that made me blush. The ethos of the Texas Rangers probably belonged in a museum. They weren't unsophisticated or unaware of that. They didn't find me surprising after three minutes. They wished I wasn't there, but I was.

Holland kicked around an iconography that essentially justified violent colonialism. Then again, I couldn't let go of a garage-wall-length closet of pristine burlesque costumes I hadn't looked at in fifteen years.

Some selves are a lot to let go of.

33

THE RIOTS

LOS ANGELES, CALIFORNIA
MAY 1992

Diane, Sarah, Carolyn, Mary, Sarah, Emily, Linda, Norwegian baby, Air Force baby, Marianne, Maryland baby, Prince George baby, Sarah Brown, Agatha White Buffalo, Cuban Donna, Cincinnati baby, Savannah baby, Martha, the other Knoxville baby, Pamela, Mary-Anne, Bobbie, Jo, cowgirl, Angela, pipefitting baby, Macon baby, Carver Village baby, Carver Village baby, Plant City baby, Charleston baby, Clearwater baby, Evelyn, Julia, Cleveland baby, Hilda, Leila, Brenda, billboard baby, Chattanooga Choo Choo baby, Gulfport baby, Jackson ladyboy baby, Tennessee baby, Linda Sue, Atlanta baby, Anna Lee, Dorothy, Fredonia, Rosie, Ohio baby, Nawlins baby, Little Woods baby, Mindy, Patricia Anne, Atlanta stripper baby, Atlanta college baby, Savannah sand pile baby, West Memphis blues baby, Kentucky Vegas baby, Fort Myers baby, San Berdu baby, li'l Savannah baby, Tampa Bay baby, Mary Jo, big yellow LA gal, Laurie, Tonya, Granny, li'l LA banger, Bronco Motel baby, Griffith Park baby, Monroe baby, Carol, Linda Sue...

Sam cruised the streets of South Central, slow as a shark in spite of the rock dancing in his blood, making his jaws ache to bite someone's head off. The rock gets you spinning, gets you thinking, Lord, not straight. But when was anyone ever straight? Can't even build a straight road in this country.

The rock gets your blood rushing like them Colorado River rapids. Gets the molecules in the very air jumping and jiving. Makes you want to leap up and... What did Old Blue Eyes say? Swing on a star. Moonbeams in a jar. Better idea—take the moonbeams home, put them in your pipe, and smoke 'em.

On the radio, some scratchy-ass station, couple of stupid kids with their pants on backward singing about jump, jump. Whatever happened to Old Blue Eyes?

The Mac Dad? The Daddy Mac?

The fuck these sissy kids talking about? Catchy though.

"Jump, jump!" Sam shouted out the window of the car as he pulled up right on the tail of a working girl, shorts halfway up her ass. No riot gonna put them off their game. Nearly leaped out of her leotard. Ha-haaaa!

Sam drove on. Too skittish, that one.

Georgia, Ohio, Florida, Ohio, Florida, Maryland, DC, Florida, Ohio, Florida, Massachusetts, Connecticut, Florida, Maryland, Florida, Colorado, Ohio, Georgia, California, Oregon, Pennsylvania, New Jersey, Nebraska, California, Louisiana, Florida, Mississippi, Louisiana, Florida, New York, Florida, Georgia, California, Michigan, Nevada, Florida, California, Arizona, Georgia, Florida, Illinois, Florida, Ohio, Georgia, California, Georgia, Tennessee, Florida, New Jersey, Missouri, Florida, Illinois, Texas,

Florida, Mississippi, Florida, Mississippi, Georgia, Mississippi, South Carolina, Florida, Mississippi, Georgia, Alabama, South Carolina, Ohio, Florida, Alabama, Ohio, Florida, Alabama, Georgia, Ohio, Mississippi, Georgia, Louisiana, Ohio, Georgia, Mississippi, Kentucky, Mississippi, Ohio, Mississippi, Tennessee, Georgia, Arkansas, Florida, Georgia, Louisiana, Mississippi, Florida, Louisiana, Arkansas, Louisiana, Florida, Georgia, Florida, Georgia, Ohio, California, Ohio, Arkansas, Georgia, Kentucky, Florida, California, Georgia, Florida, California, Mississippi, Ohio, California, California, CALIFORNIA...

California was supposed to be some kind of sun-kissed Beach Boys blond bikini baby dream. Sam crawled the whore strolls and crack alleys, shadowy no matter how blinding the midday glare.

Jean had loved Hollywood enough to name herself for that cupcake Jean Harlow. She had looked due north most Saturday nights, hoping to see the floodlights of a movie premiere. Brought a tear to his eye, now that she was gone.

At Good Samaritan Hospital, they'd told him he wasn't responsible for the aneurysm that killed her, in spite of the multiple head injuries he'd inflicted. It hadn't been that final time he'd pushed her over a rail or any of the times before, when he slammed her head into pavement or had held her underwater. Or peeled off as she slipped from the hood of his car like a sack of potatoes.

Within a month, he'd moved in with Blind Barbara. Blind as a bat, but pretty little thing—honey-colored and soft-haired. He dressed her up like a doll, put lipstick on her, walked her around, and showed her off. Blind girls worked great if you had plenty to hide.

Once, he said he was just going to the restroom and left her sitting at a diner while he killed a new baby lickety-split and still showed up in time to use Blind Barbara's wallet to pay the bill. What a gas life was. Take it or leave it, you had to laugh.

Pretty as she was, he still couldn't fuck her, but she seemed to care less than the others.

Why did it make him sick to think about fucking the ones he kept?

Barbara's sister Helen turned him on to crack. His first couple times were like seeing the face of God. If something feels so good, how can it be wrong? It's all from God. Crack and hos and fields of motherfucking flowers and necks and him and all of it, all of it. He'd figured out not to crush a larynx or a voice box or break a hyoid bone before you were ready to come. Otherwise it kills them too quick. Leaves you with a bad case of blue balls.

He ran his tongue over the scar on his lower lip as his raggedy-ass Cadillac slid through puddles of streetlight. Through the glare on the windshield, he stalked fresh meat.

Sam did sometimes consider the possibility that if there was a Sam Little, there might not be a God at all.

To question your faith was blasphemy. Mama had always taught him that. If there was no God, how had he lived through the five times people had tried to kill him? He was blessed by God. It was the meaning of his name: *named by God. God heard.*

Fire from the buildings burning nearby lit the sky up orange. The full moon was bloodred, and a slight drizzle brought black raindrops, heavy with soot.

It was May 2, 1992. For four days, South Central had burned around him. He'd seen things!

He'd seen a man dragged from a truck and beaten, and he had driven around the roadblock, unnoticed. He heard glass shards of smashed windows hit his passenger-side door like so many pebbles, leaving them pocked and scratched. Beat-up old hooptie anyway. Nothing like the cars he used to drive when Jean kept him in style. Still. These mad-ass Negros. Them madder-ass crazy Koreans on the tops of their roofs with AKs.

The George HW idjit president was sending in actual tanks and soldiers onto the streets of South Central like this flip-flop-wearing mob of diaper looters was that Saddam Who-ville in Iraq.

Even the tanks couldn't begin to fuck with them Koreans though. Had to give it to them.

They didn't know he was the auteur of an even crazier show, but it was good to be underestimated. What was that picture with the boa constrictor strangling the girl? Ohhh right—*I Married a Savage*. That was a pretty picture. Crazy whore. Sam sneaked into the theater over and over to see her and that snake of hers when he wasn't but nine.

The drizzle turned to a light rain. What was that line about the gentle rain from heaven his mama used to say? The mist caught the revolving red-and-blue beams from the tops of the cop cars all around, stripes of color shooting out into the night.

What was the name of the guy who sparked the powder keg? That can't we all get along guy? Some cops beat the shit out of you—what the fuck you care about getting along? They'd been down and dissed long enough. Let 'em tear it all down.

It was a riot or a revolution or whatever you wanted to call it. If you were a serial killer, it was an opportunity. Who would be paying attention to the nefarious escapades of one lone predator or the loss of one easily forgettable piece of ass? If there was one thing he had mastered, it was becoming the Black man no one saw, finding the Black woman no one would miss.

Ford Mercury, Ford Fairlane, Pontiac Bonneville, Ford Fairlane, Ford Mercury, Ford, convertible Pontiac Bonneville, Buick Riviera, Buick Wildcat, Pontiac Bonneville, Oldsmobile Delta, Pontiac LeMans, Ford Thunderbird, Chrysler Imperial, Chevy Bel Air, Ford Galaxie, Ford Pinto, Lincoln Continental Mark III, Lincoln Continental Mark IV, Ford Thunderbird, Ford Mercury, Cadillac Eldorado...

Keep moving and they may nab you once in a while, but they will never really know you. The day before, Sam had seen a man tie a chain around an ATM machine, attach it to a piece of heavy machinery, and drive until the entire apparatus broke loose and scattered twenty-dollar bills to the wind. Made him sort of sad. Used to be all juke joints and prettied-up strolls. Hos, sure, bangers, sure, but solid folk too.

Now all them dumb motherfuckers getting arrested for stealing a six-pack of wine coolers. Before that, it was a dime bag. All their women left behind, needing a shoulder to cry on.

Long before he got to them and finished the job, his babies had basically been murdered by the streets where he left their shells. Like when you had a sick dog, it was the humane thing to do.

Sam cruised down Fig, past burned-out cars, curled in on themselves.

He locked his crosshairs on a starry-eyed, big-legged, kind of sloppy old baby in a velour housedress and slippers, hanging on her stairwell at a motel on Fig and Imperial.

She leaned forward, took a drag on her cig, looked to the left like she didn't care.

It was almost too easy. But what do they say about sex and pizza?

She wore a red turban. He rolled down his window to the smell of burning plastic.

"Go on up and change," he said.

She turned without a word. When she came back, she looked the same. Either she didn't give a fuck, or she had three identical nightgowns.

Sam let her draw on the pipe first. Long as it took for her to get her fix on. He was a gentleman that way. Wasn't going to put a baby to bed hungry. He watched the Brillo glow orange at the end of the pipe as the rock sizzled, foamed, and dissolved. He even put on another rock, though a smaller one, and waited. It would never be enough. He'd take it from her eventually, and it wouldn't be enough for him either, but something would be. Crack was just an aphrodisiac.

They headed down Central, left on Compton, past the courthouse, took a sharp turn near Long Beach Avenue somewhere, not even he knew where, and parked in front of a liquor store he thought was closed. The baby next to him lolled her head back with the relief of her fix. Sam blistered his lip on the hot pipe. When he reached for her throat, she sprang to life as if someone put the paddles to her chest.

"Calm down now. I ain't gonna hurt you."

Usually, it took them a while to figure it out, and by the time they did, it was too late. That was his favorite. The look on their faces when they realized.

It gave him a pang in his heart too. He wasn't without feeling. As hard as it made his dick, it still hurt to watch them suffer. He would have even let this one draw breath for another moment if she hadn't popped up like some kind of zombie coming out of a grave and screamed bloody murder, reaching over and honking the horn.

Sam was not a violent man, not a rapist. He was a lover, not a fighter. In extreme circumstances, he was regretfully forced to backhand a bitch so hard her head cracked the passenger-side window. That crazy zombie did not miss a beat, came back at him, honked the horn as he batted her hands away and tried to grab her wrists.

In the scuffle, he knocked her turban sideways. Her hands instinctively went to her hair. Sam—always the boxer, even though he wouldn't box—found the opening. In a nanosecond, he had her by the throat.

A few minutes later, he had propped her up against the seat when some crazy brown guy came running out of the store pointing a Kalashnikov, screaming in Swahili or something. Sam put his arm around the corpse as if at the drive-in, waved, and peeled out. An eyewitness. He was trying not to leave those littered around anymore. Oh well, at least it was a brown guy whose store was probably about to catch fire.

It was a strange sort of peaceful loneliness when the only breath left was your own. When all you could hear was your own breath. He smelled faint smoke.

Tucked away behind a bank or loan building, a poison-green lawn caught his eye. A world or a globe floated by, and he didn't know if it was in front of him or in his head. There were no stars. The lawn was marbled in shadows, glistening with rain. No one in sight. Sirens and gunshots punctuated the curfew silence. He was out past curfew. Get home. No time for games.

They were angry. Who wouldn't be? Motherfuckers were barely done being slaves, and the police now beating them down for no big thing while all the pretty people party it up not two miles north, with their own whores and their own cocaine. They got off with a slap on the lily-white wrist while down here, motherfuckers went to prison for a dime bag of weed, were dying with the AIDS right and left from fucking and dirty needles. Don't tell Sam the CIA didn't plant the seeds of that shit. Poisoned the Black man. Could make a mother-fucker mad enough to toss tables and break windows.

If you were an amateur.

If you were a professional, you never let them see you mad. Never let them see you at all.

What would it be like to be one of these fools who actually cared? He'd never know. The whole natural world was an ecosystem of pre-dation, decay, rebirth. He was the prince of destruction.

He looked back at the limp body in the passenger seat. Dead, they were heavier than the garbage cans he hauled for Dade County Sanitation and more cumbersome. He wouldn't have to drag her far. With the riots, by the time they found her, there would be dozens of unidentified dead piling up at the morgue every day, thousands more injured. By the time they figured out her name, if they ever did, he'd be a ghost.

34

ZIGGITY BOOM

The Texas Department of Public Safety is located in a redbrick building with lots of straight lines. I was wrong about my first trip to Decatur being my last. I visited Sam in Wise County once more before he went to Odessa for his sentencing. The second time, I was meant to meet Holland at his DPS office. He was hours late again. His text yanked me around on my way out of town and would likely make me late for my flight.

When I arrived at DPS, I asked Holland how nice a bottle of whiskey it took to bribe the county sheriff to babysit. I'd spent the last hour at the coffee shop with Sheriff Akin. He'd bought me an iced tea, charmed me with local stories. He had come to the conclusion his high school sweetheart wife would have a thing or two to say to me about how I spoil my boys. She sounded like a pip. He tipped his hat on the way out.

While we were talking, the Ector County DA's office issued a press release about the Brothers case in which they said the FBI believed Samuel Little to be the most prolific serial killer in American history. Ziggity boom, the media was on it.

"You saw the story broke," said Holland. "Crazy day."

I followed him through a fluorescent labyrinth. He wore his college sweatshirt, with a few stray dog hairs on it. I guessed golden Lab. No double belt or endangered animals that day.

He wore no hat, but one white and one black hung on the wall over his kingly maroon padded desk chair. If it was consciously symbolic, it was a little on the nose. Maybe it was as simple as white hats were daywear and black hats were for formal occasions, like Garth Brooks concerts.

I meant to ask him about the hats, but you never get to everything. Beneath them were Sam's portraits in a haphazard configuration, printouts of newspaper articles. The floor was a minefield of papers and folders. Stacks of binders two feet high leaned against the wall.

Holland sat, folded his hands across his chest, and apologized for both his lateness and appearance. His mother had fallen and broken her wrist, pins in it and everything, and he came straight from the hospital. I picked my way around the papers on the industrial grade carpet, sat in a hard-backed chair facing him.

"I'm a Texan, so I was worried I'd been impolite and you'd feel unwelcome."

It was the same thing he'd said before. This time, he had a five-o'clock shadow and I believed him. He'd been up all night.

I decided to skip the warm-up. I wasn't leaving, but I wasn't about playing with his time.

I wanted my who, what, when, where, why of the confessions and the matching process before everyone else descended to pick at the leftovers. Sure, I wanted to talk psycho with the wizard of psychos, but that got moved to the bucket list. Sam was being extradited the following day to Ector County Jail.

"Are you done with your part in this? Will you see him again?"

"He's off to Odessa. I talked to him Sunday and he was pretty good. I don't know if he's mad at me or what. I'll go back, but not for a while. I guess it was forty-nine days I spent with him. It got better, like training for a marathon."

"He gave you all of them now, right? Ninety, you said?"

"Ninety-three is what we're at. It's a lot of detective work. I think based on the definitive matches, we're probably right about sixty right now."

"Sixty definitive?"

"No. No, so definitive I think is somewhere around thirty."

"Thirty-four."

"We're right at the edge of getting most of them. Now it's a lot of days of emails and phone calls and sorting through the stuff that fell through the cracks: agencies and case reports, of matching them up, but the thing that…"

"…makes it challenging is?"

"Well now, here's the little reporter all of a sudden. Nice to meet you. Nothing's challenging once you figure out how it works."

"You said, 'all murder is sexual.' Can you clarify?"

"There's some type of sexual undertone in criminal everything."

"Criminal everything? Or serial killing everything?"

"You walk into a convenience store, and the clerk fights you. You don't mean to shoot him, but in the scuffle, the gun goes off. I don't know that there's anything sexual about that. When you start planning things out, when you have that sociopathic or psychopathic mindset, I think, yeah. There's always some type of sexual element."

He cut me off before I even started the next question.

"You know what? You're never going to get there. If you think you know what you're doing and what he's going to bite on, you're wrong. Opinions are fine, but only if I can use them to understand people.

How do we understand someone who lacks remorse? Okay, were his crimes spontaneous? I think some were, but for the most part, he planned what he was going to do and he knew. 'I didn't kill that university student. I didn't kill that nurse or that lawyer or anything like that.' Because he knew that would get him caught. He talked about how stupid Bundy was because he's killing…"

"College girls."

"Exactly, college girls. We had college girls I never even put in front of him. He went into great detail about, 'No, I wouldn't do that. I'd get caught right away.' He's very intelligent. He's manipulative. But the sociopathic side of that is that he doesn't ever succeed. I mean, his achievement is the fact that he was able to kill ninety women and not get caught. Could he have gone to college? Could he have gotten a job? Yeah. Could he have been a professional boxer? Absolutely, but he didn't do that. That's the sociopath. I'm sure a psychiatrist would have a heart attack. Everything for me is how to understand them, to open them. You know. You know how to get them to confess."

"Thank you?"

"You sit in the room with this person who's a machine, and he's always looking for the weakness. He's always trying to manipulate and control you and to get you to move into a light that he wants you or a light he wants you to see him in. Bundy is successful, he gets into law school, and he's got that false charm. You sit down with Little, he also has that charm. Is he abducting women? Women are getting in his vehicle. Granted a lot of those women are prostitutes and they're going to get into the vehicle no matter what. But he's putting them at ease enough that they're getting in there, and he's taking them to dinner, maybe getting them a dress or doing things for them, before he kills them."

"What light does he want you to see him in?"

"As the killer. He's not the rapist, not the woman beater. He's the killer. He doesn't have to take anything from anyone. Now, he's got that back kind of curve to him, in which he's saying they're all wanting to die. He let up on that. I think he read me and knew I thought that was bullshit and decided to be seen by me as a killer. He wants to be seen as a normal guy but his vice for whatever reason is strangulation."

"What's your vice?"

"I don't know, probably my personality. Ask my wife."

"Fair enough. What's your takeaway from the Little investigation? Was it just one more case? Was it particularly meaningful?"

"I would have to sit back and judge it up at the end of the day."

"There isn't an end of the day though."

"Do you hear the silence?"

"I'm not scared of silence."

"You don't judge things up when you're in the middle of a game. I'm doing what I need to do to get through this and prove up what I can prove up. It's a job and you get through it. I'm trying to get to the finish line. When I get there, I'll definitely turn around and look back and I'll have some thoughts."

"What would you dream those thoughts might be?"

"I don't dream of those thoughts."

"You don't say, 'At the end of the game, I want to win'?"

"Well, have we won or have we lost? I'm not at the finish line."

"I don't know. I mean, yes, no, and there is no winning or losing, there are...just a lot of dead women."

"Well, if that's how you want to look at it. Then how do you win?"

"I don't, usually."

I looked at the group photo of the Texas Rangers, stacked three rows high. I counted one and a half Black men and I think one woman.

"You in here?"

"Somewhere. I always go to the top. That beautiful picture of me there. I think they do that photoshop if you close your eyes. Makes you look like Mr. Magoo."

"Do you happen to have any photos lying around? Case files? Just whatever's around real quick."

"No. No, that's not... Jillian, stop asking me that like I didn't already say no a dozen times. No. It's boxes and boxes."

"In that room?"

"I said no."

"How many notebooks do you think there are on Sam here?"

"No. And there's a couple more up front that the secretaries are still putting together, ten or fifteen four-inch, three-ringed binders. That's since I started my stuff. What else is out there? I don't know yet. Go on and find out for yourself."

I scrolled through the news on the plane. On November 27, the FBI announced they'd matched thirty of Sam Little's ninety-three jail-house confessions. The closed cases—meaning the court had either dismissed them or there was a completed sentence, whether by arrest or exceptional means—were a bit of a mystery.

There was no list per se. As the weeks went on, I formally requested the publicly available records on the closed cases but got few responses. Most of the ones I did get said the cases were still open, the coroners' reports unavailable. I sometimes had better luck calling the detectives myself, sometimes not. I know that among the first thirty confirmed cases were the following:

Jane Doe, 20–25, Prince George's County, Maryland, 1972
Agatha White Buffalo, 34, South Omaha, Nebraska, 1973

Miriam "Angela" Chapman, 25, Miami, Florida, 1976

Julia Critchfield, 36, Saucier, Mississippi, 1978

Brenda Alexander, 23, Phenix City, Alabama, 1979

Linda Sue Boards, 23, Smiths Grove, Kentucky, 1981

Patricia Parker (then a Jane Doe), 30, Dade County, Georgia, 1981

Dorothy Richards, 55, Houma, Louisiana, 1982

Patricia Mount, 26, Forest Grove, Florida, 1982

Rosie Hill, 20, Marion County, Florida, 1982

Fredonia Smith, 18, Macon, Georgia, 1982

Melinda LaPree, 22, Pascagoula, Mississippi, 1982

Hannah Mae Bonner, 23, Mobile, Alabama, 1984

Ida Mae Campbell, 34, Mobile, Alabama, 1984

Carol Alford, 41, Los Angeles, California, 1987

Audrey Nelson, 35, Los Angeles, California, 1989

Guadalupe Apodaca, 46, Los Angeles, California, 1989

Denise Christie Brothers, 38, Odessa, Texas, 1994

Daisy McGuire, 40, Houma, Louisiana, 1996

Melissa Thomas, 24, Opelousas, Louisiana, 1996

Nancy Carol Stevens, 46, Tupelo, Mississippi, 2005

On December 13, 2018, in the Ector County Courthouse, Samuel Little entered a plea of guilty and was sentenced to life in prison for the murder of Denise Brothers. They gave him a choice of where he wanted to go from there.

On January 1, 2019, they extradited that snake back to California State Prison, Los Angeles County, because he decided he liked it better here after all.

I couldn't believe it. They were sending him back to me.

35

THE PEOPLE OF THE STATE OF CALIFORNIA V. SAMUEL LITTLE: TRYING TO LIVE

LOS ANGELES, CALIFORNIA
AUGUST 20, 2014

The People called Leila McClain for the second time.

The first time McClain had entered, she took one look at Sam and dropped as if tasered.

Hilda Nelson and Darren Versiga lifted her by the elbows and led her out.

"You don't gotta be scared of him no more. I know we didn't come all this way for you to fall apart," said Nelson.

"I'm not scared," said McClain. "I'm so..." She reached for the word. "I straight want to kill him. I want to kill that motherfucker."

She pinned her shoulders back, dusted them off, reapplied her coral lipstick for the twelfth time.

All five foot three of her had scrapped with Samuel Little that long-ago night before running half-naked across four lanes of heavy traffic. The other three living victims had been left for dead or a third party intervened.

McClain was the only one of almost a hundred victims who got away by boxing him. She wasn't the only one who tried. Plenty of Sam's victims fought with all they had, as evidenced by his epithelial cells beneath their fingernails. They'd lost.

McClain's heels on the polished hardwood floor were the only sound in the room. On the second try, her storied bowlegs carried a now middle-aged woman with a straightened coif, fussy magenta suit, and thin gap between her front teeth to the witness stand. Finally.

On the stand, McClain turned her back to Sam. A victim's advocate sat behind her. McClain shrank into her suit, looked down at the hands folded in her lap.

She told a story of the night a predator had caught her scent, homed in on her, offered her a fifty for a date, charmed her into his car.

This spectacular fighter shook like a Chihuahua when facing a jury of...of who?

Why was she always on trial? The jury's responsibility was to hold the presumption of innocence for her attacker. They had no such obligation to her. They had failed her again and again in this regard. She was guilty before she was born. And even so, she had come this far.

SILVERMAN: Leila, you seem nervous. Are you nervous?

MCCLAIN: Yes, ma'am.

SILVERMAN: Okay. I'm just going to ask you some questions. Okay?

MCCLAIN: (No audible response.)

SILVERMAN: Is that alright with you?

MCCLAIN: Yes, ma'am.

SILVERMAN: Okay. Did you fly in yesterday from out of state?

MCCLAIN: Yes, ma'am.

SILVERMAN: Did you fly in with a friend of yours, Hilda Nelson?

MCCLAIN: Yes, ma'am.

SILVERMAN: And also Detective Darren Versiga?

MCCLAIN: Yes, ma'am.

SILVERMAN: Can you tell us how old you are?

MCCLAIN: 54.

SILVERMAN: Can you also please tell us where you were living back in November of 1981.

MCCLAIN: I had two residences. Which one would you like?

SILVERMAN: Let me ask you this: in terms of those two residences, were they both in the city of Pascagoula, Mississippi?

MCCLAIN: Yes, ma'am.

SILVERMAN: And how old were you back in November of 1981?

MCCLAIN: I'm thinking I was about 19, 20.

SILVERMAN: Now, you said that you had two residences. Tell me where one was, and then we'll talk about the second.

MCCLAIN: I had one residence where I was taking care of business. 147 Carver Village.

SILVERMAN: And where was your second residence?

MCCLAIN: 6900 Robinhood Drive, Regency Woods Apartments.

SILVERMAN: And which apartment did you actually live at?

MCCLAIN: Regency Woods.

SILVERMAN: And who did you live there with?

MCCLAIN: Along with three childrens.

SILVERMAN: Whose children?

MCCLAIN: Mines.

SILVERMAN: How far away was the Regency Woods residence from the Carver Village apartment, approximately?

MCCLAIN: Approximately—approximately 3 miles.

SILVERMAN: Now, you said that the apartment at 147 Carver Village was where you were "taking care of business." What does that mean?

MCCLAIN: That means that—turn tricks, date for cash.

SILVERMAN: When you say "turn tricks" or "date for cash," you're talking about prostitution?

MCCLAIN: Yes, ma'am.

SILVERMAN: And at that point in time in 1981, how were you making a living?

MCCLAIN: I ran a nightclub. I had just got laid off. I sold shoes out the trunk of my car. And I prostituted.

SILVERMAN: Why do you think you engaged in prostitution back then?

MCCLAIN: Because it was hardship. I had got laid off from the shipyard. I had three children. I am not the kind to kiss nobody's behind for money. I don't want to be on the welfare. That was my way for me and my kids to have the essentials that we needed.

SILVERMAN: Were you a single mother?

MCCLAIN: Yes.

SILVERMAN: Did you have any family around in the area that were supporting or helping you?

MCCLAIN: No, ma'am.

SILVERMAN: I want to direct your attention back
to November 19 of 1981, let's say a week before
Thanksgiving. Do you remember that time period?

MCCLAIN: Yes, ma'am.

SILVERMAN: Do you remember on that evening where
you were?

MCCLAIN: Okay. I was at my nightclub at the beginning of
the night. And then after it turned dark, I went walking
through the path to the Front. That's the Village.

In the day, thumping bass and the rise and fall of laughter spilled
from the twenty-four seven juke joints, gambling dens, and brothels
of the Front. Hustlers and whores of all stripes slinging every imaginable vice crawled the sidewalks. They called it a "Small California."

If you wanted it, you could find it in Carver Village.

Booze, hos, Ts and blues, guns and dope, boosted goods sold
cheap. It was a world under a bell jar, so ignored by law enforcement that its women formed a sacred pact to look out for each other,
because they well knew no one else would.

MCCLAIN: I was renting a nightclub where you make as
much money as you want in the club, you only have to
pay one rate that month for rent.

SILVERMAN: Okay. And what was going on in the nightclub? Was that the normal atmosphere that we would
expect to have in any type of bar?

MCCLAIN: No, ma'am. Not my bar. It was different
because it was an old house. And it had rooms in the

back, and the whole front was tooled out nice with a pool table and a bar. And sometimes, late at night, I stayed there.

SILVERMAN: So you had a—some rooms that you rented in the back, basically, of the nightclub?

MCCLAIN: Yes, ma'am, to other girls.

SILVERMAN: And what was the name of that nightclub? If you remember.

MCCLAIN: B&B.

SILVERMAN: And was that near the Village, Carver Village?

MCCLAIN: Yes, ma'am.

SILVERMAN: How far was it, would you say, from Carver Village?

MCCLAIN: The nightclub?

SILVERMAN: Yes.

MCCLAIN: It was a pathway. From me to that picture of George Washington. It was a pathway.

SILVERMAN: So it was very close?

MCCLAIN: Yes, ma'am.

THE COURT: That's 36—You're talking about the picture in the back here?

MCCLAIN: Yes, sir. Straight path.

THE COURT: 36 feet from the witness stand.

SILVERMAN: Thank you, your honor. And so were you there for a period of time that night. Were you drinking at all?

MCCLAIN: No, ma'am. I'm not really a drinker.

SILVERMAN: How about doing any drugs? Were you doing any drugs?

MCCLAIN: At that time, I was not doing drugs.

SILVERMAN: Would it be safe to say that today, yesterday, the day before, you're not using any drugs or alcohol, at this point?

MCCLAIN: I'm 19 years clean, December the 16th.

SILVERMAN: Congratulations. Let me ask you—that night, you said you left the B&B at some point?

MCCLAIN: Yes, ma'am.

SILVERMAN: So back on the night of November 19 of 1981, you mentioned that you walked away from the B&B and you were walking through the Village; is that right?

MCCLAIN: Yes, ma'am.

SILVERMAN: At some point did you come in contact with a male?

MCCLAIN: Yes, ma'am.

SILVERMAN: And tell me about that.

MCCLAIN: It was this guy, an old lady, and a young boy kept driving past my club earlier that day. And when I went through the path—as I was coming through the path, the station wagon came through the path. The station wagon came around again, but it was only a man in it. He parked and got out.

SILVERMAN: Okay. Now, can you describe this vehicle?

MCCLAIN: It was a long, old station wagon with a hatch in—hatchback. And it had paneling, like this, on the sides.

SILVERMAN: Like wood paneling?

MCCLAIN: Yes, ma'am.

SILVERMAN: And this man, once he departed the vehicle, did he speak with you?

MCCLAIN: Yes, ma'am. I was walking along the road, and then, you know, the strip was so small, we kind of came in contact with each other.

SILVERMAN: You passed him?

MCCLAIN: Yes, ma'am. And he say, "How you doing?" And I say, "Fine. And you?" He say, "Do you date?" I say, "Yes, I do."

SILVERMAN: And what did you take that to mean when he said, "Do you date?"

MCCLAIN: "Do you prostitute?"

SILVERMAN: Okay. And you said?

MCCLAIN: "Yes."

SILVERMAN: And what was the conversation at that point?

MCCLAIN: He said, "How much will it be?" I said, "$50." He said, "No problem." And then I said, "Well, I live right around the corner." He said, "No. We going to the Shamrock Hotel." It's right across the street, so I'm figuring, you know, I'm in close distance to the strip, so I tells him yes.

SILVERMAN: So he told you that he wanted to go to the Shamrock. Where was the Shamrock in relationship to the Village?

MCCLAIN: One street over, with woods and clubs in between it.

SILVERMAN: "Woods," meaning a rural area, with trees and things of that nature?

MCCLAIN: Yes, ma'am. Brush.

SILVERMAN: Okay. So what did you do at that point?

MCCLAIN: At that point, him and I—well, him and I got in the station wagon and we was headed towards the Shamrock.

SILVERMAN: Was it just the two of you in the vehicle?

MCCLAIN: Yes, ma'am.

SILVERMAN: Who was driving?

MCCLAIN: He was.

SILVERMAN: Okay. And you told him it was going to be $50. Before you got in the vehicle, did he give you any money?

MCCLAIN: No, ma'am.

SILVERMAN: And he started driving towards the Shamrock?

MCCLAIN: Yes, ma'am.

SILVERMAN: And then what happened?

MCCLAIN: And as we was going around the corner, he passed the Shamrock, and I said, "You just passed it, turn around." I say, "Go back that way." He say, "I don't need to turn around for what I want to do to you." And he hit me right here, in between my eyes, and then coldcocked me behind my head. He fought me.

SILVERMAN: Let me ask you this: when you said that he made a comment to you, you showed us with your left—

MCCLAIN: My left—

SILVERMAN: Which arm? If you remember.

MCCLAIN: All right. I got it—I got to set myself up. He drive and he say, "…Not for what I want to do to you." But the way he came around with that hand, pop—pops you in the head somewhere right there, that makes you just... It will either wake you up or knock you out. I woke up.

SILVERMAN: In terms of the way that you described it, for the record—Take a deep breath.

MCCLAIN: Yes, ma'am.

SILVERMAN:—Your right hand, you showed us being on the steering wheel. Is that what he had?

MCCLAIN: Right hand on the steering wheel.

SILVERMAN: And left hand across you?

MCCLAIN: I'm facing him. He comes around, coldcocks me here, somewhere there (indicating). The next hit in between the eyes. And he knew he had stung me enough that he could go like—like his thumbs up in this part of your throat... And we in between an area—sorry—so small, he just jammed the car up in gear and went to wailing on me.

SILVERMAN: And when he was hitting you, did he hit you with an open hand or with a closed fist?

MCCLAIN: Ma'am, he was boxing me.

SILVERMAN: He was boxing you?

MCCLAIN: He was boxing my face and head and when he opened his hands, he use 'em to choke you.

SILVERMAN: When you said he was boxing you, is that a term that you would use for someone that's hitting you with—

MCCLAIN: That I would use for hitting me.

SILVERMAN:—with both the right and the left fists?

Sam alternately muffled giggles or sneered as McClain spoke.

Juror #7 wept. It wasn't just the woman's wrenching testimony. Something about the viciousness in the set of Sam's jaw, watching her speak. Those hateful eyes were the last things these women saw? After all the trying, even if they failed. Look at Audrey Nelson's body. It was nothing if not a body that had tried everything. She had to leave under that monstrous gaze?

MCCLAIN: He was choking me, choking the life out of me. And I'm still fighting, scratching and kicking and biting, and he have to turn me loose because I'm biting his hands. If I can—anywhere I can get me a piece of him, I'm trying to get him like he was trying get me.

SILVERMAN: So you fought back?

MCCLAIN: With everything I had.

SILVERMAN: Did you think that he was trying to kill you, choke you to death?

MCCLAIN: Definitely. He was going to kill me.

SILVERMAN: And so what did you do?

MCCLAIN: I fought with him. We was jumping in and out of the station wagon.

SILVERMAN: You got out of the vehicle at some point?

MCCLAIN: Yes, ma'am. But this man was so quick, he could catch me before I could get from here to here, from the station wagon, and drag me back. At one point, it was a guy came by on a bicycle, a little white boy come by on a bicycle, and he asked me did I need some help, and I couldn't say nothing because at this time I couldn't talk.

SILVERMAN: Because of the pressure that he had put on your throat?

MCCLAIN: Yes, ma'am. And he say, "She drunk. That's my
   ol' lady."

SILVERMAN: Who said that?

MCCLAIN: The guy.

SILVERMAN: Do you see that guy here today in court?

MCCLAIN: That's him sitting right there in that chair, with
   that blue shirt on.

THE COURT: All right. Identifying the defendant, for the
   record.

McClain pointed, her entire arm shaking. Silverman said, "Look
at me, now. Look at me."

SILVERMAN: You seem to be shaking. Are you nervous?

MCCLAIN: I'm good, but I am nervous.

SILVERMAN: Okay. Don't be nervous. Okay?

MCCLAIN: (No audible response.)

SILVERMAN: I know those are cheap words. Back in 1981,
   did the defendant look like he looks now?

MCCLAIN: No, ma'am.

SILVERMAN: Was he in a wheelchair?

MCCLAIN: No, ma'am. He was a big, healthy, strong Black
   man. He had hair on his head. He not standing up, but
   he about six-two or six-three. He was weighing 170
   pounds. With them big hands.

SILVERMAN: So you said that you got out—actually out of
   the car at some point, and then he would drag you back in?

MCCLAIN: Yes, ma'am. It was like ring around the rosies;
   in and out, in and out, in and out. And I'm talking about

fighting me in between the time and laying me up on the car, choking me. You know how you push somebody up against something? And choking me. And—but I wouldn't give up.

SILVERMAN: So how many times would you say you actually tried or did get out of the car? If you can remember.

MCCLAIN: I don't want to tell a lie, but, frankly, I think it was about three times I got out and he'd get me back in. But I got a chance to get in that little small part of the back of the station wagon. He couldn't get in there. And he was trying to get all up in there and whip me, and I come out through a little window about this big. By the time he got over from that seat part, reaching at me, I done got loose. I'm going across highway 90, no clothes on, just my bottoms and flip flops. I'm gone.

SILVERMAN: Okay. So when you got out, were you at all concerned that you were naked from the waist up?

MCCLAIN: No, ma'am. I'm trying to live. I don't care about being naked. I want to live.

SILVERMAN: When the assault is going on and you're in and out of the car, where in relation to the Village is the vehicle parked? This is the brown station wagon hatchback.

MCCLAIN: It's on a little service road from highway 90. I think highway 90 only had two lanes—two or four lanes. I'm not really sure, but—it was two lanes on each side. That's what it was, two lanes on each side. And it was the shipyard traffic coming. And I knew if I could make it across that shipyard traffic, I was going to be at home. So

I just ran in front of all the traffic, because it was time for them to get off.

SILVERMAN: And you then ran across the lanes of traffic?

MCCLAIN: Yes, ma'am.

SILVERMAN: You didn't get hit by anybody?

MCCLAIN: No, ma'am. Cars were swerving everywhere, but I did not get hit.

SILVERMAN: And where did you run to?

MCCLAIN: I ran back to the Village, which would have been across the street. I had to run through some bushes and brush and a little wooded area, but it landed me right back on the Front. I fell down because I ran into a guy that was urinating; he almost peed on me.

SILVERMAN: A man that was urinating on the sidewalk?

MCCLAIN: He was urinating between where the clubs was and the woods was. Because they had been in—to be honest, they was gambling or drinking, whatever they doing in there, and he had to use it so he came outside to use it. I thank God he came outside to use it. I said, "That man trying to kill me."

SILVERMAN: What happened at that point?

MCCLAIN: They said, "Who?" I said, "I don't know his name. That man in that station wagon." Then everybody start coming out, club-by-club-by-club. And they say, "Take her to the hospital. Take her to the hospital."

SILVERMAN: After these people came out of the clubs, did someone actually take you to the hospital?

MCCLAIN: Yes, ma'am.

SILVERMAN: And were you treated at the hospital?

MCCLAIN: Yes, ma'am.

SILVERMAN: And can you describe for us what kind of injuries you had as a result of this?

MCCLAIN: I had migraine headaches at that time. And then my eyes, they closed, with blood coming out of them like tears. The white part of my eyes was red. And this went on for approximately two weeks. I couldn't eat. I was—

SILVERMAN: Why couldn't you eat?

MCCLAIN: I couldn't hardly swallow.

SILVERMAN: Did you also have any problems in terms of your vision?

MCCLAIN: Yes, ma'am.

SILVERMAN: When the defendant was hitting you in the head, did you ever lose consciousness?

MCCLAIN: No, ma'am.

SILVERMAN: Did you see, what some people call it, stars?

MCCLAIN: I seen stars and clovers.

SILVERMAN: Did you tell anybody in the hospital what had happened to you?

MCCLAIN: No, ma'am.

SILVERMAN: Well, let me ask you this question: did anybody ask you?

MCCLAIN: No, ma'am.

SILVERMAN: Nobody asked you what happened?

MCCLAIN: Hmm. No, ma'am. I don't believe nobody really asked me nothing about that.

SILVERMAN: So, you had headaches, migraines. You had problems with your vision. You had red where the white part of your eyes should be. How long were you there?

MCCLAIN: In the hospital?

SILVERMAN: Yes.

MCCLAIN: That night, and released early that morning up in the day.

SILVERMAN: So, the next morning?

MCCLAIN: If I'm thinking right, yes, ma'am.

SILVERMAN: Did any police come to the hospital to interview you?

MCCLAIN: No, ma'am.

SILVERMAN: Did you ever go to the police after you were released from the hospital and report this?

MCCLAIN: No, ma'am.

SILVERMAN: Can you tell us, explain to us, why not.

MCCLAIN: I'm Black. I live in a Black neighborhood that one side of the street is nothing but clubs, the other side is projects. They don't know my condition of why I'm out there, but I'm out there trying to take care of my family. They—I can't go downtown and tell them that I've been a prostitute to feed my children. They don't care nothing about no Black prostitute in Pascagoula. No, ma'am.

36

THE PEOPLE OF THE STATE OF CALIFORNIA V. SAMUEL LITTLE: THREE AND A HALF MINUTES

LOS ANGELES, CALIFORNIA
AUGUST 20, 2014

Dr. Eugene Carpenter, formerly a medical examiner with the LA County coroner's office, performed the autopsy on Audrey Nelson, a.k.a. Audrey Everett. He explained his findings with a laser pointer aimed at projections of her emaciated, scarred body on a steel slab.

Silverman knew Audrey's daughter and sister would be in the room. The doctor testified about the fingernail kit, the drag marks, the myriad of injuries, many of them premortem.

He introduced the third-party culpability evidence of the distinctive stamp mark on her neck that looked like a ring or belt buckle, neither belonging to Little. Bruising and crescent-shaped nail marks surrounded it. Silverman suggested alternative theories for how it might have gotten there.

Audrey was beaten plenty. It hadn't started with Sam Little. That was just where it had ended. Even Silverman had rarely seen a body so battered.

The doctor explained the bruising and areas of bleeding in the chest cavity, on her back, were so deep as to appear to be caused by a blunt-force weapon, not excluding feet, elbows, or hands. Severe blunt-force trauma to the central abdomen. No signs of petechial hemorrhaging, so it was like a hanging, where the pressure was so great the blood never built up in the head. You don't have the pressure that causes the little hemorrhages. Severe hemorrhaging in the neck muscles, hyoid bone snapped in three places.

> SILVERMAN: How would you describe that, given that
>   you've been practicing forensic pathology for approxi-
>   mately 27 years now, on a scale of 1 to 10? What are we
>   talking about in terms of the level of force used in this
>   particular case given the extent of hemorrhaging that
>   you saw, along with fractures of three of the four bones
>   in the neck?
> CARPENTER: Okay. I'm going to be careful because these
>   cases are not frequent. Maybe I've seen ten, 12 cases; but
>   of those ten or 12, these signs of force are the greatest
>   that I have seen in a 27-year practice.
> SILVERMAN: Okay. Tell us, in terms of your determination
>   with respect to the observations that you made in your
>   examination at autopsy, what you determined was the
>   cause of death.
> CARPENTER: Death was caused by strangulation.
> SILVERMAN: How long, approximately, would it take with
>   that type of extreme pressure held constant around the
>   neck before you would expect death to occur?
> CARPENTER: By convention, it's acceptable that about
>   three and a half minutes is a reasonable answer.

37

AUDREY

Audrey's thoughts rolled around in her head like marbles, scattered and too slow. The man in the driver's seat didn't seem to have much to say anyway.

They called her first baby Pearl now. The name rose to the surface, the house with blue shutters—a morning punctured by memories of dreams from the previous night.

Her mother changed her baby's name. Unique was the name Audrey had given her. Unique Libertene, and yes, she knew how to fucking spell it right. She spelled it wrong because she wanted to. Because she could. Because no one could tell her how to do anything anymore. All those years up at four in the morning milking the cows. No TV, no magazines, no radio, no nothing. Get on a school bus and go to school and then get back on it and come home. Old-fashioned hard work and none of this artsy bullshit.

By the time she was sixteen, she would have crawled the length of New York State on broken glass to escape the farm. She ran away to the big city four hours south. Didn't exactly work out. She met Preston there, like you do. Always some Preston waiting for the next farm girl. Got strung out even easier. He got into all manner of shit, jewelry, drugs, the rest. She'd followed him out here, to the edge of the fucking continent.

All for this glorious experience of freedom.

An iron pendulum knocked back and forth in her gut.

Pools of streetlight shifted to darkness. The car wasn't moving. Was the car moving?

She regained consciousness as the man kneeling over her in the back seat let go of her throat to unzip his pants.

Man, she'd been off her game that night. She'd pegged this one as gay—something about his vibration. Figured he just wanted to pick up some whore to help him score drugs, then look in the other direction and imagine his friend from work while you blew him. She was usually good at reading a face, if you didn't count Pres.

The threadbare black headliner of the Thunderbird turned to a staticky screen as he once again seized her throat, then released. She thrashed her arms, went for his hands, his face with her nails.

She'd sent Unique a letter with a palm leaf in it sometime not so long ago for her birthday, or close enough. *The palm leaf signifies strength*, she'd told her. *Be strong, my love. I love you I love you I love you.*

The palm trees in LA towered above gated Bel Air communities and high schools on the city's ragged outskirts alike. The edges of the palm fronds shone in the twilight like knife blades.

She knew the letter would never reach her baby. Her first. There had been two more, snatched straight from her arms at birth. Unique she had held almost a year before getting arrested for prostitution. She called her little koala bear for how she clung to her.

Unique was no baby now. Pearl was her name. Who gets to name a person? The last time she'd seen Unique, her koala was seven years old.

Audrey had an epiphany one day, having been riding the crest of one of her wild pinks rather than her mean blues. Her mother was the same way. She lived up or down. It was slow or fast, soft or hard, rarely predictable and never gentle.

She was not yet burned. She was a mess, sure, but she was still a gorgeous mess, which was the easiest kind of mess to be, even if it doesn't make you safer. She convinced some sulking trick to drive her four hours north. She rummaged through drawers as he'd impatiently honked the horn under her window. She grabbed a fistful of necklaces—she'd always liked chunky jewelry, stones, beads, crystals, magic.

She sang along with the radio the entire way. When there were too many commercials on the radio, she sang the Carpenters and the Rolling Stones. She opened the windows and fucked her careful hairdo. She sang to the yellows and reds and browns of the fall foliage. Even as he calculated the excuses he'd have to make to his wife, Audrey knew he loved her instantly. She was freedom. Freedom is a powerful fantasy.

She ran to the window of the ornate, white Victorian farmhouse with navy-blue shutters that her family had owned for nearly a century. Once stately, those hundred years had left it looking like a wedding cake in the rain.

She'd colored a hundred pictures of that house, climbed every tree on the farm. "Pearl!" she cried out. "Pearl, my love!"

The girl wouldn't have answered to Unique.

Pearl had flown to the window and thrown it open.

"I'm your mommy!"

"Mommy!"

Audrey threw her the beads.

"I love you, I love you, I love you, I love you."

Pearl caught them, looked behind her, and shuttered the windows without a backward glance.

Unique was thirteen now.

Audrey gained momentary focus, and wow. What a shithole to die in.

"Time," said the man on top of her, wedging her between the back seat and the floorboards, the small of her spine propped on the hump in the middle.

Time, like that song she liked, "Time After Time."

A parking lot. Not even lipstick on, and a fuckwad trick on a shitty night saying cheesy shit like, "Time."

Her little brother Billy would be lonely without her.

Audrey had seen him only sporadically over the last chaotic years, but all their lives, he'd been her one true friend. There had been no school friends allowed for either of them, so why bother trying? No sleepovers. No dances.

Except the one junior prom.

Billy made a case for her. What could go wrong if he went as her chaperone, with a pocketful of shiny dimes and a promise to call their mother if anything untoward occurred? Mother reluctantly agreed. Behind closed doors, the siblings rolled their eyes, locked fingers, jumped up and down with silent screams. Billy weighed in on her gown, her corsage. He made sure they were a splash.

It was the first time she'd danced anywhere but tap class, her bedroom, or her front yard. The first time she danced with a boy.

Oh, my love. My darling. I've hungered for your touch...

She sang and twirled into the parlor when they arrived home.

"You took their breath away," said Billy, sitting in the most uncomfortable chair in the room and crossing his arms like a toddler. Since the moment her soccer coach had gently told her it was time to get a bra, Audrey had turned the boys' heads. Her brother and best friend was jealous.

How could he not be sore? Boys, boys, boys, she got 'em. Boys, boys, boys, he wanted them and couldn't figure out how to say it. Even if he could, she'd have him bested any day. Boys, boys, boys. No end to them.

A cracking sound. A trickle of wet down her face. No end.

She realized the man choking the life from her wasn't saying "Time." He was saying "Mine. You are mine."

She wasn't bound by him. She was no longer even bound by time. How about that? She was back at junior prom. Her life was hers again.

Poor Billy, ever the brother, ever the bridesmaid.

"Whaaaat? Oh, come on," she said. "No way, really?"

She spun around, still in her bell dress, and wedged herself into his lap, throwing her arms around his neck.

"Can you let up on that bitchy pose?" she asked. He softened and she tucked her forehead into his neck. He wrapped his arms around her and told her she was too bony and should eat a sandwich.

She was maddening, but she knew it was hard to resent her for long—a thing so bright and wild. They'd all loved her because she was almost sure to fail. She was the one who took the bullet for the sober and sensible.

Audrey knew her mother. She knew Unique would be forced to stand in the backyard and burn those necklaces. But maybe one day,

Unique would remember them catching the autumn sunlight as they flew to her small hands and would hear I love you, I love you, I love you.

"You did, honey," Billy said, stroking her hair. "You took their breath away."

38

THE PEOPLE OF THE STATE OF CALIFORNIA V. SAMUEL LITTLE: THE VERDICT

LOS ANGELES, CALIFORNIA
AUGUST AND SEPTEMBER 2014

Hilda Nelson's and Laurie Barros's testimony echoed Leila McClain's. It also took Barros two tries to make it to the stand. She collapsed like a rag doll three steps into the courtroom and hyperventilated. Roberts lifted her to her feet.

Barros took the stand with the simmering fury of a dismissed victim of attempted murder who was forced to face her attacker in court yet again. He'd served a paltry eighteen months of his four-year sentence for assaulting and attempting to murder her and had gone on to kill and kill again.

Speaking for MIA Tonya Jackson were Louis Antonio Tamagni and Wayne Spees, former members of the San Diego Police Department who had worked as patrol officers on the night of October 25, 1984, in the area of Thirty-Sixth and G Streets, exactly the same patch of scrub and trash where Laurie Barros had been dumped by the side of the road only a month earlier. In an isolated area lit only by the moon and the headlights of the patrol car, the silhouette of a black Thunderbird appeared in front of them. They hit the high beams and the red light, and when Sam exited the vehicle and pulled his usual routine about having makeup sex after having a fight with his old lady, these cops actually checked. He'd had others pull away, no questions asked.

Spees stayed with Sam while Tamagni found Tonya Jackson, upper torso and head crammed onto the floorboard of the back seat, legs spread, beaten unconscious, gurgling blood and gasping. They called an ambulance, followed behind with Sam. He told them the hospital exam wasn't going to show any rape, just hands around her neck, and that he should have killed the bitch. Neither one of them would ever forget that night nor the debacle that followed. They had done everything right, from their model first response to dotting every last *i* and crossing every *t* in the reports. They'd not only caught him in the act, they'd done a heroic job with the follow-through, and still, they'd watched him walk away. Now look at this mess.

A flurry of other prosecution witnesses offered both forensic and law enforcement testimony. Roberts took the stand and explained her role in the CCSS, the investigatory steps, and the chain of custody surrounding the evidence.

Pentz called a criminalist and trace analysis expert in shoeprint and tire track examination who testified to the footprint and a criminalist who testified to an unidentified male DNA profile in the original Apodaca genital swabs. Sam did not testify on his own behalf. He'd done so before with positive results, appearing forthcoming, casual, unconcerned, so it was anyone's guess if they'd put him up there again, but he remained silent.

On August 29, 2014, Silverman wove the narrative and the science piece by piece into a half-day-long closing argument that presented the evidence both physical and circumstantial. She humanized the victims and appealed to common sense. What were the chances all three victims would be found murdered with the same MO in a five-mile radius with Sam's DNA on them?

Silverman's steady pace was most people's sprint: willful, deliberate, premeditated.

> SILVERMAN: All of the evidence that we've presented over the course of the last week or two proves that this particular defendant is guilty beyond any reasonable doubt. If there is another reasonable interpretation of the evidence and therefore you decide the defendant is not guilty, that's one thing; but I would think you would be hard-pressed in a case like this to be able to find another reasonable interpretation of the evidence.
>
> These victims in this case have been dead for over 25 years. It is time—and you are the jury—it is time that justice is served in this case. In this case, justice demands that you find this particular defendant guilty of three counts of first-degree murder, along with the multiple murder special circumstance, and that you finally find some resolution for this case.

When Pentz was up, he took a little dig, promising to be to the point. He acknowledged the horror and emotion brought up by the graphic and disturbing testimony, distinguished between direct and circumstantial evidence.

> PENTZ: As I ask you now to spend the next few minutes listening to my comments, I'm fully aware that some of

you are saying to yourselves: why should we render justice to him? Why should we set aside our emotions for him? Why should we be careful for him?

Well, everybody comes to justice at some point. And she has, lady justice, a blindfold over her eyes. And she holds a scale. The idea is that you weigh without attending to who it is that comes before justice; neither rich, poor, powerful, meek, the saintly or the worst sinner.

Someone with the worst imaginable past comes for justice, and still justice requires we close our eyes and weigh objectively, without emotion, without passion, fear, prejudice.

Well, we start here. We start with this idea.

We start with the idea that whoever it is that comes before you starts out innocent.

———

Starting out innocent or not, after a difficult day of deliberating, grappling with the physical and circumstantial evidence, the jury reached the opposite verdict. Guilty. Guilty. Guilty.

Sam stared ahead with a flat expression as the clerk repeated three times, "We the jury in the entitled action find the defendant, Samuel Little, guilty of the crime of murder in the first degree with special circumstances."

Sam muttered under his breath—must have messed up his deal with God to wind up in this room full of crooks, whores, liars, dogs. Even right then, the bitch detective popped an M&M into her mouth and winked at him. He shot her a curiously goofy smile and waved as he was wheeled out. The jury, the families, and the prosecution team hugged and cried outside.

The next time Sam saw any of them was almost a month later at his sentencing. He held a crumpled piece of paper in his hands.

Family members held their victim's impact statements.

Pearl Nelson teared up. The paper in front of her and her voice shook in tandem.

> NELSON: Audrey Nelson, she's my mother. She is a beautiful soul. We all have paths taken in life, do we not? Audrey had a hard path. She got caught up in the world. She was badly burned in a fire. She was away from her family, and on June 16, 1976, she gave birth to me, and she loved me so much. I was in her arms for a year before she had to give me to her parents.
>
> I know this was a hard choice for her to make. She did this so I could have a better life. Audrey knew that she couldn't give me all she dreamed for me. Times were hard, and we were separated for many years. I was 13 when the police showed up. That day I found out that she had been murdered and nobody knew who had done this.
>
> What I did know is that I was bonded to her and I yearned for her daily. The reason why my mom was in Los Angeles in the first place is because she had gotten her life back together and she was on her way to reunite with me. She always loved me and I loved her, and this long-awaited reunion was taken from my fingertips.
>
> All I ever wanted was my mom. Instead of saying hello and hugging her, I had to say good-bye. How can

I ever forget that moment when I put down that rose at
her burial. I never buried anyone before, let alone my
own mother. I had been waiting for her.

Laurie Barros didn't have anything prepared, but she stood and
claimed the years of shame and blame and pain back, in Jesus' name,
for all the victims.

Guadalupe Apodaca's family went next. Sam shifted in his chair,
asked Pentz how much of this bullshit he had to take. Sam began
interrupting the proceedings. He shouted, "I didn't do it!"

Sam called on God as his only true judge.

ZAMBRANO: Your honor, my name is Tony Zambrano.
I am the son of Guadalupe Apodaca Zambrano. And
I want to tell that piece of shit right here: you fucked
up… You think this is over? It is not over by a long shot.
I have been looking for you for a very long time. Fuck
you. Remember me. You will see me again.

The judge cautioned Sam to behave before he spoke.

LITTLE: This conviction was brought on by lies. And liars
coached by liars. I hope that in the new trial, if I get one,
the evidence that was withheld and looked over will be
brought up by my attorneys in a fair trial. The obsession
of labeling me as a serial killer without any proof, any
bodies, was a legal lynching. Speculation and surmising
is not proof.

On September 25, 2014, Samuel Little received three consecutive life sentences without the possibility of parole. Maintaining his innocence, he held up a defiant fist against the injustice as he was wheeled out.

39

THE RABBIT HOLE:
THE NATIONAL INVESTIGATION

ACROSS THE UNITED STATES
2018–2020

By the fall of 2019, nearly two years had passed since I first heard the name Sam Little. It had been a year since his extradition to Texas and back again. The FBI had made a few major media pushes, seeding national and local media outlets with Sam's drawings of the unmatched confessions in hopes tips from the public might help identify the victims.

"He's hard not to like," said a law enforcement officer. "He's like Bill Cosby, before." Before what? Before we knew. But with Sam, we already knew, in elaborate and mind-numbing detail. In spite of this, he is indeed hard not to like.

In my professional estimation, likability is an indicator of exactly nothing.

Holland coached the law enforcement teams—detectives and prosecutors—who still filed in to talk to Sam: no rape, no beating. He's a killer. Don't start talking about remorse. He'll get bored. Just let him go off on tangents if he wants to.

"He might flirt with you," Holland told the female detectives. "Let it happen."

There was a nuance to Sam's confessions. I'm sure Holland caught it, but no one else seemed to.

I listened to his sordid tales, time and time again. Sam would flirt with the women around him, but what really got him off was talking to the *men* about the murders. They listened raptly to his sexual fantasies. He talked nonstop about pussy and titties and big thighs. He'd mock women, get the cops to egg him on.

No shit. Really, man?

It excited him to have men lean in and swallow hard.

Local newscasters offered ten cent psychoanalysis: deep down he hated women. He hated his mother.

Big whoop. Him and everyone else.

Sexual predation and serial murder are like a nesting doll: reason upon reason, until you finally reach the center and find it ultimately inscrutable. Somewhere in the shadows, a rough beast you can't understand is at play. Count yourself lucky that you cannot ultimately solve this puzzle.

As for me... What reckless and over-eager writer develops a deeply personal and complex relationship with a sexual strangler just to get a jump on a story? Who seeds interviews with a hateful and vicious killer, with nicknames and in-jokes, and special songs? My office walls were lined with pinned maps and ghastly portraits. What drove me to pursue this story at the expense of other, healthier aspects of my life?

There was nothing remotely sexual in our rapport. Our Big Daddy and his little kitty cat routine was a vaudeville act. We held currency for one another. I wanted my book. He begrudged me nothing at all. He wanted canteen money, he wanted his "sugar," which was warm fuzzies and kissy noises and songs. He bragged about me to the guards and inmates. He had a well-put-together white lady in a skirt visiting him, hanging on his every word. I made him "famous."

Was the way I worked him morally reprehensible? Revenge porn meets amateur detective work? Good journalism? Shape-shifting? Plain shifty?

The product of my efforts will be tried by a jury of my peers.

On one of my last visits to the California State Prison, Los Angeles County, a female deputy I'd nicknamed Nurse Ratched pulled me into what was essentially a closet with a desk and a chair. It was the room where they check you with a wand if you have a pacemaker or a medical device.

"Take a seat."

A dozen deputies closed ranks behind her.

"Suspend her!" came a peppy male voice from the back of the mob. What? For what?

Standing beside Nurse Ratched was a deputy I'd nicknamed Li'l Danger—the one I always hoped would call my number. About 115 pounds wet, wire-rimmed glasses, no makeup, never a hint of expression, never a hint of gratuitous shade. I was nearly perfect with my protocols by then. A few of the female deputies still found imaginary reasons to bust my balls because I was there for Sam, and Sam was all over the news. He was a monster. They worked at a men's maximum-security correctional facility. You punish monsters. I didn't look much like punishment.

"Well, wait now," said Li'l Danger.

Nurse Ratched narrowed her eyes, "I watch you on nineteen cameras."

It was kinda kinky. The only thing harder than getting into trouble is getting out. All the characters are sexy in my world-leader, pretend-disco life remix. How was I going to talk my way out of a genuinely scary situation if I was busy writing a novel in real time?

I pulled myself to the present by playing my fives. Five famous sheriffs, real or fictional. Five saints. Five synonyms for screwed.

Ratched held up two pictures I had brought with me. You're allowed ten photographs, and the guidelines are basically no porn, no gang stuff, and no maps.

These particular photos were given to me by a woman named Bobbi with whom I'd become friendly.

She was a self-styled citizen sleuth, investigating her own rape and assault. The photos were of her around 1979 in Key West. I was almost sure her attacker wasn't Sam from MO alone, but after dozens of women had reached out to me, only two remained possibilities, and Bobbi was one. There were too many holes in the story, and the MO diverged, but I couldn't definitively say no based on the facts. She'd gone the route of both local and federal law enforcement, with no conclusive result. It wasn't for lack of trying on the part of the detectives or the feds. It probably wasn't his case, and even if it was, it would have been impossible to prove.

Bobbi was sure she had recognized Sam in the paper. This was not an uncommon call for me to get. Many were sure it was him who attacked them, and most were wrong. They weren't liars. They had been waiting for a desperately long time to learn who had hurt them while they did the unthinkable—survived, built lives and families.

The plasticity of memory is widely studied by some of the most brilliant minds in the world, and we're still only piecing together a cursory understanding of how it works. Particularly important is the relationship between memory and veracity in a criminal justice context.

Eyewitness testimony is a tricky thing, as illuminated by Dr. Elizabeth Loftus in her landmark studies that dismantled the "Satanic panic" of the eighties as well as its foundational psychological tenet: "repressed memories."

We're all suggestible. We're all vulnerable.

When I received these calls, I could almost always rule out Sam quickly. For instance, he never drove an eighteen-wheeler, or he was in jail at the time, or he was killing someone else clear across the country on that same night. I always listened to the whole story, responded with whatever information I had that was a matter of public record, often shared a personal story to mitigate the shame that inevitably comes after you spill—the buyer's remorse of confession. I told them it was not their fault and referred them to victims' advocacy organizations and support services.

Bobbi asked me if I would please put her pictures in front of him. See if they sparked anything.

The deputy held up the photos. "Who is this?"

"A friend."

"She hesitated!" shouted a voice from the mob—okay, a small mob, but in tactical gear.

"She's lying!"

"Suspend her!"

The colosseum was giving me the thumbs-down?

"Okay, okay, let's just," said Li'l Danger, making a "bring it down" motion with her hands.

Li'l Danger had a light touch. She brought the slightest hint of shame to her otherwise unremarkable de-escalation tactics. Like, what is wrong with you hysterical-ass little girls bullying this woman?

"Do you know? That he gets off on these photos of women? We

don't want him to have these. These are sick. These are perverted. You don't know the kind of person you're dealing with."

"I'm sorry, ma'am. Thank you very much for explaining that to me. I can see now that you're right. I won't let it happen again."

I have no idea what else I said as I stood and edged sideways along the filing cabinets toward the door.

The mob disbanded, bummed. I waved and sort of bowed, walking backward. I learned that from a prince who literally made women bow and walk out of a room backward. Who knew it would come in handy?

"Always so impressed by how you all handle this stressful work. Keep up the good work! Thanks again!"

———

I still took almost daily calls from the prison. The years of conversation, plus the fact that I never knew how long he was going to last, made me bolder. I'd heard the same reinventions, justifications, and sociopathic garbage for years. There was a limit to how far I could push him before he angered, but he wasn't getting any younger. When I asked what he wanted the world to know about him, he waxed poetic about how much he loved women.

"Stop boring me with this already. I live up to my side of the bargain. You gotta give me something good. What does it feel like to be you? What does it feel like to kill people? What's the weirdest one you ever did? What's the worst? Don't bullshit me. Do it."

"But I'd tell the world something good. I'd tell them I wish I was a lawyer."

"Okay, fine, you wish you were a lawyer. Why?"

"I could help people move big cases."

"Yeah, well, no one likes being a lawyer. Do better."

"Shut your damn mouth. I'll tell you what I want people to know. Something good is that I met you and I love you. You're so pretty and good. I'll tell all the world I love you."

"I love you too. Who do you think you're talking to? You know what no one is going to pay me for? A book about how pretty and good I am. They're going to pay me for a book about how awful you are."

The automated voice that interrupted the calls every five minutes to advise that the call was being recorded said, "You have ten seconds remaining."

Fuck.

The LAPD was slammed with the #MeToo task force, though still combing for the Little cases on their off moments. Trying to match these confessions obtained by a Texas Ranger who didn't know Los Angeles at all, out of the mouth of someone on so much crack by the eighties he barely knew north from south, didn't provide much hope. Tensions built between different jurisdictions.

Static crackled between Holland and me, between lawyers and agents I didn't even know I had, between increasing demands from both family and work.

The FBI and DOJ were still hung up on an angry email I'd sent a year back but apparently never got old.

"Hoooeee!" Holland laughed. "Dug this up and haven't laughed so hard since the first time I read it."

I had called to follow up on a lead.

"Still? Snore! I was angry. They lied to me. I apologized!"

"I'll give you all that."

"If you don't blow your stack with this story at some point," I said,

"I have a handy-dandy questionnaire for you right here. One, do you display excess glibness or superficial charm?"

While the oven heated to a blistering five hundred degrees, I towel-dried, trussed, and seasoned a chicken in a cast iron pan.

"What you got?" he asked.

"Some leads," I told him. "Nothing terrific."

"Shoot."

"Now, why would I do that? Every time I have a perfectly good relationship with a local jurisdiction, you tell them I told the DOJ to fuck off."

I aggressively chopped brussels sprouts in quarters, grabbed the ingredients for a quick corn bread.

"True or not true?" he asked.

"False! I told them to go get fucked."

"I say the exact same thing I say to your face, Jillian. How could anyone stay mad at you?"

"People manage."

"You give me a headache. That describes it the best. You sure you want to get into that right now? Question: were you hitting up some shrooms when you wrote that note?"

"Question: were you born eighty years old? First of all, you don't 'hit up' shrooms. Second of all… No, of course not. Or, I don't think so."

"You told the *federal government* to get fucked, Jillian. You cannot *tell* the federal government to get fucked. They take that shit *personal*."

"Who in the federal fuck cares about me? This sounds like your doing."

Holland laughed so hard he choked on his whiskey. "No, you can't blame it on me. No, no, no, no, not me. Not this one. This is one hundred and fifty percent you, young lady. Got a little less boring around here at least, I'll tell ya."

I minced garlic to pulp, scraped it into a satisfying pyramid. My oldest dog, Calvin, lay on his side panting. He had always been close to the food. He made it over for the smell of the chicken but couldn't stay on his feet. I tripped over him as I maneuvered around the island and almost dropped the whole pan.

Each day, Calvin was starting to lose his legs from under him and not get back up. Our dog was dying.

"I'm nice when I talk about you," said Holland. "I say you're an incredibly intelligent person. I say you're very driven, and I say you're slightly out there. Maybe I say you're pretty *far* out there."

"That's not a compliment. It's a warning."

"What now?"

"I'm crazy but smart? That's like saying I'm ugly but interesting."

"I never called you interesting."

In early October 2019, the FBI announced they had verified fifty of Samuel Little's ninety-three confessions, including the original three in Los Angeles. Sam had topped Gary Ridgway, the Green River Killer, with a confirmed forty-nine, to officially become the most prolific serial killer in the history of the United States.

Suddenly everyone remembered that birthday party to which I showed up late because I was at the prison. They texted: *Is this your guy?!?*

The FBI released five-minute-long, carefully crafted segments of interviews with Holland leading Sam through the facts of five different confessions that had yet to be solved:

1. Marianne, 19, transgender Black woman, Miami, Florida, 1971 or 1972

2. Unknown, 30–40, Black woman, New Orleans, Louisiana, 1983

3. Unknown, 25, white woman, Covington, Kentucky, 1984

4. Unknown, 24, Black woman, North Little Rock, Arkansas, 1992–1994

5. Unknown, 40, Black woman, Las Vegas, Nevada, 1993

Every case was a rabbit hole, lined with red tape.

I could recite the Los Angeles victims in order by nickname: Mobile Home Girl, 1984; Granny, 1987; Skinny Girl, 1987; 7-Eleven Fence Girl, 1987; Shelf Girl, 1987; Hollywood Hills Girl, 1987; Griffith Park Girl, 1987; Alice, 1991; Bald Head Hill Girl, 1991–1992; Turban Riot Girl, 1992; Observatory Girl, 1992–1993; Helicopter Girl, 1992–1993; Bathtub Girl, 1996; Sheila Sweater Girl, 1996; Truck Girl, 1996; T-Money, 1996.

I wrote, spent days at a time on the phone, and organized art, letters, phone calls, law enforcement contacts, the ever-growing forty-five-page timeline, the confessions, the press, the victims, the interviews.

Time became as slippery as Sam himself. The circles under my eyes were a mixture of puce and lavender. I assembled chapters but not quickly enough for anyone. I was way past my deadline, trying to finish a book while standing smack in the middle of the story. Furthermore, it was a world upended, as the COVID-19 virus waged its ruthless early attack. I couldn't make the face-to-face contact I relied on to get information from people. Our dining room turned into a makeshift classroom, and suddenly it was as if Scott and I both had four impossible jobs, and the pay sucked.

A job playing live music is awesome…until the world shuts down. It lit a fire under my ass. I sat down in front of a database one day and furiously began to look beyond the boundaries of LA County for articles to match details in the stack of the sixteen Los Angeles confessions in front of me. Without being able to move around much, the crime rates in the city leapt. Widespread protests broke out in the streets against institutionalized racism. Protestors butted heads with MAGA yahoos in paramilitary gear.

I turned my attention to the whys and hows and wheres and whens and cars and scars and bars rather than God and sexual nightmares and listening to Sam mimic his mommy. I witnessed, listened, wrote, made connections. While I hadn't started with the intention of any real investigative work beyond ferreting out the story, I caught the bug along the way. Billy Jensen's book *Chase Darkness with Me: How One True-Crime Writer Started Solving Murders* provides an excellent blueprint for embarking on a civilian murder investigation in an ethical and effective way.

All of Sam's Los Angeles melted into the pulsing center of South LA as he talked about different strolls interchangeably: Manchester and Figueroa Street (Sam called it Figaro Street), the Tam's Burgers at Central and Fifty-First, the Tam's on Century. Florence and Figueroa, the heart of the ho stroll. He remembered his girlfriend's houses: Sixty-Second and Vermont, then Eighty-First and Vermont, Eighty-First and Figueroa, Fifty-First between McKinley and Avalon.

He remembered he dumped that body off San Pedro, off Fig, off

Main, way out Central to the country, up into the Hollywood Hills, into Griffith Park.

The Million Dollar Hotel with the glowing neon heart (now the Rosslyn). South Park and pool halls and juke joints. Fletcher's bar on Central—everyone went to Fletcher's. Everyone stuck around Central.

Between the 1920s and the 1950s, Central Avenue north of Slauson clear to downtown was known as just "the Avenue." It was the West Coast hub of jazz music and culture. Famous jazz and blues musicians came out of Jefferson High onto the national stage. It was a middle-class neighborhood by day, until the streetlights came on and the respectable folk locked their doors. Ellington, Count Basie, Billie Holiday, and Charles Mingus all played the Avenue. Jelly Roll Morton had a hotel there he used to pimp women out of while he went and played the Avenue. Out-of-town jazz musicians all stayed at the Dunbar Hotel, where Ellington's band popped corks and twirled the starry-eyed local girls every time the jukebox played their version of "It Don't Mean a Thing (If It Ain't Got That Swing)."

By the late eighties, when Sam made LA his hub for the next decade, the Avenue had turned to just Central, fractured into corners with chop shops and dollar stores. The famous serial killers of Los Angeles picked their way through the wreckage. The Dunbar turned to a single room occupancy (SRO) facility. Residents of SROs have government assistance. Those in the downtown and South LA areas are often converted, crumbling art deco hotels.

The distorted lens of crack cocaine blurred the edges between the victims, the years, the hills, the graffiti, the dumpsters, the elephant grass.

I sometimes located the places he described, such as the liquor store at Manchester and San Pedro where he picked up T-Money. I found a restaurant and the health clinic on the corner of Slauson and San Pedro where he said he dumped her body in an alley. Except the clinic was down the block, on another corner, and there was no alley where he described it.

Sam had set his coordinates for opportunity. The names of the streets shifted, as did the years.

The LAPD was having many of the same frustrations. With an offender who leaves few or no rape kits, in a city where six or seven serial predators were operating at the same time, it's hard to work backward from a confession. The original CCSS started with the evidence and followed the trail to a suspect. There was no CCSS anymore, and even if there were, the Little case involved working backward while mobilizing a department to put coveted resources toward a guy who was no longer an imminent threat.

Tim Marcia and Mitzi Roberts had gone to see Sam the previous week and days later had him in the car for a ride-along. He had called me the next day, proud of himself for helping the police but confused. His memories of LA were part drug-addled delusion to begin with, but everything had also physically changed. Facing those same streets looked like a funhouse mirror version of the world he once prowled. Marcia and Roberts walked away with five front-runners for case files but scant actionable information.

"That wasn't LA," he told me later, sounding letdown. He'd wanted to help them and get a pat on the head. He felt he had disappointed the cops, disappointed me. He wanted to relive the past, only to find he never understood it in the first place.

"I'm soft," he'd said to Marcia. Like any confused old man. "I'm soft on it. I don't know nothin' here."

Marcia said, bottom line, they didn't have it unless they had a strong enough case to present to Beth Silverman. Silverman had prosecuted Sam Little, the Southside Slayer, Blake Leibel, Harold Holman. She prosecuted the Grim Sleeper, *twice*.

Marcia told me, "You don't just go dig up eighteen cases that match pretty much what he's saying. He's good on certain aspects of the female or location…date and time ain't gonna be there. Repetitive details across confessions, something is always right and something is wrong—how do you tease that apart? Finding these cases isn't as easy in LA. It's not Odessa."

My attention kept turning to a victim named Alice. I had a detailed confession, a drawing, and—most unusual for Sam—a name. I circled it.

Alice.

40

THE PEOPLE OF THE STATE OF OHIO V. SAMUEL LITTLE

CLEVELAND, OHIO
AUGUST 2019

"Why don't they just kill him?" T asked as I packed for Ohio. "He's a bad guy. He's an asshole."

My older son is not an angel, but he wants to be a Navy pilot, and swearing is not his thing. I knew he must have been angry, confused. T loves Black Panther, Transformers, the Avengers...the military. In those worlds, the solution is you kill the bad guys.

"Because as a society, we judge ourselves by the humanity with which we treat the worst of our assholes," I said. "It's easy to say just kill someone bad. I think that too sometimes. But who decides that? When does it stop? And then what makes us different from someone like him?"

"That he's an asshole."

"First of all, 'asshole' does not begin to describe Sam. You can work on your vocabulary. More importantly, there is no clause in our Constitution that says, 'except for assholes.' You treat an asshole with dignity not because they're worthy of it but because you have dignity.

It's called due process, and it means we should all be treated fairly under the law."

"What's justice?" asked my increasingly politicized Black son, who both made signs for BLM protests and still played with Transformers. "What's fair?"

I was supposed to have a developmentally appropriate answer for that. I know I used to. I went for the hug instead, because nothing came to me.

———

Only a small percentage of criminal cases resemble a classic three-act piece of theater with a crescendo of redemption. We all love it. Holland loves it, with his, "You can't handle the truth!" Silverman loves it, and she actually does it, but she's the exception.

What's not to love? Wave a magic gavel, say that order prevails and justice is something more than an interesting abstraction.

Legal documents are a gauntlet of loopholes and stonewalls, and I wasn't the legal genius I'd secretly suspected myself to be. How could you read this shit, much less write it, without wanting to drown yourself in a bucket of your own tears? Give up, call four lawyers you know, and ask them to explain? You'll get four different answers.

I had learned by then that if I could just hang out for a minute with a police report, a coroner's report, a bazillion-page legal document—all essentially in a foreign language—it would eventually click. The click wasn't usually a conclusion; it was whatever I was missing. I stared into the bowl of alphabet soup until the letters started to make words, which made sentences, which told a story.

The proceedings in Ohio weren't a nail-biter. He did it. By Skype, he'd plead guilty to two murders in Cleveland, then do the same in

Cincinnati. His lesser charges would be dismissed, and he'd be sentenced. I was more interested in who might attend.

Deputy DA Richard Bell had indicted, though he could more cheaply and easily have exceptionally cleared the cases. It took some oomph on the part of the Cleveland DA to pursue this level of public accountability for the murders of Mary Jo Peyton and Rose Evans and on that of Cincinnati DA Joseph Deters's office for the murders of Annie Lee Stewart and Cincinnati Jane Doe.

I had spoken recently with Detective Kellyanne Best. I'd heard about her from Sam—she was his new best friend, but he told me not to be jealous. We'd all live together in his palace in heaven. Best was warm and empathetic, looking for the checkable facts but willing to talk for hours to get even one. He'd read her letters to me, so I can speak to her pitch-perfect rapport, sharing just enough about her lasagna and love of football. She solved two of Sam's thirty-year-old cold cases.

"How many detectives do you have in your cold case department?" I asked her.

"Me."

I got that answer from detectives all over the country. Most departments didn't have a cold case anything. Cold case solves were more often than not driven by passion, curiosity, and that unidentifiable thing that draws some of us backward, backward, backward.

An unidentified victim remained in both cities.

The night before the trial, I quizzed my friend Jon Feldon, a brilliant and passionate public defender. I always paid for his legal advice with a shiny nickel.

"They worked all this out. He's in front of a judge in a courtroom. The judge is going to hear the plea and sentence. Okay, so in your case, it would be an alien invasion if anything else happened, right? The judge might phone it in, or he might thoroughly explain the proceedings to your guy. You're going to be there. That's press, and that helps. I hope he does. You'll find it interesting.

"So your guy states for the record that he is making an intelligent and knowing decision, of sound mind and all that. Understands waiving his rights, jury trial, self-incrimination. Hang on…"

Dishes clattered into a sink in the background.

"A good judge will make sure your guy understands the proceedings and potential consequences. If that's all good, he'll be sentenced. Talk about narrative," he said. "When you're a public defender, you fight for your client with all you have, and memory is a tricky thing."

"Explain."

"You have to believe in a narrative to sell it. You believe your story. Or it's his story, but you're telling it. It can take some emotional acrobatics. What you need to understand is the other side is doing their job to fight for him too, with all they have."

"What now?"

"They're fighting for something that is human and essential. Justice. He is a human."

"They're fighting for him, theoretically."

"Correct. Y'know, one connection between writers and lawyers. We witness or arbitrate the human condition and somehow still have to find a way to be a part of it."

In expectation of the upcoming trials, the FBI announced more than sixty verified cases. I wanted to understand what put the CLOSED stamp on a file in terms of long cold cases. What were the evidentiary expectations? What could make a case for reasonable doubt? What was the impact of community, media, departmental interest, clearance rates?

According to the FBI's website on the Uniform Crime Reporting (UCR) Program, there are basically two ways to clear a criminal case: by arrest or by exceptional means.

Cleared by arrest

In the UCR Program, a law enforcement agency reports that an offense is cleared by arrest, or solved for crime reporting purposes, when three specific conditions have been met. The three conditions are that at least one person has been:

- Arrested.
- Charged with the commission of the offense.
- Turned over to the court for prosecution (whether following arrest, court summons, or police notice).

Cleared by exceptional means

In certain situations, elements beyond law enforcement's control prevent the agency from arresting and formally charging the offender. When this occurs, the agency can clear the offense exceptionally. Law enforcement agencies must meet the following four conditions in order to clear an offense by exceptional means. The agency must have:

- Identified the offender.
- Gathered enough evidence to support an arrest, make a charge, and turn over the offender to the court for prosecution.
- Identified the offender's exact location so that the suspect could be taken into custody immediately.

- Encountered a circumstance outside the control of law enforcement that prohibits the agency from arresting, charging, and prosecuting the offender.

Examples of exceptional clearances include, but are not limited to, the death of the offender (e.g., suicide or justifiably killed by police or citizen); the victim's refusal to cooperate with the prosecution after the offender has been identified; or the denial of extradition because the offender committed a crime in another jurisdiction and is being prosecuted for that offense. In the UCR Program, the recovery of property alone does not clear an offense.

From my hotel room, I looked out over the sunset-painted Cuyahoga River that fed into the same Lake Erie on which I'd seen the Lorain Lighthouse. I'd always liked Cleveland. There were good restaurants, a thousand microbreweries, a kickin' art museum, those cool brick buildings I always wish I had at least one wall of in my house.

It was just over a year after I first sat face-to-face with Sam Little. My research assistant Amaia and I went over the notes in the hotel the night before. I made sure I had the names and dates down:

Cleveland:
- Mary Jo Peyton, twenty-one-year-old white woman. Peyton met Sam at a bar. Her body was found in the basement stairwell of an abandoned factory in May 1984. Peyton's death was not classified as a homicide at the time.
- Rose Evans, thirty-two-year-old white woman. Sam

offered Evans a ride, then strangled her in a vacant lot where she was discovered by a pedestrian on August 24, 1991. Evans's sister scattered her ashes at a small lake years ago.

Cincinnati:

- Annie Lee Stewart, thirty-three-year-old Black woman. Stewart was picked up by Sam in Cincinnati because it was raining. She was last seen getting out of a cab at the University of Cincinnati Medical Center on October 6, 1981. She told the cab driver that she was going to see her sister in the hospital. Her body was found six days later in Grove City. Stewart was a single mother of three.
- Unknown Black woman. Her body was left beside a Kool cigarette billboard.

In both cities, an unmatched confession remained:

- Unknown Black woman, 1974.
- Unknown Black woman, age 20–35, 1982

———

Black-and-white photos of the city lined the wood-paneled walls of the courtroom. A plaque on the front of the bench read, JUDGE JOHN J. RUSSO. The flags of the United States of America and the State of Ohio flanked his Aeron chair.

The assistant DA and a paralegal set up their displays, which consisted of excerpts of prosecutor Rick Bell and investigator Jack Bromfield's interviews with Sam during which he confessed to the murders of Mary Jo Peyton and Rose Evans. The other boards each represented a victim, including the unidentified woman. They included a shoe, a watch, a ring, a cross, a facial reconstruction, a newspaper article, a pile of autumn leaves I imagine were from the crime scene.

Judge Russo came out of chambers to greet us. We shook hands, and he promised to show us his signed Bruce Springsteen poster later. He was bald, handsome, judicial enough to make you automatically feel like you did something wrong, but chill enough that you're pretty sure it was jaywalking. He wore a well-tailored gray suit and sneakers. He apologized for his footwear, holding his hands out.

"I was playing basketball and made a shot like a jerk! I've got a weight-bearing cast!"

When he left, Amaia and I each dropped into an orange cushioned seat and dug in our purses for notebooks, pens, phones.

Colorful blobs floated across a seventy-inch flat-screen TV. A few local reporters filed into the press box. A couple more with laptops or notebooks sat in the seats farthest from us. One white-haired man fell asleep with his fingers still on his keyboard.

I craned my head toward the door to see a family member, a friend, anyone not media. There is a lot of talk about "closure for families" being the purpose of a courtroom hearing, the purpose of investigating cold cases in general. Watch any true-crime documentary. It's the go-to for detectives and prosecutors: we do it for the families.

A detective in Charleston once told me, "I say that sometimes, because it's easy and takes less explaining to the press. The truth. Family or no family, I work for God's children."

For a full fifteen minutes after the last local reporter ambled into the courtroom, the door of the court never opened again. I suppose I hadn't expected it to.

We stood for the judge.

There was the usual fiddling with the Skype before a blurry Sam appeared with a female defense attorney on either side of him, framed by the concrete blocks of the prison interview room. Holland appeared close to the screen and said hi to Rick Bell.

Sam had arranged through the federal government to be guaranteed no death penalty. He required a letter stating as much from each prosecutor in order to secure his confession. He was far from stupid and knew he'd never be executed. He was seventy-nine years old, in poor health, and incarcerated in California. Since the death penalty was struck down, then reinstated a few months later in 1972, there have been only thirteen executions. The last, at San Quentin, was in 2006, and there are currently 707 inmates on California's death row, with a gubernatorial moratorium on executions. Even if Sam was in Florida or Texas or Indiana, where they execute enthusiastically, it takes an average of fifteen years for a capital case to move through the appeals process.

Sam was playing games, making people jump through hoops and promise him things. Just as I'd promised him I'd be in the courtroom when he pled, and he decided on a gesture—a secret signal. I would tell him if he'd done it or not, and then he would know if I was telling the truth. He did the signal and looked into the camera.

PTSD symptoms vary widely. One of mine is my skin goes numb. I pinched my thigh as hard as I could, a trick to bring me back from my limbic brain. I was relieved it hurt. The hypothalamus, the amygdala, the thalamus, the hippocampus: danger, need, bald emotion. Fight. Flight. Freeze. I sometimes snap a rubber band on my wrist. When I was a teenager, I used a fork on my thigh, but I don't recommend that. The pinch is a happy medium and can sometimes wake me up, or it can feel like nothing at all. When I get nothing at all, I take notes upon notes so I don't lose hours in a traumatized fugue state.

When we rose for the judge, Amaia and I spontaneously clasped hands. We weren't touchy-feely on a daily basis, but we had spent a long time together with a lot of dead women. There were also too many we hadn't met yet and many we never would. It haunted me. If I could just be brighter, harder, more relentless, I could find them. I knew it wasn't my job. It wasn't my place. It wasn't the time. I had a book to finish. I had young children.

Sam and his counsel, Mary K. Tylee and Terri Webb, identified themselves. Almost everyone who sits next to Sam unconsciously leans away from him as if repelled by a force field. When I encountered disgust around my rapport with Sam, I believe it was simply a reaction to the fact that I didn't lean away. It wasn't normal.

I wasn't on trial for being abnormal. Sam was on trial for committing multiple murders.

The judge confirmed Sam had ample time to consult with counsel.

Richard Bell for the State of Ohio, Cuyahoga County, representing prosecutor Michael C. O'Malley, identified himself.

For the next hour or so, we watched Judge Russo patiently explain constitutional rights to a hard-of-hearing, old psycho. Russo was concise, not condescending, repeating himself several times with different verbiage. Sam indicated he understood his right to a defense, what exactly was meant by a right to a trial by a jury of his peers, what it meant to waive that right. Judge Russo explained what constituted "reasonable doubt" and then broke down each of the ten charges and the potential penalties.

JUDGE: And then, finally, Mr. Little, you have a
    Constitutional right here in the United States to remain
    silent. Nobody could force you to testify against yourself.
    The state could never force you to the witness stand,
    your lawyers could never force you to the witness stand.
    And, in fact, sir, I could not force you to the witness
    stand. The state of Ohio could never use that against
    you. So, they couldn't say to a jury—Hey, Mr. Little
    didn't testify. So, the guy must be guilty. Nobody could
    ever comment about your right to remain silent. Do you
    understand you give that right up when you change your
    plea?

LITTLE: Yes, sir.

It was a script, but there are different ways to deliver lines. It's
impossible to be a fair and impartial anything. We take our best shot.
Russo listened hard, took Sam's responses seriously, and presided over a
respectful proceeding for a man many would argue didn't deserve one.

JUDGE: Finally, if you have a question of me, something
    you don't understand, please make sure you ask. Because,
    at the end, I want to be very clear that your plea is being
    offered to this court, knowingly, intelligently and volun-
    tarily, okay, sir?

LITTLE: Yes, sir.

JUDGE: And then, finally, the state of Ohio and counsel
    for yourself, sir, agreed that your time would be run
    consecutive to the sentences handed down in the fol-
    lowing cases. There were two cases in Hamilton County

that you plead guilty to today. Case number 1902957, 1902543. There's a case in Los Angeles, California. That is case, B as in boy, A…as in Angela, 400148. And a case out of Texas, Ector County Texas, uh…

The room paused and there was a mad shuffling of papers. The original Denise Brothers case number was missing.

"Hang on there just a second," said Holland from his end.

Amaia and I scrolled.

"Let's get it first."

"Shush. Duh."

In thirteen seconds, we had it. I wrote it down in my notebook, tore out the sheet, and handed it to the assistant DA. *TX case # A-18–1415-CR, 70th District CT, Ector County.*

Holland showed up a millisecond later with a piece of paper in his hands.

"I believe that's A as in Adam, 181415CR," said Bell.

"Well, yes. That is correct. That's what I have."

———

Judge Russo's tone pivoted a hair, from someone doing their due diligence to someone pronouncing judgment.

JUDGE: All right, so then this afternoon I'll note for the record that I'm satisfied, that I've informed Mr. Little of his Constitutional rights… That he understands the nature of the two offenses that he's going to change his plea to. The effects of that plea and the maximum penalties the court can impose. I'm also going to find that his

plea, this afternoon, is being made knowing, intelligently and voluntarily. Mr. Little, on case 6, 40008, sir, how do you now plead to count one, the aggravated murder charge causing the death with purpose and prior calculation and design of Mary Jo Peyton, sir. How do you plead, guilty or not guilty?
LITTLE: Guilty.
JUDGE: All right, sir, I accept your plea to guilty and find you guilty. Sir, how do you plead to count six, aggravated murder where you purposefully, with prior calculation, design, did cause the death of Rose Evans. Guilty or not guilty?

I knew the end from the start, hadn't expected to shed a single crocodile tear, even for the record. I'd survived having Sam's brutality poured into my head every day, had cried until I didn't have a drop of salt water left in me. Amaia stood next to me, stone-faced, very pregnant, in a trench coat and four-inch heels, wielding an arsenal of spreadsheets in her purse. You'd not likely squeeze a tear from that one either.

LITTLE: Guilty.
JUDGE: Alright, sir, I'll accept your plea to guilty on six and find you guilty.

We both brought our hands to our faces.
Bell acknowledged the assistant prosecutor, Hannah Smith, and their paralegal, Susan Jacobson, thanked law enforcement and Holland, and asked that there be no reduction from aggravated

murder and no agreement the sentences be held concurrent to each other or with anything else. He expressed his horror and disbelief at the callousness of the crimes.

> TYLEE: Mr. Little sincerely apologizes for the two Cleveland deaths of Mary Jo Peyton and Rose Evans. He worked intensively with law enforcement officials to provide pertinent information. Which resulted in a resolution of the Cleveland cases. In pleading today, accepting life sentences, he wishes to provide closure to the families of the deceased women as well as ensuring that no one else is falsely charged for his act. He's making amends in the only way possible under his current incarceration circumstances... To provide any and all information which he possesses. Again, he sincerely apologizes for causing the deaths of Mary Jo Peyton and Rose Evans.

> JUDGE: All right, Mr. Little. You know, I asked Mr. Bell, are we going to have family here? He said to me, Judge, you know, these are such old cases that there aren't family that either we can find or that want to be here. And that...that just gives pause. Anybody that would have been here has been affected by your actions. The heinous crimes that you committed against these women, all across the United States, have left many people with...what I would say, is a hole in their lives. Some of those people that went to their graves not having closure and this does bring closure to not only Cuyahoga County and to the city of Cleveland and to whatever family members that may still be alive for the

Peyton family or the Evans family...it brings closure
for you, you've accepted responsibility, you have been
cooperative. 93 women and the pain and suffering you've
caused the families from 1970 to 2005... I think all of us
here in the courtroom and anybody who would imagine
that any one person could commit this type of crime
over the course of 34 years is indescribable, unacceptable
and again, inhuman. And so, understanding you accepted
this responsibility, the court will hand down the sentence
as the parties have agreed to hear this afternoon.

Sam was sentenced to two life sentences, to run consecutively
with the four he already carried.

Bell was a snazzy dresser, generous with his answers, and proud
of the case. His team glowed with it. I'd seen their poster boards. I
knew they'd worked hard for this empty courtroom, with no one to
cry, hug, and thank them. The People included the people no one
showed up for.

The reporters were asking the same questions as usual. How did
he evade the police for so long? Why did he do it? They all eventually
come around to that sexy beast: evil.

One reporter said, "Okay, and you're face-to-face with him.
Could you feel the evil emanating from him when you looked at him
in the face and the eyes? Could you feel human to human that there
was something very evil about this man?"

Bell replied, "You felt it when he explained...killing the women.
He lives in two different worlds. He's able to somehow compartmen-
talize his thoughts and feelings. He'd be talking about the Browns
and our great quarterback and what type of season we're gonna have.

He would talk about the burning river. He would talk with fondness about the Cleveland area. But when he would start describing those killings, he would relive them in his mind and uh...at that point in time, yes, Yes, he'd give you a glimpse into the darkness."

I don't usually fight my way through reporters shouting questions. But I figured I was there.

"Mr. Bell, do you feel this is representative of a new era, where cold cases are being prioritized and we have the information-sharing capabilities and the science to possibly go back and seek justice for them?"

"I can tell you that in this case, it's because of the willingness to give the police this information. You have some DNA on the California case or cases. This particular offender here did not usually leave his DNA. The only way to really solve it is being able and willing to play the game. To sit down with him. To peel the onion and see what he might tell you. Then to go back and confirm and corroborate. There's nothing really new in law enforcement's strategy. There's just the diligence and the willingness, and that's what the investigators had in this case, from the Ranger to the investigator in our office."

"Was there ever a question in your mind whether or not you would indict?"

"No. We were going to indict. We were going to indict even if he didn't talk. We were going to find some way to pull these cases together and to indict. We had enough evidence initially that he had done these three killings. We were able to take what little we had and then go back and marry them to the two cases that were unsolved, to those homicide files that we were able to find. We did have some evidence. But in order to prove what was his intent...and the prior calculation and design, the premeditation, we had to be willing to engage in those conversations and learn from them. And that also gave us the corroboration and the confirmation to be able to verify specifics."

———

Amaia and I walked the two blocks back to the hotel, where we freshened up, dressed down, and went to meet Betty and Inez for dinner at the Moosehead Saloon.

Over ribs, Betty showed me the tattoo on her arm she'd gotten of the Georgia O'Keeffe orchid on the thank-you note I'd sent her. Amaia and I were exhausted. The ribs were great.

That's most of what I remember beyond the margaritas. They asked about the trial, eventually. "How many?"

"Ninety-three. Around ninety-three"

"You think that?"

The teenager with the chocolate eyes closed them and slowly shook her head back and forth.

"My mama said he was lying about a lot of that. A lot of that, can't get her brain wrapped around that. He was a rolling stone. He didn't stay nowhere long," said Betty, twirling a lock.

"He did do it, Betty."

"I know he did, but I don't think he did as many. How would you remember that?"

"He was good at it."

"I couldn't tell you how many times I got my hair done, and it takes a whole day!"

"What about your tattoos? Do you remember getting those?"

"Now, you can ask me about any one of these tattoos on my body, and I can tell you exactly why they're about, what was happening. Everything here has a meaning."

"It's more about that, you know? I mean they're more like tattoos. He does remember them."

"They knew he was a criminal and a perv. That uncle he claimed molested him, yeah, he was a well-known perv too, and he got banished to the basement. But it was a couple of girls, not Sammy. My granddad knew something about something, and that's why he ran him off for good. We can't do anything for them girls, them people. They gotta live with that pain forever. He gotta figure that out with his maker. I know he loved his family, he painted that in pictures. He painted that picture of me. It's like, was I on the list?"

I had no idea where the list ended.

"I don't know."

———

Amaia and I visited the Ohio State Reformatory at Mansfield.

OSR, where at seventeen years old, Sam had turned his mattress up to the wall in his cell next to Boxing Betty and learned how to throw a proper right cross. Wilbert, Boxing Betty, is the only person about whom I've heard him speak with real tenderness. Boxing Betty is now dead, but there are poems written about her. She was something of a local legend in Cleveland. Everyone loved her rape revenge story. Everyone loved the sissy who was so tough and witty, even in a famously brutal prison, no one would dare touch her. She called Sam a lion. She taught him to box. She saw something in him. It wasn't the thing that won out.

OSR is now a museum and a tourist attraction. They shot the film *The Shawshank Redemption* there. Amaia and I had no idea it was *Shawshank Redemption* weekend. The line to get into this 1886 Victorian stone castle of a former prison wound all the way down the driveway, beside which you could view a remnant of the twenty-five-foot-tall wall that once surrounded it. A carnival with a monster fun-house and a Tilt-A-Whirl was being set up on the extensive grounds. Mannequins dressed in sexy prison guard costumes leaned against food trucks selling Korean tacos.

"Is a *Shawshank Redemption* carnival a thing?" I asked Amaia, whose bloated feet were blistering in her shoes. I luckily had Band-Aids in my purse, because I was already a mom. "Welcome to life with a first aid kit in your purse. Should you be going in here?"

"Why?"

"Because who knows what kind of mold or asbestos…"

"Are you fucking kidding me?"

"Or ghost slime or…"

"After all this?"

We entered through the Victorian mansion that served as the warden's quarters until the facility was ordered closed in 1990. Paint peeled from walls inlaid with stained glass windows framed by mahogany moldings.

The library, dining room, and parlor are now lined with historical photos and display cases that include iron shackles and frayed prison uniforms. They preserved the bathroom exactly, with a pink plastic rose in a vase that read HELEN. The last warden's wife accidentally shot and killed herself while opening a cabinet the wrong way? Because that happens a lot?

In what was the warden's sitting room, behind a wall of plexiglass, stood "Old Sparky," a vintage electric chair. Displayed also were with the sponge and harness they used to more efficiently deliver the electric current and the leather hood they put over the condemned men's—and a few women's—faces. There was a giant switch on the wall next to Old Sparky, framed by round dressing-room mirror lights.

As far as we could tell by their T-shirts, everyone else visiting that day was a Shawshank enthusiast. There were life-size cardboard cutouts of Tim Robbins and Morgan Freeman around every corner for photo ops. I took mine at the dining table, where I sat next to Tim Robbins and pretended to drink from the tin cup glued to the table.

A tunnel led from the warden's quarters to the main cellblock, where elongated ovals of buttery afternoon light poured through cathedral-high windows. In the middle of the cavernous fortress stood the world's largest freestanding steel cellblock in the world, made of steel from Lorain. A spiral staircase connected each floor. The only thing between us and the ground was a set of bars. The walkways shook.

I knew from Sam we were in the "penthouse," where they put the new prisoners until they figured out where they belonged: Sissies? Black guys? White guys? Teachers' pets? With the guys who would sharpen them up and fast?

I couldn't decide what was worse: touching a surface in this horrific room or my vertigo. I stood in the tiny cells, paint peeling off the walls, black mold shooting tentacles from every corner.

I'd heard too many of Sam's stories to stay in the shower room for long. On our way from the shower to solitary, we passed the cell where in 1962, a boy had killed himself by self-immolation. Sam had described the sound, the smell. I counted: bottom floor, north side, three cells in. Sam's was the one above.

I doubted anyone else there was counting cells to figure out which one had housed a boy who self-immolated and the future serial killer above him, breathing in the ashes.

If I remembered, *The Shawshank Redemption* was about fairness or the lack of it, justice or the lack of it, friendship, persistence, the ability to think critically under pressure. Maybe freedom? Oh, and probably redemption. If you have to get caught with a crowd of tourists, this was an awfully nice crowd.

In OSR solitary, you can stand in a pitch-black cell and shut the door if you want to see what it was like. I walked into a cell behind a pink-cheeked gal with blue eyeliner and a *Shawshank* shirt. We barely fit.

"Isn't this weird?!" she asked me. She turned to her husband. "How many seconds?"

"How many you want?"

She took my hands, pulled me into a huddle.

"Wager something on it."

"Huh?"

Why does this never occur to people? Why suffer for free?

"Dinner at the Cheesecake Factory," I said. "Or an anklet from the mall. A foot massage."

Must I think of everything myself?

Nope. She caught right on and turned around with her eyes all naughty. "How many do you think I can do?"

"Thirty secs max, babe."

He seemed like a nice, matching husband, in a matching T-shirt. That was a sensible answer.

"I'll last a minute if you take me to the Cheesecake Factory!"

That's my girl!

"Okay, babe?"

"Two if you throw in a movie!"

Whoa, there, sister. Slow down. First, never go up that fast. Second, two minutes feels like two hours when you're frightened.

Manual strangulation can take anywhere from three to ten to fifteen minutes. Faster with a ligature. It can take as long as you want it to. By then, I tended to view minutes in terms of strangulation.

I was now going to be standing in the pitch-dark for two minutes. I'd coached her poorly.

"Are we on?" she said, and I think she might even have done a little Beyoncé thing with her hand. I was sure she'd raise another minute if he agreed to get the popcorn, and three minutes would have been too long.

I filed in behind her and we faced forward. Her husband closed the metal door, and complete darkness engulfed us. I closed my eyes. The jolly blond behind me gasped and grabbed for my shoulder. She scraped her knuckles on the wall with a yelp. When she found my shoulder with her hand, I placed mine on it. The cell smelled like mold and misery. I tried not to retch. I was not going to fuck up the date that woman had coming to her.

Beth Silverman asked the jury at Little's LA trial to sit in silence for three minutes. To feel how long that is.

When my cellie's husband opened the door, she and I linked arms and beelined out of the building and into the sun.

41

FOR THE LOVE OF MONEY

LONG BEACH, CALIFORNIA
November 2019

The maps were codes to be cracked, and the streets were rivers, the stories they kept lying somewhere in the deep waters. I took images back to Sam, checked and rechecked, went back to the maps, to the databases, the news archives.

I wandered Sam's old strolls, drove his routes, pictured building after building no longer there, looked for overpasses and underpasses. Sometimes I knocked on doors and talked to people. When I wasn't in the mood, I'd take a walk on the main streets of South LA in the early evening, not turning off onto an alley or a side street with no traffic. I didn't want to be there after dark for too long, but no one with anything interesting to say would be out much earlier. I started going to Tam's and getting two orders of fries, extra Thousand Island for each, and a Diet Coke.

If there was an empty table, I'd go sit and read a book. Someone usually walked over to inquire who in the actual fuck I was.

If there were no empty tables, I'd approach a table with a woman sitting at it, and I'd ask if they minded.

"You a cop?"

"Nope."

"You a realtor?"

"No. Fries?"

Usually my name—Jillian—would break the ice, because they all watched *Good Day LA* and were invested in the personal life of Jillian Barberie. They thought that ex-husband of hers was a snake, and she was a good girl, and did I know whatever happened with her boobs? She okay now? Boobs healthy? Got a bad deal, poor thing. Always liked her.

I suspected a large problem with cracking the LA cases was Sam often drove much farther than he remembered.

These are my original notes on the Alice confession:

8. LA, BLACK FEMALE, 1990/1991 "ALICE"

Little stated while driving his 1977 Ford F-250 camper van in approximately 1990 or 1991, he met a slender 5'7" 120 pound, approximately 40 to 45 year old black female named "Alice" in Los Angeles, California. Little stated he was with Barbara when he met her. Little stated she was very neat in appearance and he made a date with the woman at a nearby corner/bus bench at 4:00 PM that day. Little stated at the time his Probation Officer was Felicia McNeal, and that he had just gotten out of prison or off parole. Little stated he took the woman way down Central Avenue almost halfway to Dominique College. Little stated that he took the woman into the county, and that she had a square purse. Little stated he drove onto a dirt road that led to a field. Little stated the woman was wearing stockings and high heels. Little stated he strangled the woman to death and left her face up, on her side, fully clothed in the field. Little stated that the field was near an overpass. Little stated that he heard the woman was found by a guy on a bicycle that was riding across the overpass.

- Inconsistency: Age
- Year also mentioned as possibly '91–'92.
- Age potentially younger? 25?
- Bubble-top camper van.
- "Drive on Central toward the beach and keep going—cross over Century, cross over Imperial." Did he mean Century and drove toward Loyola?
- Picked her up at a liquor store on 55th and Central.
- "Dominique" College? Loyola? Cal State Dominguez?
- Classic beauty, beautiful dress, square pocketbook.
- Says that past Imperial is a bridge. He dumped her beneath the bridge/overpass.
- Found by a cyclist.

While I drove, I listened to the music that would have been on a radio station in 1990, 1991, cycled through some of what would have been on the news, tried to remember where I had been. Germany reunified, the Soviet Union collapsed, HW was president, we went to war with Iraq. Grunge was a new thing. I was the mistress of the prince of Brunei.

Sam probably listened to an oldies station, though he also liked pop tunes. He could have been listening to "Nothing Compares 2 U," "U Can't Touch This," "Thieves in the Temple," "O.P.P.," "Smells Like Teen Spirit."

I was pretty sure I had the liquor store, the pink motel, and the bus stop. I could not find the body dump.

"Girl!"

A pretty, young Black woman with chapped lips, wearing a synthetic bob wig and a G-string bathing suit, bounced from behind a car and put her head in my window.

"The fuck? Girl, you scared the shit out of me," I said.

"Baby, baby," she said, regulating her volume. "You can't be out here by yourself! You looking for some dope? I can help you."

"I'm not looking to get high, but here." I pulled a twenty out of my bra. I always kept folded twenties in my bra. It kept me from having to take out my purse, and I also thought it was a nice touch, stolen from my nana Anna. I held it up. "There anyone who used to work around here in the late nineties?"

"Here?"

"Around here, near here. A corner, a wall. Anyone who knew girls working back then?"

She gave me directions to where some of the old-timers hung out, and I gave her the twenty, then I gave her another, which you should never do, because word of a sucker gets around. I did it anyway.

"You tell your cop friends that we know who they sending down here all pretending like they're working! Tell 'em we know straight off they dress too nice. Not you—why you wearing a turtleneck?"

"Really? Because it's cold. Put some fucking pants on!"

We laughed too hard, and she waved goodbye before ducking back out of sight.

I called my patrol cop friends down at Newton Division for fun and because I was in the neighborhood. I got to know them during my first ride-alongs as a journalist, and we'd stayed in touch.

"Hey, these hookers here are all over your sting. They told me to pass it on. You dress too nice! I'm around the corner. Are you working?"

"You down here? Jillian, why you gotta be a fucking idiot all the time? Call *before* you're coming so we know at least, or next time I swear I'll send a black-and-white for you."

"No one will ever talk to me again. I can't be seen hanging around with you riffraff."

"Fuck you. Be safe out there. How's Scott? Boys still givin' ya hell?"

———

When I showed Rick Jackson my earnest pile of binders, he took pity on me and brought me under his illustrious wing. Jackson has been called the "godfather" of LA crime writers, and is widely referenced by James Ellroy, Joseph Wambaugh, and, of course, Michael Connelly, who based his character Harry Bosch on Jackson. He is an encyclopedia of historic LA crime.

Jackson worked the original Little case with Mitzi Roberts, and he taught me step-by-step how to puzzle through an investigation report. He walked me through what an original investigation would have looked like, coaxed from me the kinds of questions one might ask when looking through a cold case file.

"Say you don't even have any original evidence to test for DNA. Okay, take a step back in time."

"Fingerprints?"

"Sure. Of course. What else? What was his blood type?"

"Um."

"You should know that."

"I do. I do. It's A, A positive."

"Okay, file that. Let's look at every line, one at a time."

When Jackson came to LA to see Connelly, he dropped by to visit the kids, flashed them his reserve badge, checked in on my progress. He told them just gross enough but not too gross stories. He brought some buoyancy back to the frustrating hunt, encouraged me to dig deeper, follow the curiosity that got me here in the first place.

"Don't start getting worn down now."

We bounced around LA together. When you obviously stick out, the best thing you can do is be the coolest version of what you are. From across a football field, you could tell Jackson was a cop. He still rocked the original cop mustache, which was now snow white. He'd take out his reserve badge and wave it around. He was forthright without being threatening, and he approached everyone as if they were already buddies.

One morning, we stepped out of my mom SUV next to a tent city in South LA. A woman cooking franks on a grill asked, "You two movie stars?"

"Yeah!" replied Jackson. "It's a porno! I know I'm an old man and you'd never guess, but it's this big!" He held his hands out to indicate a good two feet.

"That's right! That's what I'm saying!" she laughed.

"It's tucked into my sock right now so I don't step on it!"

"Can I star in Part 2?" she shot back.

"Hey, speaking of long, how long you been in this neighborhood?" asked Jackson. A masterful transition if I'd ever heard one.

We gathered a few tidbits here and there, found a Chinese restaurant that had been around at the time Alice disappeared, and the mom still worked in the back. We stumbled on an LA treasure: Granny's Kitchen Southern Style Soul Food. We ran through the possibilities over cornbread and short ribs.

I was certain we'd nailed the liquor store, the bus stop, and the pink motel, which was now a stucco hardware store with apartments above and tile displays out front. Centrale De Materiales, 5425 Central at Fifty-Fifth.

When I next visited Sam, I brought pictures. He told me Barbara was a pretty thing. He dressed her up like a doll. One hundred percent blind as a doll too. He tapped his finger on the second window from the street side.

"That was where that bull dyke lived who hollered at Alice. Alice was down in this alley right here. That's why she met me at the bus stop later in the day and ducked all down in the seat so no one would see her go."

"You said it was a motel."

"Oh, it was always that. That's it."

"This is why you make me crazy."

"Blind Barbara's godmother's dress shop occupied the ground floor. The neighborhood kids would steal when she had to leave Blind Barbara at the desk."

I had the liquor store. I had the pink motel. I even had the killer.

What I did not have was a body dump, and what I really did not have was a body. He caught me by phone out on the road one day, and I had him walk me through it.

"I am in front of a pink motel," I told Sam. "Can you imagine what that was?"

"Oh, wait a minute. Hold on. A pink motel? Yeah, on Central Avenue?"

"On Central Avenue. That's right."

"Do you remember my old lady, the blind girl? That was her godmother's motel. She liked everything pink: a pink Cadillac, a pink motel, and a gift shop out in front, on Central Avenue. It was pink."

"Did you meet one of your babies at that motel? Was she staying there?"

"She wasn't staying there," Sam said. "Her girlfriend was staying there. I met her right across the street, down one block, on Fifty-Fifth Street. On that corner was a liquor store. That's where the hangout was for us. That's where I met Alice."

"Tell me more about Alice. Tell me all about Alice. What did she look like?"

"She's kind of slim and tall, not real tall, but dark skin. She wore glasses and looked real neat, like a school teacher. She had nice clothes. It was a square purse she had, like a box. I met her down at that corner, and I looked at her and that was the first time I ever seen her hanging out with other people down there."

"What made you notice Alice?"

"Oh, man. I notice her body and her purse. I seen the look, and her neck was slim like a swan. She had the coolest neck you ever wanted to lay eyes on. My God, what's wrong with me? Me and Barbara had a late seventies Ford bubble-top van. It had a refrigerator, bed, and everything in it. And I was parked right there on the corner of Fifty-Fifth and Central. And she was standing there and our eyes met through the windshield. I got out of the van and walked over to the sidewalk. I started talking to her. Then she told me just walk… meet me over… She went across the street, which was that motel, the pink motel. It was over across the street."

"It's not a motel anymore, but I'm looking at it right now."

"Her girlfriend Sweet Pea was staying there. We walked across the street to an alley somewhere back there. They had a couple chairs. People had been back there smoking and probably doing everything else back there. So she sat down on one of them chairs, and I walked up to her and I was talking to her, kissed her on the cheek and rubbed my hand over her neck. And she said, 'Wait, we'll have time to do all that when you come back, baby.' I was supposed to meet her at four down the street—"

"This call and your telephone number will be monitored and recorded," the automated voice interrupted.

"They was hollering and talking to each other. She went up and I left. I came back down there around four. She was sitting on that bus bench down the street almost to Slauson, on the same side of the street the motel is on. Across the street was some kind of little factory or tire building there, the railroad tracks. All right, got me?"

"Yeah, yeah, I got you. I'm here. I see it."

"A lot of stuff has changed down there. So I haven't been down there since 2006 before I was there with them cops the other day." He was referring to his recent drive-along with the LAPD. "Anyway, she saw me come down in my van. She gets up from the bench and waves me over. We turn into that little road across the street by the railroad tracks. She came over and jumped in the van real fast. Bent down low so nobody could see her."

"She was hiding?"

"She didn't want nobody to know that she was out there hustling, I guess. Because I think she had a husband or a boyfriend once. I think they were mad at each other, plus she was going around with this woman that's a degenerate."

"She was busy?"

"Yeah, but she was a real nice-looking Black girl. She wore glasses, had a long, slim body. She said, 'Go down the other way. Down toward Slauson and Florence.' I took her all the way out Central."

"Right, right. How far did you get past Imperial?"

"Wait a minute. Listen. I turned down Florence Avenue. You got to go down past the post office. Then you make a left and a left. People out there were standing selling cocaine. I bought her a twenty-dollar piece. We went back to Central. Got back on Central and went straight up Central way down past Compton. And we turned right down... We seen a little turn off and way down over there. And that's where it had happened. They found the body over there."

"Way past Imperial or just past Imperial?"

"No. Past Imperial, past Rosecrans, all the way out. Past those projects, far out, way out, almost to the edge. You can see a sign. Domeroing [sic] College is out there somewhere. I pulled out there in that field right next... You can see Central Avenue from that field. There's a field. Central Avenue was on a little bridge. There's a little bridge there. And you turn off Central Avenue, down that little bridge, and there's a field down there, and the weeds halfway covers, conceals your car. We were sitting down there talking. She went in the back of the van where the beds crossways, all the way in the back, where I slept at. She was smoking her rock cocaine, and I was too. I gave her sex, and she became freakish and careless and she let me play with her throat and I was getting off."

"So when you say you gave her sex, Mr. Sam, are you talking about—did you actually have intercourse with her?"

"No, I didn't. I didn't. I was getting off by just my ultimate desire."

"So you were touching her throat, and you were touching yourself, correct?"

"Yeah. I sat down on the floor, leaning against the bed, both of us. She laid back, and she laid her head back on the bed and let me feel her throat. She was putting her hands around my penis and she was jacking my dick off. She was jacking my dick off, and I squeezed her neck, and I had a climax like that. I strangled her there."

"Did she say anything?"

"Let me see. Yeah. Well, when I was kissing her—I kissed her mouth. No, she didn't say nothing. After I kissed her mouth and was holding her throat and choking her, the only thing she did was struggle in my arms. She squirmed around and pulled at my hands. We were looking into each other's eyes and I was loving that. I did that until her eyes got large as a peppermint candy, staring up at me. I stared down at her, and I bent down and kissed her again. She was looking desperate for air. I couldn't stop. Afterward, I shook her and looked at her and pushed her chest in and out, but she didn't breathe no more. The air came in and out of her chest as I pushed on it. I could hear it coming in and out of her chest, but she couldn't breathe. Like a drowning person, you push their chest, but she was gone. I just put my arms around her and hugged her. I held her for a long time and looked at her hair. Then I had—"

"This call and your telephone number will be monitored and recorded."

"I just did what I wanted to do to her. I ran my hands through her hair and smelled her hair, smelled her body, looked at her. She no longer was there, so she didn't know I was doing all that. I kept holding her, and then I took her out of the van and laid her on the side so I wouldn't run over her. And I eased out away from her body, and it was laying there where I left it by the side of that dirt road right off of Central Avenue. You can look over that little bridge. I nudged her down the hill."

"Right."

"I read about that in the paper," said Sam.

"That was in the paper?" I asked. *That* was what I needed.

I was right. It was neither of the overpasses on Central. He'd described the drive the same way dozens of times, and each time, he had forgotten taking a turn. One curious comment tipped me off. As I kept asking him about it and he got progressively annoyed, one day he said, "All the way down Central to the *beach*."

The Pacific Ocean is generally "the beach" around here. It's as west as you can get without falling off the edge of the continent. But Central Avenue ran north-south, not east-west. There was no beach anywhere near Central. Maybe he meant Century Boulevard and the college was Loyola. Maybe he was just deranged. Or maybe he'd taken a turn.

As I widened the search parameters, I found this:

Los Angeles Times
12 June 1991

A man walking with his wife and child near the Metro Rail Blue Line in Long Beach stumbled across the body of a woman Monday night, and detectives believe that she died elsewhere and that her body was dumped near the tracks.

The man, whose name was not released, was walking his bicycle, accompanied by his wife and small child, when he stumbled across the woman's body near the Metro Rail Blue Line tracks about 500 feet south of the dead end of Dominguez Street about 7:30 p.m. Monday, Police Detective Roy Hamand said.

The man notified sheriff's deputies, who provide security for the Metro Rail, and deputies called Long Beach police, he said. There were no visible signs of trauma on the woman, who appeared to be 20 to 30 years old. She may have been dead for up to 24 hours when she was found, he said. The woman was fully clothed but had no shoes, purse, money or identification.

The beach was the town of Long Beach.

If you swung onto the second overpass on Central, it was just a quick hop from State Route 91 to Interstate 710 to a turnoff that led to a street called Dominguez. All along the route were signs for California State University, Dominguez.

I ordered historic aerials of the area from the early nineties, and they differed very little.

Dominguez Street reached a dead end in an industrial area, stacked with shipping containers. A train trestle ran over the freeway, and on the other side was a snarl of overpasses, one of which over-looked the exact area next to the freeway. On it, was a bike path.

I found a second article:

Woman's body found near Blue Line tracks
Newspaper June 11, 1991 | Daily Breeze (Torrance, CA)
Author: UPI MetroWire | Page: B4 | Section: NEWS

A man walking with his wife and child near the Metro Rail Blue Line in Long Beach stumbled across the body of a woman Monday night and detectives believe she died else-where and her body was dumped near the tracks.

The man, whose name was not released, found the clothed body about 500 feet south of the dead end of Dominguez Street about 7:30 p.m. Monday, detective Roy Hamand said.

There were no visible signs of trauma on the woman, who

appeared to be 20 to 30 years old, Hamand said. She may have been dead for up to 24 hours when she was found, he said.

The woman was wearing a light blue body suit, a black skirt printed with brown flowers and a red blouse printed with black flowers. But she wore no shoes, had no purse, money or identification on her, Hamand said.

Her one piece of jewelry was a small gold seashell earring in her left ear. Her right earlobe looked as if it had been pierced at one point, but the hole had been torn and then healed, he said.

There was evidence that the woman had been dragged on her back, but not through the brush where the body was found, Hamand said.

An autopsy and toxicology tests will be conducted. Investigators were trying to identify her through fingerprints, he said. The man notified Sheriff's deputies who called Long Beach police, Hamand said.

It was already dark. I called our friend Justin at the gym. He was just finishing training. Justin is a former U.S. Marine combat veteran with PTSD and hearing loss from an IED explosion in Afghanistan. He'd been a heavy artillery operator—the guy on the top of the Humvee with the giant weapon. He was thrown, and that had saved him. His platoonmates in the vehicle hadn't been as lucky.

Justin was also a Black guy who looked like a superhero. When I had to drive into South LA at night, I swung by the gym and took him along if he had the time.

I told him I needed him. I called his wife and apologized for keeping him out late. She was a bombshell blond hairstylist concerned for my safety and always game to loan out her man and reheat the lasagna. She told us to be careful and to please consider letting her give me a few highlights next time we were over. They'd brighten me up! I might not like to be obvious, but maybe I could consider a little brightness?

Justin and I exited the 710 South into a neighborhood of neat, single family houses with chain-link fences. We turned off the main street and wound through an industrial area, punctuated with swaths of undeveloped land. The sounds of trains and trucks floated over our heads—a city of highways in the sky.

Sam called.

"I'm in Long Beach!" I told him. "I am looking at one other overpass that I found in an article."

"What year was that?" Sam asked.

"1991."

"They found a body in Long Beach in 1991?"

"Long Beach and an overpass, with a bike path. Do you remember what Alice was wearing?"

The automated voice chimed in before he could reply. "This call and your telephone number will be monitored and recorded."

"She was wearing a dress."

"Did it have any kind of—"

"Oh my God," Sam interrupted. "Oh Lord. Oh Lord. I might've too. I might've drove completely to Long Beach. Oh man, oh man. You know what? You may have found her because I may have drove to Long Beach without knowing it because… Yeah. Oh my God. You did a good job, baby."

When Justin and I crawled the last bit to reach the patch of green on the side of the freeway, I hoped everything sharp I kneeled on was a thorn, not a needle. Though disoriented in the dark, the freeway streaked with light and the barreling trucks too close, the incline toward the street looked right. Sam had told me he'd given her a kick from the brush into the clearing and that she'd rolled nearly into the street and he'd felt bad about that. Dominguez Street, the dead end, the brush, the incline, the overpass, the bike path, the articles. I had enough.

When I got home, I crouched over the oversize historic aerial photograph, uncapped a Sharpie, and drew an X. I called Rick Jackson. He agreed—we had enough. He called a buddy of his at the Long Beach PD.

Twenty minutes later, he called back.

"The case is still open. The cold case matches all your details. The victim was identified at the time. Sit down. Her name was Alice Denise Duvall. I dub you an honorary member of the Detective's Club. You solved a murder, kiddo."

Alice Denise Duvall. Born June 23, 1956, died June 10, 1991. Someone had uploaded her photo onto Ancestry.com, a portrait from when she must have been five or six, in a white pinafore and matching bonnet, a dark bow around her neck, prim as a princess, hands folded in her lap, ankles crossed. Alice.

42

DEBBIE

Within the next week, I met with a couple of million-dollar-smile Long Beach cold case detectives. Detective Michael Hubble was a nice guy with Calvin Klein model looks and lots of kids. Detective Leticia Gamboa was a compact Latinx downplayed beauty who could smoke you with her liquid liner stare down. She was almost certainly the bad cop. I liked them immediately.

They showed me into an interview room. It contained only plastic chairs on either side of a table, on one side of which is what I can only describe as a white rectangular handle for an IKEA kitchen cabinet, but oversize and made for handcuffs.

We went over the dates, the articles, my notes. They couldn't share details of the open case, but they'd give me the first interview when it closed.

I got a second drawing of Alice the next day, sent them a copy. I met up with them the next month to check in and because they needed to see the original and the postmark. They'd gone to visit

Sam in prison. They resubmitted evidence, received partial results, and had been granted funding for a more expensive and conclusive Y-STR DNA test. They assured me they had enough to file, even if there was no DNA at all.

The case was back-burnered when social and political sea change hit police departments across the country as the Black Lives Matter movement challenged the inherent bias against people of color throughout the criminal justice system while a deadly pandemic put the world on hold.

Increasingly polarized political campaigns began to look like the Nuremberg rallies. Already impoverished communities turned to scorched earth. When daily life looks like a scene from *The Stand*, cold cases go to the bottom of the list. In a year, yet again, South LA was unrecognizable.

Under the circumstances, it seemed reasonable to reach out and at least tell Alice's family I was investigating the story and her sister's name had come up.

The detectives were sure. I was sure. I moved Alice Duvall to our confirmed victims spreadsheet and left a message for her sister Deborah. I answered a call from a Virginia number on an early evening in July 2020.

I gave Debbie my background and told her that I had been working on a story that involved her sister Alice. She asked to have a few days to consider whether she was ready to discuss this but called me back sooner than that. We gabbed for a bit—kids, grandkids, my family, my job. She and her husband both had lifelong military careers she couldn't talk about. She told me whatever I imagined that meant, I was right. She's a grandma now and trains tactical ops at Quantico.

She switched gears.

"I've thought on this carefully and talked to my husband and children. I'm ready to hear whatever you have to tell me about my sister Alice."

I'd walked a few people step-by-step through their mother's or sister's murders, but all of them already knew their loved one had been murdered and that the killer was Sam. They didn't know the details. Some of them wanted to know, some didn't. I looked straight into the eyes of the ones who did and told them everything I knew. I'm not a stranger to pain, nor am I afraid of the pain of others. Thresholds vary, curiosity varies.

There are many ways to tell a story. I tell stories of this magnitude slowly. I give people a chance to say uncle, which is a tough call as a journalist. Sometimes, the element of surprise can give you an advantage. Then again, this is the relative of a murder victim, not an exclusive with Bashar al-Assad. What will the jugular get you? The last drop of blood this person has to offer?

I tried to follow the lead of a victim or their loved ones.

Debbie had been in a specialized career of some kind, judging by her fortitude, her lightning-quick calculations, and the forensics questions with which she opened when she called. Looking back, the fact that she worked for the Department of Justice was a bigger clue.

I told her everything I knew. We sat silently for a while.

Debbie took a deep breath and walked me back through her childhood in the fifties in Watts. She was the youngest and least favored daughter of a disabled mother whose failure to thrive as an infant left her without the use of one arm, among other medical problems.

Debbie loved her older sister Alice. She also loathed her sister Alice. They had different daddies, neither anywhere to be found.

Why was Alice always the golden child?

Debbie said, "I know, I know. It's so hard to be so good, so pretty, everyone loves you too much? Yeah. It can be. I know it can be. But it makes me angry."

"It does, doesn't it?"

Finally. Finally, I interviewed someone who didn't say their sister had been perfect, kind, loved every animal, her smile lit up a room, beautiful inside and out, liked rainbows and pistachio ice cream. They rarely had a guess for why she had been in so much pain, but they knew she'd loved lilacs. I'd seen their crime scenes. I noticed no lilacs.

Debbie's famous, favored, gorgeous, addicted, murdered prostitute sister *pissed her off*. Of course she did! Alice was that brief, bright candle. What breaks your heart more than that?

Between Alice and Debbie, there'd been a middle sister named Doris, who'd been placed with a cousin. Debbie and Doris were still close.

"Would you say your mother wasn't present?"

"She was for Alice."

"What's your first memory of your mother?"

"Her pulling my hair out by the roots."

Three years younger than Alice, Debbie was a target for her mother's rage, which was aggravated by the regular seizures that eventually killed her at the age of twenty-six. Debbie found her mother's body and thought she was playing the Frankenstein game, where she pretended to be dead, then came to life and chased them. She never reanimated.

Alice and Debbie went to their grandmother. They went from bonnets to pigtails to braids to foot-high afros. Alice was a fiery beauty with classic features. Debbie was a beauty as well, elegant and steely, but she'd never been at all interested in that life.

"Alice loved singing. I used to tell her, excuse my French, 'Shut the hell up.'"

"That's French? Not in my house."

"She loved Chaka Khan. One time, I met Chaka Khan. I told her, I said, 'My sister is no longer living, but she loved you. That's all she did was sing your songs, and I had to tell her, 'Shut up, because you ain't Chaka Khan.' Chaka Khan was laughing. She says, 'Well, I hope she's in heaven singing my songs.' I said, 'I know she is.'"

Alice ironed her clothes every day.

"Neat as a pin. Wild as the wind." Debbie said, "That would be something like the lyrics she'd write. She was a songwriter. That's what she wanted. She wrote so many songs."

By the time they were in Washington High School, Alice, Doris, and Debbie danced on *Soul Train* in clothes their grandmother made. "Was it as fun as it looked?" I asked.

"It sure was. It was that fun! I can take you on a full ride. A *Soul Train* ride. Yep."

"You guys were teenagers?"

"I'm going to say Alice was eighteen, Doris was seventeen, I was sixteen. Oh, and it *was* fun. It was so much fun, meeting different people and entertainers. These kids to this day don't know what they're missing—the camaraderie. Don Cornelius was a bandit to be around. He was just a mean dude anyway. But the people on the show for the most part, all we wanted to do was dance together and have fun."

Debbie remembered Marvin Gaye, the O'Jays, the Whispers, Chaka Khan...

Debbie sent me an old clip of Alice dancing the famous *Soul Train* line in yellow bell-bottoms and a red halter shirt. She did a high kick at the end, her hands up in what looks like a boxing guard. It was the first time I had seen any of Sam's victims alive and in motion. She danced to the O'Jays, "For the Love of Money."

"Alice held a lot of her feelings in. She always had that sadness. She really never talked to me. She thought of me as the baby. We went out one time, first time I ever went out with my sister. She used to hang around that entertainment crowd. To me, that entertainment crowd just looked seedy."

Alice got into that free kind of life that tightens around you like a finger trap.

"She took me to the Comedy Club. That's comedy? She introduced me to this older guy. I was nineteen? Yeah, because I just graduated, and I was starting to work. He had to be in his fifties. He says, 'You know who I am?' I said, 'No, and I really don't care.' He says, 'Well, I'm Richard Pryor's manager.' 'You're not Richard Pryor, so why should I care?' He says, 'Oh, you're so cute. I want you to be my eye candy.'"

Debbie took a taxi home then and there. She didn't go back. Alice stayed.

I asked Debbie if there could have been something that happened to Alice as a kid to make her so angry. Teachers or preachers or coaches or cousins...?

Debbie didn't rule it out, but she didn't think so, because there hadn't been a marked personality change. Alice came as she was.

"I am very tuned into people. I can read you like a book when I meet you. I know whether to walk on or stay there. Like I know you're good people. If Alice was hurt, I would have known."

"Alice did not have that same intuitive gift."

"No, she did not."

"Did that scare you?"

"I wasn't scared. I was angry. I think the drugs were a solution to what she was dealing with on a daily basis. I think she got into it accidentally, hanging out with different groups of people. My understanding is, once you get that first high, you want to get even higher and higher. I got married and we moved overseas. I didn't know how bad it was until my aunt called. I came home for her. I got her into my car, and we talked, and I said, 'Why are you living your life like this? You don't have to do this. If you want to, I will buy you and Tony a ticket to Germany, and you can get yourself together. You don't have to be on these streets. I'm asking you to change your life.'"

Debbie offered Alice a ticket out, but she needed to get her own passport. Debbie even left instructions exactly how.

When Debbie left, she knew it was the last time she'd see Alice. She'd been wearing all black, which she almost never did, when she got the call. No detectives ever contacted her. She came home for the funeral, then went back to Germany. She called her aunt a couple of times a month asking after any news. Did the cops have any leads? Who had done this thing to her sister? They called the cops for a year or so but gave up when they never heard back. Never heard another word until I'd reached out.

"I raised my children to be aware that there's drugs out there. There's people that take advantage of you, so forth and so on. They know everything, for the most part, that happened to their aunt."

She rattled off what sounded like four amazing kids with four terrific jobs, all serving in the public sector.

"They are all good, productive citizens. It's all I hoped for them. The thing that finally settled my mind was, she doesn't have to deal with the craziness and hurt that she was going through all her life. The things that were happening to her. You can't live that life for that long, and then think you're going to get out of it. Some women, I guess."

"Very few."

"Very few. I didn't think she was coming out of that. You know what just came to mind? Alice and I was walking. And she looked at me and she says, 'You know, little sister, I had a dream about Jesus.' She was never like that. I thought: she is not going to be on this planet long. I tried to get as much life out of her as I could at the time. I knew Alice wouldn't ever be sixty years old. I knew that much."

43

AS IT STANDS

LOS ANGELES, CALIFORNIA
JANUARY 2021

Georgia, Ohio, Florida, Ohio, Florida, Maryland, DC, Florida, Ohio, Florida, Massachusetts, Connecticut, Florida, Maryland, Florida, Colorado, Ohio, Georgia, California, Oregon, Pennsylvania, New Jersey, Nebraska, California, Louisiana, Florida, Mississippi, Louisiana, Florida, New York, Florida, Georgia, California, Michigan, Nevada, Florida, California, Arizona, Georgia, Florida, Illinois, Florida, Ohio, Georgia, California, Georgia, Tennessee, Florida, New Jersey, Missouri, Florida, Illinois, Texas, Florida, Mississippi, Florida, Mississippi, Georgia, Mississippi, South Carolina, Florida, Mississippi, Georgia, Alabama, South Carolina, Ohio, Florida, Alabama, Ohio, Florida, Alabama, Georgia, Ohio, Mississippi, Georgia, Louisiana, Ohio, Georgia, Mississippi, Kentucky, Mississippi, Ohio, Mississippi, Tennessee, Georgia, Arkansas, Florida, Georgia, Louisiana, Mississippi, Florida, Louisiana, Arkansas, Louisiana, Florida, Georgia, Florida, Georgia, Ohio, California, Ohio, Arkansas, Georgia, Kentucky, Florida, California, Georgia,

Florida, California, Mississippi, Ohio, California, California, California...

'49 Ford Mercury, '57 Ford Fairlane, '64 Pontiac Grand Prix, '59 Pontiac Bonneville, '57 Ford Fairlane, '58 Ford Mercury, '59 Ford, '64 convertible Pontiac Bonneville, '65 Buick Riviera, '63 Mercury, '64 Buick Wildcat, '68 Pontiac Bonneville, '64 Wildcat Buick, '69 Oldsmobile Delta, Pontiac LeMans, '71 Ford Thunderbird, '70 Pontiac Grand Prix, '67 Cadillac Eldorado, '73 Ford Thunderbird, '69 Ford Thunderbird, '68 Chrysler Imperial, '67 Chrysler 300, '56 Chevy Bel Air, '72 Ford Galaxie, '67 Ford Pinto, '70 Lincoln Continental Mark III, '75 Lincoln Continental Mark IV, '76 Ford Thunderbird, Ford Mercury, '78 Cadillac Eldorado, '76 Ford F-150 bubble-top van, '79 Cadillac Eldorado, '85 Buick Riviera, '78 Cadillac Fleetwood, Cadillac, '85 Buick, '77 Dodge motorhome, '85 Chrysler, '96 Cadillac, '82 Nissan Maxima, '95 Oldsmobile, '89 Oldsmobile 88, '84 Buick LeSabre, '87 Ford F-150, '99 Buick...

Diane, Sarah, Carolyn, Mary, Sarah, Emily, Linda, Norwegian baby, Air Force baby, Marianne, Maryland baby, Prince George baby, Sarah Brown, Agatha White Buffalo, Cuban Donna, Cincinnati baby, Savannah baby, Martha, the other Knoxville baby, Pamela, Mary-Anne, Bobbie, Jo, cowgirl, Angela, pipefitting baby, Macon baby, Carver Village baby, Carver Village baby, Plant City baby, Charleston baby, Clearwater baby, Evelyn, Julia, Cleveland baby, Hilda, Leila, Brenda, billboard baby, Chattanooga Choo Choo baby, Gulfport baby, Jackson ladyboy baby, Tennessee baby, Linda Sue, Atlanta baby, Anna Lee, Dorothy, Fredonia, Rosie, Ohio baby, Nawlins baby, Little Woods baby, Mindy, Patricia

*Anne, Atlanta stripper baby, Atlanta college baby, Savannah sand
pile baby, West Memphis blues baby, Kentucky Vegas baby, Fort
Myers baby, San Berdu baby, li'l Savannah baby, Tampa Bay baby,
Mary Jo, big yellow LA gal, Laurie, Tonya, Granny, skinny li'l
LA banger, Bronco Motel baby, Griffith Park baby, Monroe baby,
Carol, Linda Sue, Audrey, Guadalupe, Pine Bluff baby, LA baby,
Rose, Alice, Tina, Tracy, Ruby, Bobbie, Denise, Jolanda, Daisy,
Melissa, Priscilla, Sheila, T-Money, Ann, Nancy Carol...*

*Unnamed, Unnamed, Unnamed, Unnamed, Unnamed, Unnamed,
Unnamed, Unnamed...*

Samuel Little died at California State Prison, Los Angeles County,
on December 30, 2020, at approximately 4:35 in the morning due to
complications from COVID-19, according to a press release from the
prison. He was eighty years old.

Sam sometimes said to his victims, "Take my breath."

If they weren't already gone, his breath only meant more suffering. He sometimes gave them CPR postmortem.

The drive between my home and the prison could take anywhere
from an hour and fifteen minutes to two hours. During the years I
traveled between hell and home every weekend, I came to loathe that
journey with every cell of my body. Even as I loathed it, it was, at times,
beautiful.

In the early spring, orange poppies frost the desert hills. Once,
when they were newly in bloom—luscious and vibrant enough to take
your breath away—I pulled the car over to a precarious shoulder and
tore my stockings to shreds running through a bramble patch in a pair
of heels that suddenly seemed much less sensible. I wanted to see the

poppy field from its center. I imagined Glinda's famous first question of Dorothy upon her entrance to Oz.

Are you a good witch or a bad witch?

I write this final chapter from a world unimaginably different from the world in which I first heard Sam's name. We are a country ravaged by a virus, caught in the grips of political discord, isolated, destabilized, attempting to become both teachers and breadwinners in an educational system and economy that are changing before our eyes.

Scott and I euthanized our dog Calvin two days before I got the call about Sam. Calvin kept me awake those final nights, pacing, getting stuck in corners. I heard the jingle of his tags, woke, and carried him onto the lawn to pee. I waited as he sniffed at the night breeze, looked at the trees beyond the gate.

I rubbed his ears until he fell asleep in the downstairs corridor and slept the last night on the floor beside him. I wanted one more day, just one more, just one more again, until no one could look me in the eye anymore.

Calvin was our first dog, in our first house. We got him as practice for the baby we were going to have any second, except we didn't. I stuck a couch in what was supposed to be the baby's room so it wouldn't be empty, and we got our second dog, Peanut. Doggy had been Tariku's first word of English when we finally brought him home from Ethiopia.

The vet was especially kind, allowing us to come in on short notice. I had called him the day before half hysterical, asking about the exact drug regimen, explaining that I knew a little too much about larger mammals being put to sleep, and it often didn't go so well. He assured me if he used the drug regimen used in human executions, he'd be sued for malpractice. He talked me through it step-by-step.

Stay-at-home orders were in full effect, masks were required, and no patients passed each other. Only for euthanasia did they allow the owners inside with their pets.

It went exactly as planned. I asked for a little extra time when it was done. "I can't leave while he's still warm."

The doctor and Scott both left, and I kept my palms on Calvin's head until he started to cool. I kissed him and thanked the staff.

I put Calvin's tag on my necklace. The jingle shook me awake early the second morning, the morning I found out Sam died.

The most prolific serial killer in United States history spent the last few years of his life a star, showered in love letters and milkshakes and still complaining from his cell about the speed of his mail. He called me ten days before he died. He was ranting, confused. After that, he was in quarantine. I never talked to him again.

If he died, as they say, from COVID-19 complications, he died by suffocation.

In October 2019, the FBI updated the map on their twenty-one-page Samuel Little website to include five removed cases and two added, one in Willoughby Hills, Ohio, and another in New Orleans. Eight new portraits have been added.

The FBI claims to have confirmed sixty-one of Little's murders at the time I write this. Forty-five of Little's cases were cleared by exceptional means. He carried eight life sentences.

T-Money?
Bald Head Hill Girl?
Bathtub Girl?
Turban Girl?
Helicopter/Observatory Girl?

I have one or two points on the map for each, but I am missing a third and last. I am missing the location of the body dump and the body itself.

Detective Mitzi Roberts recently secured a new RHD Cold Case Unit, configured in a unique way. The new CCU will be led by Roberts and consist of an all-volunteer squad of retired reserve detectives and officers, including Tim Marcia. Together they'll chip away at the six thousand unsolved cases that remain on the books in Los Angeles alone.

———

What was it like talking to a violent psychopath?

Was I frightened? Did I feel like I was staring at the devil himself?

It's reckless arrogance to think you know the devil. The devil does not dress in red sequined horns and a pitchfork from Halloween Headquarters.

You listen when the devil talks. You let him tell you who he needs you to be. You mustn't be boring, because murder is many things, but it is not boring. You assemble, piece by piece from genuine facets of yourself, a fictional creation. You hope she is a worthy avatar who will protect you from the inevitable manipulation and annihilation you will face at the hands of someone who is human, but just barely.

Sam Little was a toddler, a wild man, a hustler. He was lazy, vicious, and a murderer to his core. Sam was the classic expression of the id, the cliché Oedipus, the longest shadow, the ultimate psychopath.

I spoke with Debbie on New Year's Eve 2021 as she was getting ready for a stroll with her husband. There was a light flurry, the kind of snowflakes that land on your eyelashes and make streetlights sparkle, and they wanted to try to catch some on their tongues. We laughed, hoped for a day we might travel again and meet up, and she could show Jovi a dance move or two. She thanked me.

"I never have to wonder again if Alice is okay," said Debbie. "I know she is."

Epilogue

On the morning of December 30, 2020, at 5:30 a.m., lieutenant something or other from California State Prison, Los Angeles County, called. I had been designated as the next of kin for inmate Samuel Little #AV22258, who had passed away at approximately 4:59 that morning from COVID-related complications. The voice on the other end of the line was sorry for my loss. I did not know what to say.

Alone in bed, I watched the pale light of dawn crawl in through the part in the curtains, my legs dissected by a stripe of sunlight. A mockingbird perched outside the window, its grating, shifting call precluding any further rest or even contemplation. How perfect. If Sam were a bird, he'd be that obnoxious.

Exactly two years, four months, and twelve days before he died, I faced Sam for the first time in person. During the intervening time, the FBI, LAPD, Texas Rangers, and local law enforcement across the country had worked tirelessly. The connections of his confessions to cold cases were far from done, and they had just lost their only witness. Luckily, the silent witness—emerging forensic DNA science—has allowed the investigations to continue.

Since the first day I talked to Sam, Sammy, Mr. Sam, I'd long since stopped turning off my phone. My life had become one of hypervigilance and gambler's reinforcement. Days without even one much-coveted call were countered by days soaked in hours of mind-bending confessions. A cop or two actually called me back some days. I never knew what I was going to get. I took to carrying a cross-body purse around my own house with my recorder, my phone, my pen, and my notebook in it. No one liked me much.

Though my dreams were steeped in drowning, smothering, strangling, I knew I'd done a real thing. I'd helped solve murders. Sleep seemed a paltry sacrifice. I'd traveled from Pascagoula to Lorain and back, toured storage rooms of cold case files and evidence boxes.

I'd become adept with a handgun.

I wasn't sure if I was wiser, but I was sharper.

By the time Sam died, I'd become so entangled in the investigation that I'd been served two subpoenas (ignored the first one—highly discourage this) for Sam's San Bernardino homicide of Sonja Collette Austin. I refused to turn over my unpublished records or reveal my sources, and the Reporters Committee for Freedom of the Press sent celebrity attorney Michael Dore, who rode a white horse all the way to a shithole in the middle of the desert in his Ferragamo shoes, in the middle of a pandemic, to keep me out of jail on a First Amendment basis.

I was supposed to be designated Little's next of kin. I'd made arrangements to donate his brain to the top neuroscientists in the country, at both Stanford and UC Irvine, depending on the conditions under which the brain could be preserved.

Sam fucked up the paperwork.

I called lawyers, doctors, the LAPD, Jim Holland, UC Irvine, the FBI, Stanford. Nothing worked. In the end, Sam's brain and its mysteries died with him.

Due to the overflow of bodies during the height of COVID-19 in LA, *no autopsy* was conducted on one of the most pernicious criminals in American history.

I talked to many of the detectives involved after Sam's death. I talked to the family members I'd stayed in touch with. "Good riddance" was the most popular response. I wondered if that was shorthand for relief from the justifiable anger that the man who brutally tortured their loved ones lived to the end of his days with three hot meals, a cot, and a cell wall plastered with photos of women's asses and drawings of victim's faces. I now have those photos and drawings in my garage, next to the Tilex and the sponges.

Samuel Little, at the end of his life, got belligerent about squeezing me to put more money on his books, write him more letters, sing him more lullabies, do more anything. I sent him cookies. He said prettier girls were sending more…for tracings of his penis. For tracings of his hands. Those hands that murdered and murdered are worth a lot on eBay. Not everybody just goes ahead and murders, but they can place their hands in the outline of someone who most certainly did.

He was always running a hustle, even on me. One week, he had run out of paper. Could I send him just a few dollars?

He was starving. I had sent him ramen but no hot pot. What kind of a bitch was I anyway? Just like the rest of them?

He shucked and jived until his last breath.

Sometime after his death, I opened an envelope from the California Department of Corrections. He left me one thousand and ninety-seven dollars on his death.

He'd had plenty of money the whole time.

In the face of Samuel Little's serial murders and thousands of other cold cases, law enforcement communities around the country struggle with dwindling resources. The cold case murder books of the ignored, dismissed, and marginalized often remain in stacks in dusty storage rooms.

There are also passionate scientists, dedicated members of law enforcement, community activists, and self-described web sleuths combining cutting-edge forensic technology with innovative ideas about information sharing.

Detective III Mitzi Roberts, officer in charge of the new Cold Case Homicide Unit at LAPD's Robbery Homicide Division, heads up just such an initiative. Similar programs being pioneered across the country may inch us closer to the ideal of Lady Justice wearing a true blindfold.

Nearly a year after Sam's brain became worthless to science, I had turned in my final pages and was putting in that desperate catching up work you do when you almost ruined your life, but not quite.

Therapy. Decluttering. Shooting guns. Rereading Camus.

A captain from the coroner's investigation office called.

"I understand that you originally had problems with the remains of Samuel Little, and I apologize for that. I've been assigned to the case. I worked up in Corcoran when Manson died, and what happened there was distasteful. Frankly, it was a disgrace. I thought we'd avoid the circus, and it seems that you might handle it respectfully."

I thanked the captain and said I'd be right there.

My younger son was home sick from school the day I got the call to pick up Sam's remains. I walked to the door of the LA County coroner's office, holding my ten-year-old's feverish hand. With the other, I shook the hand of the coroner and walked back to the car with the ashes of a two-hundred-pound serial killer tucked under my arm.

"Nice," my son said when we hit the freeway.

"This is my job. Don't like it? Get a job. McNuggets?"

He shrugged.

I still don't know what to do with the ashes. They sit on a shelf in my garage, between the holiday lights and the party plates. The brown plastic box the coroner handed me is about nine inches by seven inches by five inches, and it reads:

Historic Union Cemetery, est. 1872
Crematory and Funeral Home
Samuel Little #21836

The plastic bag of tagged ashes in the container weighs 8.2 lbs. I thought about the weight of ash, the meaning of a pound of flesh, and how the words *weight* and *worth* can be synonymous.

I continue to work on Sam's unsolved murders while adding my foibles and occasional successes to the amateur detective toolbox I carry forward to the next story.

As someone who marks significant moments of my life with tattoos, I chose a tattoo for Sam's victims. In many traditions, birds travel between the worlds of the living and the dead. They are often messengers of the gods, or conversely, they carry the spirits of the dead to the next world. In the traditional tattoos of American sailors, swallows carry the souls of the drowned to heaven.

Audrey, Alice, Denise, Guadalupe…

I tattooed swallows on my chest to remind me that when you reach into the dark waters, turn your face to the sky.

VICTIM LIST

SOLVED

MARY BROSLEY, 33

Location: Miami, Florida

DOD: January 1, 1971

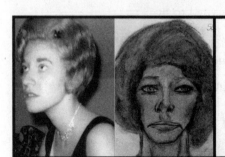

KAREN O'DONOGHUE, 26

Location: Miami, Florida

DOD: May, 1971

SARAH BROWN
Location: New Orleans, Louisiana
DOD: 1973

AGATHA WHITE BUFFALO, 34
Location: South Omaha, Nebraska
DOD: November 1, 1973

LINDA BELCHER, 22
Location: Phoenix, Arizona
DOD: March 2, 1974

MARTHA CUNNINGHAM, 34
Location: Knox County, Tennessee
DOD: January 1, 1975

MIRIAM "ANGELA" CHAPMAN, 25

Location: Miami, Florida

DOD: May 6, 1976

MARY ANN JENKINS, 22

Location: East St. Louis, Illinois

DOD: April 1977

DOROTHY GIBSON, 17

Location: Miami, Florida

DOD: June 1977

LEE ANN HELMS, 21

Location: Atlanta, Georgia

DOD: June 26, 1977

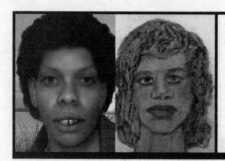

CLARA BIRDLONG, 44
Location: Escatawpa, Mississippi
DOD: 1977

JULIA CRITCHFIELD, 36
Location: Saucier, Mississippi
DOD: January 21, 1978

EVELYN WESTON, 19
Location: Columbia, South Carolina
DOD: September 5, 1978

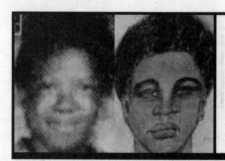

KARLEEN JONES, 14
Location: Plaquemine, Louisiana
DOD: November 23, 1978

BRENDA ALEXANDER, 23

Location: Phenix City, Alabama

DOD: August 27, 1979

VALERIA BOYD, 18

Location: Fort Wayne, Indiana

DOD: October 28, 1980

MARY ANN PORTER, 31

Location: Fort Wayne, Indiana

DOD: October 28, 1980

LINDA SUE BOARDS, 23

Location: Smiths Grove, Kentucky

DOD: May 12, 1981

PATRICIA PARKER, 30
Location: Dade County, Georgia
DOD: September 28, 1981

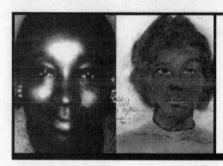

ANNIE "ANNA" LEE STEWART, 33
Location: Grove City, Ohio
DOD: October 11, 1981

FREDONIA SMITH, 18
Location: Macon, Georgia
DOD: July 10, 1982

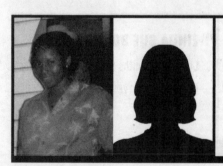

ROSIE HILL, 21
Location: Marion County, Florida
DOD: August 16, 1982

DOROTHY RICHARDS, 55
Location: Houma, Louisiana
DOD: September 1, 1982

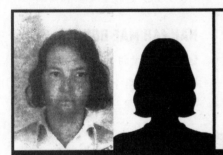

PATRICIA ANN MOUNT, 26
Location: Forest Grove, Florida
DOD: September 10, 1982

MELINDA LAPREE, 22
Location: Pascagoula, Mississippi
DOD: September 17, 1982

WILLIE MAE BIVINS, 32
Location: Tallahassee, Florida
DOD: May 12, 1984

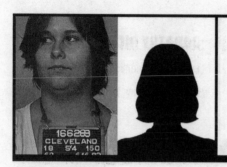

MARY JO PEYTON, 21

Location: Cleveland, Ohio

DOD: May–June 1984

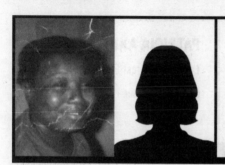

HANNAH MAE BONNER, 23

Location: Mobile, Alabama

DOD: August 10, 1984

IDA MAE CAMPBELL, 34

Location: Mobile, Alabama

DOD: August 10, 1984

FRANCES CAMPBELL, 22

Location: Savannah, Georgia

DOD: 1984

SONJA COLLETTE AUSTIN, 28

Location: San Bernadino, California

DOD: April 12, 1987

CAROL ALFORD, 41

Location: Los Angeles, California

DOD: July 13, 1987

AUDREY NELSON, 35

Location: Los Angeles, California

DOD: August 14, 1989

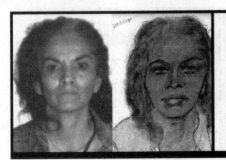

GUADALUPE APODACA, 46

Location: Los Angeles, California

DOD: September 3, 1989

ZENA MARIE JONES, 36

Location: West Memphis, Arkansas

DOD: 1990

ALICE DENISE DUVALL, 34

Location: Long Beach, California

DOD: June 10, 1991

ROSE EVANS, 32

Location: Cleveland, Ohio

DOD: August 24, 1991

ROBERTA TANDARICH, 34

Location: Akron, Ohio

DOD: September 1991

ALICE DENISE "TINA" TAYLOR, 27

Location: Gulfport, Mississippi

DOD: December 11, 1992

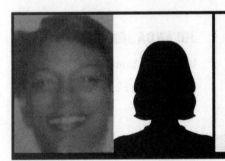

TRACY LYNN JOHNSON, 19

Location: Gulfport, Mississippi

DOD: December 11, 1992

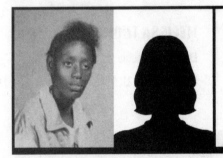

RUBY LANE, 19

Location: Perry, Florida

DOD: May 3, 1993

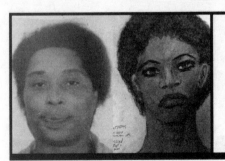

BOBBIE ANN FIELDS-WILSON, 37

Location: Lubbock, Texas

DOD: August 7, 1993

DENISE CHRISTIE BROTHERS, 38

Location: Odessa, Texas

DOD: January 12, 1994

JOLANDA JONES, 26

Location: Pine Bluff, Arkansas

DOD: February 24, 1994

MELISSA THOMAS, 24

Location: Opelousas, Louisiana

DOD: January 31, 1996

DAISY MCGUIRE, 40

Location: Houma, Louisiana

DOD: February 6, 1996

NANCY CAROL STEVENS, 46

Location: Tupelo, Mississippi

DOD: August 8, 2005

UNSOLVED

UNNAMED BLACK FEMALE ("Emily"), 23–24

Location: Miami, Florida

DOD: 1970s

UNNAMED WHITE FEMALE

Location: Homestead, Florida

DOD: 1970–1971

UNNAMED BLACK FEMALE ("Linda"), 22

Location: Miami, Florida

DOD: 1971

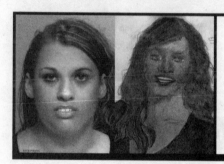

UNNAMED WHITE FEMALE ("Sarah" or "Donna"), 25–35

Location: Kendall, Florida

DOD: 1971

UNNAMED BLACK TRANSGENDER FEMALE ("Marianne"), 18

Location: Miami, Florida

DOD: 1971–1972

UNNAMED BLACK FEMALE, 28

Location: Miami, Florida

DOD: 1971–1972

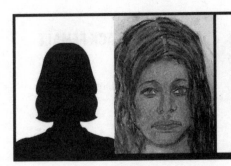

UNNAMED WHITE FEMALE, 20–25

Location: Prince George's County, Maryland

DOD: 1972

UNNAMED BLACK FEMALE

Location: Cincinnati, Ohio

DOD: 1974

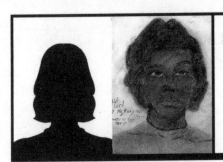

UNNAMED BLACK FEMALE, 22–23

Location: Savannah, Georgia

DOD: 1974

UNNAMED BLACK FEMALE, 25

Location: Knoxville, Tennessee

DOD: 1975

UNNAMED BLACK FEMALE ("Jo"), 26

Location: Granite City, Illinois
DOD: 1976–1979

UNNAMED BLACK FEMALE

Location: East St. Louis, Illinois
DOD: 1976–1979

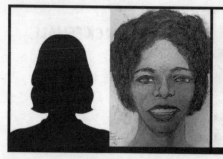

UNNAMED BLACK FEMALE, 25–28

Location: Houston, Texas
DOD: 1976–1979 or 1993

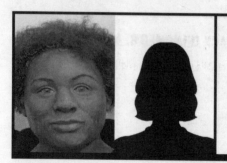

UNNAMED BLACK FEMALE, 30–40

Location: Macon, Georgia
DOD: 1977

UNNAMED BLACK FEMALE,
35–45
Location: Pascagoula, Mississippi
DOD: 1977

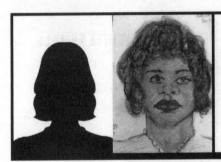

UNNAMED BLACK FEMALE
Location: Plant City, Florida
DOD: 1977–1978

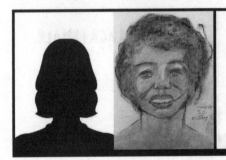

UNNAMED BLACK FEMALE, 28
Location: Charleston, South
Carolina
DOD: 1977–1982

UNNAMED BLACK FEMALE, 22
Location: Gulfport, Mississippi
DOD: 1980–1984

UNNAMED BLACK FEMALE, 35–40

Location: Atlanta, Georgia

DOD: 1981

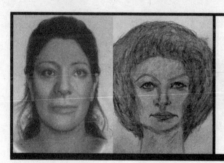

UNNAMED WHITE FEMALE, 33–44

Location: New Orleans, Louisiana

DOD: 1982

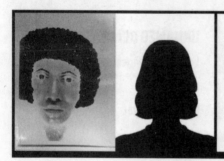

UNNAMED BLACK FEMALE, 20–35

Location: Willoughby Hills, Ohio

DOD: 1982

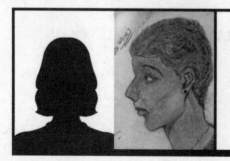

UNNAMED BLACK FEMALE, 30–40

Location: New Orleans, Louisiana

DOD: 1982

UNNAMED BLACK FEMALE,
18–32

Location: San Bernadino, California

DOD: 1984

UNNAMED BLACK FEMALE

Location: Fort Myers, Florida

DOD: 1984

UNNAMED BLACK FEMALE

Location: Tampa Bay, Florida

DOD: 1984

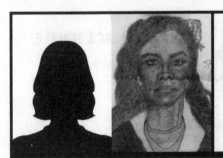

UNNAMED BLACK FEMALE, 23

Location: Savannah, Georgia

DOD: 1984

UNNAMED BLACK FEMALE, 23–25

Location: Atlanta, Georgia

DOD: 1984

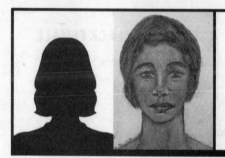

UNNAMED WHITE FEMALE

Location: Covington, Kentucky

DOD: 1984

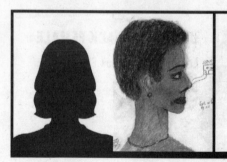

UNNAMED BLACK FEMALE

Location: Los Angeles, California

DOD: 1987

UNNAMED BLACK FEMALE

Location: Los Angeles, California

DOD: 1987

UNNAMED BLACK FEMALE, 19

Location: Los Angeles, California

DOD: 1987

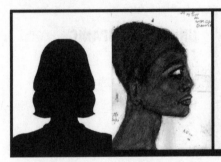

UNNAMED BLACK FEMALE ("Granny"), 50

Location: Los Angeles, California

DOD: 1987

UNNAMED BLACK FEMALE, 22–23

Location: Los Angeles, California

DOD: 1987

UNNAMED BLACK FEMALE, 26–27

Location: Los Angeles, California

DOD: 1987

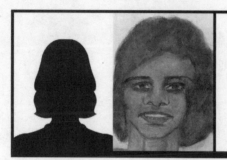

UNNAMED BLACK FEMALE, 24

Location: Monroe, Louisiana

DOD: 1987–early 1990s

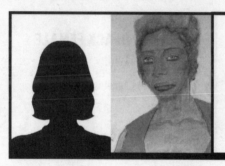

UNNAMED HISPANIC FEMALE, 40s

Location: Phoenix, Arizona

DOD: 1988 or 1996

UNNAMED BLACK FEMALE, 20–22

Location: Los Angeles, California

DOD: 1991–1992

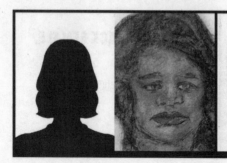

UNNAMED BLACK FEMALE

Location: North Little Rock, Arkansas

DOD: 1992–1993

UNNAMED BLACK FEMALE

Location: Los Angeles, California

DOD: 1992

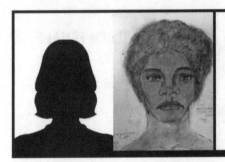

UNNAMED BLACK FEMALE

Location: Los Angeles, California

DOD: 1992–1993

UNNAMED HISPANIC FEMALE, 24–25

Location: Los Angeles, California

DOD: 1992–1993

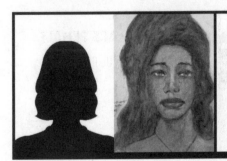

UNNAMED BLACK FEMALE, 40

Location: Las Vegas, Nevada

DOD: 1993

UNNAMED BLACK FEMALE ("Sheila"), 23–25
Location: Los Angeles, California
DOD: 1996

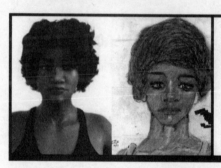

UNNAMED BLACK FEMALE ("T-Money"), 23–24
Location: Los Angeles, California
DOD: 1996

UNNAMED WHITE FEMALE, 23–25
Location: Los Angeles, California
DOD: 1996

UNNAMED BLACK FEMALE, 25
Location: Los Angeles, California
DOD: 1996

SURVIVING VICTIMS

PAMELA KAY SMITH

Location: Sunset Hills, Missouri

Assaulted: September 11, 1976

HILDA NELSON, December 5, 1953–July 21, 2020

Location: Pascagoula, Mississippi

Assaulted: July 31, 1980

LEILA MAE (MCCLAIN) JOHNSON, September 1, 1959–January 14, 2018

Location: Pascagoula, Mississippi

Assaulted: November 19, 1981

LAURIE KERRIDGE (BARROS)

Location: San Diego, California
Assaulted: September 17, 1984

TONYA JACKSON

Location: San Diego, CA
Assaulted: October 25, 1984

Reading Group Guide

1. Why do you think author Jillian Lauren chose to open the book with her own fight (and near-death by strangulation) with a boyfriend?

2. What is the allure of the cold case—for detectives, journalists, and true crime fanatics? How does Detective Mitzi Roberts describe it? How can cold cases compete for resources against active investigations?

3. How does Jillian's approach to telling Little's story differ from other true crime accounts? Where is her focus, and how does that change our impressions of each crime?

4. One of the most shocking facts about Sam Little's crimes is how poorly hidden they were. Why, after so many arrests, did he continue to get released from jurisdictions all over the country?

5. Despite knowing the risks, Jillian builds a relationship with

Little over time. What is the most challenging aspect of that relationship for her? What motivates her to maintain it?

6. Texas Ranger Jim Holland's interview techniques are revered by his colleagues, but also described in the following way, "Makes you fucking sure you did something wrong." Why is the discomfort of the interviewee, and the *creation* of a feeling of guilt, one of the measures of interview success?

7. What was Jean's motivation for teaming up with Little until her eventual death? Do you agree with Jillian that Jean was fully aware of Little's murders?

8. Little tries to convince Jillian that all crimes are equal, from stealing a cookie to murder, because they are all equally sinful in the eyes of his religion. Do you agree with his argument?

9. Sam Little perished in prison, where his sentence reflected only a few of the many murders he committed. Do you think justice was served?

A Conversation with the Author

You are, yourself, a character in the narrative. How did you decide which parts of your long relationship with Little would be included and how much of your internal narrative would be shared?

You don't choose the story. The story finds you. I didn't set out to unravel the unimaginable carnage of a serial killer as the news cameras looked on. After two memoirs, the spotlight of public scrutiny had worn on me, and I desperately wanted to write myself out of the center of the narrative.

I always face the blank page with the hubris of already knowing the ending of the story, or at the very least, the beginning. I'm wrong every time. I began with the goal of writing a classic piece of journalistic reportage: eight thousand words for *New York Magazine*.

My initial interview with Detective Mitzi Roberts, had been on a different subject completely. When she told me about a serial killer she had collared who she suspected of many more murders across the country, I saw a chance to jump on an underreported story and bring some heat to the failure of the justice system to protect the most vulnerable among us. A chance to do some real good.

I didn't plan to cast myself as the story's central lens, but as the events unfolded in real time, my foibles and triumphs, and the relationships I developed along the way, organically took a more central place in the narrative.

Little was inconsistent about admitting his guilt, alternately confessing to stranglings, protesting charges of rape, and denying his culpability at sentencing. Was there a rhyme or reason to these stances, or you think he would say whatever served him best in the moment?

Little was a dyed-in-the-wool psychopath. I believe his inconsistencies were sometimes a result of legitimate confusion. Even with what has been referred to as his "photographic memory," ninety-three victims are a lot to keep straight.

I know sometimes he messed around with certain DAs and detectives on purpose. He could clock a phony from a cell block away, and he loved watching people chase their tails.

His memory failed in specific ways. For instance, he was a poor judge of distance and time. He almost never remembered names. He described many victims as wearing black dresses, but that was often his fantasy, not a memory.

When talking about the years that crack took a hold of him—predominately the eighties in Los Angeles—Little's memory became more addled. I suspect a couple of the unsolved confessions are actually the same person.

Sometimes he messed with me—gave me a piece of false information to see if I caught on. I believe that by the end of our talks, he was as honest with me as he was capable of being.

It was important to Little that he not be perceived as a

woman-beater or a rapist. He insisted to his dying day he never raped or beat a woman in his life—except his long-tern girlfriend Jean. Anyone who said otherwise was a "lying whore." In order to get the cold case murder convictions based on Little's confessions, Little demanded letters from DAs across the country promising him they wouldn't seek the death penalty. In most cases, he pled to murder in the first degree in exchange for dropping the rape/kidnapping/you-name-it lesser charges.

He wanted to be perceived as a killer. He didn't need to beat or rape women, unless in the rare case they had a "poor disposition." He loved and worshipped women. He wouldn't accept a narrative that threatened his positive self-concept. He didn't rape women—he didn't need to. More to the point…he couldn't. It was nearly impossible for him to become sexually aroused when not engaged in strangulation.

Some stories changed, some were remarkably consistent. Some drawings looked identical to the identified victims, some looked nothing of the sort.

Still, a remarkable sixty-one cases have been cleared. The information he provided, consistent or not, combined with the tireless work of detectives, the DOJ, and the FBI across the country have proved fruitful.

The basic answer is: every interaction was a transaction. So, yes, he said what served him best in the moment. What served him best in this case was this series of jailhouse confessions. He spent his last days getting attention and McDonald's breakfasts.

How does your previous writing compare to writing true crime? What were the most surprising similarities and differences when you started writing?

I write in all genres. I even pulled some old, published poetry off the shelf the other day! I'm working a lot in the screenplay world. This true crime book is itself a hybrid of genres. At the center of all my work is the desire to reach toward universal themes.

Then real difference was in the exactitude of the research and investigation process. I've always been a little more loosey-goosey, and all of a sudden I was facing police reports and interviewing famous neuroscientists, storied LAPD cops, victim's families...subjects that took delicacy, empathy, determination, and fighting through departmental bullshit. Learning criminal law on the fly was pretty interesting! I had forty white, four-inch, three ring binders lining a wall of my office, all organized by victim, by public records, family interviews...

I felt beholden to these women. I had seen the lists and lists of Jane Does. I was compelled to follow the story to its end and hopefully help to restore the names and dignity of the victims.

Little often seems to have taken an antagonistic tone towards you during your dialogues. Did you ever actually lose your cool with him? How did you keep your composure across all of the conversations?

Little was a boxer in his youth, and at any moment he could throw a surprise jab, metaphorically that is. He only ever threw a real jab at me once and missed my cheekbone by an inch. He did that because I stepped over the line. I disagreed with him. As many murders to which he, often gleefully, recounted to me in great detail, he maintained his innocence around the three LA victims for which he was finally put away for good. They set him up. He could rant about it for hours.

I told him he wasn't set up, he was caught and those are different things. He did kill those women and I knew it. That was when he threw the jab.

Sam got belligerent when he felt a loss of control. He was constantly hustling something from someone. Charging "fans" money for his handprints. The dick tracings were free though, I hear.

In my final conversations with him, he was ragged-voiced and paranoid, asking me to put ten dollars on his books. Did I forget about him? Was I a lying bitch like all the rest of them in the end? After all, I had been a ho, as he never ceased to remind me. Usually in response to me calling him a homicidal maniac.

There were so many conversations, and we had a unique way of talking to each other: secret code words and nick names and songs. It's the most effective way I know to get in the ring with a psychopath.

As my aunt said: He'll steal the shirt off your back, tell you he's stealing the shirt off your back, and yet you will feel inexplicably compelled to give him the shirt.

I wouldn't say I kept my composure all the time. I made a hundred mistakes. The thing that kept me going was a powerful sense of meaning.

Samuel Little died of COVID in prison. He left me his worldly possessions, including $1047.99.

Till the end of his days, he had plenty of money, and he still hustled me for ten dollars.

How do you talk to someone like that? Don't lie if you can help it, don't bore them, know what you ultimately want, and play the game that gets you the answer.

What was your very first thought when you were able to successfully match Little's account of Alice to her cold case?

I write this from the spot in which I sat when I received the call from retired LAPD detective Rick Jackson, who had rung up the Long Beach police department for me as a favor. They're more likely to talk to a cop.

Rick had been following the Alice case with me—he used it to teach me how to properly read between the lines of a police report. We drove around South LA together, seeking landmarks, interviews, signposts to the murder scenes, body dumps, clubs, and pool halls long closed down.

Rick set the scene for me (he's a master storyteller) and then said, "Are you sitting down? The case is open. The victim is identified. Her name is Alice Denise Duvall".

The endorphins swimming in my head were like helium, lifting me from the couch. Rick got off the phone to call them back. I cried and hugged my assistant. Checked and double checked all my information. We'd done it.

There are so many failures along the way: in writing, in life, with justice. Solving Alice's murder was a thrill and then a crash. This was a horribly murdered woman. I've since become close with Alice's family, and they buoy me with their support and encouragement.

What draws you to true crime as a reader and writer? What perspective does the genre give you?

I've always been fascinated by criminal deviance. *Helter Skelter* off my parents' shelf was the gateway drug for me, and *In Cold Blood* sealed the deal. Stories about murder have built in high stakes. We can't turn away. I've encountered the perspective that true crime is exploitative by nature. I disagree. Violence isn't monstrous, it's all too human. As a reader and writer of true crime, I am able to explore the stories of those existing on the fringes of society and see up close both the failures and progress of the criminal justice system. It has been a harrowing ride and one of great personal significance. I'm afraid I'm hooked.

Bibliography

I walk with gratitude in the footsteps of the unflinching pioneers in this strange field that requires facing utter lunacy with meticulous exactitude. Where I've used exact quotes, I've noted them in the manuscript.

Aggrawal, Anil. *Forensic and Medico-legal Aspects of Sexual Crimes and Unusual Sexual Practices*. Boca Raton, FL: CRC Press, 2009.

Aggrawal, Anil. *Necrophilia: Forensic and Medico-legal Aspects*. Boca Raton, FL: CRC Press, 2011.

American Psychiatric Association. *Diagnostic and Statistical Manual of Mental Disorders*. 5th ed. Arlington, VA: American Psychiatric Association, 2013.

"Antisocial Personality Disorder." Mayo Clinic. Accessed July 1, 2022. https://www.mayoclinic.org/diseases-conditions /antisocial-personality-disorder/symptoms-causes /syc-20353928.

Berman, Mark, Wesley Lowery, and Hannah Knowles. "Indifferent Justice, Pt. 2: Through the Cracks." *Washington Post*, December 2, 2020. https://www.washingtonpost.com /graphics/2020/national/samuel-little-serial-killer /part-two/?itid=gr_samuel-little_enhanced-template_2.

Brake, Sherri. *The Haunted History of the Ohio State Reformatory*. Charleston, SC: Haunted America, 1995.

Clover, Carol J. *Men, Women, and Chain Saws: Gender in the Modern Horror Film*. Princeton, NJ: Princeton University Press, 1992.

"Confessions of a Killer." Federal Bureau of Investigation. October 6, 2019. https://www.fbi.gov/news/stories/samuel-little-most-prolific-serial-killer-in-us-history-100619.

Darbey, Nancy K. *Ohio State Reformatory*. Mount Pleasant, SC: Arcadia Publishing, 2016.

De Becker, Gavin. *The Gift of Fear: And Other Survival Signals That Protect Us from Violence*. New York: Random House, 1995.

Diamond, Jared. *Guns, Germs, and Steel: The Fates of Human Societies*. New York: New York University Press, 2007.

Dunne, Dominick. *Justice: Crimes, Trials, and Punishments*. New York: Three Rivers, 2001.

Egger, Steven A. *The Killers Among Us: Examination of Serial Murder and Its Investigations*. Upper Saddle River, NJ: Prentice Hall, 1998.

Fallon, James. *The Psychopath Inside: A Neuroscientist's Personal Journey into the Dark Side of the Brain*. New York: Penguin, 2014.

Foer, Joshua. *Moonwalking with Einstein: The Art and Science of Remembering Everything*. New York: Penguin, 2011.

"Frequently Asked Questions on CODIS and NDIS." Federal Bureau of Investigation. Accessed June 15, 2022. https://www.fbi.gov/services/laboratory/biometric-analysis/codis/codis-and-ndis-fact-sheet.

Graeber, Charles. *The Good Nurse: A True Story of Medicine, Madness, and Murder*. New York: Hachette, 2013.

Hannan, Sheehan. "The Crimes of America's Most Prolific Serial

Killer." The Read, *Cleveland Magazine*, January 28, 2020. https://clevelandmagazine.com/in-the-cle/the-read/articles/in-the-shadows.

Hargrove, Thomas. "Cold Case Homicide Statistics." Project: Cold Case. Accessed May 25, 2022. https://projectcoldcase.org/cold-case-homicide-stats/.

Hitchcock, Alfred, dir. *Psycho*. Shamley Productions, 1960.

Hunt, Darnell, and Ana-Christina Ramón, eds. *Black Los Angeles: American Dreams and Racial Realities*. New York: New York University Press, 2010.

Inbau, Fred E., John E. Reid, Joseph P. Buckley, and Brian C. Jayne. *Criminal Interrogation and Confession: Essentials of the Reid Technique*. Burlington, MA: Jones and Bartlett Learning, 2015.

Jensen, Billy. *Chase Darkness with Me: How One True-Crime Writer Started Solving Murders*. Naperville, IL: Sourcebooks, 2019.

Jillette, Penn, and Teller. *Penn and Teller's Cruel Tricks for Dear Friends*. New York: Villard, 1989.

Jung, Carl Gustav. *The Archetypes and the Collective Unconscious*. Translated by R. F. C. Hull. Bollingen Series 20. Princeton, NJ: Princeton University Press, 1959.

Knowles, Hannah, Wesley Lowery, and Mark Berman. "Indifferent Justice, Pt. 3: Still Unsolved." *Washington Post*, December 4, 2020. https://www.washingtonpost.com/graphics/2020/national/samuel-little-serial-killer/part-three/?itid=gr_samuel-little_enhanced-template_3.

Leopold, Nathan F. *Life Plus 99 Years*. Garden City, NY: Doubleday, 1958.

Loftus, Elizabeth, and Katherine Ketcham. *The Myth of Repressed Memory: False Memories and Allegations of Sexual Abuse*. New York: St. Mark's, 1994.

Longfellow, Henry Wadsworth. "Paul Revere's Ride." Paul Revere House. https://www.paulreverehouse.org /longfellows-poem/.

Lowery, Wesley, Hannah Knowles, and Mark Berman. "Indifferent Justice, Pt. 1: The Perfect Victim." *Washington Post*, November 30, 2020. https://www.washingtonpost.com /graphics/2020/national/samuel-little-serial-killer/part-one/.

Michaud, Stephen G., and Hugh Aynesworth. *Ted Bundy: Conversations with a Killer*. Irving, TX: Authorlink Press, 2000.

Myers, David, and Elise Myers. *Central Ohio's Historic Prisons*. Mount Pleasant, SC: Arcadia Publishing, 2009.

The People of the State of California v. Samuel McDowell. CR 71823, 11 (Sup. Cal. 1985).

The People of the State of California v. Samuel Little. BA400148–1, 4 (Cal. Ct. App. 2014).

The People of the State of California v. Samuel Little. B259209 (Cal. Ct. App. Jan. 30, 2017).

Petrie, Daniel, dir. *Sybil*. Aired November 14 and 15, 1976, on NBC.

Sides, Josh. *L.A. City Limits: African American Los Angeles from the Great Depression to the Present*. Berkeley: University of California Press, 2003.

Slotkin, Richard. *Gunfighter Nation: The Myth of the Frontier in Twentieth-Century America*. New York: Atheneum, 1992.

State of Florida v. Sam McDowell. 83–1445-CF (7th Cir. 1983).

Stevenson, Robert Louis. *The Strange Case of Dr. Jekyll and Mr. Hyde*. Mineola, NY: Dover Thrift Editions, 1991.

Taupin, Jane Moira. *Introduction to Forensic DNA Evidence for Criminal Justice Professionals*. Boca Raton, FL: CRC Press, 2014.

Texas Department of Public Safety (website). https://www.dps.texas .gov.

Venrick, Bill, and Jean Venrick. *Echoes from the Hill: History of the Ohio Boys' Industrial School*. Lancaster, OH: Wordwright Press, 2014.

"Violent Criminal Apprehension Program." Federal Bureau of Investigation. May 3, 2016. https://www.fbi.gov/news /stories/violent-criminal-apprehension-program-part-1.

Wieseltier, Leon. *Kaddish*. New York: Vintage Books, 1998.

Wilkerson, Isabel. *The Warmth of Other Suns: The Epic Story of America's Great Migration*. New York: Random House, 2010.

Resources

We urge agencies to call the ViCAP tip line at 1-800-634-4097 or email vicap@fbi.gov. Call your local FBI field offices or local police departments to report information that may be connected to a crime of this nature. Agencies will be able to close some of their cold cases if they commit to thoroughly search their case files. ViCAP continues to offer assistance in that effort as well as analytical support on other serial cases. All of ViCAP's services are free of charge and are available to any law enforcement agency in the country.

ViCAP
https://www.fbi.gov/wanted/vicap

NATIONAL DOMESTIC VIOLENCE HOTLINE
CALL: 1-800-799-7233 // TEXT: 1-800-787-3224

NATIONAL TEEN DATING ABUSE HOTLINE
CALL: 1-866-331-4673

RAPE, ABUSE, AND INCEST NATIONAL HOTLINE

CALL: 1-800-656-4673

NATIONAL CENTER FOR VICTIMS OF VIOLENT CRIME

CALL: 1-855-484-2846

VICTIMSOFCRIME.ORG

CALL: 1-202-467-8700

CHARLEY PROJECT

EMAIL: goodmeaghan@gmail.com

DOE PROJECT

EMAIL: admin@dnadoeproject.org

NaMUS (National Missing and Unidentified Persons System)

CALL: 1-833-872-5176

Image Credits

Samuel Little's USA map

Courtesy of McKenzie O'Connor

Birth certificate

Taylor County, GA, public records

Samuel Little self-portrait

Courtesy of the author

Samuel Little mug shots

Public record, FBI.gov

Polaroid of Samuel Little

Courtesy of the author

Boy's Industrial School

Courtesy of the Columbus
Metropolitan Library, Fairfield County
Heritage Association Collection

Ohio State Reformatory

Courtesy of the author

List of Samuel Little's cars

Courtesy of the author

1967 Pinto

Courtesy of the Pascagoula
Police Department

Sam and Jean

Courtesy of the author

**Patricia Mount mug shot
and crime scene**

Courtesy of the
Alachau County Police
Department

Sarah Brown

Public record, FBI.gov

Agatha White Buffalo

Courtesy of the White Buffalo
family

Agatha White Buffalo crime scene

Courtesy of the *Omaha
World-Herald*

Mary Brosley

Courtesy of the Miami Dad Police
Department

Marianne

Public record, FBI.gov

Carver Village

Courtesy of the Pascagoula
Police Department

Melinda LaPree

Courtesy of the Pascagoula
Police Department

Darren Versiga

Courtesy of the Pascagoula
Police Department

Eight-man lineup

Courtesy of the Pascagoula
Police Department

Denise Brothers

Courtesy of the Christie Family

Denise Brothers' children

Courtesy of the Christie Family

Hilda Nelson

Courtesy of Hilda Nelson

Drawing of Hilda Nelson

Courtesy of the author

Laurie Barros

Courtesy of Radical Media

Leila McClain

Courtesy of Leila McClain

Guadalupe Apodaca

Courtesy of the Los Angeles
Police Department

Audrey Nelson

Courtesy of the Los Angeles
Police Department

Carol Alford

Courtesy of the Los Angeles
Police Department

Duvall crime scene

Courtesy of the Duvall family

Alice Duvall

Courtesy of the Duvall family

Drawing of Alice Duvall

Courtesy of the author

Audrey Nelson

Courtesy of the Nelson family

Rick Jackson

Courtesy of Detective Rick
Jackson

**James Holland, Angela Williamson,
and Christie Palazzolo**

Courtesy of the International
Homicide Investigators
Association

Mitzi Roberts and Tim Marcia

Courtesy of Mitzi Roberts

Mitzi Roberts and group

Courtesy of the Nelson family

Jillian Lauren and Amaia Perta

Photo by Joe Berlinger, courtesy
of the author

Death certificate

Public record, Los Angeles, CA

Samuel Little letters

Courtesy of the author

Jillian Lauren and Samuel Little

Courtesy of the Author

**Photos in the Victims List were
derived from public records at
FBI.gov**

Acknowledgments

Above all, thank you to my strong and supportive Shriner men. We are wiser and stronger for our sacrifices. We play it as it lays around here.

Many family members of Little's victims welcomed me into their lives, their stories, their memories, their pain. My respect for their vulnerability and strength is immeasurable. Thank you to the Christie family, the Flores/Zambranos, the White Buffalos, and the Nelsons. Pearl Unique—you are truly both.

To Debbie and the Duvall family (of which I am proudly an honorable member), your love and faith give me the strength to keep going.

Thank you to Little's surviving victims, Laurie Kerridge and the late Hilda Nelson, for your willingness to share your stories with me, in the hope of helping others.

I extend my humble gratitude to the McDowell family, who allowed me into their homes, and into their hearts.

Deepest gratitude to LAPD Detective III Mitzi Roberts, for gifting me a life-changing story, and inspiring me to see it through.

To my cop-crush, retired LAPD Detective Rick Jackson, I treasure your belief in me, your ebullience, and your patient guidance.

MC, thank you for lighting the LA skyline for me with the flick of a switch.

Thanks to my manager Charlie Fusco—friend and force—and the crackerjack team at TGC. Laura, what would I do without you? Rachel Weintraub, there are no words. Thanks to Ethan Cohan, a scholar and a gentleman. Thank you, Anna Michels, for your sharp editorial eye, and to the team at Sourcebooks for your unflinching support. All gratitude to Shelley Venemann, Gladys Pittman, and the peeps at Provident.

It was an honor to work Joe Berlinger and his remarkable Radical Media crew on the documentary *Confronting a Serial Killer*.

All love to our Reboot mishpuchah, Nefesh kin, and Ethiopian extended family, who continue to teach me the ways of joy, community, and reverence.

Bonkers, bananas gratitude to the Reporters Committee for Freedom of the Press. In a truly heroic midnight save, Sarah Matthews told me I would not be walking into court unrepresented, while protecting my sources.

Thank you to Michael Dore of Gibson Dunn & Crutcher LLP: a pit bull in Ferragamos, a sucker for the First Amendment, and the reason this isn't written on toilet paper from San Bernardino County Jail. Thanks also to my mentors through Women in Film, Anika McClaren and Tara Cole.

Tara and Mike—don't know how you magnificent lawyers both got stuck with me. You're fucking cool.

Love to my friends, family and co-conspirators: R'Susan Goldberg, Amaia Perta (soul sister in crime), Penn Jillette, Zoe Ruiz, Trevor Noah, Jenny Feldon, Jonathan Ames, DDA Kelly Howick, Jon Feldon (owe you a shiny nickel), all my Suite 8ers and bitch night bitches, Heather Havrilesky, Annabelle Gurwitch, Del Wilber, Maurice Chammah, Claire Bidwell-Smith, Colin Summers, the LaZebniks, Billy Jensen, Garret Finney, Kurt Gutjahr, Charles Graeber, Gilly Barnes, Justin Van Hairston, Andrew Dreskin, Dr. Tina Bloom, Gary Lippman, Christophe Liglet, Anne Dailey, Renee Reeser, Randy Petee, John and Fred, Paul and Vincie, the Shriner family, the Dreskin family, the Fern family, the Fogliano-Paynter family, Sasha Zohuri, Zackary Drucker, Mitch Eisner, Judy White, Jamie Rose, Garrett Finney, and the Children of Darkness.

To my invaluable design team, Edward Kingston and Gretta Eberline, thank you for entering my life and expanding my creative world. Mckenzie O'Connor, thank you for bringing the map to life with your unique vision.

The members of the law enforcement community across the country who came together to work on the Little case are too manifest to mention.

Thanks also to DDA Beth Silverman, retired Detective Tim Marcia, the LAPD, LASD, LAPD Robbery Homicide Division, Wise County Sheriff Lane Aiken, Detective Kellyanne Best, Assistant Cuyahoga County Prosecutor Rick Bell, and the whole Cleveland team, Detective Justin Caid, Detective Michael Hubbard, Detective Leticia Gamboa, Michael Pentz, Lieutenant Detective Darren Versiga, retired Sergeant Detective Snow Robertson, Dr. Joseph Wu, and Detective Dana Harris.

The sheriff's deputies and inmates alike at California State Prison, Los Angeles largely treated me with respect and kindness. Thanks, Calvin and Everett, for always having a pencil and pulling out my chair.

Thanks to Deamer and the patrol officers at Newton Division for not sending a black and white every time I called from Tam's.

Thanks to Special Agent Shayne Buchwald for your grace and humor.

My great respect and admiration go out to DOJ ViCAP liaison Angela Williamson and BSU ViCAP analyst Christie Palazzolo for being the brainiacs, working long and hard for justice behind the scenes. Your commitment to the ViCAP and SAKI programs has already changed the world.

Thank you, Texas Ranger James B. Holland, for making me a better journalist.

Dr. Eizabeth Loftus, thank you for helping me to understand your iconoclastic/iconic insights on eyewitness testimony.

Dr. James Fallon, thank you for sharing your staggering brilliance, wit, and a wonderful afternoon.

Dr. Del Paulhus from the University of British Columbia—the world's nicest expert on Evil—thank you for sharing your innovations... and for empowering Muffin, Tootsie, and Ike to fight another day!

To Dr. Fallon, Dr. Macciardi, and Dr. Halpern: I'm sorry I failed to get you that brain. Thank you for your patience and your efforts. I would've taken a hacksaw and brought it to you myself if I could have. Next one.

About the Author

Jillian Lauren is a true crime expert, writer, storyteller, adoption advocate, and rock wife. She is the *New York Times* bestselling author of the memoirs *Everything You Ever Wanted* and *Some Girls: My Life in a Harem* and the novel *Pretty*. *Some Girls*, in which she recounts her time spent in the harem of the prince of Brunei, has been translated into eighteen languages.

She was the only journalist to extensively interview Samuel Little, the most prolific serial killer in American history. This experience is chronicled in Joe Berlinger's hit documentary series *Confronting a Serial Killer* and in Michael Connelly's podcast *Murder Book: The Women Who Brought Down Samuel Little*.

Jillian has an MFA in creative writing from Antioch University. Her writing has appeared in *New York Magazine*, the *New York Times*, *Vanity Fair*, *Paris Review*, the *Los Angeles Times*, *Los Angeles Magazine*, *Elle*, *Flaunt Magazine*, the *Daily Beast*, *Salon*, and many others. Her work has been widely anthologized, including in *The Moth Anthology* and *True Tales of Lust and Love*.

Jillian is a regular storyteller with the Moth and performs at spoken word and storytelling events across the country. She did a TEDx talk about adoption and identity at Chapman University in 2014. She has been interviewed on *The View*, *Good Morning America*, and *Howard Stern*, to name a few. She is a member of Greater Los Angeles American Mensa.

Jillian is married to Weezer bass player Scott Shriner. They live in Los Angeles with their two sons.

IG: @jillianlauren
Twitter: @jillylauren
FB: Jillian Lauren
TikTok: @jillianlaurenauthor